DIE BRAUT VON MESSINA

SCHILLER

DIE BRAUT VON MESSINA

ODER

DIE FEINDLICHEN BRÜDER

EIN TRAUERSPIEL MIT CHÖREN

EDITED BY

KARL BREUL, Litt.D., Ph.D.

SCHRÖDER PROFESSOR OF GERMAN IN THE UNIVERSITY OF CAMBRIDGE

Cambridge :
at the University Press
1913

CAMBRIDGE
UNIVERSITY PRESS

University Printing House, Cambridge CB2 8BS, United Kingdom

Published in the United States of America by Cambridge University Press, New York

Cambridge University Press is part of the University of Cambridge.

It furthers the University's mission by disseminating knowledge in the pursuit of
education, learning and research at the highest international levels of excellence.

www.cambridge.org
Information on this title: www.cambridge.org/9781107649637

© Cambridge University Press 1913

First published 1913
First paperback edition 2014

A catalogue record for this publication is available from the British Library

ISBN 978-1-107-64963-7 Paperback

PREFACE

THE present edition of Schiller's *Braut von Messina*, the first to be published in England, appears much later than was originally intended, but much as the Editor regrets the unavoidable delay he cannot but find some consolation in the fact that the postponement of his work made it possible for him to use a number of valuable essays published during the last few years on certain aspects of the drama. The titles of these essays are quoted in the Bibliographical Appendix, and it is hoped that no book or article of real importance has been overlooked.

Die Braut von Messina is a drama not so adapted for ordinary reading in schools as some other works of Schiller, such as *Maria Stuart* or *Wilhelm Tell*. So far as schools are concerned, it will probably only appeal to a few picked pupils and will hardly ever be studied by whole classes. But it is an excellent play for careful University study, and not only for men and women reading Modern Languages. It should prove of great interest to such students of the ancient classical literatures as have, as all of them ought to have, a reading knowledge of German and to whom it could not fail, any more than Goethe's *Iphigenie*, to suggest many interesting comparisons. It will also, no doubt, attract people of a more mature age who are interested in good literature and are pursuing their German studies without the help of a teacher. With a view to the needs of these various classes of serious students of classical German literature the notes to the text have often been given greater fulness than is customary in ordinary school editions. The Editor has reason to believe that many readers of Schiller's noble play will be glad of detailed explanations and of various suggestive hints and literary comparisons. For this reason many quotations and parallels from other works of Schiller have been given in the Notes and Appendices, it being the aim of the Editor in the first instance to explain Schiller by Schiller himself, and thus introduce students in the most direct way to the great poet's poetic diction and literary aims. The works of Goethe and other contemporary authors have also been frequently referred to. Many cross-references have been given in the Notes which will prove especially useful to students who, after having once read through the drama, are anxious to go through it carefully for a second time and to study certain interesting questions of language, metre, or plot in greater detail. All deviations in Schiller's poetry (1803) from modern prose usage (1913) have been carefully noted, peculiarities of diction have been indicated, foreign terms and their German equivalents pointed out, and classical terms and allusions explained throughout, the fullest use being made of Sir William Smith's excellent *Classical Dictionary*. Mere translations without explanation have not, as a rule, been given. Some of those proposed in the case of words or lines occurring in the Choruses were suggested by happy renderings of Schiller's text by Frank Nicholson, M.A., of Edinburgh. See the Introduction, page xxii. Shorter notes and a number of renderings without explanations may be found in the two useful American editions mentioned on page 265. In a few cases the pronunciation of German words has been given in the script adopted by the *Association Phonétique Internationale* which is now widely used in England and is also employed by Professors Viëtor and Siebs in their excellent books on German pronunciation.

It would be impossible in the Introduction to a volume of the 'Pitt Press Series' to discuss the many interesting problems suggested by the study of this remarkable literary experiment as fully as is done in the numerous books and articles devoted to detailed discussion of special questions. In the present Introduction, which aims at giving a succinct synopsis of all the various questions connected with the drama, the results of much thought and deliberation could often be merely indicated in the briefest possible way. But in the case of many vexed questions the copious references given in the notes to the Introduction and the Text, and in the various Appendices, should enable serious students of the play to pursue the investigation of such questions further and ultimately to form their own opinions. In the same way it was not possible to mention in every case the name of the scholar whose views were either adopted or combated.

In writing the Notes and the Introduction the Editor has derived much help from a great number of commentaries and editions, books and essays, especially from those by Düntzer, Boxberger, Heskamp, Schäfer, Tumlirz, Englert, Carruth, Palmer and Eldridge; Bellermann, Bergmann, Kühnemann, Petsch, Weitbrecht, Bulthaupt, Gloël, Hahne, Olbrich, Maaß, Kohlrausch, E. Harnack, Petersen, Imelmann; Scherer, Hoffmeister, Berger, Rea, Vaughan; Zarncke, Belling, Draheim, Fries, and others. The German literary periodicals have been found of much use on many points, and the great dictionaries of the brothers Grimm and their successors, with those of D. Sanders and Sanders-Wülfing, M. Heyne, H. Paul, Fr. Kluge, and the revised edition of K. Weigand, were of great service.

Finally the Editor desires to tender his sincerest thanks to his friends the Professors Otto Francke, Max Friedländer, Konrad Burdach, Wilhelm Seelmann and Wilhelm Creizenach, to his pupils and friends Miss Minna Steele Smith, Professor Walter Rippmann, M.A., Mr Frank Nicholson, M.A., Mr Gilbert Waterhouse, B.A., and above all to his friend, the Rev. W. A. Cox, M.A., Fellow and late Dean of St John's College, for the great kindness and care with which he read through all the proofs of this edition and contributed many valuable suggestions and criticisms while the proofs were going through the press.

K. B.

10 CRANMER ROAD, CAMBRIDGE.

March 1913.

TABLE OF CONTENTS.

INTRODUCTION

I. HISTORY OF THE PLAY.

Ich habe große Lust, mich nunmehr in der einfachen Tragödie nach der strengsten griechischen Form zu versuchen.

> Schiller to Körner, May 13, 1801.

Mein erster Versuch einer Tragödie in strenger Form....

> Schiller to Humboldt, February 17, 1803.

Die Braut von Messina is one of the results of the earnest and steadfast endeavours on the part of Schiller and his friend Goethe to make the best of the ancient Greek poetry fruitful for German literature. It is one of the products of the second German *renaissance*, the Hellenic renaissance of the end of the eighteenth century, symbolized by Goethe in the second part of his Faust by the union of Faust and Helena. During this period of Graecism the Greek writers who exercised the chief influence on German literature were Homer and the great Attic tragedians, Aeschylus, Sophocles, and Euripides.

As is usual in the case of the later dramas of Schiller, we are very well informed about the genesis of Die Braut von Messina. The chief sources of information are Schiller's letters (especially those to Körner, Goethe, Humboldt, and Iffland), and also, after the play was finished, a number of short entries in his Diary. The study of the history of any of Schiller's works must always be largely based on his extensive correspondence, of which the letters written by himself have now been most carefully edited by Jonas[1]. By a study of Schiller's letters we

---

[1] See the Appendix V (Bibliography) on p. 273. Two other valuable books, both furnished with very full and conscientiously compiled indexes, are *Schillers Calender* (new edition, by Ernst Müller, Stuttgart,

are admitted to the poet's workshop, we are privileged to watch
the genesis of great works of art. The Correspondence allows
us to see how the artist pondered on his choice of a subject,
how in many cases he wavered a long time between several
subjects that attracted him equally, how ultimately some reason
determined his selection and he approached his task working—
with or without interruptions—till he had mastered the material
and shaped the drama to his own satisfaction. We see what
helped him and what hampered him, how at later stages of the
work lacunae were filled in, what points remained a long time
unsettled in his mind and what new motives suggested themselves to his thought while he was working out his original plan,
even after the greater part of it was finished[2]. It is true, a great
work of art can well be enjoyed, and indeed is enjoyed by the
majority of people, without any knowledge of the processes
through which it passed before its author presented it to the
world; but those students who are privileged to enter the workshop and watch the master at work will be filled with admiration
not only of the genius of Schiller but also of the infinite pains
with which, in spite of his frequent bad health, he gave to each
work of his, whether essay, poem or play, the highest degree of
perfection which it was possible for him to attain.

A tragedy such as Die Braut von Messina should also be
studied with frequent reference to Schiller's aesthetic writings,
such as Über den Grund des Vergnügens an tragischen
Gegenständen and Über das Erhabene, not to mention the
essay Über den Gebrauch des Chors in der Tragödie (see the
Appendix I, pp. 239—247), and, again, many parallels with
thoughts expressed in his ballads and his philosophical poems
should be noticed; many of them have been pointed out in
the Notes.

The original conception of the play is considerably older

[2]1893) and *Regesten zu Friedrich Schillers Leben und Werken, mit
einem kurzen Überblick über die gleichzeitige Litteratur, in tabellarischer
Anordnung* (by Ernst Müller, Leipzig, 1900).

[2] A few characteristic extracts from Schiller's letters are given in
Appendix II, on pp. 248—257.

than the middle of August, 1802, the time when Schiller
seriously set about writing the drama. As early as the summer
of 1788, when Schiller was at Rudolstadt, reading Homer
with the help of the masterly translation of Voss and, at the
request of his future wife, Charlotte von Lengefeld, trying his
hand at the translation of two dramas of Euripides, he wrote
(in August) to his intimate friend Körner that he had conceived
the plan of writing a play in the style of the Greek tragedy (in
griechischer Manier). He had finished his Don Carlos in 1787;
the period of storm and stress now lay definitely behind him, and
he was for the first time in his life deeply stirred by his Greek
studies. He was anxious to assimilate, as far as was possible
for him, the simple and grand manner of the ancient Greek
masters, to learn from them a new style and a new art, and to
improve his own style of writing by translating from Euripides
for his Rudolstadt friends, the sisters Lengefeld. Thus he
turned into German blank verse Iphigenie in Aulis and a few
scenes of Die Phönizierinnen, the latter a fine tragedy on the
subject of the Hostile Brothers of Thebes. He lamented the
lost serenity and loftiness of classical Greek poetry and longed
for the dawn of an age of true art, simple, plastic, natural,
beautiful, ideas that found eloquent expression in his poem Die
Götter Griechenlands (1788). It was but natural that Schiller
should at once turn his thoughts to the plan of himself writing
a drama in the simple and lofty style of the Greek tragedians.
At that time, however, he very probably did not as yet think
of treating the subject of the Hostile Brothers, but he very likely
intended to treat in this manner Die Malteser, a favourite theme
of his, to be worked out as a grand tragedy, with Choruses of
the Knights of Malta (die Malteser), the heroic defenders of their
island against the overwhelming power of the Turks. This
fascinating subject was from time to time taken up by the poet,
but it was never fully treated by him. Numerous sketches that
he has left allow us to form a tolerably good idea of his changing
plans, and also of his reason for ultimately abandoning the
subject. After 1788, the thought of writing a drama in the Greek
style was laid aside for a time. Not only did Schiller's increased

attention to historical studies, in consequence of his appointment to the Jena Chair (in 1789), prevent him from proceeding with the idea, but the poet also hesitated, as he wrote to Körner in 1789, because he did not yet know the Greek drama well enough and because his ideas about dramatic art were not yet sufficiently matured. Thus it happened that his next great play, 𝔚𝔞𝔩𝔩𝔢𝔫𝔰𝔱𝔢𝔦𝔫[3], was an historical tragedy which grew out of his historical studies and at which he worked on and off for fully thirty months between October 22, 1796 and March 17, 1799. Before he undertook the composition of his drama he had devoted much time and thought to the study of dramatic theory and also to the study of the masterpieces of Hellenic and modern literature. His essays Über die tragische Kunst (1792), Über Anmut und Würde and Über das Erhabene (both in 1793), and above all his masterly and truly classic treatise Über naive und sentimentalische Dichtung (1794), in which the peculiarities of ancient and modern, objective and subjective, classical and romantic poetry were for the first time treated with wonderful critical insight and acumen, were for Schiller himself important steps in the constant endeavour to attain a thorough understanding of Greek art, of Goethe's art, and, in contrast with this, of his own peculiar poetic talent. On October 2, 1797, when still at work on his 𝔚𝔞𝔩𝔩𝔢𝔫-𝔰𝔱𝔢𝔦𝔫, he wrote to Goethe[4] that he had recently taken much trouble to discover a tragic subject of the same kind as the *Oedipus Rex* of Sophocles and offering a poet the same dramatic advantages. No definite plan is here mentioned by Schiller, but we see that, while busy with a great drama, the poet liked, in spare moments, and as a sort of relaxation, to turn over in his mind the possibilities of new dramatic subjects.

After he had finished 𝔚𝔞𝔩𝔩𝔢𝔫𝔰𝔱𝔢𝔦𝔫 on March 17, 1799, Schiller wrote to Goethe on the 19th[5] that he was now thinking of

---

[3] For the genesis of 𝔚𝔞𝔩𝔩𝔢𝔫𝔰𝔱𝔢𝔦𝔫 see my edition of this play in the Pitt Press Series, Vol. I (Cambridge, 1894, [2]1896), Introduction, chapter iii.

[4] Schiller's Letters, ed. Jonas, Vol. V, 271.

[5] See Jonas, Vol. VI, 20.

writing a play on a subject of his own invention, the interest
of which would be of a purely imaginative and human
character, for of soldiers, heroes and commanders he was
heartily tired. He was anxious to show Goethe some tragic
material of his own creation and to obtain his friend's advice
as to its suitability. In this letter no subject of pure fancy is
definitely mentioned, but that he had in his mind the story
of Die Braut von Messina is proved from Goethe. On
March 22, 1799, while on a visit to Schiller at Jena, he wrote[6]
to a mutual friend, the Swiss art-critic Meyer: Schiller ist
kaum von dem Wallenstein entbunden, so hat er sich schon wieder nach
einem neuen tragischen Gegenstande umgesehen und, von dem obligaten
historischen ermüdet, seine Fabel in dem Felde der freien Erfindung gesucht.
Der Stoff ist tragisch genug, die Anlage gut, und er will den Plan genau
durcharbeiten, ehe die Ausführung anfängt. He did not inform Meyer
of the name of the subject chosen by Schiller, but in his Diary[7]
we read under the date of March 21 : Früh neun Uhr von Weimar
weg, vor Mittag in Jena. Kurze Promenade, nachher zu Schiller. Die
feindlichen Brüder. Über Tragödie und Epopee. Gegen Abend die
vier ersten Akte von Wallenstein zusammen gelesen. This is the first
definite mention of the subject which Schiller proposed to take
up immediately after his great historical tragedy. On June 14,
1799, he asked Goethe[8] for a copy of the plays of Aeschylus,
but he did not for some time go on with the Hostile Brothers.
Other plans and interests once more gained the upper hand,
and two more historical plays were completed, the principal
figures of which were women. Maria Stuart was finished[9] on
June 9, 1800, and Die Jungfrau von Orleans on April 16,
1801. To the last-mentioned 'romantic tragedy' his next
great play, Die Braut von Messina, forms in some respects a

[6] See the large Weimar Edition of Goethe's Works : Division IV
(Letters), Volume XIV, page 50.
[7] See the large Weimar Edition of Goethe's Works: Division III
(Diaries), Volume II, page 238.
[8] See Jonas, Vol. VI, 45.
[9] See my edition of this drama in the Pitt Press Series (Cambridge,
1893, ²1896), Introduction, p. xix.

counterpart and in others a strong contrast. In 1800 Schiller had moved from Jena to Weimar in order to be nearer to Goethe and the excellent theatre to the perfecting of which he and Goethe devoted their best energies and at which all Schiller's later dramas were first performed. After the completion of the *Maid of Orleans*, on April 16, 1801, Schiller was able to turn at last to a simple drama in the strictest Greek form treating of a subject that was entirely his own. An important letter to Körner, dated May 13, 1801, contains full information about Schiller's plans as they stood then[10]. From it we learn Schiller's conception of Die Braut von Messina, as well as of the treatment of two other tragic subjects, Die Malteser and Warbeck, both of which occupied him for some considerable time and neither of which was ultimately carried out. The subject of the Hostile Brothers did not yet interest him sufficiently to make him definitely set aside all other plans—the reason being that, as in the *Oedipus Rex*, the interest was centred not so much in the persons of the drama as in the plot; thus the play was to him still lacking in human interest. The poet's general plan was, however, now quite clear before his mind: the play was to be of a simple structure and to consist of five persons and twenty scenes (including the Chorus). Between May 1801 and September 1802 very little was done. Schiller's health caused him much trouble and prevented his devoting himself, as much as usual, to the working out of a great original drama. He was, however, never idle, and if he did not feel strong enough to proceed with a great play of his own, he spent his time in writing smaller poems, such as the ballads Hero und Leander (1801) and Kassandra (1802), and in translating and adapting the plays of others, such as Gozzi's Italian play Turandot, and Goethe's Iphigenie. He also considered, as was his wont, several subjects, old and new, and these for a time attracted his interest more than the Hostile Brothers. These were the subjects of Warbeck and of Wilhelm Tell, the latter of

---

[10] See Jonas, Vol. VI, 277. The most important portion of this letter is given in Appendix II under *b*.

which was actually carried out as soon as 𝔇𝔦𝔢 𝔅𝔯𝔞𝔲𝔱 𝔳𝔬𝔫 𝔐𝔢𝔣𝔣𝔦𝔫𝔞 was completed. However, he never ceased to think of the play. Thus he gave Körner a full account of it on the occasion of a visit to his friend at Dresden, in September 1801. The last stage in the composition of 𝔇𝔦𝔢 𝔅𝔯𝔞𝔲𝔱 𝔳𝔬𝔫 𝔐𝔢𝔣𝔣𝔦𝔫𝔞, that in fact in which the play was actually written, begins in the middle of August 1802, and extends, with occasional breaks caused by bad health, over about 5½ months, to February 1, 1803, when the drama was at last completed. The first important letter telling us of Schiller's plans and progress is one to Körner, dated September 9, 1802[11]. In this letter the title is for the first time given as 𝔇𝔦𝔢 𝔅𝔯𝔞𝔲𝔱 𝔳𝔬𝔫 𝔐𝔢𝔣𝔣𝔦𝔫𝔞 instead of 𝔇𝔦𝔢 𝔣𝔢𝔦𝔫𝔡𝔩𝔦𝔠𝔥𝔢𝔫 𝔅𝔯𝔲̈𝔟𝔢𝔯[12]. Schiller was anxious to finish the play by the end of 1802 in order to have it acted on January 30, 1803, on the occasion of the birthday of the Duchess Luise of Weimar, for which day Goethe and Schiller always were anxious to prepare, if possible, some special performance at the theatre. In October he worked very hard; on November 5 he received a copy of Sophocles from Professor Süvern, and on November 15 he joyfully informed Körner[13] that 1500 lines were finished (a little more than one half of the present 2840) and that he felt himself rejuvenated by the use of the new form. The study of the splendid translation of four Aeschylean tragedies[14] by Count Friedrich Stolberg, which had just been published, exercised a powerful stimulus on him, and he was also influenced to some extent by the Spanish metre of Calderon, with which he became acquainted in 1802 by the production of Friedrich Schlegel's tragedy 𝔄𝔩𝔞𝔯𝔣𝔬𝔰, which is pervaded by the spirit and style of the great Spanish

[11] See the Appendix II, under *c*.

[12] See the discussion of the double title of the play on page xxv.

[13] See Jonas, Vol. VI, 427.

[14] 𝔙𝔦𝔢𝔯 𝔗𝔯𝔞𝔤𝔬̈𝔡𝔦𝔢𝔫 𝔡𝔢𝔰 𝔄𝔢𝔣𝔠𝔥𝔶𝔩𝔬𝔰, 𝔲̈𝔟𝔢𝔯𝔣𝔢𝔱𝔷𝔱 𝔳𝔬𝔫 𝔉𝔯𝔦𝔢𝔡𝔯𝔦𝔠𝔥 𝔏𝔢𝔬𝔭𝔬𝔩𝔡 𝔊𝔯𝔞𝔣𝔢𝔫 𝔷𝔲 𝔖𝔱𝔬𝔩𝔟𝔢𝔯𝔤. Hamburg, 1802. (𝔓𝔯𝔬𝔪𝔢𝔱𝔥𝔢𝔲𝔰 𝔦𝔫 𝔅𝔞𝔫𝔡𝔢𝔫, 𝔖𝔦𝔢𝔟𝔢𝔫 𝔤𝔢𝔤𝔢𝔫 𝔗𝔥𝔢𝔟𝔢𝔫, 𝔇𝔦𝔢 𝔓𝔢𝔯𝔣𝔢𝔯, 𝔇𝔦𝔢 𝔈𝔲𝔪𝔢𝔫𝔦𝔡𝔢𝔫.) See also Appendix II, *e*.

dramatist[15]. On November 27 he told his publisher, Cotta, that he hoped to let him have the play by the beginning of February 1803 at the very latest. On December 31, the last evening of the year, he was able to read what was finished, i.e. nearly the whole of the drama, to his wife and sister-in-law. During the month of January 1803 Schiller was busy filling in lacunae and making various important alterations and improvements in the latter part of his drama[16]. On February 4 he was, at last, able to enter in his Diary[17]: Heute habe die Braut vollendet; it was too late for the intended performance in celebration of the birthday of the Duchess. On February 4 it was read for the first time with great success to a private circle of friends, while Goethe read it alone and afterwards discussed it with Schiller. Several other private readings followed, including one on February 11 when Schiller read his play to the Duchess; and copies were sent during the latter half of the month to friends at a distance such as Körner, Humboldt, Iffland and others, in most cases accompanied by some characteristic utterance of Schiller concerning his artistic intentions[18]. At first Schiller, who well knew that in the *Oedipus Rex* a musical accompaniment had not been wanting to the songs of the Chorus, had hesitated as to the best way of producing his Choruses, and had modestly hoped that it might be found possible to have the lyrical intermezzos of the Chorus recited in a musical way and accompanied by a musical instrument. He as well as Goethe had been looking for the advice and collaboration of Goethe's musical Berlin friend Zelter, whose visit to Weimar they expected in February and with whom they wished to discuss the whole question[19]. But he was unable

[15] See the note to l. 1057 on page 178.

[16] See the important letter to Goethe dated January (26?), 1803, given in the Appendix II, *d*.

[17] *Schillers Calender* ([2]1893), p. 140; see also page 225[b].

[18] See Appendix II, *e, f, g, k, m*.

[19] See Appendix II, *g*. Zelter was a composer. His (not very helpful or practical) answer dated Berlin, March 16, 1803, is printed in the *Marbacher Schillerbuch*, Vol. II (1907), p. 367.

to come, and the idea of a musical accompaniment had to be
abandoned. It was now found necessary to distribute the
speeches of the Chorus among single persons who became
leaders, and for these leaders characteristic names were invented.

On March 19, 1803, Die Braut von Messina was performed
for the first time at Weimar and obtained a great success[20].
Henry Crabb Robinson entered in his Diary[21] : 'I attended
(on March 20) the first performance and wrote to my brother
that this tragedy surpassed all Schiller's former works. But
this feeling must have been caught from my companions, for
it did not remain.' Especially loud in their praise were the
students from the neighbouring university of Jena, who were
wont to regard the performance of a new tragedy by Schiller
as a special treat for which they never failed to tramp or
drive over to Weimar in large numbers. These young men,
fresh from the study of the classical dramas and full of youthful
enthusiasm, were so delighted with the lyrical beauties of the
songs of the Chorus and so deeply impressed by the grandeur
of the last act that they gave three cheers for the poet in the
theatre[22]. Schiller himself was deeply moved, and when the
first semi-chorus with solemn song bore the corpse of Don
Manuel on a bier covered with a black pall into the presence
of the unsuspecting Isabella, he said to his wife and sister-
in-law, who witnessed with him the impressive performance :
Das ist doch nun wirklich ein Trauerspiel[23] ! Goethe was also

[20] See the letter to Körner, dated March 28, 1803, given in Ap
pendix II, under *l.*

[21] H. C. Robinson, *Diary* (London, 1869), Vol. I. 152. The date
is a mistake for March 19. Robinson was then staying at Jena.

[22] For this ovation, started by young Dr Schütz of Jena, the leader
received an official reprimand. The Duke had been displeased with the
noisy scene in his theatre, and Goethe, as the chief official connected
with the Weimar stage, was obliged to request the authorities at Jena
to administer a severe rebuke. See his letter, dated March 21, 1803,
Weimar edition, IV. 16, pp. 202—204.

[23] See *Schillers Leben*, by Karoline von Wolzogen (Schiller's sister-
in-law), in Cotta's ' Bibliothek der Weltlitteratur,' p. 250.

much impressed, and so were those who witnessed the first performances in Berlin, on June 14 and 16, as is clear from Iffland's letter to Schiller, dated June 18, 1803[24]. Early in July the tragedy was performed by the Weimar actors at their summer theatre at Lauchstädt, not far from Halle, from which town, and also from Leipzig, many students came to see the play. Schiller was present too and was the object of a great ovation. One performance (on July 3) was particularly impressive on account of a terrible thunderstorm, which swept over the frail theatre during the most stirring part of the drama and made an ineffaceable impression on all present[25]. The representations at Hamburg and Vienna were also successful. At the first representation in the Austrian capital the part of Beatrice was acted by the charming Toni Adamberger, who subsequently became the *fiancée* of the poet Theodor Körner. The drama is still to-day on the *répertoire* of all the better German theatres, although it is not so often acted as 𝔚𝔦𝔩𝔥𝔢𝔩𝔪 𝔗𝔢𝔩𝔩, 𝔇𝔦𝔢 𝔍𝔲𝔫𝔤𝔣𝔯𝔞𝔲 𝔳𝔬𝔫 𝔒𝔯𝔩𝔢𝔞𝔫𝔰 and some other plays of Schiller. The reason is not only that the acting is more difficult for modern actors trained in the ways of the naturalistic modern drama, but also that it does not appeal so strongly to the ordinary play-goer as the great historical dramas. Still even at the present day 𝔇𝔦𝔢 𝔅𝔯𝔞𝔲𝔱 𝔳𝔬𝔫 𝔐𝔢𝔰𝔰𝔦𝔫𝔞 may not infrequently be seen in the best German theatres and, in spite of the many objections raised by learned critics, like all Schiller's dramas never fails to draw large and appreciative audiences.

The reception of the drama by the reading public and by the

---

[24] See the Appendix II, *o*. See also E. Genast, *Aus Weimars klassischer und nachklassischer Zeit. Erinnerungen eines alten Schauspielers* (new ed. by R. Kohlrausch), I, 83—86.

[25] See the note to l. 2299. Graff's own interesting account is reprinted (as No. 392, on pp. 352—3) in Julius Petersen, *Schillers Gespräche*, Leipzig, 1911; and the account of Ludwig Krahn, a divinity student of Halle, in the same book (as No. 393, on pp. 353—6). The latter account is also given, with a few explanatory notes, by Theodor Distel, in *Studien zur Vergleichenden Literaturgeschichte*, Vol. v (1905), Ergänzungsheft, pp. 350—354.

critics was very various, and even now opinions differ very widely on many points [26]. The warmest reception was accorded to the new work by Schiller's personal friends Körner [27] and Humboldt [28]. The opinions of other contemporaries were less favourable. The Duke of Weimar, Karl August, who had a great predilection for the classical French drama, objected to this play and judged it most severely and unjustly; the same was done, though with less excuse, by Herder, who during the last years of his life felt rather bitterly towards Goethe and Schiller, and did not approve of their artistic and literary aims. The Romanticists, especially A. W. Schlegel and his friends, did not withhold very unfavourable criticism, although their own dramatic productions in the same style, e.g. August Wilhelm Schlegel's *Ion* and Friedrich Schlegel's *Alarkos*, proved to be hopeless failures on the Weimar stage and cannot for a moment be compared with Schiller's grand tragedy. Even his friend Iffland, the great actor and experienced manager of the Royal Theatre of Berlin, who admired the play sincerely, had his doubts about the advisability of pursuing this new style and recommended Schiller not to proceed on this road any further, as the public was too sadly lacking in artistic feeling and would be sure to misunderstand him. Nearly the whole of the first half of the nineteenth century the drama was underrated; but to-day, after the play has been acted and studied again and again, the general opinion has become much more fair

[26] See especially Albert Ludwig, *Schiller und die deutsche Nachwelt*, Berlin, 1909 (with a full table of contents and a good index), and also the works enumerated in the Appendix V (Bibliography) under F. [Ernst Bergmann's Braunschweig 'Programme' of 1906 gives a very valuable survey of the various critical opinions.]

[27] See Appendix II, *h, i, k.*

[28] See Appendix II, *n.* It is not possible to reprint the two very long and very important letters on the drama which Humboldt wrote to Schiller on October 22, 1803, and to Goethe, after Schiller's death, on June 4. 1805. They are both easily accessible in Albert Leitzmann's excellent edition of the Correspondence between Schiller and Humboldt. See p. 273.

and intelligent, and consequently much more favourable. Although modern critics disagree—and probably will continue to disagree very widely—about the idea of Fate in the drama and about the expediency of introducing the Chorus into a modern tragedy[29], all now readily admit that this drama is a work of unusual poetic beauty, the heart-stirring creation of a lofty spirit, full of noble thought and lyric charm, of a perfection in style and metre which has never been surpassed in German, the grand production of a thoughtful and mature artist which is in its way unique and constitutes a lasting gain to German literature.

II. THE TEXT AND ITS SOURCES.

The drama was published for the first time by Cotta, at Tübingen, in June, 1803[30]. At the same time a cheaper edition was published, with Cotta's consent, at Vienna (by Geistinger) in order to take the wind out of the sails of publishers of piratical editions which at that time were not uncommon. 6000 copies were sold before the poet's death, and two more separate editions appeared, in 1810 and 1818, before 1825 when the drama was published among Schiller's collected works. There are now a large number of excellent German editions, many of them provided with useful introductions and notes.

The text of the present edition is mainly based on that of Oskar Walzel in Cotta's recent *Säkular-Ausgabe*, Vol. VII. All the best critical modern texts are based on the first printed edition, correcting its misprints, modernizing its spelling and punctuation, and borrowing from the Hamburg acting copy the division into acts and scenes, and also the names of the speakers in the two semi-choruses.

The only texts of any interest to the student beside the original printed edition of the drama are two acting copies in

---

[29] See chapters V and VI.

[30] See the Appendix V (Bibliography), under A, *a*.

manuscript, the Regensburg and the Hamburg stage manuscripts. These manuscripts were carefully revised by the poet himself before they were sent out, and represent as a rule a version of the text which is earlier than that of the printed editions. In some cases, however, the text in the acting copies was altered by Schiller to make it more easily intelligible to a theatrical audience, while an original and more poetic version was reserved for the printed editions. The deviations of the acting copies from the text of the printed editions are, on the whole, quite insignificant. Their chief importance lies in what they tell us about the poet's intentions concerning the dividing up of the portions spoken by the Chorus. A complete list of the various deviations of the acting copies from the printed editions was carefully compiled by Wilhelm Vollmer, which was utilized for H. Oesterley's critical edition of the drama in Vol. XIV of Karl Goedeke's monumental edition of Schiller's collected works, Stuttgart, 1872. The deviations of the important Hamburg theatre manuscript are recorded in the Hesse edition, Vol. XX, pp. 251—61 (by Georg Witkowski). Only when they are of some importance have they been referred to in the Notes contained in this edition.

III. ENGLISH TRANSLATIONS OF SCHILLER'S *BRAUT VON MESSINA* [31].

Die Braut von Meffina has been received with less interest in England than most of Schiller's dramas. It has excited far less attention than Die Räuber on the one hand and Don Carlos, Wallenstein, Maria Stuart, Die Jungfrau von Orleans or Wilhelm Tell on the other. The first

---

[31] See the Appendix V (Bibliography), under B, and Thomas Rea, *Schiller's Dramas and Poems in England*, London, 1906, pp. 91—96 and 149. Among recent English appreciations of the drama the few pages (286—88) by Charles E. Vaughan, in his thoughtful book *The Romantic Revolt*, Edinburgh and London, 1907, deserve to be specially mentioned.

who, in 1830, published a translation of one song of the Chorus (Act IV, Sc. 4) was William Taylor (of Norwich), the early interpreter of German poetry to his countrymen. He was followed by Ch. Hodges who, in 1834 and 1836, brought out translations of large portions, amounting to about two-thirds of Schiller's drama, in various publications in Germany. His renderings are not of high excellence. Indeed, the same must be said of most of the translations enumerated in the Appendix. The most faithful is the anonymous translation published at Munich in 1838 and 1839, in which the German and the English texts are given on opposite pages. The most spirited rendering of the Choruses is no doubt the one by Frank C. Nicholson, of Edinburgh, the translator of *Old German Love Songs* (1907), whose fine translation has not yet been published, but was placed at my disposal by the kindness of the author. A. Lodge's rendering can hardly be called a translation. It is frequently an adaptation—and not a very successful one—of Schiller's drama, the translator stating himself that 'he has sometimes amplified, more frequently condensed, the original, in one or two passages slightly varied the sense....' Several scenes, including Beatrice's monologue, are considerably abridged and fine parts of the Choruses omitted. G. Irvine's translation is, on the whole, more faithful, but it, too, is guilty of omissions. Two translations were inaccessible to the present Editor. No less than three of the six translations (not counting Nos. 1 and 8, which are only renderings of Choruses) were published not in England but in Germany.

IV. SCHILLER'S *BRAUT VON MESSINA* IN ART.

Two scenes in this drama, the brightest and the gloomiest, have attracted the draughtsman and the painter. The first meeting of Don Manuel and Beatrice in the precincts of the convent (I. 7, ll. 696—703) has been made the subject of a capital sketch by C. Jäger which is reproduced in the *Schiller-Galerie* (see note to l. 701) and makes a very charming picture. The

grand pathetic scene in the Palace (IV. 5) in which Don Cesar
learns, beside the bier of Don Manuel, that Beatrice is his
sister, is the subject of an impressive painting, by Johann
Friedrich Matthaei, called 𝔅𝔢𝔞𝔱𝔯𝔦𝔠𝔢 𝔞𝔫 𝔐𝔞𝔫𝔲𝔢𝔩𝔰 𝔏𝔢𝔦𝔠𝔥𝔢, which
hangs in the Weimar State Library, and of which an etching
(by C. Müller) is preserved at Weimar in the Schiller House.
A reproduction of it may be seen in Bellermann's *Life of
Schiller*, on page 225. Two copper-plate engravings from the
Calendar for 1804 (Offenbach) are given in Wychgram's *Life of
Schiller*, on page 467.

Incidental music was written for Schiller's drama by several
composers, but much of it was only used for certain performances and never published[32]. The music for the first Weimar
performance, written by Franz Destouches, was never printed,
and was probably lost in the great fire at the Court Theatre
(1825). The music for the first Berlin performance was written
by Bernard Anselm Weber, that for Vienna by Johann Fuss,
and that for Leipzig by Friedrich Schneider. Some hitherto unprinted music was written for a Berlin performance in 1825 by
Christian Urban. Apart from these compositions of incidental
music, there are several overtures to the tragedy. One by
Ferdinand Ries (*opus* 162), which was performed for the first
time, in 1830, at Düsseldorf, met with much approval, and
was often heard in the middle of the last century. Another overture, by Karl Borromaeus von Miltitz, was performed in 1838, at
Dresden ; it was never printed and, although well spoken of at
the time, is now practically unknown. Robert Schumann also
composed an overture (*opus* 100, C-minor) during the winter of
1850/51 which was performed in March, 1851, at Düsseldorf.
But it is a work of his declining powers and not easy to
appreciate without careful study. Three other overtures, bringing the total of independent overtures up to six, were composed
by Isidor Rosenfeld (*opus* 25, F-minor), Karl Schulz, of Schwerin,

[32] For information about the music and a short appreciation, see
especially Albert Schaefer's exhaustive work quoted in the Appendix
V, p. 273. For particulars about Berneker's fine music, see Victor
Laudien, *Constanz Berneker*, Charlottenburg, 1909, pp. 75—88.

and Theobald Rehbaum (G-minor), the last mentioned so far
unpublished, but well spoken of; it was for the first time performed at Berlin in 1884.

The subject was no less than four times treated in the form
of an opera. In 1839 *La Sposa di Messina*, by Nicolo Vaccaj,
was performed, at the Scala theatre, at Milan, but was only
repeated once. In 1840, at the Court theatre of Neu-Strelitz,
was given Die Fürsten von Messina, tragische Oper in 4 Aften,
frei nach Schiller bearbeitet von J. F. Bahrdt, Musik vom Grafen
C. L. von Oertzen. Only the overture of this work appeared in
print (Lübeck, 1871). The third opera was called Die Braut
von Messina, tragische Oper nach Schillers gleichnamiger Tragödie, von
Hermann Miller, Musik von Johann Heinrich Bonewitz. It was performed for the first time early in 1874 in the Academy of Music
at Philadelphia and met with a favourable reception. The last
opera was Die Braut von Messina, Oper nach Schillers gleichnamigem
Trauerspiele, Text von Professor Hoftinchy, Musik von Zdeněk Fibich (*op.*
18). This opera was first performed in April, 1884, at Prague and
met with a great success. Only the Funeral March from it (Act IV,
Sc. 4) has as yet been published (see the note to l. 2268). The
grand Chorus in the same scene was also set to music by Georg
Schumann, and by Constanz Berneker.

The fine monologue of Beatrice with which the Second Act
opens was composed by Franz Holstein (*opus* 38) under the
title Beatrice, eine Scene aus der „Braut von Messina," to be sung at
concerts by a soprano voice.

Perhaps the finest of all the music that has hitherto been produced in connexion with our drama is the magnificent setting of
the Choruses by the late Constanz Berneker of Königsberg.
His impressive Chorgesänge aus Schillers Braut von Messina,
für Männer-Chor, Soli und Orchester, were for the first time performed at Königsberg in December, 1892, and several times
repeated in the same town. They were intended by the composer to be used at performances of the drama on the stage,
but, owing to the difficulty of the music for ordinary theatre
choruses, they have so far never been heard on the stage
itself, but only in the concert room. They have not yet been

performed outside Germany, but it is to be hoped that they will soon be attempted by some well-trained choir in England. They would form a fine counterpart to Mendelssohn's choruses in the *Antigone* which are now not infrequently heard at performances of the great tragedy of Sophocles. Berneker made a selection from the Choruses and divided them into seven parts that have the following titles: I. Eintritt in bie Königs= burg (ll. 132 sqq.); II. Begrüßung ber Königin (ll. 255 sqq.); III. Waffenruf (ll. 871 sqq.); IV. Brautchor (ll. 1174 sqq.); V. Brubermorb (ll. 1906 sqq., especially l. 1962); VI *a*. Toten= flage (ll. 2268 sqq.) and *b*. Friebensfehnfucht (l. 2562); VII. Sühne (ll. 2803 and 2836—40).

From Schiller's essay Über ben Gebrauch bes Chores in ber Tragöbie (see pages 239—47) it is clear that the poet himself was at any rate not averse to the aid of music in the performance of his drama (see p. 245, 17 and p. 251, under II, *g*). It was Berneker's wish to contribute by his setting of the chief songs of the Chorus to the fuller conquest of the German stage by Schiller's most solemn and most lyrical drama[33].

V. CRITICAL DISCUSSION OF THE DRAMA.

Der Sinnenbe, ber alles burchgeprobt.
Goethe on Schiller, *Maskenzug.*

The TITLE OF THE DRAMA, originally intended to be Die feinblichen Brüber, was first altered to Die feinblichen Brüber zu Meffina, and finally changed to the present title: Die Braut von Meffina ober bie feinblichen Brüber. In this title the original designation is placed last, the first place being given to the heroine of the play, while the second title is added to indicate the subject of the tragedy. Schiller does not like to give merely a name, e.g. Beatrice, unless this name is historically well known

---

[33] See also the learned and suggestive observations of Konrad Burdach in his stimulating essay in the *Deutsche Rundschau*, Vol. 143 (1910), pp. 108—112.

as in the case of Maria Stuart or Wallenstein, but prefers to add
a brief indication of the scene of action, such as Die Ritter von
Malta, Die Jungfrau von Orleans, or Die Braut von Messina.

Long before he thought of placing the SCENE OF ACTION of
his drama in Sicily, Schiller had bestowed much thought
upon the political, religious and social conditions of the island
in the middle ages, and had, in 1790, given a masterly
picture of the medieval Sicilian world in one of his historical
essays[34]. The vivid imagination of the poet and his power of
giving a plastic representation of scenery which he had never
seen and of conditions that had long passed away was the
wonder of all his friends. From the observation of a mill-
stream and the reading of a few lines of Homer's *Odyssey* he
was able to conjure up that wonderful picture of the gigantic
whirlpool of the Charybdis in his stirring ballad Der Taucher.
He had never seen Switzerland, but a few pictures, the study
of many books, and the accounts supplied by his wife and
Goethe, enabled him to give the grand and true descriptions of
Swiss scenery and customs in Wilhelm Tell which delight all
readers, and none more than the Swiss themselves. His task in
Die Braut von Messina was, however, still more difficult and
his achievement still more wonderful, for the Sicilian scenery
was to him even stranger than the Switzerland of Wilhelm
Tell. Before all it was the mixed civilisation in medieval Sicily
that attracted him. It seemed to him to be particularly suitable
for a drama in which he wished to introduce remnants of ancient
Greek civilisation, medieval Christian beliefs, and Mahommedan
superstitions all existing side by side[35]. The Sicilians had ever

[34] See Cotta's *Säkular-Ausgabe*, XIII. 149 sqq., especially pp.
155—6. A short extract from it is given on page 247. Compare also
R. Fester's essay, 'Schillers historische Schriften als Vorstudien des
Dramatikers,' in *Deutsche Rundschau*, Vol. 138 (1909), pp. 148—158.

[35] See Schiller's 'Essay on the use of the Chorus,' Appendix I,
p. 247, 8—19, and his letter to Körner of March 10, 1803, given in the
Appendix II, *k*, on pages 254—5. For similar reasons Lessing chose
Jerusalem as the scene of action for his religious drama, Nathan der
Weise.

been noted for their valour, heroism and stoicism, but also for
their jealousy, revengefulness and gloomy superstitions, and
thus were particularly well fitted to furnish the persons suitable for the purposes of the tragic poet. The assumed co-
existence in Sicily of the various religious faiths, the occurrence
of terms now pagan and now Christian in the mouth of the same
persons, is really *not* historical, but the mistake was that of
Schiller's time, and he certainly used the assumed mixture of
religious ideas to the very best poetic advantage. This seems
indeed to have prompted his choice of Sicily as the scene of
action of his play. The official religion of the ruling family in his
drama is Christian, and Christian conceptions prevail throughout ; in moments of crisis all the characters use terms and utter
ideas that are peculiar to the medieval Roman Catholic Church,
although an orthodox Roman Catholic would in some cases not
express himself as they do. Yet it does not seem astonishing
that some pagan beliefs of earlier centuries were still held by the
Sicilians along with Christian ideas, as several of the ancient
temples had been transformed into Christian churches and the
old and the new seemed to blend in many other ways. In
choosing subjects such as the Maid of Orleans, the Bride of
Messina, and Wilhelm Tell, not from the clear daylight of
history, but from the twilight of legend and superstition, Schiller
was no doubt influenced by the romantic spirit. Sicily held
a prominent part in Schiller's poetic imagination and is also
the scene of two of his ballads, viz. Der Taucher and Die
Bürgschaft, written a few years before the drama. Among his
left papers there was found a sheet on which the Sicilian Vespers
(commenced at Palermo on March 30, 1282) is jotted down,
among others, as a possible subject of dramatic treatment. The
scene of Julius von Tarent (by Leisewitz), which had a great
influence on Schiller's tragedy of the Hostile Brothers, is in
the south of Italy, almost opposite Sicily, and Malta, the scene
of his own drama Die Malteser, is quite close to Sicily.

The TIME OF ACTION has purposely not been clearly indicated by the poet. It must be one of the later centuries of
the middle ages and the choice seems to lie between the twelfth

and the fourteenth century. Messina is imagined as being the capital of a small principality which is sometimes in feud with other small Sicilian states and liable to the raids of daring pirates. The rulers are a race of fierce, passionate and haughty men, despots and egotists, who in olden times had come 'from the sunset's ruddy glow'; but it would be useless to look for any definite historical personages as prototypes of the brothers, or even to attempt to say whether they were Normans of the twelfth or Spaniards of the fourteenth century. The actual political conditions were with good reason left vague by Schiller, as he wished to divert attention from the past and from public life to the private affairs of the ruling house. Thus we do not even see quite clearly who at the beginning of the action is the ruler of Messina. Is it Isabella, or are her sons joint rulers? What did they really quarrel about? All this remains almost entirely in the background; each of the brothers calls himself in turn 'the highest in Messina,' and we are nowhere told that their quarrel was a quarrel for rulership. Obviously Schiller did not wish to complicate matters by adding to their rivalry in love the rivalry for the throne. The capital of the Norman Princes was really Palermo, where also traces of Arabic civilisation and customs are numerous, and are even visible in the royal palace. Messina in Schiller's play may thus really be taken to be a mixture of Messina, Palermo and other Sicilian towns, and if the stage-manager were to draw inspiration and ideas from the ancient royal palace of Palermo, in which Oriental, Norman and German art are blended, he would not be far wrong[36]. The names of the chief personages and of the leaders of the Chorus do not throw any light on the question of nationality; they are free inventions of the poet, and they too point to different races. While Cesar, Beatrice and Cajetan (Gaetano) sound Italian, Manuel, Diego and Isabella have a Spanish ring, although a Byzantine Emperor (Manuel I Komnenos) was also called Manuel. Bohemund and Roger are Norman (Roger being the name of the first Norman ruler in Sicily), Hippolyt represents

[36] See Robert Kohlrausch in *Deutsche Rundschau*, Vol. 122 (1905), pp. 118 sqq.

the old Greek tradition, while Manfred reminds us of the glorious reign of the Hohenstaufen in Sicily. The names of the messengers, Lanzelot and Olivier, that are given in the Hamburg acting copy, carry us forward to the short time of the French rulership of Charles of Anjou (1268—82) that followed upon the sway of the Hohenstaufen and preceded that of the Spaniards. If we assume the brothers to be Spaniards, they would be princes of the fourteenth century and members of the house of Aragon, which ruled at Palermo for a considerable time. Usually, however, the brothers are taken to be Normans and the time of action the twelfth or early thirteenth century.

There is but very little CHANGE OF SCENE in this play, partly on account of the intentional simplicity of the dramatic plot (see the note to l. 1629), partly on account of the Chorus which is nearly always present. The scene changes only four times in the drama; it returns twice to places where the action had taken place before, so that there are only three different scenes of action in the whole play. The TIME OF ACTION occupies one day and the following night, less than twenty-four hours. It has been questioned whether so many events could possibly have happened during those few hours. The answer is that in a drama the steady sequence of events is alone important and that it would be pedantic to calculate exactly, watch in hand, how much time each event would require in real life. Just as futile would it be to attempt to draw any conclusions from l. 192 (see the note) as to the season when the action is supposed to take place. The UNITY OF ACTION is unbroken throughout the play; nothing could be omitted, everything is well linked together as it stands. Objections have been raised to two Scenes in the Second Act, viz. II. 2 and II. 6, about which the Notes should be consulted. The Third and Fourth Acts are models of masterly dramatic structure. In the printed edition Schiller had intentionally abstained from dividing the tragedy into Acts, but had printed Scene after Scene without a break, in the manner of the ancient classical dramas. During Schiller's lifetime and indeed until 1869 the various printed editions of the drama did not give the division into Acts. But for the representation of the play at Berlin, Hamburg, and elsewhere the author divided the play into four Acts, and on the original play-bill of the Weimar theatre it was described as : Trauerspiel mit drei Pausen, which is equivalent to Four Acts. When he was writing the play he seems to have thought of five sections, and in a letter to Goethe (see Appendix II, *d*, p. 250) he speaks of the first four Acts as occupying five-sixths of the whole play, thus implying its completion by a fifth Act that would take the remaining one-sixth part. It seems probable that in the ultimate division into four Acts the fourth and a short fifth Act (IV. 8 to 9) were united in the present Act IV; some scholars are of opinion that the present Act II contains the original Acts II and III (II. 1—4 and II. 5), but this seems less probable. (See the introductory note to Scene 5 on p. 185.)

The PLOT of the play was this time not taken from history, as had been the case with Wallenstein, Maria Stuart, and Die Jungfrau von Orleans, nor was it mythological and borrowed from some well-known Greek legend, as was the case with Goethe's Iphigenie. Die Braut von Messina is a domestic tragedy after the model of the ancients, and the plot is an invention of Schiller's[37]. Schiller had not treated an original subject since the days of his early revolutionary social dramas Die Räuber and Kabale und Liebe, and among the great finished tragedies of his last period Die Braut von Messina is the only one of this type. In many ways it bears a resemblance to the greatest of Schiller's dramas, Wallenstein; as in that play the subject is the utter ruin of a noble house. But there are many more romantic elements in Die Braut than in Wallenstein.

It was Schiller's aim to attempt the writing of a tragedy in the strictest Greek form, after the manner of the ancient Attic tragedies[38]. In order to do this, his first task was to invent a

[37] See Schiller's letter to Körner dated May 13, 1801, printed in the Appendix II, *b*, p. 248. As early as March 21, 1799, Goethe had told their common friend H. Meyer that the plot of Schiller's new drama was his own free invention.

[38] See his letters given in the Appendix II, *b*, II, *e*, and II, *f*, pp. 248—51.

plot that should be similar to plots treated by Aeschylus, Sophocles, and Euripides, and should, if possible, ' offer all the advantages of the *Oedipus Rex* of Sophocles.' He had carefully read the masterpieces of the Greek tragedians, mostly in German translations, had himself translated large portions of two Euripidean tragedies, had carefully considered the character and possibilities of the *Oedipus*[39], and studied four Aeschylean tragedies (in Stolberg's translation) with great enthusiasm just at the time when he was engaged upon his new drama[40]. Thus he believed that he had thoroughly entered into the spirit of the ancients and felt inclined to attempt to rival them on their own ground and, as he put it jestingly to Humboldt, to see if he, ' the most modern of all modern poets,' might not perhaps ' as a contemporary of Sophocles have won a prize[41].' Hence it is but natural that much of the plot which he invented for his special purpose shows similarities with incidents and peculiarities of style and conception that are found in the ancient classical dramas. ' Karoline von Wolzogen, Schiller's highly-cultured sister-in-law, says in her *Life of Schiller*: Man müsse eine tragische Familie erfinden, fiel ihm einmal ein, ähnlich der des Atreus und Lajus, durch die sich eine Verkettung von Unglück fortzöge. Am Rhein, wo die Revolution so viele edle Geschlechter vom Gipfel des Glücks herabgestürzt, und wo in schwankenden Verhältnissen der Doppelsinn des Lebens die ebne Bahn leicht verwirren könne, sei der passendste Platz für ein solches Gemälde des Menschengeschicks in seiner Allgemeinheit[42]. He did in fact conceive

[39] See the letter to Professor Süvern in the Appendix II, *a*, p. 248.

[40] See his letter to W. von Humboldt, in the Appendix II, *e*, p. 250.

[41] See Appendix II, *e*, p. 250.

[42] Karoline von Wolzogen, *Schillers Leben* (in Cotta's ' Bibliothek der Weltlitteratur '), p. 250. The passage quoted above occurs in connexion with Schiller's plan of writing a continuation of Die Räuber. See p. lxxii of this edition. This conception in the poet's mind of a tragic family was realized in Die Braut von Messina, but in order to make the conditions of life more similar to those found in the ancient classical tragedies Schiller abandoned the idea of making the Rhine country

the idea of such a 'tragic family,' similar to that of Atreus and Laios, but laid the scene of action, for the reasons given above, in medieval Sicily.

The ELEMENTS FROM WHICH SCHILLER CONSTRUCTED HIS PLOT are numerous; they are partly modern and romantic, and partly classical. There was no old story in existence which he could have adopted for his purpose.

The subject of the Hostile Brothers is one of the oldest in the literature of the world. It is at once Biblical (Cain slays Abel), legendary (Romulus kills Remus), and literary (as in the hostile brothers of Thebes, also Atreus and Thyestes[43]). But Schiller treated the subject in its modern and romantic form, as Leisewitz and Klinger had done, and as he himself had treated it in his earliest drama, Die Räuber. In this modern handling the element of love, which is entirely absent from the ancient legends and dramas, is introduced. In the modern tragedies the brothers, apart from other points of difference, love the same maiden. This brings about the catastrophe. One brother kills the other and has to atone for the murder with his own life. In Die Braut von Messina Schiller added the new tragic feature that the maiden is the sister of the hostile brothers, so that neither of them can ultimately possess her. The suggestion that, in imitation of the relationship of Oedipus and Iocasta, Schiller intended to introduce into his drama even an incest, in the relation of Don Manuel to Beatrice[44], should be rejected (see the note to l. 842).

Thus the groundwork of the plot is modern and romantic, but it is interwoven with many classical motives, borrowed partly from Homer and partly from the Greek tragedians. The curse of an ancestor (l. 964) may have been taken from Homer's

of the end of the eighteeenth century the scene of action and chose instead medieval Sicily which had for many years strongly attracted him.

[43] See chapter viii on pp. lxiv sqq.

[44] See Erich Harnack's article in the *Internationale Wochenschrift*, quoted on p. 271.

Iliad (IX. 454—57)[45], but ancestral curses are not uncommon in popular traditions or in literature, as is seen in the well-known Greek legend of Hippolytus and his father Theseus. The dream of the mother before the birth of the child that will cause the ruin of her house, the interpretation of her dream, the casting out of the child, its preservation and ultimate return to the house of its parents, are likewise found in various ancient traditions. This part of the story reminds us throughout of the legend of Oedipus, also the old tradition about the youth of the great Persian King Cyrus, and furthermore of a legend which seems to have been treated by Sophocles in his lost tragedy *Alexandros*, the outlines of the plot of which have been preserved in the short and dry account given by Hyginus[46]. Schiller knew the famous collection of ancient plots in the so-called *Fabulae* of Hyginus very well, and in shaping the plot of his Braut von Messina he may perhaps have thought of the *Alexander-Paris* Fable (No. 91); but there is no reason to assume that Schiller based the Greek portion of his plot mainly on Hyginus, as the greater part of the Alexander-Paris story has nothing whatever in common with Schiller's drama. The fourth element of importance in Schiller's plot is the peculiar atmosphere of the medieval Sicilian world which, by an ingenious idea of the poet, was used as a magnificent setting for his moving domestic tragedy. The life of the people of Messina in a

[45] In Homer's *Iliad* the curse of the father was that his son who had appropriated to himself the woman beloved by his sire should never have a child of his own.

[46] In order to facilitate comparison the whole 'fable' has been printed in the Appendix IV, on p. 262. See the essay of Ernst Maass, in *Deutsche Rundschau*, Vol. 134, quoted on p. 272. It seems to have formed the subject of the first drama of a trilogy on the subject of Troy, which fell through the reckless abduction of fair Helen of Sparta by Priam's son Alexandros (Paris). Paris is thus destined to become the ruin of his family and of his country: this is foretold by a dream before he is born. Beatrice too is destined to be the cause of the downfall of her house, but it is brought about not so much by her action as by her mere existence.

country that is most beautiful and fertile, but at the same time constantly exposed to the danger of terrible eruptions of Mount Etna and the sudden raids of pirates, forms the lurid background to the rapidly approaching doom of its passionate rulers.

These are the principal elements upon which Schiller draws for his plot. In addition his diction was strongly influenced by Goethe's Jphigenie (see p. xciv), and that of one scene (Act II. Scene 2) by the Spanish metre of Calderon and his German imitators (see the note to l. 1057). There are other points in which Schiller may or may not have been indebted to the works of other poets, but not one of them is of real importance. Thus it is possible that the meeting of Beatrice with Don Cesar in the church was suggested by the similar meeting of Emilia with the Prince of Guastalla in Lessing's domestic tragedy Emilia Galotti (Act II, Scene 6), about which the note to l. 1118 should be consulted. It is also very likely that Isabella's impressive address to the elders of the town of Messina (in the opening scene of our drama) was consciously modelled on similar opening scenes which Schiller had read in ancient Greek tragedies. See the note on p. 124. But it must be added that Isabella's speech is much more dramatic and more closely bound up with the action of the play than the speeches of Atossa and Iocasta.

Thus we see that in Schiller's plot the finest spirit of the ancient Greek poets, as found in Homer and Attic tragedy, is blended with a distinctly modern element, the romantic treatment of the subject of the Hostile Brothers by the writers of the Storm and Stress drama. All these elements were finally welded together, with important modifications and additions of his own, by the master-mind of the mature artist, the most modern and at the same time the most profound of all modern German poets, who desired for once to leave his usual sphere of dramatic production in order to try how far it was possible for him to write a play in the style of the ancients and to what extent the most valuable features of the ancient Greek tragedies, the simpleness of their structure and, above all, their lyrical elements could be made fruitful for modern dramatic art[47].

The LEADING IDEA of $\mathfrak{D}$ie $\mathfrak{B}$raut von $\mathfrak{M}$essina is the downfall of a noble reigning house through lack of self-control on the part of its members. In order to give to his drama an antique colouring and to conform to some extent to the methods of the ancient tragedians, Schiller introduced into his tragedy the idea of Fate which brings about the ruin of all the members of this 'tragic family.' Their unavoidable doom is said to be due to the curse of an ancestor whose son (the father of Don Manuel and Don Cesar) had carried off and married, apparently against her will, the girl whom his father had selected for his own bride[48]. The incensed ancestor had thereupon poured terrible curses on this wretched marriage and had said that Isabella should give birth to hatred and strife[49]. At the end of the drama, when the two unhappy women stand mourning by the side of the dead brothers and behold the male line of their race extinct, the destiny of the family seems fulfilled; the curse has destroyed the sons of the offender and ruined the happiness of those who are left. But in this classical *motif* of an ancient family curse Schiller has really emphasized a very important modern idea. According to a tolerably well authenticated utterance of his intentions to Böttiger, then headmaster

[47] In making the attempt to introduce the Chorus into a drama of the highest type, and with this lyrical element to call in the aid of music, Schiller was not merely influenced by Greek ideas and Greek models, but his 'experiment' must above all be looked upon as the supreme effort in a series of similar attempts in which several modern poets and critics had preceded him. See chapter VI.

[48] In an earlier tragedy of Schiller's, $\mathfrak{D}$on $\mathfrak{C}$arlos, just the opposite had taken place. Here Don Philip II, the King of Spain, had married Elizabeth of Valois, who was the *fiancée* of his son and heir, Don Carlos. By doing this he wrecked his son's life.

[49] See lines 960—76, and compare Isabella's brief corroboration, lines 2504—6, although she does not, with good reason, ever directly refer to the curse.

of the Weimar Grammar School[50], Schiller wished to develop in Die Braut von Messina the idea of heredity. The curse laid on the members of this family is in reality their innate passionate temper, their secrecy, and their utter inability to exercise moderation and self-control. The brothers have inherited their egotistical and masterful ways from their stern and ruthless father whose doings, although he is dead when the action begins, are of the greatest importance for the drama; even Beatrice is not free from the family failing, and each of the three children contributes something to the completion of the doom of the family. In every tragedy there must be a conflict between the will of the hero and the resistance to its free play by outside limitations and unavoidable influences arising from his inherited moral temper, from the surroundings among which he has grown up, and from the actual conditions of life in which he must work. Thus a modern writer may with reason call inherited physical and moral family gifts or weaknesses a person's 'fate.' As certain diseases are

---

[50] Given in the *Minerva*, 1814, p. 8. See Jakob Minor, in the *Grillparzer-Jahrbuch*, IX (1899), 61—62. Böttiger asserts that in writing Die Braut von Messina Schiller had been actuated by the thought, daß ein Volk, ein Geschlecht, physisch und moralisch immer mehr ausarte, aber in dieser Ausartung auch selbst schon den unvermeidlichen Fluch seiner Vorfahren trage, und endlich, wenn das Maß voll sei, ohne Rettung untergehe. Es sei hier eine wunderbare Wechselwirkung: denn so wie es geschehe, daß selbst ausgeartete Kinder noch des Segens ihrer frommen und gerechten Vorfahren teilhaftig würden, so sei Schuld und Ruchlosigkeit der Väter auch noch ein verderbendes Erbteil für eine dem Anschein nach schuldlose Nachkommenschaft geworden. Man müsse hier nur das Animalische, das in der Fortpflanzung, in der Rasse liege, und bei den Menschen Stammescharakter heißt, von dem unterscheiden, das die frühe Angewöhnung, Erziehung, Beispiele dem Stämmchen noch überdies einimpfen. Beides wirke gemeinschaftlich, beides liege gewiß schon im Blute. So wie es Familiengesichter und Familienkrankheiten gebe, so auch forterbende moralische Gebrechen, und bei der zunehmenden physischen Schwäche auch ein moralisches Unvermögen. See also Erich Harnack's essay, '*Über das Problem der Vererbung in Schiller's Braut von Messina*,' quoted in the Appendix V, on p. 271.

often transmitted from father to son, so also moral deficiencies, evil dispositions, uncontrollable passions are inherited, and are further accentuated by an education in which moderation and love are wanting. This is what Schiller wished to bring out in his play, this is really the meaning of the old family curse from which none of the children of the offending father is free, and which ultimately ruins the lives of all of them. Here we see a new and intelligible form given to the old idea of destiny. Thus we have no longer a blind and incomprehensible *moira* ruling over the lives of the principal persons in the drama as in the case of the *Oedipus Rex*, but we have the connexion between cause and effect. Hard and cruel as the law of heredity no doubt sometimes is, still it is reasonable. The moral order of things is respected. The curse is fulfilled in the misery caused by the hereditary want of moderation and self-control, the rash yielding to the promptings of the heart from which the sister suffers no less than her brothers. Each of them acts as his innermost nature makes him act and thus precipitates the impending doom. For each of them Don Cesar's confession holds good: bie Freiheit hab' ich und die Wahl ver= loren (l. 1154). In transforming the old idea of the 'fate' of a person in this modern and scientific manner, making the hereditary constitution the real curse transmitted by the ancestor, Schiller seems to have been influenced by an important essay by Herder[51]. This essay Das eigene Schicksal had

---

[51] Herder contributed to the third number of Schiller's monthly periodical Die Horen (1795) a very thoughtful article called Das eigene Schicksal (III. I sqq.). On p. 2 we read Jeder Mensch hat sein eigenes Schicksal, weil jeder Mensch seine Art zu sein und zu handeln hat..... On p. 5: dein Schicksal ist das Resultat deines Charakters. On p. 18: Man spricht oft von unglücklichen Familien; und warum sollte es deren nicht geben? Erben sich nicht falsche Grundsätze und Gedankenverwirrungen, böse Anlagen und Leidenschaften wie Seuchen und Gebrechen fort? und werden sie nicht oft durch Erziehung genährt?...Kannst du, so heile das Familien-Übel, und es wird eine gesunde Sprosse hervorblühen, die den Unglücksnamen hinwegnimmt, die vom bösen Dämon das Haus reinigt. And in an essay in his Abrastea, written in 1802, when Schiller was at work on his drama, Herder calls die

already been of importance for Schiller's Wallenstein[52], and there is no doubt that really Die Braut von Messina stands in much closer relationship to Wallenstein than to the *Oedipus Rex*. The ruin of the children of Isabella arises from their own characters and is not brought about, as in the Sophoclean tragedy, chiefly by outward circumstances[53]. Beatrice might have said, like her more clear-sighted sister Thekla in Wallenstein:

> Es geht ein finstrer Geist durch unser Haus,
> Und schleunig will das Schicksal mit uns enden.
> (Die Piccolomini, III. 9, ll. 1899—1900.)

The question is often asked: Is Die Braut von Messina a 'FATE-TRAGEDY'? From what has been said it is clear that the term is inappropriate if it is taken to mean, as it usually is, a drama in which the reasonable exercise of the free-will of the persons of the drama is paralysed by some arbitrary, cruel and inexorable fate that crushes every attempt of the chief persons to escape from their predestined terrible end and drags them through parricide and incest to wretchedness and ruin. Such caricatures of a tragedy were the silly 'fate-tragedies' of Werner, Müllner, Houwald and others which, to Goethe's disgust, appeared soon after Schiller's death and ostensibly followed the example set by Schiller in Die Braut

---

Umstände, unter denen Oedipus geboren wurde, sein Verhängnis, den Stammes-charakter sein Schicksal. Cp. also Minor in the *Jahrbuch der Grillparzer-Gesellschaft*, IX. 61.

[52] See my Pitt Press edition of Wallenstein, Vol. II. (1901), Introd. xlviii.

[53] It should, however, be noted that the conception of the *rôle* played by fate in the *Oedipus Rex* is not by any means typical of Greek tragedies in general. The *Oedipus Rex* is an exceptional play in this respect, and it is a one-sided view that draws general conclusions about the 'Greek fate-tragedy' from this drama alone. See J. Minor in the *Grillparzer-Jahrbuch*, IX, p. 11; and Ulrich von Wilamowitz in his *Griechische Tragödien übersetzt*, Vol. I (Berlin, 1899), especially pages 10 sqq.

von 𝔐effina⁵⁴. Schiller's great tragedy is very different from
these. In it the characters act with entire freedom⁵⁵ and are, one
and all, not without moral guilt, more or less serious, although
it must be admitted that what they have to suffer greatly exceeds
in each case what, in strict justice, they have individually
deserved. Don Cesar incurs most actual guilt, Isabella least.
But in the case of both mother and children it is clear that their
characters are their fate and they shape it. Schiller's own view
is clearly expressed in the concluding lines of the drama, in
which, after an impressive pause, the Chorus deliberately state
as their conviction:

> Das Leben ist der Güter höchstes nicht,
> Der Übel aber höchstes ist die Schuld.

What else can this mean but that the poet wished to point the
moral that a life lived under the sense of a load of guilt is not
worth living? The lesson which is to be learned from Schiller's
Braut von 𝔐effina is therefore: Control your passions,
keep clear from guilt, do not wreck the happiness of your life
by want of self-control! All this is very different from the
impression obtained from reading the *Oedipus Rex* or seeing it
acted.

Still it cannot be denied that in Die Braut von 𝔐effina the
importance of Fate is more accentuated than in any other drama
of Schiller, even in Wallenstein. In the latter drama only a few
persons seem to believe in Fate, but in Die Braut von 𝔐effina
the word Fate occurs on the lips of every person and is frequently used by leaders of the Chorus in passages where they

---

[54] See the strong expression of this feeling in the (suppressed)
stanza to his *Maskenzug vom 18ten Dezember*, 1818, printed on p. 257
(under II, *p*, ll. 1—8).

[55] The best articles recently written on this vexed but very important question are those by C. Weitbrecht, E. Bergmann, R.
Petsch, H. Gloël, and F. Hahne. The full titles are given in the
Appendix V, on pp. 270—73. Bergmann's essay of 1906 contains
a very useful classification and discussion of previous essays and different
views.

clearly speak not as blind partisans and ignorant children of the people, but in which they rise to the higher level of dispassionate reflexion. While in all tragedies there must be a conflict between freedom and necessity, the only difference between them consisting in the different mixture of these two elements and the different prominence given by the poet to the one or the other, it is clear that in 𝔇𝔦𝔢 𝔅𝔯𝔞𝔲𝔱 𝔳𝔬𝔫 𝔐𝔢𝔣𝔣𝔦𝔫𝔞 Schiller has purposely given to the element of necessity an unusually large space. He was obviously anxious to approach, as far as his Kantian and modern convictions allowed him, to the stern conception of the ancients in a play by which he wished to enter into competition with Sophocles. Thus a number of accidents and misunderstandings are introduced which all prevent a timely recognition and a happy solution, and the two dreams (which in this play replace the oracles of the ancients) have a much greater importance than in his other plays. They are meant to be more than a mere poetic ornament. They both come true. This cannot be mere accident. Schiller obviously intended not only Isabella and her children, but also the spectators, to assume that these dreams were sent to the Prince and Princess as indications of the future. Thus Schiller, in his wish to assimilate his drama as much as possible to the conceptions of the ancients, seems actually to have gone so far as to represent in it Fate not merely as the subjective belief in an unalterable Destiny held by some .persons of the play, but rather as an objective and independent power shaping the destinies of the princely family. The work of Fate in our drama is shown in the inexplicable early hatred of the brothers and the irresistible attraction exercised on both brothers by Beatrice whom they both meet by accident and without suspecting who is. The irresistible attraction can be explained by Beatrice's unusual beauty and also by a certain physiological element, a family likeness, which is mysterious to the brothers, but not to the onlookers. Still, although Schiller made these concessions to the spirit of the ancients (and we should not shut our eyes to this fact[56]), they are not the essential

[56] This has recently been well brought out by H. Gloël.

features of his drama. The first meeting of the brothers with
Beatrice was due to a mere chance, and the brothers cannot
but be strongly attracted by her; but all that follows these
meetings springs entirely from the characters of all the persons
concerned. Beatrice's two secret visits (the one to the funeral
of the Prince and the other to the church near the garden which
she was told not to leave), by which the whole disaster is brought
upon her, are due merely to her own inability to deny herself a
wish. The way in which Isabella deals with the two dreams and,
while believing in the truth of her own, attempts to frustrate
the prediction of the other, is characteristic of her autocratic
nature. Everywhere we see that Schiller has taken the greatest
care not to diminish the full responsibility of his dramatic
characters and has consequently taken unusual pains with the
characterisation of the principal persons[57]. Nowhere do they
appear as mere tools in the hands of a blind Fate. Schiller,
the ardent disciple of Kant, the manly poet who always in-
sisted on the supreme importance of human responsibility and
who demanded that the will of man should rise superior to
the various limitations imposed by his temperament and his
surroundings, would never have consented to degrade the
children of Isabella to mere irresponsible puppets. In the end
Don Cesar heroically breaks the power of the curse by his
voluntary death—and we must admit that for a character such
as his no other solution is possible (ll. 2724—28). Thus in his
attitude towards the conflict between freedom and necessity the
poet of Die Braut von Messina shows the great importance in
every human life of what may be called a person's *fate*: his
inherited disposition and the powerful moulding influence of
his surroundings, without, however, entirely exonerating the
characters from the sad consequences of their passion-prompted

[57] The best discussion of the characters of the brothers is the one
by F. Hahne. For the characterisation of Isabella and Beatrice the
book by Julius Burggraf should be consulted, and for the Choruses
the excellent essay by K. Olbrich. For the exact references see the
Appendix V, pp. 270—2.

B. *d*

actions. As in 𝔚𝔞𝔩𝔩𝔢𝔫𝔰𝔱𝔢𝔦𝔫, and here even more than in 𝔚𝔞𝔩𝔩𝔢𝔫𝔰𝔱𝔢𝔦𝔫, Schiller

> ſieht den Menſchen in des Lebens Drang
> Und wälzt die gröſʒre Hälfte ſeiner Schuld
> Den unglückſeligen Geſtirnen zu[58].

In conclusion we may admit that this attempt to emphasize the idea of necessity by introducing something of the ancient conception of fate into a modern drama and so treat a romantic subject in an antique style is occasionally rather confusing, and hence not quite successful. At the end of the tragedy we are more depressed than elevated, and feel the deepest pity for the two lonely women, above all for Isabella, whose suffering is quite out of proportion to her apparent deserts. Goethe expressed this natural feeling in his Maskenzug of 1818[59], and there can be no doubt that the blending of the ancient and the modern in his own Iphigenie auf Tauris is more satisfactory to modern feeling. Here an ancient subject has been filled with Goethe's own soul. In Schiller's drama, too, the spirit is not Greek, but modern, romantic, and even philosophical and scientific; so is the idea of heredity which pervades it. It remains a production that appeals to a smaller public than the other dramas of Schiller. No doubt Die Braut von Meſſina is a lofty work of art, unique in its way in German literature; for Schiller, however, it was but a poetic experiment, and in his subsequent plays he did not repeat this, but struck out new lines.

All the members of this family tower above their retainers, among whom they cannot have any confidential friends, but only more or less devoted servants. Mother and children must therefore be bound to one another by ties all the closer, and

[58] See the *Prologue* to 𝔚𝔞𝔩𝔩𝔢𝔫𝔰𝔱𝔢𝔦𝔫 Lager, ll. 108—10, and compare my note in the Pitt Press edition (1896), p. 176.

[59] The final stanzas of it are given on p. 257 under II, *p*. The two bereaved women, Isabella and Beatrice, appear in the stately procession of figures from Schiller's dramas, and Aurora pronounces in their name some reflexions on their sad fate.

must exercise the strongest influence on one another—they are impassioned and hot-blooded people and cannot help either passionately loving or hating each other. All the CHARACTERS are skilfully drawn, often by but a few strokes. Schiller originally felt that the development of the plot and the preparation for the various recognitions was more interesting than the drawing of the characters[60], but in the final form of the drama each person has become an interesting personality. Isabella is especially well drawn. Schiller's older women are as a rule better than his girls; the Countess Terzky, Gertrud Stauffacher, Hedwig Tell, Marfa are all drawn with a master hand. Beatrice is much less resolute than Thekla, Wallenstein's high-minded daughter, but still she has a distinct individuality of her own. The brothers are well contrasted[61]. They have certain family characteristics in common, their unruly disposition and their autocratic ways, but Don Manuel is the gentler character, he is more of a dreamer and schemer, he has certain characteristics that appeal to women, and he understands how to win their confidence and affection; while Don Cesar is direct and ruthless, the born ruler, who commands peremptorily and acts quickly, and in his lordly manner has but little consideration for the feeling of a woman. He and Beatrice are greatly under the influence of their hot blood, while Don Manuel keeps cooler and calmer. It is very doubtful whether he, in Don Cesar's place, would have killed his brother without first demanding a word of expla-nation. This would have made the murder impossible, and Schiller, for whose plan the fratricide was necessary, allotted the *rôles* of the brothers accordingly.

In this drama it is more difficult than in Die Jungfrau von Orleans or in Wilhelm Tell to say who should be called the HERO of the play. By changing the title from Die feindlichen Brüder von Messina into Die Braut von Messina Schiller wished to indicate that Beatrice was the principal person. It

[60] See his letter to Körner, dated May 13, 1801, printed in the Appendix II, *b*, on p. 249.
[61] See the note 56.

is she who by her very existence, and also by some of her deliberate actions, brings about the downfall of her family. Everything happens for her and on account of her. Still she is rather a passive heroine, as is fair Helen of Troy, for whose sake many of the best Greeks and Trojans perished. The active hero is Don Cesar, and he is usually called the tragic hero of the play. He does most, suffers most, and develops most during the play. In the end he is able to gain the greatest victory, the victory over his own unruly heart. He overcomes the hereditary failing of his whole race : its egotism and lack of self-control. He is the principal actor and bears the heaviest burden of guilt. He is forgiven by his mother and obtains the sisterly love of Beatrice. The most impressive figure is probably the unhappy mother, who is indeed another Niobe. In these circumstances it seems best to say that, just as in Wilhelm Tell the hero of the drama is not a single personage, the archer Wilhelm Tell, but rather the whole Swiss nation, the real hero of Die Braut von Messina is neither Beatrice nor Don Cesar, but the whole 'tragic family,' the princely house of Messina. The downfall of this proud family, so full of secrecy and unrestrained passion, is the subject of the tragedy.

Most of Schiller's dramas are distinctly historical, the scene of action being laid in different countries, viz. Italy (Fiesco), Spain (Don Carlos), Germany (Wallenstein), England (Maria Stuart), France (Die Jungfrau von Orleans), Switzerland (Wilhelm Tell), and Russia (Demetrius). The subjects of Warbeck and Die Maltefer were likewise historical, and these dramas, if completed, would have taken us once more to England and to Italy. Only three of Schiller's finished tragedies have no historical background and are based on a plot of the poet's invention. Two of these are the early plays of his 'Storm and Stress' period : his first remarkable attempt, the crude and bold revolutionary play Die Räuber, and the powerful domestic tragedy Kabale und Liebe (originally bearing the name of the heroine Luise Millerin). But while these two dramas are modern plays filled with denunciations of contemporary German

INTRODUCTION xlv

political and social abuses, Die Braut von Messina is an idealistic play, the scene of action of which is medieval Sicily, and the purpose of which was a literary experiment.

In yet another way the drama holds a position of its own among Schiller's tragedies. It is an essentially *lyrical* drama, not only on account of the songs of the Chorus, but also on account of the many fine lyric passages occurring in scenes of ordinary dialogue. Such portions are Beatrice's monologue, Don Manuel's account to the Chorus of his first meeting with Beatrice, the account given by Don Cesar to Isabella and Don Manuel of his first meeting with Beatrice, and also the kind of *terzetto* between Beatrice and the men of Don Manuel and of Don Cesar (III. 1, ll. 1725 sqq.). In these lyrical portions Die Braut von Messina stands half way between the ordinary tragedy in blank verse, such as Don Carlos or Wallenstein, and the romantic opera of Richard Wagner, and is also in this respect a most interesting experiment of the great dramatist[62].

VI. THE CHORUS IN SCHILLER'S DRAMA.

Wenn das Drama wirklich durch einen so schlechten Hang des Zeitalters in Schutz genommen wird, wie ich nicht zweifle, so müßte man die Reform beim Drama anfangen, und durch Verdrängung der gemeinen Naturnachahmung der Kunst Luft und Licht verschaffen....Ich hatte immer ein gewisses Vertrauen zur Oper, daß aus ihr, wie aus den Chören des alten Bacchusfestes, das Trauerspiel in einer edlern Gestalt sich loswickeln sollte....Die Oper stimmt durch die Macht der Musik...das Gemüt zu einer schönern Empfängnis; hier ist wirklich auch im Pathos selbst ein freieres Spiel, weil die Musik es begleitet....

Schiller to Goethe, December 29, 1797 (Jonas, *Schillers Briefe*, v. 312, 313).

Full information as to Schiller's artistic purpose in introducing the Chorus into his drama was given by himself, beside a few remarks in his correspondence, in his suggestive essay ' On the

[62] See Konrad Burdach, *Schillers Chordrama und die Geburt des tragischen Stils aus der Musik.* See Appendix V, p. 270.

use of the Chorus in Tragedy,' which he appended to the first printed edition of the drama and which since that time has always been reprinted with it. In this edition it is given in Appendix I, pp. 239—47. An anonymous English translation of this essay is prefixed to A. Lodge's translation of *The Bride of Messina* in Bohn's Standard Library (London, 1889, pp. 439 sqq.). Schiller took a great deal of pains with this critical essay[63], and without doubt it is one of the most brilliant of his aesthetic writings. It is the result of Schiller's and Goethe's fruitful exchange of views on dramatic problems and of their whole-hearted collaboration which we see reflected in their correspondence for eleven years without a break. The essay should be studied in connexion with the poet's correspondence, especially the important letter to Goethe of December 29, 1797, from which an extract has been quoted at the beginning of this chapter, and also with Schiller's and Goethe's carefully considered joint-essay, 'On Epic and Dramatic Poetry,' written towards the end of 1797, the outcome of much thought and a prolonged exchange of views. The essay 'On the use of the Chorus in Tragedy' deserves a place of honour among Schiller's best aesthetic writings (such as the illuminating and much longer essay on 'Naive and Sentimental Poetry'), as it contains Schiller's most mature views on dramatic art and the purpose of Tragedy. It has been fitly called die großartigste aller kritischen Noten, die jemals einem erhabenen Dichterwerke von der Hand seines Urhebers beigefügt worden[64].

The essay shows that Schiller realized perfectly the character and purpose of the classic Greek Chorus and that he had good reason for not introducing it into his drama exactly as it appears in the *Oedipus Rex* of Sophocles. Schiller's avowed purpose in

---

[63] See his letter to Goethe dated May 24, 1803 (Jonas, *Schillers Briefe*, VII. 43), in which he says: das ganze Theater mit samt dem ganzen Zeitalter drückt auf mich ein, und ich weiß kaum, wie ich es abfertigen soll. Übrigens interessiert mich diese Arbeit; ich will suchen, etwas recht Ordentliches zu sagen und der Sache, die uns gemeinsam wichtig ist, dadurch zu dienen.

[64] Michael Bernays, *Schriften zur Kritik und Literaturgeschichte*, Berlin, 1899, IV. 342.

introducing the Chorus was to counteract the tendency towards a shallow naturalism in contemporary dramatic poetry and to strengthen the latent symbolism of his tragedy. The use of the Chorus in this domestic tragedy was not the aberration of a modern poet and an undue concession to extreme classicism, as has often been asserted; it was a deliberate step in Schiller's attempt to reform the modern drama, by means of which he hoped to deepen its appeal to the emotions and so to bring it nearer to the greatest Greek tragedies. The Chorus, as used by Schiller, was intended to idealize the action of the play, to lift it above the commonplace in expression and feeling, to counteract crude naturalism, and to spiritualize, as it were, every-day reality. By the strong expression of lyric emotion by a number of men the Chorus was to intensify pathos. The Chorus is in fact an essential lyrical part of the drama; by its introduction Schiller sought to impart to the drama a musical element, of a moving and elevating kind, and thus an alliance, as it were, between poetry and music is effected. In Schiller's view, and not only in his but also in Goethe's, and in that of the greatest and most competent German poets and critics of his time, this combination of poetic and musical elements was calculated to produce a loftier style in tragic plays[65]. Thus the introduction of the Chorus into this play was not only a poetic device that had been carefully considered by Schiller for many years, but it was a deliberate artistic experiment, in harmony with many previous attempts of the same kind made in Germany and abroad during the eighteenth century, attempts advocated not only by extreme classicists. The use of the Chorus in Die Braut von Meffina may be called the supreme effort in a long series of important endeavours to blend once again in the drama words and melody, poetry and music. These efforts were not by any means limited to Germany, but had originated in Italy and in England as a reaction against the French rhetorical drama of the seventeenth

[65] This has been shown convincingly by Konrad Burdach in his learned and brilliant articles contributed to the *Deutsche Rundschau*, under the title 'Schillers Chordrama und die Geburt des tragischen Stils aus der Musik.' See the Appendix V, p. 270.

century; they also spread to France itself[66]. In Germany the first
serious attempt to combine poetry and music, the spoken dialogue
and the chanted choruses in serious drama, was made by no less
a person than Klopstock in his bardic dramas (𝔅𝔞𝔯𝔟𝔦𝔢𝔱𝔢) on
Hermann, the Cheruscan liberator of Germany. This 'musical
poet,' as he was called by Schiller, attempted to create a German
national drama in his 'Hermann' trilogy, in which plays there
was a combination of prose-dialogue, of monodic song, and of
'songs of the bards,' i.e. choruses, in a dignified free metre.
Lessing subsequently recommended the use of free lyric metre
in serious dramas, as well as a combination of poetry and
music in such plays, although the great critic was unable to
write them himself. The critic Sulzer also emphatically approved
of the use of the Chorus in the spoken drama. Both Wieland
and Herder produced several plays to which a strong lyrical
element was imparted by means of songs. Of these only
Wieland's 𝔄𝔩𝔠𝔢𝔰𝔱𝔢 and Herder's 𝔅𝔯𝔲𝔱𝔲𝔰, 𝔓𝔥𝔦𝔩𝔬𝔨𝔱𝔢𝔱𝔢𝔰, 𝔇𝔢𝔯
𝔤𝔢𝔣𝔢𝔰𝔰𝔢𝔩𝔱𝔢 𝔓𝔯𝔬𝔪𝔢𝔱𝔥𝔢𝔲𝔰 and 𝔄𝔡𝔪𝔢𝔱𝔲𝔰' 𝔥𝔞𝔲𝔰 can be mentioned.
The brothers Stolberg wrote a number of plays 𝔪𝔦𝔱 𝔆𝔥𝔬̈𝔯𝔢𝔫, of
which 𝔗𝔦𝔪𝔬𝔩𝔢𝔬𝔫, by Friedrich Stolberg (1784), attracted special
attention. Goethe produced, or planned, both before and after
Schiller's choric drama, several plays containing a Chorus. He
conceived the plan of writing a drama 𝔇𝔦𝔢 𝔇𝔞𝔫𝔞𝔦𝔟𝔢𝔫 in the
manner of the ancient Greek tragedy, in which the Chorus was
to play the principal part[67]. One short chorus from another

---

[66] All this has been shown by Burdach in the before-mentioned
essay. For England he refers to the choruses in Milton's *Samson
Agonistes* and to the later work of Mason, especially his *Elfride*, in
which a chorus of maidens is introduced. This drama was translated into
German and was probably known to Schiller, among whose unfinished
sketches a plan of an 𝔈𝔩𝔣𝔯𝔦𝔡𝔢 tragedy is found. There are a number of
Italian (eighteenth century) dramas with choruses. In France Racine
introduced choruses of Jewish maidens into his biblical dramas *Esther*
and *Athalie*, set to music by Moreau, as a means of idealizing and
heightening the tragic style.

[67] See his letter to Zelter dated May 29, 1801. [Weimar ed. Part
IV, Vol. 15, p. 232.]

intended play, Die Befreiung des Prometheus, a song of the Nereids, has been preserved; it is in noble free metre[68]. The plays Helena and Pandora, which are, like Die Braut von Messina, mixtures of classical and romantic elements, both require song and music; they contain choruses and are throughout lyrical in character. Especially in the Pandora we find a combination of Classicism and Romanticism similar to that in Schiller's Braut. There are iambic trimeters as well as rimed choruses, and an extraordinary variety of rhythms, the whole play being a wonderful mixture of lyric and dramatic elements. Schiller himself, before writing his Braut, had planned another 'Chordrama,' Die Malteser, originally called Die Ritter von Malta. It was a favourite subject of his and occupied him at intervals between 1788 and 1803 when, after the publication of Die Braut von Messina, he wisely gave up the idea of completing it. Numerous sketches and parts of scenes of this interesting drama, written at different times, have come down to us[69]. After he had carried out his desired experiment in Die Braut von Messina he was not anxious to repeat himself immediately afterwards in Die Malteser.

Schiller's important deviations from the practice of the ancients are in no case due to ignorance or carelessness on the part of the poet, but were invariably the result of most careful consideration. There are two principal points in which Schiller's Chorus differs from that in the *Oedipus Rex*. On the one hand the double nature of the Chorus caused by splitting up the uniform Chorus of Sophocles into two semi-choruses consisting of the followers of the two brothers, with all that results from it; and, on the other hand, the introduction of rime and the frank adoption of German instead of Greek metres, for which Schiller deserves unqualified praise. Not only did he not adopt the complicated and rimeless metres of the classical Choruses, but he has not even retained the usual division into strophe and antistrophe. By adopting German metres, whether

[68] See Goethe's Werke [Weimar ed.], Vol. 11, p. 333.

[69] See Gustav Kettner, *Schillers kleinere dramatische Fragmente*, Weimar, 1895, pp. 1—63.

strophic structures in rime or free rhythms (about the force and
beauty of which there is but one opinion), Schiller has rendered
the songs of the Chorus easily intelligible to all modern readers
and prevented their becoming mere ancient Greek curiosities.
The songs were conceived and written by Schiller altogether in
German forms and in the German spirit. Lessing and Herder
had distinctly recommended German imitators of the classical
choruses to follow the example of Klopstock and to write such
lyrical portions in free metre. Some of the finest songs of
Schiller's Chorus (e.g. IV. 4, ll. 2268 sqq.) are composed in free
rhythm. In brilliant effect and wonderful variety they surpass
the earlier attempts of Klopstock, and rank with the best achieve-
ments of Goethe's youth and early manhood in this style.

The double nature of the Chorus has often been objected to
by contemporary and later critics. But, first of all, it is not fair
to judge and condemn Schiller for dividing the Chorus simply
because in this case he has not kept close to the practice of
Sophocles as seen in the *Oedipus Rex*, for this is by no means to be
regarded as the exclusive practice of the Greek tragedians. For
instance, at the conclusion of the 'Seven against Thebes[70]' the
chorus of Theban maidens is likewise split up into two semi-
choruses who, the one against and the other with the consent of
the authorities, go off in different directions in order to escort
the corpse of each of the hostile brothers to the tomb. It is
possible that also in Die Malteſer Schiller may, at least for a
time, have intended to introduce a dissension between the host
of knights. There is a sketch of a scene in which the Provençal
knights are ready to fight the Spanish knights at Malta, a strong
antagonism between these two groups being clearly noticeable,
and where stichomythia of one or two lines in each case is used
as effectively and pointedly for taunt and scorn[71] as in Die Braut,
ll. 1707 sqq. But as they are coming to blows 'the Chorus,'
consisting of sixteen ecclesiastical knights, clad in the long robes
of their order, enter and separate the fighters. In Die Braut

---

[70] See W. Headlam's translation, p. 108.
[71] See Kettner's edition, pp. 61, 62.

the Chorus is divided into two semi-choruses, consisting of the older and the younger knights, followers of Don Manuel and Don Cesar; but at the same time they are conscious of being citizens of the same town and are united in a common regard for the ruling family. In this way Schiller gave to his Choruses a real dramatic personality and allowed them a much more prominent part in the dramatic action than they had had with the ancients, even with Aeschylus, in whose tragedies the Chorus is on the whole more active and of greater importance than in the later plays of Sophocles and Euripides. In Berneker's music the older knights naturally have bass voices while the younger semi-chorus consists of tenors. It has been shown[72] that in the divided Chorus, wherever the knights speak and act as partisans, they reflect exactly the characters of their lords. The men of the older Chorus share many of Don Manuel's peculiarities, the younger Chorus are exactly what Don Cesar has made them. This characteristic feature strongly reminds us of Schiller's Wallen= ſtein, in which the private soldiers in Wallenstein's camp corres-pond very closely to the characters of their generals. Schiller could not bring himself to introduce the Chorus simply for its own sake as in the classical drama of the ancient Greeks, in which the appearance of the Chorus was a matter of course, and was taken for granted 'like the sky in a landscape[73].' To the modern dramatist it appeared necessary that there should be a reason in the scheme of the play for their presence and that they should not merely observe and comment on the action, but have their share in it. A Chorus that does nothing but utter calm reflexions on the actions of the chief personages in a tragedy is merely a sort of intermediary between the chief persons of the play and the spectators. But by giving reasons for the appear-ance and withdrawal of the Chorus, and by dividing it into the followers of each of the two princely brothers, Schiller makes his Chorus represent the young and the middle-aged among the people of Messina, which was in this way shown to be itself split

[72] See K. Olbrich's essay mentioned in the Appendix V, p. 272.
[73] Sime's Life of Schiller, p. 200.

into conflicting parties. It thus stands for a large portion of the common people, the armed citizens of Messina. As such the Chorus is unfit to rise to the calm heights of dispassionate reflexion[74]. It does not represent the poet's own mature and elevated views of life—these are contained in Schiller's philosophical poems and in some of his finest ballads, both of which should be compared with the utterances of the Chorus wherever occasion offers[75]. The views of the men of Messina, however well expressed, are as a rule but the Philistine views of the common herd or express the loyal attachment of warriors to their lords. The speeches are neither wise nor full of insight. The deepest reflexions in the play are not put into the mouth of the Chorus; rather do we hear them towards the end of the tragedy from the lips of Don Cesar. Thus the Chorus stands for the mere populace and lacks the wise and grave character of some of the choruses of elders in the ancient tragedies. Schiller has therefore in his later dramas rightly decided *not* to repeat the experiment of introducing the Chorus as such, but returned, in Wilhelm Tell and Demetrius, to the practice of Wallenstein. As a matter of fact, the band of robbers in his earliest play, Die Räuber, the conspirators in Fiesco, and subsequently the soldiers in Wallenstein and in Die Jungfrau von Orleans, had supplied a background to the hero that was very similar to the armed men of the Chorus in Die Braut von Messina, and the same holds good of the Swiss confederates on the Rütli in Wilhelm Tell and of the Polish diet in Demetrius. The Chorus in Die Braut von Messina is thus more than a halfway house between the ancient classical Chorus and the Robbers, the Wallensteiners and the Swiss. Everywhere Schiller shows

[74] See R. Petsch's suggestive essay on *Chor und Volk im antiken und modernen Drama*, mentioned in the Appendix V, p. 272. Petsch has also pointed out that Christian Weise (in his Masaniello) anticipated Schiller in putting on the German stage the populace as such, not in the form of a classical chorus.

[75] This has been done to some extent in the Notes to this edition. Some of the reflexions of the Master Bell-founder in *The Song of the Bell* may also be compared.

the same mastery in marshalling large numbers of men who in each case are intimately bound up with the action of the play. The few passages in Die Braut von Messina in which the members of the Chorus do not speak as partisans, but rise to the discussion of general themes, stand apart, and these general reflexions of the armed men are felt, especially on the stage, as rather incongruous. Karl August, the Duke of Weimar, was amused at the bewaffnete Poeten, and this discrepancy between the utterances of the Chorus constitutes a real crux for stage-manager[76] and actors, no less than for the composer, which is more difficult of solution than most problems presented by Schiller's tragedies. With Schiller's discussion of the double nature of the Chorus (see p. 247) his letter to Körner of March 10, 1803, should be compared[77].

From the first the chief difficulty in the staging of Die Braut von Messina was, and is still, the way in which the lyrical portions of the drama, i.e. the utterances of the Chorus, should be delivered. According to Schiller's original intentions (that were shared by Goethe), the lyrical portions of the drama were to be set to music. If the Chorus was to fulfil effectively the purpose intended by Schiller, it must raise the tragic style of the play to a higher level; if it was to perform in any way the part played by the ancient Greek Chorus, it must not be recited, but sung. The Braut, if performed in this way, would thus have been a return to the ancient combination of the spoken word (in the serious and reflective monologues and in the ordinary dialogue) with the lyrical element (the lyrical monologue of Beatrice and the utterances of the Chorus) that was sung. In order to produce the play in this manner the Weimar friends had counted on the assistance of their musical friend, the composer Zelter of Berlin[78]. To their regret he was unable to help them,

---

[76] Cp. the observations of Eugen Kilian, *Schillers Massenszenen auf der Bühne*, pp. 108 sqq.; and Heinrich Bulthaupt, *Dramaturgie des Schauspiels*, [8]I. (1902), 416—8, quoted in the Appendix V, pp. 267 and 271.

[77] See the Appendix II, *k*, on p. 254.

[78] See the Appendix II, *g*, p. 251, and also Introd. p. xvi.

for reasons that may partly be due to his own inability to write the music desired by the poet, partly owing to the state of musical composition in the early years of the nineteenth century. Music such as was required for an effective polyphonic setting of Schiller's choruses to the full accompaniment by a good orchestra did not exist in Schiller's time. Not until much later was this kind of music created (on the basis of the work of the great masters Bach and Handel, Gluck, Haydn and Mozart), by Beethoven, Schubert, Schumann and Wagner. Only modern music with its infinite resources could breathe fulness of life into Schiller's Choruses and let them blossom out into what Schiller had in mind, but Zelter was unable to execute, in 1803. In the setting of the lyric choral parts of 𝔇ie 𝔅raut von 𝔐effina by Constanz Berneker the full effect that the grand and varied songs of the Chorus are able to produce has at last been realized. Filled with the lofty spirit of Schiller, schooled in all the possibilities that Richard Wagner had taught the younger generation of composers, devoted all his life to the study and composition of serious choral music, Berneker produced his masterpiece[79] in the spirited setting of Schiller's Choruses to the accompaniment of a full orchestra. As this music is not easy to perform, it is not practicable on every stage, but it should be attempted on all the better stages where it is possible to call in the help of a trained chorus of singers and a good orchestra. The choruses have more than once been sung with great success in German concert rooms, but their effect would be greater if they could be heard on the stage. If the words of the Chorus are not sung, but large portions of it are spoken *unisono* together by a number of persons, its success on the stage is extremely precarious and the result has often been far from effective. To the reader of the drama the question of whether the choruses should be said or sung is of no moment, but it presents a very serious difficulty for the stage manager and the actors. As soon as Schiller saw that his Chorus could not be sung but

---

[79] See Konrad Burdach in *Deutsche Rundschau*, pp. 108—111, and cp. this Introduction, pp. xxiv—xxv.

had to be spoken on the stages of Weimar, Berlin, Hamburg, and other towns, he felt it necessary to subdivide it further and to assign the chief parts to the best speakers, to six of whom he gave names, and whom he made, three on each side, leaders of their part of the Chorus. But it is clear that this arrangement was only a makeshift, introduced by Schiller at the eleventh hour, and forced upon him by the existing conditions of the stage. There can be no doubt that by these subdivisions he largely destroyed the effectiveness of the Chorus as a whole and greatly reduced the impressiveness of their utterances. He and Goethe were forced to adopt this expedient, as they did not see at the time how the drama could be performed otherwise on their stage. But in the circumstances it is not to be wondered at that Herder and his circle raised grave objections to the appearance of such a divided and subdivided Chorus, which yet was supposed to be a revival of the Chorus of the ancient Greeks. Granting that these critics of Schiller, above all Herder, were unduly severe, and did not make a fair allowance for the disadvantages under which the Chorus had to appear, it must nevertheless be admitted that Schiller's Chorus, as it appeared on the German stage, did not and could not fulfil the ideal *rôle* which Schiller had claimed for it in his essay. In theory he and Herder agreed much more closely than Herder would acknowledge.

In conclusion we may say that it is unjust to blame Schiller for the mere fact that the Chorus in his Braut von Messina differs in various important respects from the Chorus as it appears in Sophocles. His tragedy was not intended to be in every particular a reproduction of the ancient classical drama. It was conceived by a modern poet who wrote for modern spectators and readers, and was a poetic experiment, which in the nature of things could only be a compromise between the ancient and the modern, between the Greek and the Romantic. If the influences of Homer, Aeschylus, Sophocles and Euripides can be recognized in his tragedy, so also can those of Goethe, Stolberg, Calderon and his German imitators. A great deal, and that not the least valuable portion, is entirely Schiller's

own. Schiller resembles the ancients in lofty conception,
he differs from, but is not inferior to them by adapting their
Chorus to his own purpose of spiritualizing reality and of
counteracting crude naturalism. He was anxious to create in
this way a new and higher drama that should combine all the
best features of ancient poetry with his own world-embracing
modern conceptions and so give to the new drama a peculiar
depth and beauty of its own[80]. Schiller never dreamt of suggest-
ing that the Chorus should or could be re-introduced into *all*
tragedies of the higher style[81]. It has clearly no place in the
historical drama, which was really the field in which Schiller's
genius garnered the richest harvests and to which he returned
when he saw that his friends and his nation were not prepared
to follow him on the path which he had tentatively trodden. He
well recognized that in a modern German drama the Chorus as
such was out of place, and a freer representation of the people
was needed in its stead. After his experience of the extraordinary difficulties connected with the proper representation of
the Chorus on the stage, Schiller had little hesitation in returning to his old style and in endeavouring to perfect it in the two
great plays that immediately followed the completion of his choral
drama, Wilhelm Tell and Demetrius. Instead of a limited
Chorus consisting of a small number of Knights[82] we have in

[80] See Humboldt's letter given in the Appendix II, *n,* on
p. 256.

[81] See his important letter to Iffland, dated April 22, 1803 [Jonas,
Schillers Briefe, VII. 35]: Bei der Braut von Messina habe ich, ich will
es Ihnen aufrichtig gestehen, einen kleinen Wettstreit mit den alten Tragikern
versucht, wobei ich mehr an mich selbst als an ein Publikum außer mir dachte,
wiewohl ich innerlich überzeugt bin, daß bloß ein Dutzend lyrischer Stücke nötig
sein würden, um auch [this is important!] diese Gattung, die uns jetzt fremd
ist, bei den Deutschen in Aufnahme zu bringen, und ich würde dieses allerdings für
einen großen Schritt zum Vollkommenen halten. Übrigens aber werde ich es vor
der Hand dabei bewenden lassen, da Einer allein nun einmal nicht hinreicht, den
Krieg mit der ganzen Welt aufzunehmen.

[82] In the text of the Hamburg acting copy each semi-chorus consists
of three leaders and five other knights, total number sixteen. [See

these dramas of world-interest glimpses of men of all kinds representing great nations, and we watch Schiller handling these judiciously organized large masses with the consummate skill of a great master.

But if the practicability of Schiller's bold attempt to elevate the modern stage by a revival of the Chorus of ancient tragedy may well be doubted, the supreme beauty of the lyrical passages, rimed and rimeless, has been freely acknowledged on all hands from the very first. The metre is wonderfully varied and euphonious, the diction lofty and yet plastic, the rhythm marvellously expressive of every changing mood, offering splendid opportunities to the musical composer. The musical element of rime is usually present, but some of the most tragic and impressive passages are written in the rimeless free metre. Nowhere in Schiller's poetry, nor indeed in the whole of German poetry, has the beauty and force of some of the songs of the Chorus been surpassed.

VII. SCHILLER'S DRAMA AND ANCIENT GREEK TRAGEDY.

Griechheit, was war sie? Verstand und Maß und Klarheit.
Schiller, *Griechheit*, 1796.

In the preceding chapters it has been clearly shown that Schiller's Braut von Messina is not in any way a slavish and spiritless imitation of ancient Greek tragedy. The German poet was anxious to see how far it was possible for a modern dramatist to enter into the spirit and style of the classical

Goedeke's Critical ed. Vol. xiv, p. 20.] In the 'Personenverzeichnis' each semi-chorus has, besides its three leaders, seven other knights, which raises the total to twenty. In the last performance of the drama (on November 9, 1912) at the Weimar Court-Theatre the numbers in each semi-chorus were fifteen (3 + 12), and the total thus increased to thirty. The names of the leaders were fixed by Schiller as follows:— Cajetan, Berengar, Manfred (Don Manuel's knights); Bohemund, Roger, Hippolyt (Don Cesar's knights). See pp. xxviii—xxix.

tragedians, and to compete with them on their own ground[83]. Hence it was natural that Schiller sought not only to invent a plot similar in general character to plots treated by the great Attic tragedians, but that he intentionally borrowed or adapted a number of features which he found in the ancient dramas and considered suitable for his own. These features partly concern language, metre, and style, partly plot, structure, and a number of technical devices, partly they are certain general characteristics of the classical tragedies of Aeschylus, Sophocles, and Euripides. Schiller was well versed in the theory and practice of these great writers. He had read all their master-pieces very carefully, and also the fables of Hyginus in which a number of plots of lost Greek dramas have been preserved in extremely small compass. Besides he had for years thought most carefully about the chief characteristics of classical as opposed to modern poetry and had discussed them with Goethe. All the three Attic tragedians had influenced him in turn, Euripides first, Aeschylus last and perhaps most strongly of all. In 1791 he had intended to translate the *Agamemnon* of Aeschylus; in 1793 he read and admired Humboldt's trans-lation of the magnificent Chorus from the *Eumenides* and, in 1797, used portions of it in the finest of his ballads on classical subjects, Die Kraniche des Ibykus[84]. In 1802, when engaged upon his Braut von Messina, he studied four plays of Aeschylus (in Stolberg's translation) with the keenest appreciation. He gradually became less Sophoclean and more Aeschylean in his style, and in a letter to Körner, dated September 9, 1802, he told his friend, that his new play was acquiring the character of an Aeschylean tragedy[85].

[83] Goethe had made a similar attempt to write in the epic style of Homer in his Achilleis (1797—99). See Cotta's Jubilee edition, Vol. VI.

[84] See the Appendix III, pp. 258—61, where the description of the Furies from Aeschylus (in Humboldt's translation), Schiller's Kraniche and Goethe's Iphigenie are given as parallels to the fine passage in Die Braut von Messina, III. 5, ll. 2012—2028.

[85] See the Appendix II, *c*, p. 249.

GREEK INFLUENCE on 𝔇 𝔦𝔢 𝔅𝔯𝔞𝔲𝔱 𝔳𝔬𝔫 𝔐𝔢𝔣𝔣𝔦𝔫𝔞 is traceable in the following respects :

(a) *On metre, language and style :*

1. The use of the Greek iambic *trimeter* (the ordinary metre of the Greek tragedians) in one of the grandest scenes of his drama. See p. lxxxiv of this Introd. and cp. the note before l. 2592 on p. 230.

2. The frequent use of various kinds of *stichomythia*. As this special form of carrying on a pointed dialogue is frequently found in the old Greek plays, it should be mentioned here. But it also occurs in Shakespeare and in Goethe, and it had been used by Schiller himself in several of his earlier dramas. See p. xc—xci of this Introduction.

3. A large number of classical idioms and expressions to which attention has been called in the Notes. See the Index to the Notes.

(b) *On structure, plot and technical devices :*

1. The great simplicity of structure, which Schiller considered to be a great advantage to the poet.

2. The limitation of the action to the simple conditions of a domestic tragedy.

3. The limited number of persons, the interest being entirely concentrated upon the four members of the 'tragic family'[86].

4. The compression of the action into less than twenty-four hours.

5. The comparatively small change of scene—there are only three scenes of action.

6. The relegation of many points of importance for the plot to a period before the beginning of the dramatic action[87].

[86] There are, as in Goethe's 𝔍𝔭𝔥𝔦𝔤𝔢𝔫𝔦𝔢, four principal actors and one old and confidential servant.

[87] Schiller admired the art of Sophocles in the *Oedipus Rex*, in which everything of importance for the life of Oedipus happened long

7. The opening speech (*prologos*) of the Queen. See the Note on p. 124. Compare also the (very different) monologue of Beatrice with which Act II opens.

8. The regular announcement of a new comer before he enters the scene.

9. The two typical 'messenger scenes' (I. 6, IV. 2)[88].

10. The introduction of the Chorus. See the discussion of this important feature in Chapter VI.

11. The frequent use, especially towards the end, of 'tragic irony.' The chief cases have been discussed in the Notes. See the Index to the Notes.

12. The many cases of 'tragic recognition.' In the Greek tragedies an important part is played by the so-called *anagnorisis*, the 'tragic recognition,' of which good use was made by Goethe in his Iphigenie (Act III, Scene 1). The grandest example among the ancients is found in the *Oedipus Rex* where the revelations come blow upon blow in quick succession. But similar soul-stirring revelations, following close upon each other, occur in Schiller's drama. There are the following five tragic recognitions in the play—apart from what is gradually learned by the Chorus: (*a*) Don Manuel realizes that Beatrice is his sister and is the maiden loved by his brother (Act III, Scene 3); (*b*) Beatrice learns that Don Manuel and Don Cesar are brothers (III. 3); (*c*) Beatrice learns that Isabella is the Princess of Messina and her own mother as well as the mother of the brothers (III. 3); (*d*) Isabella learns that Don Cesar has killed his brother (IV. 5); (*e*) Don Cesar learns that Beatrice is his sister (IV. 5).

before the beginning of the play, while the drama itself only gives a 'tragical analysis' in a number of revelations. Something similar was to be attempted in Schiller's intended play Die Braut in Trauer, which was never written. See p. lxxii.

[88] A most effective imitation of the 'messengers' reports' in the Greek tragedies occurs in Wallensteins Tod, IV. 10. See the note in my edition of the play in the Pitt Press Series, on pp. 260—61.

(c) *On certain general characteristics of the tragedy:*

1. The idealistic and lofty treatment of the subject.

2. The frequent allusions to ancient Greek legends and mythology (among others the impressive introduction of the Furies pursuing the murderer. See Appendix III).

3. The introduction of the disastrous ancestral curse which is found in Greek tragedies, but also in Homer's *Iliad*. See p. xxxiii of this Introduction.

4. The creation of a 'tragic family' after the pattern of the famous tragic families of Laius (Oedipus, the Hostile Brothers) and of Tantalus (Atreus, Orestes, Iphigenia). See the Introd. p. xxxi. A number of important *motifs* (dreams before the birth of a child predicting its destiny to ruin the family, command of the father to have it killed, the saving of the child and its final return home in order to bring about the prophesied 'thundering downfall' (l. 239) of a noble race) were introduced into the drama by a skilful blending of material taken from various old stories, especially from the *Oedipus* with a possible admixture from the Alexandros-Paris fable of Hyginus. In shaping the plot of his drama Schiller seems to have thought especially of the tragic fate of the Theban family of Laius. In lines 450—52 he directly reminds us of the hostile sons of Oedipus. Goethe, in his 3phigenie, had treated the fate of the descendants of the other great tragic family, the house of Tantalus (in l. 306 Iphigenie informs King Thoas : Vernimm! 3ch bin aus Tantalus' Geschlecht). We are also reminded of Schiller's earlier treatment of the downfall of the House of Wallenstein. Isabella is drawn into the ruin of her family as well as the Duchess of Friedland. Our pity for the members of the family doomed by the terrible hereditary curse is not undeserved, for

the characters of the Princess and her children are
neither base nor repellent. The really repulsive
figure, the tyrannical and self-seeking father, stands
grimly in the background ; he is dead when the play
opens.

5. The introduction of the idea of Fate, interpreted by
Schiller in a modern spirit, has been fully discussed
in Chapter v, p. xxxv.

There are, however, a number of important DEPARTURES
FROM THE PRACTICE OF THE GREEK TRAGEDIANS that must
not be overlooked. Some of these have been discussed above;
others are :

1. Death—in this case the actual murder—is allowed to
take place on the stage.

Schiller had followed this practice in Die Jungfrau von
Orleans, and allowed it again to take place before the eyes of
the spectators in Wilhelm Tell and in Demetrius; but he had
avoided it in Wallenstein and, for obvious reasons, in Maria
Stuart.

2. The divine oracles of the Greeks could not be used by
the modern poet in the ancient sense of official institutions.
Consequently they were replaced by two important prophetic
dreams and their interpretation.   To the same category belongs
the symbolic and ominous action of the old hermit in Act IV
(Scene 2, ll. 2133—41).

Although, as has been stated, in tone and conception Die
Braut von Messina comes nearer to the lofty spirit of the
Aeschylean tragedies than to those of the highly polished
Sophocles, yet, when Schiller first seriously contemplated the
.production of a tragedy 'after the strict manner of the ancients,'
he was anxious to invent a plot that should offer him all the
advantages of the grand Sophoclean tragedy *Oedipus Rex*[89].
As we have seen, he actually borrowed a number of *motifs* from
it, and in writing his modern play he continually thought of the

[89] See his important letter to Goethe, dated October 2, 1797 [Jonas,
Schillers Briefe, v. 271].

masterly technique of the stern ancient tragedy. Die Braut von Messina has consequently often been compared with the *Oedipus Rex*[90]. Some POINTS OF SIMILARITY are the following: (1) It had been predicted that Oedipus would kill his father and marry his mother. In the same way it had been foretold that the brothers would destroy each other and their race (the exact way in which this was to be brought about is not mentioned). (2) In the ancient drama we have an unnatural marriage, in the modern an unnatural love. (3) At the end of the drama Oedipus punishes himself, so does Don Cesar. But there are also many important POINTS OF DIFFERENCE between the two plays—apart from the general characteristics noticed above. These are: (1) Oedipus can in no way be called morally guilty, as he has no idea that he is and has been doing wrong[91]. In Schiller's drama Destiny acts on the unruly souls of the younger generation through their inherited passionate temper. Here the lack of self-control constitutes real moral guilt[92]. (2) Oedipus knows of the prophecy, but is ignorant of the fact that it has actually been fulfilled, while the children of Isabella either do not know of it at all or hear of it when it is too late. (3) Little is said by Sophocles about the father of Oedipus who, according to Greek tradition, had deliberately acted against the will of the Gods and thus prepared his own doom and that of his race, while in Schiller's drama the terrible curse of the grandfather on the father and his descendants plays a most important part. (4) All the deeds of Oedipus for which he suffers have been done before the drama begins, and are only gradually disclosed during the play. In the German play many of the deeds which bring about the

[90] See some of the books and essays mentioned in the Appendix V, pp. 270—73.

[91] For this reason the end of the Sophoclean tragedy leaves a jarring and harassing effect on the mind, at least of modern spectators and readers. But Sophocles wrote in later years a serene and conciliating counterpart to this crushing tragedy in the noble play *Oedipus at Colonus*.

[92] But compare the observation on p. xxxix.

ruin of the house of Isabella are committed in the course of
the action of the play and only some of them belong to the
𝔙𝔬𝔯𝔣𝔞𝔟𝔢𝔩. The most guilty deed does not here lie in the remote
past, nor are its bearings unknown to the murderer, but it is
quickly done, quickly discovered, and is expiated within the
course of a few hours. It is also worthy of notice that Schiller
shrank from bringing before the eyes of modern spectators the
horrors and gruesome sights which occur in the *Oedipus Rex* and
other Greek tragedies. He strongly objected to crude naturalistic representations of this kind in which he could not see any
gain to serious drama.

VIII. SCHILLER'S 'BRAUT VON MESSINA' AND GERMAN LITERATURE.

The two most important German poets[93] who were, like
Schiller, inspired by the ancient Greek tragedians and wrote
dramas on Greek subjects are Goethe and Grillparzer. In some
respects their plays are more nearly related to the Greek drama
than Schiller's 𝔅𝔯𝔞𝔲𝔱 𝔳𝔬𝔫 𝔐𝔢𝔣𝔣𝔦𝔫𝔞, but in other respects they are
more modern in spirit and, in hardly any case, was an attempt
made to introduce the ancient classical chorus.

The best known of the dramas of Goethe is his exquisite
𝔍𝔭𝔥𝔦𝔤𝔢𝔫𝔦𝔢[94]. It was very well known to Schiller, by whom it
was adapted for the Weimar stage in the early part of 1802,
and on whose diction in 𝔇𝔦𝔢 𝔅𝔯𝔞𝔲𝔱 𝔳𝔬𝔫 𝔐𝔢𝔣𝔣𝔦𝔫𝔞 (at which he
was soon afterwards working) it exercised a not inconsiderable
influence. Otherwise the two plays have nothing in common.
While in Italy, Goethe conceived the idea of writing two other
dramas treating of a Greek subject. The one was to be a
continuation of 𝔍𝔭𝔥𝔦𝔤𝔢𝔫𝔦𝔢 𝔞𝔲𝔣 𝔗𝔞𝔲𝔯𝔦𝔰, and was to be called
𝔍𝔭𝔥𝔦𝔤𝔢𝔫𝔦𝔢 𝔞𝔲𝔣 𝔇𝔢𝔩𝔭𝔥𝔬𝔰 (which title was subsequently altered to

[93] On other dramas see Vol. II of the book by Carl Leo Cholevius
quoted in the Appendix V, on p. 268.

[94] For further information concerning this drama see my edition of
it in tne Pitt Press Series, Cambridge, [2]1904.

Iphigenie auf Delphi). This drama, about the plan of which we are fully informed by Goethe himself, was carefully considered in 1786 during his Italian journey, but was never written[95]. The heroine of the other drama was to be Naufikaa, the daughter of Alkinoos, the Phaeakian king, one of the most attractive figures of Homer's *Odyssey*. Of this Sicilian play, which was begun during Goethe's visit to Sicily (1787), only a few fragments were written, and it is much to be regretted that other interests prevented Goethe from carrying out the design of this Homeric-Sophoclean play, as the few fragmentary scenes that were written are of great beauty[96].

Some of Goethe's later attempts to make Greek personages the heroes of dramas come much nearer than Iphigenie and Naufikaa to the writers of ancient tragedy (with regard to structure and metrical form) and bear for this reason a closer resemblance to Schiller's Greek-Sicilian tragedy. The figure of the Homeric Helena plays the chief part in the Third Act of the Second Part of Faust. This Act, representing the reappearance of fair Helen of Troy, the incarnation of Hellenic beauty, in the modern world and her short-lived union with Faust, is in some respects a play within the play. Goethe read portions of this Helena-drama (in September 1800) to Schiller from his manuscript, and here Schiller found a nearer approach to the ancient Greek tragedians than any modern German poet had ever attempted or attained before. Not only were the language and style of these portions of the Helena written in close imitation of the Attic drama, but several metrical devices of the ancient poets were successfully imitated: the iambic trimeter was adopted throughout for this portion of the drama, and the chorus of the attendant maidens of fair Helen was very similar to the choruses found in Euripides ; their songs were without rime, and adhered in every respect more strictly to the ancient models than do the choruses of Schiller. Still the Helena act in Faust was never intended by Goethe to be a close imitation of the technique of the ancients in every

[95] See the Introduction to my edition of Iphigenie, pp. xxxiii—v.
[96] See *ibidem*, p. xxxv.

important detail[97]. Goethe's last play in classical style, written after Schiller's death, was the unfinished ᛈᚪᚾᛒᛟᚱᚪ (1807), a striking, but difficult play, in which Prometheus, an old favourite of Goethe's, was again introduced[98] and whose character as a realist and indefatigable worker formed an effective contrast to that of his dreamy brother Epimetheus, the husband of the fair Pandora whose loss he never ceases to lament.

Franz Grillparzer, the gifted Viennese dramatist, wrote several *gräcisierende Dramen* which show, however, the influence of Goethe's ᛃᛈᚻᛁᚷᛖᚾᛁᛖ rather than that of Schiller's ᛒᚱᚪᚢᛏ ᚢᛟᚾ ᛗᛖᚠᚠᛁᚾᚪ. He made three women of classical times the heroines of three striking plays : ᛋᚪᛈᛈᚻᛟ, in the play of the same name (1818), Medea, in the trilogy ᛞᚪᛋ ᚷᛟᛚᛒᛖᚾᛖ ᛒᛚᛁᛖᚦ (1822), and Hero, in ᛞᛖᛋ ᛗᛖᛖᚱᛖᛋ ᚢᚾᛒ ᛒᛖᚱ ᛚᛁᛖᛒᛖ·ᚹᛖᛚᛚᛖᚾ (1831). Sappho, Medea, Hero are, like Iphigenia, Helena, Nausikaa, Pandora, all three celebrated heroines of legend and poetry. These Greek women were represented by Grillparzer in a romantic spirit, with a minute study of character reminding us of Goethe and of Racine. In no play of his did he make use of the chorus.

Thus we see that neither Schiller's great friend, Goethe, nor Grillparzer, the gifted and original Austrian playwright, was his predecessor or his imitator in his attempt to write a tragedy after the strict style of the ancients. He himself never thought fit to repeat the experiment, in spite of the deep impression that was

---

[97] See H. Morsch, *Goethe und die griechischen Bühnendichter*, Berlin, 1888; Franz Thalmayr, *Goethe und das klassische Altertum*, Leipzig, 1897 ; and Calvin Thomas, *Goethes Faust*, Part II (Boston, 1901), pp. 409 sqq. On September 23 Schiller wrote to Goethe (Jonas, VI. 202) concerning the impression made on him by Goethe's reading from his ᚻᛖᛚᛖᚾᚪ : ᛁᚻᚱᛖ ᚾᛖᚢᛚᛁᚳᛖ ᚢᛟᚱᛚᛖᚠᚢᚾᚷ ᚻᚪᛏ ᛗᛁᚳ ᛗᛁᛏ ᛖᛁᚾᛖᛗ ᚷᚱᛟᚦᛖᚾ ᚢᚾᛒ ᚢᛟᚱᚾᛖᚻᛗᛖᚾ ᛖᛁᚾᛒᚱᚢᚲ ᛖᚾᛏᛚᚪᚠᚠᛖᚾ; ᛒᛖᚱ ᛖᛒᛚᛖ, ᚻᛟᚻᛖ ᚷᛖᛁᛋᛏ ᛒᛖᚱ ᚪᛚᛏᛖᚾ ᚥᚱᚪᚷᛟᛒᛁᛖ ᚹᛖᚻᛏ ᚪᚢᛋ ᛒᛖᛗ ᛗᛟᚾᛟᛚᛟᚷ ᛖᛁᚾᛖᛗ ᛖᚾᛏᚷᛖᚷᛖᚾ ᚢᚾᛒ ᛗᚪᚳᛏ ᛒᛖᚾ ᚷᛖᚻᛟᚱᛁᚷᛖᚾ ᛖᚠᚠᛖᚲᛏ, ᛁᚾᛒᛖᛗ ᛖᚱ ᚱᚢᚻᛁᚷ ᛗᚪᚳᛏᛁᚷ ᛒᚪᛋ ᚥᛁᛖᚠᚠᛏᛖ ᚪᚢᚠᚱᛖᚷᛏ....

[98] The early scenes of a ᛈᚱᛟᛗᛖᛏᚻᛖᚢᛋ drama were written during Goethe's youth, and their 'Storm and Stress' style has nothing in common with the style adopted in the poet's maturity.

produced on himself and others by the representation of Die Braut von Meffina, and soon after the appearance of this play Schiller complained bitterly of insipid imitators who had completely misunderstood his aims in writing the drama. Ever since the time of the German romanticists it has been customary to call Die Braut von Meffina the parent-play of the silly 'fate-tragedies' by Zacharias Werner, A. Müllner, A. Houwald, and others which for a time had great vogue in Germany. Even if Schiller's noble play was really the cause of the many poor and ridiculous fate-tragedies, it is yet not right to put the blame for this fact on Schiller. The spirit of the later plays, in which the various horrors are brought about by the mere mechanical operation of a blind and mysterious fate, is altogether different from the manly and moral spirit in which Schiller created his drama. Schiller's play, although it has often been classed as a 'fate-tragedy,' is by no means a 'fate-tragedy' in the same sense as the *Oedipus Rex*. Although the word Schickfal is frequently used, Die Braut von Meffina is essentially a character-tragedy. All the events spring quite naturally from the disposition of the different members of the family and every action is fully accounted for by their secrecy or want of self-control. When August von Platen exposed the German 'fate-tragedies' to universal ridicule by the publication of his two ingenious Aristophanic comedies Die verhängnisvolle Gabel and Der romantische Ödipus, he did not dream of including Schiller in his withering condemnation. But he wittily proposed that the last two lines from Die Braut von Meffina should be put as a motto under the bust of Adolf Müllner, the author of the much-read fate-tragedy Die Schuld. Grillparzer, after a youthful attempt in this style, soon left it never to return to it again. But his Ahnfrau (1817), although a fate-tragedy, is a much finer production than all the other fate-tragedies[99]. Goethe, in the before-mentioned Maskenzug (December 18, 1818), originally intended to express very strongly, with regard to Schiller's Braut von Meffina and

[99] See Jakob Minor's essay in the *Grillparzer-Jahrbuch*, Vol. IX, quoted in the Appendix V, p. 269.

the ridiculous imitators of a play that they failed to understand, the opinion:

Was Er getan, soll keiner wiederholen[100]!

The subject of 'the Hostile Brothers' has often been the theme of tragic treatment in German as well as in other literatures, ancient and modern. Some of the most important of these will be briefly noticed in the following chapter.

IX. THE *MOTIF* OF 'THE HOSTILE BROTHERS' IN LITERATURE.

Hostility between two brothers leading to the murder of one by the hand of the other is one of the oldest tragic subjects. In the Bible the story is interwoven with the early history of the human race; in historical legend we meet it by the cradle of a great nation; in early poetry it tells of the downfall of an ancient house. Reference need only be made to the stories of Cain and Abel, Romulus and Remus, Eteocles and Polynices. In all the older legends and dramas the cause of fratricide is jealousy, either felt by one brother only or by both, but invariably springing from a desire to be first, to be lord and ruler. In no case is the hatred of the brothers due to any rivalry caused by love for a woman. In these legends all the three great Athenian writers of tragedy found abundant material, and some of their splendid plays have come down to our times. Two plays treating of the jealousy and mutual murder of the sons of Oedipus, Eteocles and Polynices, the brothers of Thebes, were written by Aeschylus and by Euripides. The tragedy of Aeschylus, the first part of a somewhat loosely connected trilogy, was called *The Seven against Thebes*, and with this drama the poet won the prize in the Athenian competition among tragic writers in 477 B.C. Schiller, while at work on Die Braut von Meffina, was greatly stimulated by the study of this

[100] See Appendix II, p. 257, l. 8.

noble work which he read in Friedrich Stolberg's impressive translation[101]. The *Phoenissae* of Euripides was known to him as early as 1788 (see p. xi), and his own translation of portions of this play into blank verse, called Szenen aus den Phönizierinnen, was not without influence on Die Braut von Messina[102]. One stirring scene in his Braut (Act I, Scene 4) corresponds exactly to an important scene (II. 4) in the *Phoenissae*[103]. In Latin literature the story of the brothers of Thebes was treated by Seneca in dramatic form, and by Publius Papinius Statius in a rather frigid and lengthy epic poem in twelve cantos, called *Thebais*. He spent ten years in writing it, and it was for a long time held in much esteem. In modern literature the same subject was treated by Racine in his drama *La Thébaïde ou les Frères ennemis*, acted in 1664 by Molière's company. This was Racine's first play, and it was based on Statius. On French soil the conflict of the Theban brothers was subsequently treated by Crébillon and Voltaire, while the death of Abel became the subject of a tragedy by Legouvé, called *La mort d'Abel*[104].

In English literature the theme of the hostile brothers seems to have been chosen much less frequently, although a pair of jealous brothers appear in the secondary action of *King Lear*. A certain similarity to Die Braut von Messina may be noticed in *The Mysterious Mother* by Walpole. But it is not in the introduction of two brothers who hate each other that this similarity is apparent, but in the suppressed knowledge of the existence of a sister and the resulting love of the brother for her: the impending incest in the English play is prevented by

[101] See Jonas, *Schillers Briefe*, VI. 428, VII. 2 and 14; and Appendix II, *e*, p. 250. Cp. also p. xv of this Introduction.

[102] See the Cotta Jubilee edition of Schiller's works, Vol. X. Introd. xiv—xv.

[103] Compare the Cotta Jubilee ed. x. 161 sqq.

[104] This play was based on Salomon Gessner's epic tale Der Tod Abels (1758) and may have influenced Schiller in one or two small points. See the essays of F. Liebrecht and of F. Imelmann mentioned in Appendix V, on pp. 272 and 271.

a revelation of their relationship; the sister is sent to a convent and the brother into exile[105].

In GERMAN literature the murder of one brother by the other has very often been the subject of poetic treatment. From the sixteenth to the eighteenth century the biblical story of Cain and Abel was a favourite theme with German writers. In the century of the Reformation the Nürnberg bootmaker and poet Hans Sachs had introduced the murder of the good son Abel into the fifth act of his play Die ungleichen Kinder Evae[106], while in the eighteenth century Salomon Gessner wrote an epic tale Der Tod Abels, and the 'painter' Müller an idyl Der erschlagene Abel. In these productions the *motif* of love naturally found no place. For the writers of the Storm and Stress period the subject of the hostile brothers had quite a special fascination[107], and here the youthful Schiller found the models for his first revolutionary play. The two most important dramas on this subject before Schiller's Räuber were Die Zwillinge by Klinger, and Julius von Tarent by Leisewitz. These two impressive plays, both written in prose, became known in the same year. In 1775 they were both sent up to the excellent stage-manager and actor Schröder of Hamburg who had offered a prize for the best original German play. Klinger's tragedy obtained the prize because it seemed to offer greater possibilities for an effective representation on the stage, but the play of Leisewitz was accorded high praise also, and it is in fact the more mature and artistic production of the two[108].

[105] See W. H. Carruth's edition of Die Braut von Messina, p. 140.

[106] On the sources of this *Comedia* and other treatments of the same subject by Sachs, see A. L. Stiefel's essay in *Germania*, XXXVI. 32 sqq.

[107] See Erich Schmidt, *Lenz und Klinger*, Berlin, 1878, pp. 85 sqq., and *Anzeiger für das deutsche Altertum*, III. (1877), 198 sqq., and A. Sauer, *Stürmer und Dränger*, Vol. I, Introduction, p. 45 (in Kürschner's Deutsche National-Litteratur, Vol. 79).

[108] See Sauer, pp. 310—11, and Walther Kühlhorn, *J. A. Leisewitzens 'Julius von Tarent,' Erläuterung und literarhistorische*

Klinger had heard of Leisewitz's intention to compete for the prize, and also of his source[109]; he did not hesitate to make use of the latter, and this explains the fact that both plays have much in common and that in both the scene of action is laid in Italy. The youthful Schiller knew both plays well, especially Julius von Tarent, which he could almost say by heart. Thus it happened that five years after the publication of these two remarkable dramas in 1776 Schiller, deeply moved by them, wrote his first great domestic drama, Die Räuber (1781), in prose, in which, however, the scene of action is laid in Germany. This play took the whole of Germany by storm. Again we have in it the *motif* of the hostile brothers and their love for the same maiden, but the end is different and no fratricide is committed. From the time of Die Räuber the subject of the love of two brothers for the same woman was never absent from Schiller's mind. In 1782 he published a somewhat tame and moralizing version of it in the short prose story Eine groß= mütige Handlung aus der neuften Geschichte[110], which was based upon an actual occurrence in a family well known to the poet. In it two brothers, who are on the best of terms, love the same maiden, yet manage to arrive at a solution of the difficulty by which a tragic issue is avoided. In his first tragedy in blank verse, Don Carlos (1787), we find the motive differently handled. Here the father of the hero, King Philip II of Spain, has himself married the charming Elisabeth of Valois who was loved by and destined for his son, Don Carlos. This wrecks the life of the prince and brings about the ruin of the royal house. We are reminded of Die Braut von Messina

Würdigung, Halle, 1912 (Vol. X of F. Saran's *Bausteine zur Geschichte der neueren deutschen Literatur*), with a very full and useful bibliographical chapter.

[109] In the Histories of Thuanus there is an account of the tragedy in the Medici family through which two sons of the Duke Cosimo I. perished in 1562. Hence the scene of action in the tragedies of Leisewitz and Klinger is laid in Italy.

[110] See Schiller's *Sämtliche Werke*, *Säkular-Ausgabe*, Vol. II. 145 sqq., and the Introd. xiv—xv.

where, in the older generation, the exact opposite had happened (ll. 960—66). But nowhere in the whole range of German poetry has the tragic subject of the conflict of the Hostile Brothers been elevated into a higher sphere than in the lofty tragedy which the mature poet produced towards the end of his fruitful life. Here the old and favourite subject of the poets of the Storm and Stress period, the subject to which Schiller himself had given so much thought for so long a time, received at last its definite classical form. As in the plays of Klinger and Leisewitz, the scene of action is laid on Southern soil, two hostile brothers are in love with the same maiden, and one brother is slain by the other; but Schiller has introduced important modifications. The tragic conflict is rendered still more intense by the facts that the beloved maiden proves to be the sister of the brothers[111], and the murderer, instead of being slain by the father, dies by his own hand in voluntary expiation of his rash deed. We are deeply moved

---

[111] The love of a brother for a sister whom he does not know to be his sister had been used as a dramatic motive before Schiller by Lessing in his Nathan der Weise (1779), and was used again by Grillparzer in his Ahnfrau (1817). It is also worthy of note that the passionate love of a brother for his sister was to form a tragic motive in Schiller's intended continuation of Die Räuber, which occupied him at different periods of his life and was to be called Die Braut in Trauer. In this second part of his tragedy the son of Karl Moor, an unruly youth and passionate hunter, was to be represented as a man who could be calmed and ruled only by his gentle sister Mathilda, and who could not bear the idea of seeing her the wife of another. For this see Robert Boxberger's Introd. pp. 6—7 to his edition of Die Braut von Messina in Kürschner's Deutsche National-Litteratur. The love of a brother for his sister is brought to a happy issue in Goethe's profound psychological study, Die Geschwister (i.e. brother and sister); the discovery is made at the end of the drama that the supposed sister is no relation to Wilhelm and the union of the lovers thus becomes possible. This piece, the forerunner of Iphigenie, to some extent carries out the idea, at that time so present to Goethe's mind, of representing his relation to Frau von Stein as that of a loving brother to a gentle sister.

by the tragic fate of the princely family, but Schiller did not stoop to introduce all the horrors of the 'fate-tragedy.'

It is impossible to discuss in this place any of the later German poetic productions in which the subject of the Hostile Brothers has been treated with more or less ability and success. It is, however, safe to say that, so far, Schiller's 𝔅𝔯𝔞𝔲𝔱 𝔳𝔬𝔫 𝔐𝔢𝔣𝔣𝔦𝔫𝔞 is the work in which this old subject has received its most successful treatment, uniting as it does the ancient and the modern, the Greek and the Romantic, the best to be found in Schiller's predecessors combined with what was peculiar to Schiller, his loftiness of conception, his depth of thought, his power to stir the souls of the spectators to their very depths, and the irresistible force and beauty of his poetic diction.

X. METRE AND STYLE OF DIE BRAUT VON MESSINA[112].

A. Metre.

I. The Word.

§ 1. *Preservation of older and longer forms.*

If required by the metre, the old uncontracted forms may be preserved in words which as a rule are used in a contracted form. This is the case especially with verbs, e.g. fraget (413), entschließet (423), rühret (504), ahnet (558), beugete (682), drohete (765), gefüget (836), geferschet (1116), gerächet (1907); nahe (655), zurücke (780), frühe (1596). Cp. also sahe (1498) and the note to this form.

---

[112] The instances given in the following are taken almost exclusively from the portions of the drama that are written in blank verse. They are merely intended to illustrate fully all that has been remarked under the various headings, but they are in no case intended to be complete. On the metre of the drama cp. E. Belling, *Die Metrik Schillers*, Breslau, 1883, pp. 86, 212 sqq., 242 sqq., 283 sqq., 328; H. Draheim, *Schillers Metrik*, Berlin, 1909, pp. 84—90; L. Bellermann, *Schillers Dramen*, Berlin, 1905, [3]111. 85—89; and the other books and essays that are mentioned (under C) on page 266. See also my Introductions to Schiller's 𝔚𝔞𝔩𝔩𝔢𝔫𝔣𝔱𝔢𝔦𝔫 and 𝔚𝔦𝔩𝔥𝔢𝔩𝔪 𝔗𝔢𝔩𝔩.

B. *f*

§ 2. *Shortening of words.*

Words may be shortened in various ways in order to suit the metre. They may be shortened by (*a*) *Elision*, (*b*) *Syncope*, (*c*) *Apocope*, and (*d*) otherwise.

(*a*) *Elision.*

Where a word ends with an unaccented *e*, and the next word begins with a vowel, the final *e* is generally suppressed in order to avoid the hiatus (cp. § 4). The cases of such elision are extremely numerous in poetry, and Schiller's play affords many examples, especially when a verb is followed by a pronoun, e.g. harr' ich (90), mußt' ich (301), fühlt' er (473), würd' er (473), fag' euch (52), fag' etwas (468), löf' alle (54), teil' auch (104), geh' und (1166), Löw' und (1344).

(*b*) *Syncope.*

Syncope is the omission of an unaccented vowel, usually *e*, and often *i* in the endings *-ig* and *-ifch*, in the middle of a word in order to reduce it by one syllable, e.g.

> e: gnug (98), gnügt (1599), hieltft (1637), ältre (466), Größrer (1161), Verlorne (2120), erftgebornen (1451), blühnden (1395).
>
> i: heil'gen (54), blut'gen (68), heft'ger (314), mächt'ger (2825), arab'fcher (509), neid'fchen (647).
>
> a: drum (602).

(*c*) *Apocope.*

By 'apocope' we mean the cutting off of the last vowel of a word (an unaccented *e*), not before another vowel (as in the case of *elision*), but either at the end of a line for the sake of the ending or before a consonant in order to drop a syllable. In our play apocope is not infrequently met with, e.g. heut' (1138), feh' (dich 501), denk' (nicht 566), befragt' (der 1317), Aug' (des 1657), müßt' (mich 2152), Urfach' (1641). It occurs especially frequently in the case of lang' (114, 1270, 1273, etc.).

(*d*) *Other reductions of words.*

The pronoun es is very frequently shortened to '*s*, which is also very common in colloquial, especially in South German, speech, e.g. fie'ß (86), wie'ß (93), finb'ß (129), bebarf'ß (1159), bu'ß (1490, 2036), bir'ß (2039), etc.

(*e*) *Double forms.*

According to the requirements of the metre many words occur in two forms in our play, viz. Berges (2099), Bergs (2118) ; zurücke (780), zurück (742) ; heiligen (445), heil'gen (54) ; fliehen (1874), fliehn (1875) ; brohete (765), brohte (767) ; fahe (1498), fah (1596) ; and many others. Even compounds appear occasionally in two forms, e.g. Grabestuch (1497), Grabtuch (1498).

(*f*) *Foreign words in ⸗ie, ⸗ia, ⸗ius.*

In most cases the two vowels in ⸗ie are separately sounded, viz. i⸗e, in Li⸗li⸗e (1311, 2340), Ma⸗gi⸗er (2346, 2347), Jn⸗bi⸗erß (821), Ara⸗bi⸗er (1318, 1320), Fu⸗ri⸗en (2420, 2801), Ge⸗ni⸗en (1494), also Ge⸗ni⸗uß (2087). In Pinie (982), however, the pronunciation is that of a disyllable, Pin⸗je. The word Cäcilia (1683) is to be pronounced as a trisyllable, Cä⸗cil⸗ja. Diego (Di⸗e⸗go) 101, 1564 is always trisyllabic.

(*g*) *The name Manuel.*

The name Manuel is as a rule pronounced as a trisyllabic word, viz. Ma⸗nü⸗el (624, 806, 1019, 1713, 1799, 1824, 1825, 1829, 2147, 2177, 2241), but in a number of cases the name has clearly the disyllabic pronunciation Ma⸗nuel (1821, 1822, 2126, 2179, 2245).

§ 3. *Stress.*

(*a*) *Accented and unaccented syllables.*

The rules of prosody in German poetry are very different from those which we find in Classical or Romance languages. In Greek and Latin the quantity of the syllables is everything : two short syllables may take the place of a long one, and *vice versa* ; three syllables ($- \smile \smile$), if two of them are short, do not count for more in the verse than two that are long ($- -$). In the Romance languages (e.g. French, Italian and Spanish), the Classical metres are disregarded, no difference is made between long and short syllables, but the number of syllables in a line is

f 2

counted. The common French Alexandrine, for instance, is a verse consisting of 12 syllables (a final unaccented syllable does not count), and it is incorrect to describe it as an iambic verse. In German poetry it does not matter whether syllables are long or short, any more than in French, nor is their number counted, but the accented syllables only are taken into consideration. This is especially characteristic of the old German versification, in which, as long as there was the necessary number of accented syllables (a stress syllable or *arsis* is called a Hebung), it did not matter in the least whether one or more unaccented syllables separated them or not (an unaccented syllable or *thesis* is called a Senfung). Later German poets have however given their verses a much more formal character by introducing a regular alternation between accented and unaccented syllables, so that modern German verse resembles both French verse, in so far as the line contains a more constant number of syllables, and classical metres, in so far as the German accented syllables may be taken to correspond to their long, the unaccented to their short syllables. Yet in the case of German verse it is not accurate to speak of 'feet' in the strict classical sense of the word, e.g. of iambics, trochees, dactyls, anapaests, etc. but rather of lines of a certain number of accents with an iambic or ascending, etc. rhythm (cp. § 8). If the term 'foot' is used to denote a metrical unit in German versification it means one accented syllable usually preceded or followed by one or more unaccented syllables.

In every line of verse it is necessary to have the prescribed number of accented syllables, and the accentuation assigned to these in verse should be the same as their accentuation in ordinary prose. This is another important difference between German and classical prosody. In classical poetry the rhythmical accent is independent of the prose accent, while in German prosody the two must coincide.

(b) *Fluctuating stress.*

The general rule is, that every word preserves in verse its proper prose accent, and also that a greater stress must not be laid on a word of less importance than is laid on an important word. The observance of this rule is necessary in order that the rhythm of the metrical line may appear regular and pleasant to the ear. Still in all German classical dramas written in blank verse there are a number of instances where the sense requires a stress on a word or a part of a word which, according to the metre, ought not to have any. This is the case especially at the beginning of a line, and in reading such lines it is necessary to avoid giving one syllable a much stronger accent than the others have, by keeping the voice in suspense as it were. In German this is called Schwebende Betonung ('fluctuating stress,' 'level stress') or Versetzter Rhythmus ('altered rhythm,' 'transposed rhythm,' 'fluctuating rhythm'), for instance :

Wohl läßt der Pfei'l sich au's dem Her'zen zie'hn (2720).

Here the sense requires a stronger accent on Wohl than on läßt on which it would metrically fall. The ascending rhythm is re-established in the latter half of the line. Similarly in

Langsam kehrt die Besi'nnung i'hr zurü'ck (2215).

The conflict between the natural stress (La'ngsam) and the rhythmical stress (Langsa'm) results in the compromise of ac-centuating both syllables, with a slight predominance of the pitch in uttering the first syllable. The metrical length of la'ngsa'm represents very effectively the slow recovery of the senses.

There are numerous examples of 'fluctuating stress' in our drama, especially at the beginning of a new metrical line. Schiller was very skilful in bringing out the force of important words at the beginning or in the middle of the line by making it necessary to read them with level stress. He liked to begin verses with descending rhythm and to change the rhythm in the later part of the line. By doing so he prevented the blank verse, which on the whole has ascending rhythm and has a regular sequence of accented and unaccented syllables, from becoming monotonous.

The cases of schwebende or versetzte Betonung occur especially in the case of

(a) *a noun* : Schwert (56), Leben (453), Liebe (2546);

(*b*) *a compound noun or adjective* at the beginning or in the middle of a line : Blendwerk (1900), Lebloser (2191), Bußfert'ge (2637), freundlos (2756), langsam (2215), Rohherziger (2757), Arglist'ge (2781), Trostlose (2821) ; [*medially* :] Todfeind (577), gutmeinend (595), Holdsel'ge (708), hohläugigten (1277) ;

(*c*) *a simple verb* : Find' (502), Komm (553), Laß (571), Fahre (1904), Fluche (2514), Lebe (2755) ; [*medially* :] raubt' (787), ward (1324), Fragt (1463), Weine (2521) ;

(*d*) *a compound verb* : nachholen (562), aufbläst (580), auffliegt (1272), heimkehrend (1274), ankämpfen (2185), anklagen (2512), anschmiegender (2707), aufblicken (2726) ; [*medially* :] einbohrend (454), ausholend (701), hintretend (2134) ;

(*e*) *a pronoun* : Ich (2815), du (2807), er (2814), sie (2467), wir (495), was (2265), das (2328) ; [*medially* :] meine (2468), selbst (72), mich (2797), dein (2074), dich (1115, 2792) ;

(*f*) *other words* : Nein (513), Heil (534), O (2745), Weh (1109), Wohl (2720), Hier (548), Bald (573), Wie (1523), So (2327), Ein (2698) ; [*medially* :] wohl (1417), nicht (1512, 1660), wenn (1843), dann (2699).

The adjectives compounded with un= sometimes keep their usual prose accent, but not infrequently require to be read with fluctuating stress. Some instances of the latter case are unheilbar (591) ; unfreundlichen (601), unzeitig (1381), unfern (1593), unselig (2066), Unschuldige (2358), Unglückliche (2369).

§ 4. *Hiatus.*

The Latin term 'hiatus' is used to describe a concurrence of vowel sounds in two successive syllables, one at the close of one word and the other at the beginning of the next. In classical verses the hiatus is most carefully avoided. Schiller does not avoid it very scrupulously. The most careful modern poets, e.g. Platen, Geibel, Bodenstedt, Heyse, Storm and others tolerate it much less. It must, however, be remembered that some cases of hiatus are unavoidable in German, e.g. meine Ehre, das blaue Auge, die schwere Arbeit, die blühende Erde ; it even occurs in a number of ordinary words, e.g. ſäen, gehen, wehen, Theater, etc.

Of the different kinds of vowel concurrences only one, the concurrence of a final e (having the secondary stress in a word) with another word beginning with a vowel, seems to be felt by the more careful poets as really objectionable and it is therefore mostly removed by means of elision (see § 2, *a*). In our drama there are only three cases in which an e bearing a secondary stress followed by a vowel occurs, viz.

wimmelnde, ertoſen (990); feſtliche erſchienen (1261); Neugeborene alsbald (1326).

In the first case there is a very short break which makes the hiatus a little less noticeable. Somewhat less objectionable are cases in which the final e of the first word is altogether unaccented and followed immediately by a full accented vowel, e.g. verſammle alles (115); erkenne, ober (471); Freube, und (552); heute an (569); Decke, und (850); entzweite Euch (1303); Monde aber (1368); Freube ein (1393); gebiete, alſo (2594); Dienſte alſobald (2614).

II. The Line.

§ 5. *Blank verse.*

(*a*) *Number of accented syllables.*

A metrical line is called a verse (ein Vers, from the Latin *versus* 'a turning,' viz. a turning to begin a new line). Our drama is written in so-called 'blank verse,' i.e. in lines each of which contains five 'feet,' that is to say five accented syllables preceded and followed in each case by one unaccented syllable. Generally the accented and the unaccented syllables alternate quite regularly, the line beginning with an unaccented syllable, and the metre might be described thus (' denoting an accented, × an unaccented syllable) :

$$\times \ ' \ \times \ ' \ \times \ ' \ \times \ ' \ \times \ ' \ (\times).$$

Occasionally we find two unaccented syllables following one

another before an accented one. This is especially noticeable in
the case of verſetzter Rhythmus, e.g.

′ × × ′ × ′ × ′ × ′ (×).

The number of accents, and even of syllables, is exactly the
same, but the usual rhythm × ′ × ′ is at the beginning changed
into ′ × × ′. If there is no thesis occurring before the first arsis
the beginning of the line must be read with fluctuating stress
(see § 3, *b*). After the last arsis a final thesis frequently occurs
(see § 6).

Blank verse has no rime, but only rhythm, and thus holds
the middle place between lyric and prose. Diction is elevated
above the common-place and yet not allowed to become unnatural and artificial.

Schiller's blank verse is, like Lessing's, an adaptation of the
English blank verse of Shakespeare, while Goethe's blank verse
(in Iphigenie and other plays) is an adaptation of the Italian
'endecasillabo,' ' verse of eleven syllables,' as it is found in the
epics of Ariosto and Tasso.

(*b*) *Difference of stress in the accented syllables.*

Some of the five accented syllables of each line, *two, three*
or *four* as the case may be, have as a rule a specially strong
accent in order to produce a certain variety of stress. Otherwise the lines would become intolerably monotonous.

A line in which *two* syllables take a stronger stress than the
others is :

Vor euren Mä'nnerblicken zu entſchlei'ern (5).

An instance of *three* chief stresses in a line is :

Meſſi'na teil'te ſich, die Bru'derfehde (53).

An instance of *four* chief stresses in a line is :

Empfin'det ihrer Nä'he Kra'ft und Zu'g (130).

The regular alternation between arsis and thesis gives to the
blank verse at least ten syllables and allows it in many cases
eleven. Where there are eleven syllables in a line, the last

is naturally a thesis and should therefore bear no stress. Some exceptions to this general rule are for instance :

wählt' ich (773), lebt uns (1292), nichts mehr (2495), aufschlug (1313),

Anzug (91), Zufall (2041), Anteil (2204).

(*c*) *Auftakt.*

An unaccented syllable preceding the first accented one in a line is called in German Auftakt. This 'upbeat' imparts liveliness to the verse and produces an effect similar to that of classical iambics. The rhythm of the poem is in such cases 'ascending' (aufsteigend) ; verses without Auftakt have 'descending' (absteigend or fallend) rhythm and their effect is similar to the classical trochee. In our play the rhythm is generally ascending, e.g.

Der Not gehor'chend, ni'cht dem eig'nen Trie'b (1).

A line without Auftakt which has a descending (trochaic) rhythm throughout is

Je'tzt verste'h' ich da's Entse'tzen (1216).

But there are no lines of five accents with descending rhythm throughout in our drama.

(*d*) *Unaccented syllables.*

In most lines the unaccented syllables regularly alternate with the stress syllables, e.g.

Das Le'ben i'st der Gü'ter höch'stes ni'cht (2839).

There are, however, a considerable number of lines in this play, apart from those passages that are composed in free metre and require special consideration, in which more than one unaccented syllable occurs either at the beginning or in the middle of the line. In these cases the rhythm is not 'simple' but 'mixed.' If the rhythm is generally 'ascending' its nature is no longer 'iambic' but becomes 'iambic-anapaestic.' If the simple rhythm was 'descending' or 'trochaic' it becomes in its 'mixed' form 'trochaic-dactylic.' The 'mixed' rhythm naturally imparts to the metre greater variety and is often skilfully used by Schiller to bring out the excitement and emotion of the speakers. If two unaccented syllables occur at the beginning of a line, this is called boppelter Auftact, if they occur in the middle of a line, it is called 'double thesis' (Doppelsenfung). In the classical Greek *trimeter* it was also permissible to begin the line with two unaccented syllables, but it is not likely that Schiller was directly influenced by this metrical device.

Instances of boppelter Auftact at the beginning of a line are:

> Um bie Lo'cken win'be fi'ch ein Di'abe'm (835).
> Eine Schli'nge le'gt, ein Ne'tz um fei'ne Fü'ße (1743).

See also lines 1397, 1737, 2509, 2521, 2676.

Instances of a double thesis in the middle of a line are:

> Ich ha'be bich wie'ber, u'nb ber Gei'ft verla'ffe (1141).
> Die ga'nze Kü'fte! Durch a'lle Mee're fe'tzt (1626).

See also lines 702, 1322, 1739, 1788, 2220, 2452, 2468.

(e) *Metrical stress on a weak e.*

In a number of cases one of the five accents of the line falls on an e which in prose would have only a secondary accent or none at all. Such a stress is of course much weaker than the others. Cases are especially frequent at the end of the metrical line, e.g. Glü'cklíche'n (796), Barmhe'rzíge'n (793), nä'chtliche'n (1276), Flü'chtige' (807), fü'nbíge' (2678), verei'telte' (1327), glän'zenbe'r (828), Grau'fame'r (1788), and in many other passages; also in the middle of the line they sometimes occur.

There are other cases in which, at the beginning and in the middle of lines, the metrical stress falls on an e which in ordinary prose remains altogether unaccented. In such cases the beginning of the line must be read with 'inverted stress,' i.e. ′ × × ′ instead of × ′ × ′. For instance in

> Fahre zur Hö'lle, fa'lsche Schla'ngenfee'le! (1904),

the e in Fahre should not be more strongly accented than the preceding a. The word should therefore be accented Fa'hre, and not Fahre'. There are many similar instances at the beginning of the line. In the middle, however, they are much less frequent. But note ll. 1910, 2191, 2559. In the first case the shouts Radje! Radje! make the irregularity less noticeable. Line 2191 is to be read throughout with inverted stress, and also the end of l. 2559 : Zwi'nge bidj ni'djt!

(*f*) *Irregular lines.*

(1) *The verses may have more than five accented syllables*:

(*a*) There occurs in our drama one line of *seven* syllables, viz. l. 1572 :

Isabella. Wo i'ft fie? Wo' ift Be'atri'ce?
Don Manuel. Be'atri'ce!
Diego. Blei'b!

In this case the line is divided between three speakers, and the necessary pauses prevent the excessive length from being very noticeable.

(*β*) There are many cases of lines containing *six* accented syllables, but these fall into two distinct classes.

In many cases a line containing six accented syllables occurs in the midst of a passage written in blank verse. Such lines of six accents are called in German Sedjsfüßler or Berfe von fedjs Hebungen and are in the poetry of the German classical writers merely casual intruders without any special purpose. About the middle of the eighteenth century most German dramas of the higher style were written in ascending and riming lines of six beats in imitation of the French *alexandrines* of the classical plays of Corneille, Racine, Molière. The German prosody of Schiller and Goethe was in these cases no doubt still influenced, more or less unconsciously, by the longer lines of the French and of the older German dramas with which the poets were familiar and the style of which Goethe had even adopted for his first dramatic attempts. Thus the poets and their readers were quite accustomed to the ring of these verses. Schiller's lines of this kind in our drama have frequently a break in the middle, the 'caesura' (see § 7) ; for instance

Des Himmels Braut berührt mit fündigem Berlangen (720).

Some other cases of Sedjsfüßler are ll. 363, 419, 567, 1130, 1454, 1799, etc. etc.

Very different are the so-called iambic *trimeters*, the regular metre of the classical Greek tragedies. Schiller had been interested in them for some time. When, in September, 1800, Goethe read to him a portion of his great and as yet unprinted Helena scene (which was intended for the second part of Fauſt) Schiller began to study the metre very carefully. Soon after he made excellent use of it in the three Montgomery scenes of his tragedy Die Jungfrau von Orleans which he was just then writing. He introduced the grand and solemn trimeters again into one of the most pathetic scenes of Die Braut von Meſſina (IV. 8). There is usually a break after the fifth or the seventh syllable, but this break is not necessary and is in fact often absent in Schiller's play. In other cases again the break occurs as early as after the second or as late as after the eighth syllable, e.g.

Das Recht des Herrſchers ‖ üb' ich aus zum leßten Mal (2590).
Dem Grab zu übergeben ‖ dieſen teuern Leib (2591).
Wie kam's, ‖ daß man das unglückſelige Gerüſt (2613).
Nur von dem Tod gewinnt ſich nichts. ‖ Bedenk' es wohl (2648).

Sometimes the break occurs after the sixth syllable as in the case of the French alexandrine, e.g.

Und ehrſt du fürchtend auch ‖ den Herrſcher nicht in mir (2652).

In two respects there is an important difference between the alexandrine and the trimeter. On the one hand the trimeter can never have a feminine ending (see § 6), and two trimeters are never bound together by means of rime, as is usual in the case of the alexandrine in the classical French drama. On the other hand Schiller's trimeters (like those of the Greek tragedians) sometimes begin with two unaccented syllables, which imparts to the metre an impassioned touch, but which is impossible in French, cp.

Den Verbre'cher fü'rchte, de'n der Flü'che ſchwer'ſter drü'ckt (2653).

There are no cases of two unaccented syllables *between* the stressed syllables (such as are occasionally found in Latin poetry and in the Second Part of Goethe's Fauſt) in any of Schiller's trimeters, which in this respect follow the Greek models very strictly.

Between the trimeters of ll. 2590 and 2655 occur three cases of blank verse. See also the note on l. 2656.

(2) *The verses may have less than five accented syllables.*

In Schiller's older plays there are not a few instances of short lines, but in Die Braut von Meffina there are only two instances, viz. one line of only four beats (l. 2326) and one of one accent (l. 2768). See the notes on these two lines.

(3) *The verses may be 'broken.'*

There are a number of cases (ll. 101, 394, 543, 1109, 1297, 1298, 1572, 1573, etc.) of such breaking of the metrical line in the dialogue in order to secure greater liveliness. It is, however, not very common in our play, and some scenes are quite free from it. In Die Braut von Meffina Schiller disturbs the harmony and unity of the metrical line much less frequently than in his earlier plays in blank verse, and far less than Lessing does in his Nathan der Weise (1779).

§ 6. *Masculine and feminine verses.*

If the last syllable of a line has a stress, the verse is called masculine (in German männlich or stumpf) (*a*); if on the other hand the stress falls on the last but one and the ending is 'dissyllabic' or 'double,' the verse is called feminine (weiblich or klingend, der Vers hat klingenden Ausgang) (*b*); e.g.

(*a*) Der Not gehorchend, nicht dem eignen Trieb (1).

(*b*) Der We'lt in fti'llen Mau'ern zu' verbe'rgen (9) *or*
  Was fa'gft du, Mu'tter, ei'ne Schwe'fter le'bt u'ns? (1292) *or*
  Ich mi'r gewä'hlt — den Bru'der a'ber fa'nd i'ch (2480).

The latter kind of feminine endings (le'bt u'ns, fa'nd i'ch) is rather heavy and consequently not of frequent occurrence. In nearly every case the feminine ending is provided by an unaccented e of an inflexional syllable or an i (in the endings -ig, -lich, etc.).

§ 7. *Caesura.*

In the classical languages the term *caesura* was used when a foot contained the end of one word and the beginning of another. In German metre the term Zäfur, Cäfur (Einfchnitt) is used in a different way, viz. with regard to a pause in the sense. In Schiller's drama most lines of five accents have a caesura or break which usually occurs between the second and the third arsis, less frequently between the third and the fourth.

When the break immediately follows an accented syllable it is called 'masculine' (*a*), but if it follows an unaccented syllable it is called 'feminine' (*b*), e.g.

(*a*) Ließ er den Haß — ‖ Der Starke achtet es (44).

(*b*) Der Not gehorchend, ‖ nicht dem eignen Trieb (1).

Occasionally there occurs even a double caesura in a line, e.g.

Volle'ndet ! ‖ Ihr habt frei'e Ma'cht ! ‖ geho'rcht (443),

or even three breaks in a line as in

Was ist das ? ‖ Wie ? ‖ Du zögerst ? ‖ Du verstummst ? (1569).

The caesura is most frequent after the second or after the third accented syllable, but it may occur after any stress-syllable, e.g.

1. Glaubt mi'r ! ‖ Es lie'bt ein je'der, frei' sich se'lbst (344).

2. Ließ er den Ha'ß — Der Sta'rke a'chtet e's (44).

3. Was so'llen die'se hie'r ? ‖ Ist's ei'ne Schla'cht (329).

4. Vergi'bt sich u'nd verfö'hnt sich schwe'r. ‖ Der Ma'nn (407).

It would be as easy to give instances of feminine caesurae occurring in similar positions.

§ 8. *Rhythm.*

The rhythm of the blank verse is 'ascending' (cp. §§ 3 and 5, *c*). Its effect is similar to that of classical iambics.

§ 9. *Rime.*

Rime in blank verse seems to be a contradiction, as 'blank verse' really designates 'verse devoid of rime.' Consequently it cannot be of very frequent occurrence in a blank-verse drama. Rimes have been employed by Schiller and other German dramatists, after the model of Shakespeare, with a special purpose, viz.

(*a*) *at the end of a scene :* I. 4 ; I. 6 ; I. 7 ; II. 5 ; II. 6 ; III. I. Also at the end of scenes I. 5 ; I. 8 ; III. 5 ; IV. 7, but these Scenes contain the lyrical outbursts of the chorus and are not written in blank verse.

(*b*) *at the end of a passage of importance* which marks a break within the scene: ll. 627 sqq.; 660 sqq.; 704 sqq.; 842—3; 1404 sqq.; 1416 sqq.; 1464 sqq.; 1531 sqq.; 1543 sqq.

(*c*) to emphasize some lines expressing *strong feeling* or a *general truth*: ll. 648 : 9; 1520 : 22; 2371 sqq.; 2392 : 94. The lyrical passages in which rimes are frequent occur especially in the earlier part of our drama.

In no case has Schiller inserted regular poems in Die Braut von Messina as he has in Wallenstein and Wilhelm Tell; but, apart from the scenes written in blank verse, Schiller has made abundant use of rime in his fine choruses. By introducing the modern device of rime into these he put them on a very different footing from the unrimed choruses in the ancient Greek plays, and made them thus much more readily acceptable to his contemporaries. The rime at the end of the verses is one great characteristic of modern, as compared with classical Greek poetry. In his splendid Helena scenes in the second part of Faust Goethe imitated the ancient choruses much more closely. See the Introduction, page lxv.

§ 10. *Accuracy of Rime*[113].

Two words are said to rime if their last accented vowels and all the following sounds (if any) correspond. Inaccuracy of rime may be of two kinds, viz. the vowel sounds may not be quite the same, or the following consonants may slightly differ. The latter is called assonance and does not often occur in modern German poetry. Accuracy of rime, though at all times very difficult to attain in German, is now much more sought after than it was in the time of Lessing, Goethe and Schiller. There are many inaccurate rimes in our play; as a rule they are correct according to South German pronunciation, which explains their frequent occurrence in Schiller's and Goethe's writings; but modern poets, following the North German and the stage-

[113] Compare also K. Goedeke, *Schillers Werke, historisch-kritische Ausgabe*, I. 383 sqq.; *Zeitschrift für deutsche Philologie*, XVII. 454 sqq.; *Zeitschrift für den deutschen Unterricht*, VII. 160—61; Friedrich Kluge, *Bunte Blätter*, 1912, pp. 202—3.

pronunciation [114], are careful to avoid them. Schiller preserved his strong Swabian accent during the whole of his life, and his rimes were at no time free from marked provincial peculiarities. The inaccuracy of Schiller's rimes is much greater than that of the best Middle High German poets. The chief inaccuracies are [115] :

(*a*)   *Rimes of short and long vowels of the same kind.*

ĭ : ī in bift : verbrießt (1709 : 10); ă : ā in haßt : raft (1221 : 23), warb : bewahrt (1089 : 91); ŏ : ō in Schloß : Schoß (922 : 24), schloß : Los (1021 : 23); ŭ : ū in um : Eigentum (936 : 38). Only the last of these is due to Schiller's dialect in which the u in um is long.

There are two e sounds in German. The long closed e is spelt e while the open e is usually spelt ä. Schiller did not distinguish between them in his pronunciation which was in all cases close (as in Weh, See, etc.). Thus he rimes befeelt : erzählt (1549 : 51), entseelt : vermählt (1968 : 69) ; cp. also ll. 1418 : 20 and 1996 : 97. He also rimes a short open e with long open e (spelt ä) in messen : Gefäßen (1992 : 93).

(*b*)   *Rimes of vowels of different quantity and quality.*

e (short) : ŏ (short) in Schwelle : Hölle; Fels : Gehölz (908 : 10); cp. also ll. 1011 : 13.

e (long closed) : ŏ (long) in stehen : Höhen (238 : 40); gewesen : lösen (1034 : 35) ; cp. also ll. 178 : 79 ; 1696 : 98.

e (long open, usually spelt ä) : ŏ (long) in Nähe : Höhe (2302 : 05) ; gebären : zerstören (974 : 76).

i (short) : ü (short) in sitzen : schützen (222 : 23) ; Wille : Fülle (231 : 33).

i (long) : ū (long) in Gebieter : Flurenbehüter (225 : 27); verbieten : hüten (1721 : 22).

i (short) with ū (long) in Hindernisse : Füße (1742 : 43).   See under (*a*).

---

[114] See Theodor Siebs, *Deutsche Bühnenaussprache*, Bonn, [10]1912; and Wilhelm Viëtor, *Deutsches Aussprachewörterbuch*, Leipzig, 1912.

[115] Not every possible instance is given in the following lists, but only some examples of each kind of inaccurate rimes.

ei : eu (or äu) in Freien : erneuen (169 : 70) ; reizt : durchkreuzt (219 : 21) ; heile : Säule (455 : 56) ; Geheime : Träume (952 : 54). See ll. 1016 : 17.

In South and Middle German ö has the sound of a closed e, ü sounds like i, and eu (äu) like ei ; in every case the pronunciation is 'unrounded,' the lips not being brought forward or rounded, as is the case in the North German pronunciation of ö, ü, eu (äu). Hence most of these rimes were perfectly good in Schiller's (and Goethe's) dialectic pronunciation in which sehe : Nähe : Höhe could well rime, the vowel sound of each being the same as in sehe, viz. a long close e.

(c) Rimes between consonants of different quality.

ſ : ß in Lose : Schoße (324 : 25); Los : schloß (1021 : 23); ertosen : stoßen (990 : 92).

The voiceless ß between vowels was pronounced by Schiller like the voiced s.

ſ : z in Fels : Gehölz (911 : 13) is merely an inaccurate rime.

g : ch in Schweigen : schleichen (984 : 86); entsteiget : entweichet (2426 : 29).

The voiced stop g is here (but not in the standard pronunciation of the stage) pronounced like a voiced spirant and thus rimes, though rather imperfectly, with the voiceless spirant ch.

b : t in Pfaden : verraten (1081 : 82); Boden : Toten (1958 : 61); jeder : später (2279 : 80); befehdben : töten (178 : 79). Cp. also ll. 1983 : 84.

There is little difference between medial b and t in South German pronunciation, the b being voiceless but produced with less force than t.

The rime of final b with final t, e.g. Feld : Welt (1716 : 17) is unobjectionable because in German the voiced stops b, b, g become voiceless t, p, f if placed at the end of a word. In the same way Jagden : nachten (907 : 09) was good in Schiller's pronunciation as medial gb was pronounced like cht.

III. Grouping of the Lines.

The lines are as a rule not connected by means of rime, and in most cases the sense comes to a close or to a stop of some sort with the end of each verse. But there are various ways

in which several lines are more closely connected. Such are
(*a*) *Enjambement,* and (*b*) *Stichomythia.*

§ 11. *Enjambement.*

This term means the carrying on of the same thought without
the slightest interruption from the end of one line to the following line, e.g.

> Der Augenblick ist da, wo es ans Licht
> Des Tages soll hervorgezogen werden (107—8).

or Den Mann zu täuschen, den umsichtigsten
> Der Menschen, und ins Herz zurückzubrängen (2079—80).

or Um alsobald, wenn ihr den Rücken mir
> Gekehrt, mit neuer Wut sich zu entfesseln (322—3).

Similar cases of 'overflow' verses occur occasionally in our
play and serve to break the natural monotony of a number
of consecutive 'end-stopt' lines. The language is thus to a
certain extent made to resemble the natural flow of prose. To
the ear the enjambement is hardly noticeable, and a play is of
course in the first instance written for an audience.

The large majority of Schiller's blank verses in this drama
are self-contained and 'end-stopt.' Most persons in the play
speak in one or more whole lines without their speech coming
to an end in the middle. The lines in which a strong natural
break occurs in the middle and in which there is thus a
discrepancy between the end of a line and the end of a
sentence are in a small minority. The cases of *enjambement*
are also less frequent in this than in Schiller's earlier dramas.
An excessive use of *enjambement* and breaks in the middle of
the line, such as is noticeable in Lessing's Nathan der Weise,
causes the hearer to lose his sense of the rhythm of the individual
line and the metrical unity of the verse, the language of the
poet thus coming too near ordinary prose.

§ 12. *Stichomythia.*

In most cases the dialogue or the narration is carried on in
speeches consisting of a number of lines, alternating with
passages of similar length or with short interspersed observations.
In not a few cases, however, Schiller has purposely arranged

his dialogues so that they are carried on for some time with a certain parallelism, the number of lines allotted to each speaker being the same. In some cases each speaker has two lines, in others the sentences are compressed into one, which often makes them epigrammatic and in each case gives great animation to the dialogue. This peculiarity of style is found in the old Greek dramatists and is called by a Greek name *stichomythia* (στιχομυθία) 'the speaking in (alternate) lines' (𝔚echselreden in [𝔇oppel]verfen). It has been imitated by the classical French tragedians and also by some modern English dramatists. In the plays of Goethe and Schiller there are numerous instances. Goethe has it no less in his early prose tragedy 𝔈gmont than in his 𝔍phigenie, which was finally written in blank verse and in this form exercised considerable influence on Schiller. Schiller himself has passages in *stichomythia* in 𝔚allenstein and in all the dramas following it. See my editions of 𝔚allenstein, 𝔐aria 𝔖tuart, and 𝔚ilhelm 𝔗ell.

In our play we find a considerable number of instances of *stichomythia* of the two kinds, viz. single lines and double lines.

In some cases the arrangement of the lines is somewhat different, but an intentional parallelism is always noticeable, whether the speakers are allotted one-half, one, two, or even four lines.

Half-lines: ll. 2467 sqq.

One line: ll. 486 sqq.; 1629 sqq.; 1707 sqq.; 1805 sqq.; 2208 sqq.

Two lines: ll. 466 sqq.; 502 sqq.; 739 sqq.; 1590 sqq.; 1858 sqq.; 2029 sqq.; 2639 sqq.

Four lines: ll. 2607 sqq.

This skilful use of different kinds of *stichomythia* or parallelism gives to the dialogue and thus to the whole drama a heightened dramatic character. Another means towards the same end is the frequent use of rime (see § 9).

In Act III, Scene I, ll. 1707 sqq. the single stichomythic lines are further bound together by means of rime. In this way Schiller introduced a modern element into the characteristic rimeless alternate lines of the ancients.

g 2

xcii   *INTRODUCTION*

B. Language and Style.

I. LANGUAGE.

The peculiarities of language which, apart from the use of
poetical expressions, give the diction a poetical character, may
be classified as follows[116]:

A. *Peculiarities of Word Forms.*

A number of words used by Schiller are poetic because they
are archaic and unusual, e.g. ſiehe (67), ſahe (1497), fertflung (1506);
dein (532), mein (858); der Meduſen (147), der Sonnen (199); Ceſarn
(472); das Gemahl (961).

A similar effect is produced by the use of simple verbs and
nouns instead of their more usual compounds, e.g. geſchieden for
ausgeſchieden (946), etc.

B. *Peculiarities of Syntax.*

(1) *Nouns.* lebt in einem Heldenpaare fort glorreicher Söhne (20);
den Schleier zerriß ich jungfräulicher Zucht (1009); in Lebens Glut den
Schatten beigeſellt (1029), etc.   See the notes to these lines.

(2) *Adjectives.* (a) In many cases adjectives stand without
inflexion:

(α) Before nouns, especially before neuter nouns, e.g. redlich
Herz (102), ein edler Bild (378), ein verſöhnlich Herz (484), ausſchließend
Eigentum (519), etc.

(β) Before another adjective without being connected by
means of und.   In this case the adjective without inflexion is
often mistaken for an adverb, e.g. unbekannt verhängnisvollem (24),
ſchmerzlich ſüßes (106), furchtbar kriegeriſche (328), etc.   But cp. also
Nah und Fernes (2404).

---

[116] In all the more important cases the word-forms or the syntactical
peculiarities have been discussed in the Notes. See also the Index to
the Notes, and the books and articles enumerated in the Appendix V
under C, p. 266.

(*b*) In several cases adjectives are placed with repetition of the definite article after the substantive to give them greater emphasis, e.g. baß Wort, baß heilenbe (168); bie Stabt, bie völferwim= melnbe (990); ben Anblick...ben heißerflehten (1362); bie Mutter...bie glück= liche (1438), etc.

(3) *Pronouns.* (*a*) Pronouns are occasionally placed early in a sentence and only subsequently find their proper explanation by a noun, e.g. fie...biefe Saaten (197); ihn...ben alten Haß (429); es...baß Schöne (630); fie...bie gefällige Tochter beß Schaumß (898), etc.

(*b*) The definite article and the demonstrative pronoun are not infrequently used with the sense of the possessive pronoun, e.g. baß braufenbe Blut (196); biefeß Herz (78); etc.

(4) *Verbs.* (*a*) Older constructions are used with certain verbs, e.g. fich anmaßen (343), fofen (699), warten (858), vergeffen (1613), wahren (1777), etc.

(*b*) Some verbs are used in a peculiar and poetic way, e.g. gebot (16), erhielt (85), gewähren (95), verjüngen (124), warb (232), jubereiten (330), mag (645), ermüben (1782), etc.

(*c*) Auxiliaries are frequently omitted. See the notes to ll. 7 and 459.

II. STYLE.

The chief characteristics of Schiller's poetic language in the most elevated and the most lyrical of his dramas are the following :

(*a*) It is *uniformly idealized*, i.e. all the *dramatis personae* speak the same elevated language, and the individual peculiarities of the speakers disappear in the general refined elevation of tone. In thus idealizing the language of the drama Schiller shows himself influenced by the ancient Greek tragedians as well as by Goethe's language, especially in Iphigenie.

(*b*) It is *free from all colloquial, dialectic or old German words and phrases* which are not uncommon in Wallenfteinß Lager and in Wilhelm Tell.

(*c*) *The frequent use of certain favourite words*, e.g. ſchau=
bernb (450, 1883), wunbernb (609), ſchöpfen (768, 2117, 2375), ſich
erwarten (799); Geburt (401), Haus (2754); gefällig (899).

(*d*) *The attributive adjective is often replaced by a noun and
the original subject is placed in the genitive depending on the
new noun*, e.g. ber Söhne Kraft for bie kräftigen Söhne (264), bes
Vaters Macht (682), ber Mutter Hoheit (262), bes raſchen Boten jugenb=
liche Kraft (hab' ich geſanbt) (2110), etc.

(*e*) *The abstract is sometimes used instead of the concrete*,
e.g. bes Brubermorbs Hänbe (1969) for bie Hänbe bes Brubermörbers;
beine...Unſchulb (2830) for bu Unſchulbiger.

(*f*) *Effective use is made of alliteration*, e.g. in lines 202,
871—2, 1721, 1793, 1933, 2396.

(*g*) *Emphatic use of* nicht (265), nicht wahrlich (1480), *or of a
past participle which is only later qualified by a noun at the
beginning of a sentence*, e.g. ſchnell umgewanbelt...iſt...Herz (707).
See the notes to these lines where other instances are given.

(*h*) *Schiller's language and style in* Die Braut von Meſſina
*are very strongly influenced by the Greek classics and by the
works of Goethe and Voss based on the Greek dramatic and epic
poets.* His diction in Die Braut von Meſſina abounds in
turns which are either direct imitations of the ancients or new
words and phrases conceived in the style of the classics or
words and phrases suggested by Goethe's practice in Iphigenie
auf Tauris. Particulars are mentioned in the Notes. Goethe's
influence is clearly seen in lines 330, 419, 452, [593], 985, 1271,
1354, 2312, 2390, 2503. The following cases of classical influence
may be mentioned here:

Words and phrases: mächtigwaltenb (16), ſäulengetragen (136),
himmelumwanbelnb (213), fluchbefreit (534), bumpferbrauſenb (992),
glückbekrönt (1139), nachtgewohnt (1269), bonnerſchwer (2067), etc.; ber
Söhne Kraft (264); bein herrliches Haupt (258); ein Gott (1091); ſie
rühmt ſich...zu ſein (743); bas ſchwarze Blut (2414); ſchwere Taten
(419).

Syntax: Sucht ber Ehren (2574); bir gewußt for in bir gewußt
(484); beneib' ich ihm (1244); and others.

Repetitions: Rache...Rache...falle...falle (1910); Wehe...wehe (1985, 2004).

Use of words of the same stem in close proximity: das Glück der Glücklichen (104); sie liebt den Liebenden (622), and many others.

XI. ARGUMENT.

I, 1.

Isabella, the widowed Princess of Messina, addresses the Elders of the town. She reviews the past and discusses the present situation, the old hostility of her two sons, the death of her stern husband three months ago, the bitter feud of the Princes and the anarchy reigning at Messina in the absence of a strong ruler, the threat of the impatient townspeople to look for another race of rulers if the Princes will not become reconciled, and her own ceaseless endeavours during the last three months to prevail upon her sons to give up their animosity and to meet in a spirit of reconciliation under the paternal roof. The Princess informs the Elders that at last her entreaties have been crowned with success, that the Princes have agreed to meet in the palace this very day. She commands the townspeople to receive their masters with due respect and obedience. The Elders withdraw without making any reply.

I, 2.

Isabella commands her old trusty servant Diego to go forthwith to a certain religious house in the neighbourhood of the town and to fetch from there a dear charge whom he had once helped her to conceal in this safe place. After Diego's departure a growing noise outside the palace indicates the approach of her sons with their stately following.

I, 3.

The Chorus, consisting of two groups of knights, the older being the followers of Don Manuel, the younger the retainers of Don Cesar, enter the palace and group themselves while waiting for their lords and the Princess. They express themselves willing to go on fighting the feuds of the princes, but also ready to become reconciled if their masters wish it. The Chorus of the younger knights is the more rash and aggressive of the two. The statements and reflexions of the older men supplement to some extent what has been said by Isabella to the elders and Diego. They comment on the folly of the men of Messina in destroying one another in civil war for the sake of a race of stern foreign rulers, and at the same time dwell on the necessity of obeying a strong prince, and praise the advantages of an unpretentious position in life in difficult times of trouble and feud. When Isabella and her sons enter, both Choruses unite in a short song of praise and loyal homage.

I, 4.

The Princess endeavours in every possible way to prevail upon her two sons, who seem to have nothing in common but love and reverence for their mother, to forget their old hatred and to make up their minds to become friends. When her passionate pleading apparently remains without result, she leaves the hall in deepest grief.

I, 5.

Still her eloquent words have not been spoken in vain. The brothers, deeply moved by the despair of their beloved mother, enter into conversation which gradually waxes more friendly, and in the end they become reconciled. Their reconciliation is warmly endorsed by their retainers, all of them sons of one and the same land.

I, 6.

Don Cesar learns that a maiden, whom (by his spies) he has been seeking, has just been discovered at Messina. He starts at once, with renewed assurances of brotherly affection and with strictest injunctions to all his knights never again to attempt to stir up any ill feeling towards his brother.

I, 7.

Don Manuel, who has apparently been somewhat reserved and absorbed in his own thoughts, informs his knights that he had come to the meeting without feeling any more hatred towards his brother, but that his whole heart was given up to one engrossing passion—a deep love for a beautiful maiden. He describes to his followers in enthusiastic words how, five months ago, he met her accidentally in the garden of a convent, how this love had at once completely taken possession of him, how on learning from her (who was ignorant of her own relations) that she was shortly to be removed from her safe place of retreat, he had the night before prevailed upon her to flee with him, and that he had left her concealed in a garden close by. He is anxious to proclaim her forthwith as his bride and to introduce her, in garments befitting a princess, to his mother. She is, so far, unacquainted with his high position. He starts with a small following for the bazaar in order to purchase there all the necessary articles of apparel in order to adorn his beloved one before escorting her in state to the palace.

I, 8.

The Chorus, after Don Manuel's departure, reflect on the various ways in which the knights can spend their time now that the brothers have put an end to their fighting. They discuss the pleasures of courting, hunting, and sailing, and in the end express sinister forebodings as to the ultimate fate of the race to which their lords belong and mention a terrible curse uttered by the grandfather of their lords against his son and all his descendants.

II, 1.

Beatrice, anxiously awaiting Don Manuel's return, reviews her past life and the bold step she has taken in following her unknown lover. She trusts him and is ready to sacrifice everything to her love. She mentions that she has just left the safe garden for a short time in order to pray in a church close by, and recalls with a shudder how once before, on the death of the late Prince of Messina, she had gone stealthily to the church in order to witness the funeral rites and was there to her terror addressed by a bold youth with ardent eyes. She hears approaching steps, takes them for those of her returning lover, and rushes to meet him.

II, 2.

Don Cesar enters and, without paying any attention to her fright, greets her as his lost love, declares her to be his bride elect, tells her his name and rank, and orders the Chorus to guard her for a short time till he can come back and take her to the palace. He hurries away without receiving an answer from the girl who is speechless with terror.

II, 3.

The Chorus greet Beatrice as their prospective princess. She, awaking from her stupefaction, bewails her cruel fate.

II, 4.

The Chorus praise the fortune of rulers who always obtain of all things the choicest and the most beautiful.

II, 5.

Isabella, standing between her two sons, discloses to them the secret that they have a sister. She explains to them why they have been kept in ignorance of this fact. Shortly before the birth of this daughter her husband and she had dreams concerning her which each of them had got interpreted, the prince by a Mahommedan soothsayer, and she by a Christian monk. On receiving an unfavourable explanation the stern Prince ordered the new-born child to be killed forthwith, but the mother, reassured by her oracle, succeeded in saving the child and in hiding it, with the help of the faithful Diego, in a convent where it was brought up. She informs her sons that they will presently see their sister, as now at last, their reconciliation being completed, it has been possible to send Diego to fetch her. The brothers learn this startling news with great joy and each of them informs his mother that he too will shortly bring her a daughter, a beautiful maiden whom he has chosen to be his wife. Isabella is overjoyed at this prospect and declares herself to be the happiest of mothers. When, however, she asks her sons for particulars as to their intended brides, Don Manuel gives her an evasive answer, while Don Cesar tells her of his first meeting with Beatrice (of whose name he is ignorant), showing how he fell in love at first sight, and confessing that he does not know her parentage.

II, 6.

Diego returns and informs the grief-stricken Isabella that her daughter Beatrice has disappeared from the convent. It is believed that she has been carried off by pirates. Isabella calls upon her sons to take arms and recover their sister. Don Cesar rushes off at once. Don Manuel, struck by the name Beatrice and by some other circumstances, is filled with grave misgivings and resolves to set his mind at ease by an immediate interview with his betrothed. After he has left, Don Cesar returns, learns from the mother the name of the convent where her daughter had been hidden, and rushes off again in pursuit of the pirates. Isabella remains behind in deep anxiety.

III, 1.

The knights of Don Manuel, bearing wreaths and bridal presents for Beatrice, are met at the entrance of the garden by the retainers of Don Cesar who refuse to admit them. After high words they draw their swords and Beatrice is in the greatest fear for the life of Don Manuel, whom she now expects to return every moment.

III, 2.

Don Manuel enters, enforces peace and peremptorily dismisses his brother's knights, who withdraw unwillingly.

III, 3.

He at once begins to ask Beatrice some important questions. To his horror her answers and confessions leave no doubt that she is his and Don Cesar's sister.

III, 4.

While they are still talking Don Cesar enters, and, on seeing Beatrice cling fondly to her lover, forthwith draws his dagger and stabs Don Manuel by whom he believes himself to be basely deceived. He then orders Beatrice to be taken to his mother and sets out in quest of his sister.

III, 5.

The knights of Don Manuel put their lord on a bier, bewailing his cruel fate and foreboding evil to his murderer who, as a fratricide, will henceforth be pursued and hunted down by the avenging deities.

IV, 1.

Isabella is in great anxiety, but still not without hope of a happy issue. She informs Diego that she has sent a messenger to a pious hermit on Mt Etna in order to obtain from him, if possible, some information about her lost daughter.

IV, 2.

The messenger returns and tells the Princess that the hermit bade him to return forthwith, after he had told him that the lost daughter had been discovered by Don Manuel. The messenger adds that the hermit then set fire to the hut in which he had served God for ninety years and left it lamenting.

IV, 3.

The knights of Don Cesar carry Beatrice, who is pale and unconscious, on a stretcher into the palace. Isabella, ignorant of what has happened in the garden, welcomes her joyfully as her dear daughter captured from the pirates by her valiant sons. When the girl comes to herself, she slowly recognizes her mother, but implores her not to allow her to be sent to Don Cesar's mother, the Princess of Messina. She is overcome with grief and horror when she learns that her mother is the Princess of Messina and at the same time the mother of Don Manuel and Don Cesar.

IV, 4.

The retainers of Don Manuel bring his corpse stretched on a bier and covered with a black cloth. Isabella at first thinks that he has been killed by one of the pirates in the gallant attempt to rescue his sister, and, overcome with grief, she curses the murderer, the murderer's mother and his whole race. She contemptuously declares all oracles and prophecies to be vain and devoid of truth, relates the two dreams and the two conflicting explanations of them (see II, 5) and maintains that neither of them had any truth in it. In vain do the Chorus and Beatrice endeavour to stop the violent outburst of her indignation and despair.

IV, 5.

Don Cesar appears and now learns that Beatrice is his sister, while the unsuspecting Isabella learns that Don Manuel fell by his brother's hand. Don Cesar curses his mother's secret doings by which, as he says, all the horrors were caused. Isabella in her turn defies all powers on high and severs all connexion with Don Cesar 'who had murdered her better son.' With words expressing the bitterest scorn of gods and oracles, she leaves the hall.

IV, 6.

Don Cesar entreats Beatrice (who does not speak a single word during this scene) for her sympathy. She is not to mourn for Don Manuel alone. He will be content to die if she will mourn for him too. When she remains silent, he turns away and says that he will see neither her nor his mother any more.

IV, 7.

The Chorus praise the peace and quiet of nature and of a retired life far from the turmoil of the towns that are filled with crime and trouble.

IV, 8.

Don Cesar, determined to take his own life in expiation of the murder, quietly gives all the necessary instructions for the fitting interment of his brother. When the Chorus endeavour to prevail upon him to spare his life for the benefit of his subjects, he firmly bids them to desist.

IV, 9.

Isabella comes back, revokes her curse, and entreats Don Cesar to live for her. She cannot bear to lose him too. He is deeply moved, but remains firm in his tragic determination. When her pleading proves unavailing, she calls Beatrice to her help.

IV, 10.

At her sight Don Cesar is stirred to the innermost depths of his soul. At first Beatrice asks to be allowed to die herself in order to make amends for the misery which she has brought upon all her family. At last she prevails upon herself to implore Don Cesar to live for his mother and for herself. The Chorus believes that now Don Cesar will consent to spare his own life, when suddenly the music of the funeral service of Don Manuel is heard in the chapel close by and his coffin is seen through the open portals. Don Cesar feels himself irresistibly drawn towards his dead brother and kills himself. The play is brought to an end by the Chorus, in a few solemn words.

Die Braut von Messina

oder

Die feindlichen Brüder

Ein Trauerspiel mit Chören

Perſonen.

Donna Iſabella, Fürſtin von Meſſina.

Don Manuel,
Don Ceſar, } ihre Söhne.

Beatrice.

Diego.

Boten.

Chor, beſteht aus dem Gefolge der Brüder.

Die Älteſten von Meſſina, reden nicht.

Erster Aufzug.

Die Szene ist eine geräumige Säulenhalle, auf beiden Seiten sind Eingänge, eine große Flügeltüre in der Tiefe führt zu einer Kapelle.

Erster Auftritt.

Donna Isabella in tiefer Trauer, die Ältesten von Messina stehn um sie her.

Isabella.

Der Not gehorchend, nicht dem eignen Trieb,
Tret' ich, ihr greisen Häupter dieser Stadt,
Heraus zu euch aus den verschwiegenen
Gemächern meines Frauensaals, das Antlitz
Vor euren Männerblicken zu entschleiern.   5
Denn es geziemt der Witwe, die den Gatten
Verloren, ihres Lebens Licht und Ruhm,
Die schwarzumflorte Nachtgestalt dem Aug'
Der Welt in stillen Mauern zu verbergen;
Doch unerbittlich, allgewaltig treibt   10
Des Augenblicks Gebieterstimme mich
An das entwohnte Licht der Welt hervor.
Nicht dreimal hat der Mond die Lichtgestalt

Erneut, seit ich den fürstlichen Gemahl
Zu seiner letzten Ruhestätte trug,　　　　　　　　　15
Der mächtigwaltend dieser Stadt gebot,
Mit starkem Arme gegen eine Welt
Euch schützend, die euch feindlich rings umlagert.
Er selber ist dahin, doch lebt sein Geist
In einem tapfern Heldenpaare fort　　　　　　　　20
Glorreicher Söhne, dieses Landes Stolz.
Ihr habt sie unter euch in freud'ger Kraft
Aufwachsen sehen, doch mit ihnen wuchs
Aus unbekannt verhängnisvollem Samen
Auch ein unsel'ger Bruderhaß empor,　　　　　　　25
Der Kindheit frohe Einigkeit zerreißend,
Und reifte furchtbar mit dem Ernst der Jahre.
Nie hab' ich ihrer Eintracht mich erfreut;
An diesen Brüsten nährt' ich beide gleich,
Gleich unter sie verteil' ich Lieb' und Sorge,　　　　30
Und beide weiß ich kindlich mir geneigt.
In diesem einz'gen Triebe sind sie eins,
In allem andern trennt sie blut'ger Streit.

　　Zwar, weil der Vater noch gefürchtet herrschte,
Hielt er durch gleicher Strenge furchtbare　　　　　35
Gerechtigkeit die Heftigbrausenden im Zügel,
Und unter eines Joches Eisenschwere
Bog er vereinend ihren starren Sinn.
Nicht waffentragend durften sie sich nahn,
Nicht in denselben Mauern übernachten;　　　　　40
So hemmt' er zwar mit strengem Machtgebot
Den rohen Ausbruch ihres wilden Triebs,
Doch ungebessert in der tiefen Brust
Ließ er den Haß — Der Starke achtet es

Gering, die leise Quelle zu verstopfen,   45
Weil er dem Strome mächtig wehren kann.
    Was kommen mußte, kam.   Als er die Augen
Im Tode schloß, und seine starke Hand
Sie nicht mehr bändigt, bricht der alte Groll,
Gleichwie des Feuers eingepreßte Glut,   50
Zur offnen Flamme sich entzündend los.
Ich sag' euch, was ihr alle selbst bezeugt:
Messina teilte sich, die Bruderfehde
Löst' alle heil'gen Bande der Natur,
Dem allgemeinen Streit die Losung gebend;   55
Schwert traf auf Schwert, zum Schlachtfeld ward die Stadt.
Ja diese Hallen selbst bespritzte Blut.
    Des Staates Bande sahet ihr zerreißen,
Doch mir zerriß im Innersten das Herz —
Ihr fühltet nur das öffentliche Leiden   60
Und fragtet wenig nach der Mutter Schmerz.
Ihr kamt zu mir und spracht dies harte Wort:
„Du siehst, daß deiner Söhne Bruderzwist
Die Stadt empört in bürgerlichem Streit,
Die, von dem bösen Nachbar rings umgarnt,   65
Durch Eintracht nur dem Feinde widersteht.
— Du bist die Mutter! Wohl, so siehe zu,
Wie du der Söhne blut'gen Hader stillst.
Was kümmert uns, die Friedlichen, der Zank
Der Herrscher? Sollen wir zu Grunde gehn,   70
Weil deine Söhne wütend sich befehden?
Wir wollen uns selbst raten ohne sie
Und einem andern Herrn uns übergeben,
Der unser Bestes will und schaffen kann!"
    So spracht ihr rauhen Männer, mitleidlos,   75

Für euch nur sorgend und für eure Stadt,
Und wälztet noch die öffentliche Not
Auf dieses Herz, das von der Mutter Angst
Und Sorgen schwer genug belastet war.
Ich unternahm das nicht zu Hoffende,   80
Ich warf mit dem zerrißnen Mutterherzen
Mich zwischen die Ergrimmten, Friede rufend —
Unabgeschreckt, geschäftig, unermüdlich
Beschickt' ich sie, den einen um den andern,
Bis ich erhielt durch mütterliches Flehn,   85
Daß sie's zufrieden sind, in dieser Stadt
Messina, in dem väterlichen Schloß,
Unfeindlich sich von Angesicht zu sehn,
Was nie geschah, seitdem der Fürst verschieden.

    Dies ist der Tag! Des Boten harr' ich stündlich,   90
Der mir die Kunde bringt von ihrem Anzug.
— Seid denn bereit, die Herrscher zu empfangen
Mit Ehrfurcht, wie's dem Untertanen ziemt.
Nur eure Pflicht zu leisten seid bedacht,
Fürs andre laßt uns andere gewähren.   95
Verderblich diesem Land, und ihnen selbst
Verderbenbringend war der Söhne Streit;
Versöhnt, vereinigt, sind sie mächtig gnug,
Euch zu beschützen gegen eine Welt
Und Recht sich zu verschaffen — gegen euch!   100

        (Die Ältesten entfernen sich schweigend, die Hand auf der Brust.
            Sie winkt einem alten Diener, der zurückbleibt.)

Zweiter Auftritt.

Isabella. Diego.

Isabella.

Diego!

Diego.

Was gebietet meine Fürstin?

Isabella.

Bewährter Diener! Redlich Herz! Tritt näher!
Mein Leiden hast du, meinen Schmerz geteilt,
So teil' auch jetzt das Glück der Glücklichen.
Verpfändet hab' ich deiner treuen Brust   105
Mein schmerzlich süßes, heiliges Geheimnis.
Der Augenblick ist da, wo es ans Licht
Des Tages soll hervorgezogen werden.
Zu lange schon erstickt' ich der Natur
Gewalt'ge Regung, weil noch über mich   110
Ein fremder Wille herrisch waltete;
Jetzt darf sich ihre Stimme frei erheben,
Noch heute soll dies Herz befriedigt sein,
Und dieses Haus, das lang' veröbet war,
Versammle alles, was mir teuer ist.   115
    So lenke denn die alterschweren Tritte
Nach jenem wohlbekannten Kloster hin,
Das einen teuren Schatz mir aufbewahrt.
Du warst es, treue Seele, der ihn mir
Dorthin geflüchtet hat auf beßre Tage,   120
Den traur'gen Dienst der Traurigen erzeigend.
Du bringe fröhlich jetzt der Glücklichen
Das teure Pfand zurück.
        (Man hört in der Ferne blasen.)

O eile, eile
Und laß die Freude deinen Schritt verjüngen!
Ich höre kriegerischer Hörner Schall,   125
Der meiner Söhne Einzug mir verkündigt.
(Diego geht ab. Die Musik läßt sich noch von einer entgegengesetzten
Seite immer näher und näher hören.)

Isabella.

Erregt ist ganz Messina — Horch! ein Strom
Verworrner Stimmen wälzt sich brausend her —
Sie sind's! Das Herz der Mutter, mächtig schlagend,
Empfindet ihrer Nähe Kraft und Zug.   130
Sie sind's! O meine Kinder, meine Kinder!
(Sie eilt hinaus.)

Dritter Auftritt.

Chor tritt auf.

Er besteht aus zwei Halbchören, welche zu gleicher Zeit, von zwei entgegengesetzten Seiten, der eine aus der Tiefe, der andere aus dem
Vordergrund eintreten, rund um die Bühne gehen und sich alsdann auf
derselben Seite, wo jeder eingetreten, in eine Reihe stellen. Den einen
Halbchor bilden die ältern, den andern die jüngern Ritter; beide sind
durch Farbe und Abzeichen verschieden. Wenn beide Chöre einander
gegenüberstehen, schweigt der Marsch, und die beiden Chorführer reden.

Erster Chor.

Dich begrüß' ich in Ehrfurcht,
Prangende Halle,
Dich, meiner Herrscher
Fürstliche Wiege,   135
Säulengetragenes herrliches Dach.
    Tief in der Scheide
Ruhe das Schwert,

Vor den Toren gefesselt
Liege des Streits schlangenhaarigtes Scheusal.   140
Denn des gastlichen Hauses
Unverletzliche Schwelle
Hütet der Eid, der Erinnyen Sohn,
Der furchtbarste unter den Göttern der Hölle!

Zweiter Chor.

Zürnend ergrimmt mir das Herz im Busen,   145
Zu dem Kampf ist die Faust geballt,
Denn ich sehe das Haupt der Medusen,
Meines Feindes verhaßte Gestalt.
Kaum gebiet' ich dem kochenden Blute.
Gönn' ich ihm die Ehre des Worts?   150
Oder gehorch' ich dem zürnenden Mute?
Aber mich schreckt die Eumenide,
Die Beschirmerin dieses Orts,
Und der waltende Gottesfriede.

Erster Chor.

Weisere Fassung   155
Ziemet dem Alter,
Ich, der Vernünftige, grüße zuerst.
                    (Zu dem zweiten Chor.)
Sei mir willkommen,
Der du mit mir,
Gleiche Gefühle   160
Brüderlich teilend,
Dieses Palastes
Schützende Götter
Fürchtend verehrst!
Weil sich die Fürsten gütlich besprechen,   165
Wollen auch wir jetzt Worte des Friedens

Harmlos wechseln mit ruhigem Blut,
Denn auch das Wort ist, das heilende, gut.
Aber treff' ich dich draußen im Freien,
Da mag der blutige Kampf sich erneuen,   170
Da erprobe das Eisen den Mut.

Der ganze Chor.

Aber treff' ich dich draußen im Freien,
Da mag der blutige Kampf sich erneuen,
Da erprobe das Eisen den Mut.

Erster Chor.

Dich nicht hass' ich! Nicht du bist mein Feind!   175
Eine Stadt ja hat uns geboren,
Jene sind ein fremdes Geschlecht.
Aber wenn sich die Fürsten befehden,
Müssen die Diener sich morden und töten,
Das ist die Ordnung, so will es das Recht.   180

Zweiter Chor.

Mögen sie's wissen,
Warum sie sich blutig
Hassend bekämpfen! Mich ficht es nicht an.
Aber wir fechten ihre Schlachten,
Der ist kein Tapfrer, kein Ehrenmann,   185
Der den Gebieter läßt verachten.

Der ganze Chor.

Aber wir fechten ihre Schlachten,
Der ist kein Tapfrer, kein Ehrenmann,
Der den Gebieter läßt verachten.

Einer aus dem Chor.

Hört, was ich bei mir selbst erwogen,   190
Als ich müßig dahergezogen
Durch des Korns hochwallende Gassen,

Meinen Gedanken überlassen.

Wir haben uns in des Kampfes Wut
Nicht besonnen und nicht beraten,   195
Denn uns betörte das brausende Blut.
  Sind sie nicht unser, diese Saaten?
Diese Ulmen, mit Reben umsponnen,
Sind sie nicht Kinder unsrer Sonnen?
Könnten wir nicht in frohem Genuß   200
Harmlos vergnügliche Tage spinnen,
Lustig das leichte Leben gewinnen?
Warum ziehn wir mit rasendem Beginnen
Unser Schwert für das fremde Geschlecht?
Es hat an diesen Boden kein Recht.   205
Auf dem Meerschiff ist es gekommen
Von der Sonne rötlichtem Untergang;
Gastlich haben wir's aufgenommen
(Unsre Väter! die Zeit ist lang),
Und jetzt sehen wir uns als Knechte   210
Untertan diesem fremden Geschlechte!

Ein zweiter.

Wohl! Wir bewohnen ein glückliches Land,
Das die himmelumwandelnde Sonne
Ansieht mit immer freundlicher Helle,
Und wir könnten es fröhlich genießen;   215
Aber es läßt sich nicht sperren und schließen,
Und des Meers rings umgebende Welle,
Sie verrät uns dem kühnen Korsaren,
Der die Küste verwegen durchkreuzt.
Einen Segen haben wir zu bewahren,   220
Der das Schwert nur des Fremblings reizt.
Sklaven sind wir in den eigenen Sitzen,

Das Land kann seine Kinder nicht schützen.
Nicht, wo die goldene Ceres lacht
Und der friedliche Pan, der Flurenbehüter —   225
Wo das Eisen wächst in der Berge Schacht,
Da entspringen der Erde Gebieter.

Erster Chor.

Ungleich verteilt sind des Lebens Güter
Unter der Menschen flücht'gem Geschlecht,
Aber die Natur, sie ist ewig gerecht.   230
Uns verließ sie das Mark und die Fülle,
Die sich immer erneuend erschafft,
Jenen ward der gewaltige Wille
Und die unzerbrechliche Kraft.

Mit der furchtbaren Stärke gerüstet,   235
Führen sie aus, was dem Herzen gelüstet,
Füllen die Erde mit mächtigem Schall;
Aber hinter den großen Höhen
Folgt auch der tiefe, der donnernde Fall.

   Darum lob' ich mir, niedrig zu stehen,   240
Mich verbergend in meiner Schwäche!
Jene gewaltigen Wetterbäche,
Aus des Hagels unendlichen Schloßen,
Aus den Wolkenbrüchen zusammen geflossen,
Kommen finster gerauscht und geschossen,   245
Reißen die Brücken und reißen die Dämme
Donnernd mit fort im Wogengeschwemme,
Nichts ist, das die gewaltigen hemme.
Doch nur der Augenblick hat sie geboren,
Ihres Laufes furchtbare Spur   250
Geht verrinnend im Sande verloren,
Die Zerstörung verkündigt sie nur.

— Die fremden Eroberer kommen und gehen,
Wir gehorchen, aber wir bleiben stehen.

Die hintere Türe öffnet sich, Donna Isabella erscheint zwischen ihren
Söhnen Don Manuel und Don Cesar.

Beide Chöre.

Preis ihr und Ehre, 255
Die uns dort aufgeht,
Eine glänzende Sonne!
Knieend verehr' ich dein herrliches Haupt.

Erster Chor.

Schön ist des Mondes
Mildere Klarheit 260
Unter der Sterne blitzendem Glanz,
Schön ist der Mutter
Liebliche Hoheit
Zwischen der Söhne feuriger Kraft,
Nicht auf der Erden 265
Ist ihr Bild und ihr Gleichnis zu sehn.
  Hoch auf des Lebens
Gipfel gestellt,
Schließt sie blühend den Kreis des Schönen,
Mit der Mutter und ihren Söhnen 270
Krönt sich die herrlich vollendete Welt.
  Selber die Kirche, die göttliche, stellt nicht
Schöneres dar auf dem himmlischen Thron,
Höheres bildet
Selber die Kunst nicht, die göttlich geborne, 275
Als die Mutter mit ihrem Sohn.

Zweiter Chor.

Freudig sieht sie aus ihrem Schoße
Einen blühenden Baum sich erheben,

Der sich ewig sprossend erneut.
Denn sie hat ein Geschlecht geboren,   280
Welches wandeln wird mit der Sonne
Und den Namen geben der rollenden Zeit.
Völker verrauschen,
Namen verklingen,
Finstre Vergessenheit   285
Breitet die dunkelnachtenden Schwingen
Über ganzen Geschlechtern aus.
  Aber der Fürsten
Einsame Häupter
Glänzen erhellt,   290
Und Aurora berührt sie
Mit den ewigen Strahlen
Als die ragenden Gipfel der Welt.

Vierter Auftritt.

Isabella (mit ihren Söhnen hervortretend).
Blick' nieder, hohe Königin des Himmels,
Und halte deine Hand auf dieses Herz,   295
Daß es der Übermut nicht schwellend hebe,
Denn leicht vergäße sich der Mutter Freude,
Wenn sie sich spiegelt in der Söhne Glanz;
Zum erstenmal, seitdem ich sie geboren,
Umfass' ich meines Glückes Fülle ganz.   300
Denn bis auf diesen Tag mußt' ich gewaltsam
Des Herzens fröhliche Ergießung teilen,
Vergessen ganz mußt' ich den einen Sohn,
Wenn ich der Nähe mich des andern freute.
O meine Mutterliebe ist nur eine,   305

Und meine Söhne waren ewig zwei!
— Sagt, darf ich ohne Zittern mich der süßen
Gewalt des trunknen Herzens überlassen?

(Zu Don Manuel.)

Wenn ich die Hand des Bruders freundlich drücke,
Stoß' ich den Stachel nicht in deine Brust?　　310

(Zu Don Cesar.)

Wenn ich das Herz an seinem Anblick weide,
Ist's nicht ein Raub an dir? — O, ich muß zittern,
Daß meine Liebe selbst, die ich euch zeige,
Nur eures Hasses Flammen heft'ger schüre.

(Nachdem sie beide fragend angesehen.)

Was darf ich mir von euch versprechen? Redet!　　315
Mit welchem Herzen kamet ihr hieher?
Ist's noch der alte unversöhnte Haß,
Den ihr mit herbringt in des Vaters Haus,
Und wartet draußen vor des Schlosses Toren
Der Krieg, auf Augenblicke nur gebändigt　　320
Und knirschend in das eherne Gebiß,
Um alsobald, wenn ihr den Rücken mir
Gekehrt, mit neuer Wut sich zu entfesseln?

Chor.

Krieg oder Frieden! Noch liegen die Lose
Dunkel verhüllt in der Zukunft Schoße!　　325
Doch es wird sich, noch eh' wir uns trennen, entscheiden,
Wir sind bereit und gerüstet zu beiden.

Isabella (im ganzen Kreis umherschauend).

Und welcher furchtbar kriegerische Anblick!
Was sollen diese hier? Ist's eine Schlacht,
Die sich in diesen Sälen zubereitet?　　330
Wozu die fremde Schar, wenn eine Mutter

Das Herz aufschließen will vor ihren Kindern?
Bis in den Schoß der Mutter fürchtet ihr
Der Arglist Schlingen, tückischen Verrat,
Daß ihr den Rücken euch besorglich deckt?   335
— O diese wilden Banden, die euch folgen,
Die raschen Diener eures Zorns — sie sind
Nicht eure Freunde! Glaubet nimmermehr,
Daß sie euch wohlgesinnt zum Besten raten!
Wie könnten sie's von Herzen mit euch meinen,   340
Den Fremdlingen, dem eingedrungnen Stamm,
Der aus dem eignen Erbe sie vertrieben,
Sich über sie der Herrschaft angemaßt?
Glaubt mir! Es liebt ein jeder, frei sich selbst
Zu leben nach dem eigenen Gesetz,   345
Die fremde Herrschaft wird mit Neid ertragen.
Von eurer Macht allein und ihrer Furcht
Erhaltet ihr den gern versagten Dienst.
Lernt dies Geschlecht, das herzlos falsche, kennen!
Die Schadenfreude ist's, wodurch sie sich   350
An eurem Glück, an eurer Größe rächen.
Der Herrscher Fall, der hohen Häupter Sturz
Ist ihrer Lieder Stoff und ihr Gespräch,
Was sich vom Sohn zum Enkel fort erzählt,
Womit sie sich die Winternächte kürzen.   355
— O meine Söhne! Feindlich ist die Welt
Und falsch gesinnt! Es liebt ein jeder nur
Sich selbst; unsicher, los und wandelbar
Sind alle Bande, die das leichte Glück
Geflochten — Laune löst, was Laune knüpfte —   360
Nur die Natur ist redlich! Sie allein
Liegt an dem ew'gen Ankergrunde fest,

Wenn alles andre auf den sturmbewegten Wellen
Des Lebens unstet treibt — Die Neigung gibt
Den Freund, es gibt der Vorteil den Gefährten;　　365
Wohl dem, dem die Geburt den Bruder gab,
Ihn kann das Glück nicht geben! Anerschaffen
Ist ihm der Freund, und gegen eine Welt
Voll Kriegs und Truges steht er zweifach da!

Chor.

Ja, es ist etwas Großes, ich muß es verehren,　　370
Um einer Herrscherin fürstlichen Sinn,
Über der Menschen Tun und Verkehren
Blickt sie mit ruhiger Klarheit hin.
Uns aber treibt das verworrene Streben
Blind und sinnlos durchs wüste Leben.　　375

Isabella (zu Don Cesar).

Du, der das Schwert auf seinen Bruder zückt,
Sieh dich umher in dieser ganzen Schar,
Wo ist ein edler Bild als deines Bruders?

(Zu Don Manuel.)

Wer unter diesen, die du Freunde nennst,
Darf deinem Bruder sich zur Seite stellen?　　380
Ein jeder ist ein Muster seines Alters,
Und keiner gleicht und keiner weicht dem andern.
Wagt es, euch in das Angesicht zu sehn!
O Raserei der Eifersucht; des Neides!
Ihn würdest du aus Tausenden heraus　　385
Zum Freunde dir gewählt, ihn an dein Herz
Geschlossen haben als den einzigen;
Und jetzt, da ihn die heilige Natur
Dir gab, dir in der Wiege schon ihn schenkte,
Trittst du, ein Frevler an dem eignen Blut,　　390

Mit stolzer Willkür ihr Geschenk mit Füßen,
Dich wegzuwerfen an den schlechtern Mann,
Dich an den Feind und Frembling anzuschließen!

Don Manuel.

Höre mich, Mutter.

Don Cesar.

Mutter, höre mich.

Isabella.

Nicht Worte sind's, die diesen traur'gen Streit   395
Erledigen — Hier ist das Mein und Dein,
Die Rache von der Schuld nicht mehr zu sondern.
— Wer möchte noch das alte Bette finden
Des Schwefelstroms, der glühend sich ergoß?
Des unterirb'schen Feuers schreckliche   400
Geburt ist alles, eine Lavarinde
Liegt aufgeschichtet über dem Gesunden,
Und jeder Fußtritt wandelt auf Zerstörung.
— Nur dieses Eine leg' ich euch ans Herz:
Das Böse, das der Mann, der mündige,   405
Dem Manne zufügt, das, ich will es glauben,
Vergibt sich und versöhnt sich schwer. Der Mann
Will seinen Haß, und keine Zeit verändert
Den Ratschluß, den er wohlbesonnen faßt.
Doch eures Habers Ursprung steigt hinauf   410
In unverständ'ger Kindheit frühe Zeit,
Sein Alter ist's, was ihn entwaffnen sollte.
Fraget zurück, was euch zuerst entzweite:
Ihr wißt es nicht, ja, fändet ihr's auch aus,
Ihr würdet euch des kind'schen Habers schämen.   415
Und dennoch ist's der erste Kinderstreit,
Der, fortgezeugt in unglückfel'ger Kette,

Die neuste Unbill dieses Tags geboren.
Denn alle schwere Taten, die bis jetzt geschahn,
Sind nur des Argwohns und der Rache Kinder.   420
— Und jene Knabenfehde wolltet ihr
Noch jetzt fortkämpfen, da ihr Männer seid?
(Beider Hände fassend.)
O meine Söhne! Kommt, entschließet euch,
Die Rechnung gegenseitig zu vertilgen,
Denn gleich auf beiden Seiten ist das Unrecht.   425
Seid edel, und großherzig schenkt einander
Die unabtragbar ungeheure Schuld.
Der Siege göttlichster ist das Vergeben!
In eures Vaters Gruft werft ihn hinab,
Den alten Haß der frühen Kinderzeit!   430
Der schönen Liebe sei das neue Leben,
Der Eintracht, der Versöhnung sei's geweiht.
(Sie tritt einen Schritt zwischen beiden zurück, als wollte sie ihnen Raum
geben, sich einander zu nähern. Beide blicken zur Erde, ohne einander
anzusehen.)

Chor.
Höret der Mutter vermahnende Rede,
Wahrlich, sie spricht ein gewichtiges Wort!
Laßt es genug sein und endet die Fehde,   435
Oder gefällt's euch, so setzet sie fort.
Was euch genehm ist, das ist mir gerecht,
Ihr seid die Herrscher, und ich bin der Knecht.

Isabella
(nachdem sie einige Zeit innegehalten und vergebens eine Äußerung der
Brüder erwartet, mit unterdrücktem Schmerz).
Jetzt weiß ich nichts mehr. Ausgeleert hab' ich
Der Worte Köcher und erschöpft der Bitten Kraft —   440
Im Grabe ruht, der euch gewaltsam bändigte,

Und machtlos steht die Mutter zwischen euch.
— Vollendet! Ihr habt freie Macht! Gehorcht
Dem Dämon, der euch sinnlos wütend treibt,
Ehrt nicht des Hausgotts heiligen Altar,   445
Laßt diese Halle selbst, die euch geboren,
Den Schauplatz werden eures Wechselmords.
Vor eurer Mutter Aug' zerstöret euch
Mit euren eignen, nicht durch fremde Hände.
Leib gegen Leib, wie das thebanische Paar,   450
Rückt aufeinander an und, wutvoll ringend,
Umfanget euch mit eherner Umarmung.
Leben um Leben tauschend siege jeder,
Den Dolch einbohrend in des andern Brust,
Daß selbst der Tod nicht eure Zwietracht heile,   455
Die Flamme selbst, des Feuers rote Säule,
Die sich von eurem Scheiterhaufen hebt,
Sich zweigespalten voneinander teile,
Ein schaudernd Bild, wie ihr gestorben und gelebt.

(Sie geht ab. Die Brüder bleiben noch in der vorigen Entfernung
voneinander stehen.)

Fünfter Auftritt.

Beide Brüder. Beide Chöre.

Chor.

Es sind nur Worte, die sie gesprochen,   460
Aber sie haben den fröhlichen Mut
In der felsigten Brust mir gebrochen!
Ich nicht vergoß das verwandte Blut.
Rein zum Himmel erheb' ich die Hände,
Ihr seid Brüder! Bedenket das Ende!   465

Don Cesar (ohne Don Manuel anzusehen).

Du bist der ältre Bruder, rede du!
Dem Erstgebornen weich' ich ohne Schande.

Don Manuel (in derselben Stellung).

Sag' etwas Gutes, und ich folge gern
Dem edeln Beispiel, das der Jüngre gibt.

Don Cesar.

Nicht, weil ich für den Schuldigeren mich   470
Erkenne, oder schwächer gar mich fühle —

Don Manuel.

Nicht Kleinmuts zeiht Don Cesarn, wer ihn kennt:
Fühlt' er sich schwächer, würd' er stolzer reden.

Don Cesar.

Denkst du von deinem Bruder nicht geringer?

Don Manuel.

Du bist zu stolz zur Demut, ich zur Lüge.   475

Don Cesar.

Verachtung nicht erträgt mein edles Herz.
Doch in des Kampfes heftigster Erbittrung
Gedachtest du mit Würde deines Bruders.

Don Manuel.

Du willst nicht meinen Tod, ich habe Proben.
Ein Mönch erbot sich dir, mich meuchlerisch   480
Zu morden; du bestraftest den Verräter.

Don Cesar (tritt etwas näher).

Hätt' ich dich früher so gerecht erkannt,
Es wäre vieles ungeschehn geblieben.

Don Manuel.

Und hätt' ich dir ein so versöhnlich Herz
Gewußt, viel Mühe spart' ich dann der Mutter.   485

Don Cesar.

Du wurdest mir viel stolzer abgeschildert.

Don Manuel.

Es ist der Fluch der Hohen, daß die Niedern
Sich ihres offnen Ohrs bemächtigen.

Don Cesar (lebhaft).

So ist's, die Diener tragen alle Schuld!

Don Manuel.

Die unser Herz in bitterm Haß entfremdet.   490

Don Cesar.

Die böse Worte hin und wider trugen.

Don Manuel.

Mit falscher Deutung jede Tat vergiftet.

Don Cesar.

Die Wunde nährten, die sie heilen sollten.

Don Manuel.

Die Flamme schürten, die sie löschen konnten.

Don Cesar.

Wir waren die Verführten, die Betrognen!   495

Don Manuel.

Das blinde Werkzeug fremder Leidenschaft!

Don Cesar.

Ist's wahr, daß alles andre treulos ist —

Don Manuel.

Und falsch! Die Mutter sagt's, du darfst es glauben!

Don Cesar.

So will ich diese Bruderhand ergreifen —
(Er reicht ihm die Hand hin.)

Don Manuel (ergreift sie lebhaft).

Die mir die nächste ist auf dieser Welt.   500
(Beide stehen Hand in Hand und betrachten einander eine Zeitlang
schweigend.)

Don Cesar.

Ich seh' dich an, und überrascht, erstaunt
Find' ich in dir der Mutter teure Züge.

Don Manuel.

Und eine Ähnlichkeit entdeckt sich mir
In dir, die mich noch wunderbarer rühret.

Don Cesar.

Bist du es wirklich, der dem jüngern Bruder　　　505
So hold begegnet und so gütig spricht?

Don Manuel.

Ist dieser freundlich sanftgesinnte Jüngling
Der übelwollend mir gehäss'ge Bruder?

(Wiederum Stillschweigen; jeder steht in den Anblick des andern
verloren.)

Don Cesar.

Du nahmst die Pferde von arab'scher Zucht
In Anspruch aus dem Nachlaß unsers Vaters.　　　510
Den Rittern, die du schicktest, schlug ich's ab.

Don Manuel.

Sie sind dir lieb. Ich denke nicht mehr dran.

Don Cesar.

Nein, nimm die Rosse, nimm den Wagen auch
Des Vaters, nimm sie, ich beschwöre dich.

Don Manuel.

Ich will es tun, wenn du das Schloß am Meere　　　515
Beziehen willst, um das wir heftig stritten.

Don Cesar.

Ich nehm' es nicht, doch bin ich's wohl zufrieden,
Daß wir's gemeinsam brüderlich bewohnen.

Don Manuel.

So sei's! Warum ausschließend Eigentum
Besitzen, da die Herzen einig sind?　　　520

Don Cesar.

Warum noch länger abgesondert leben,
Da wir, vereinigt, jeder reicher werden?

Don Manuel.

Wir sind nicht mehr getrennt, wir sind vereinigt.
(Er eilt in seine Arme.)

Erster Chor (zum zweiten).

Was stehen wir hier noch feindlich geschieden,
Da die Fürsten sich liebend umfassen?   525
Ihrem Beispiel folg' ich und biete dir Frieden,
Wollen wir einander denn ewig hassen?
Sind sie Brüder durch Blutes Bande,
Sind wir Bürger und Söhne von einem Lande.
(Beide Chöre umarmen sich.)

Sechster Auftritt.

Ein Bote tritt auf.

Zweiter Chor (zu Don Cesar).

Den Späher, den du ausgesendet, Herr,   530
Erblick' ich wiederkehrend. Freue dich,
Don Cesar! Gute Botschaft harret dein,
Denn fröhlich strahlt der Blick des Kommenden.

Bote.

Heil mir und Heil der fluchbefreiten Stadt!
Des schönsten Anblicks wird mein Auge froh.   535
Die Söhne meines Herrn, die Fürsten seh' ich
In friedlichem Gespräche, Hand in Hand,
Die ich in heißer Kampfeswut verlassen.

Don Cesar.

Du siehst die Liebe aus des Hasses Flammen
Wie einen neu verjüngten Phönix steigen.   540

Bote.

Ein zweites leg' ich zu dem ersten Glück!
Mein Botenstab ergrünt von frischen Zweigen!

Don Cesar (ihn beiseite führend).

Laß hören, was du bringst.

Bote.

                          Ein einz'ger Tag
Will alles, was erfreulich ist, versammeln.
Auch die Verlorene, nach der wir suchten,   545
Sie ist gefunden, Herr, sie ist nicht weit.

Don Cesar.

Sie ist gefunden! O wo ist sie? Sprich!

Bote.

Hier in Messina, Herr, verbirgt sie sich.

Don Manuel (zu dem ersten Halbchor gewendet).

Von hoher Röte Glut seh' ich die Wangen
Des Bruders glänzen, und sein Auge blitzt.   550
Ich weiß nicht, was es ist, doch ist's die Farbe
Der Freude, und mitfreuend teil' ich sie.

Don Cesar (zu dem Boten).

Komm, führe mich — Leb wohl, Don Manuel!
Im Arm der Mutter finden wir uns wieder,
Jetzt fordert mich ein bringend Werk von hier.   555

(Er will gehen.)

Don Manuel.

Verschieb es nicht. Das Glück begleite dich.

Don Cesar (besinnt sich und kommt zurück).

Don Manuel! Mehr, als ich sagen kann,

Freut mich dein Anblick — Ja mir ahnet schon,
Wir werden uns wie Herzensfreunde lieben,
Der lang' gebundne Trieb wird freud'ger nur   560
Und mächt'ger streben in der neuen Sonne,
Nachholen werd' ich das verlorne Leben.

Don Manuel.

Die Blüte deutet auf die schöne Frucht.

Don Cesar.

Es ist nicht recht, ich fühl's und table mich,
Daß ich mich jetzt aus deinen Armen reiße.   565
Denk' nicht, ich fühle weniger als du,
Weil ich die festlich schöne Stunde rasch zerschneide.

Don Manuel (mit sichtbarer Zerstreuung).

Gehorche du dem Augenblick! Der Liebe
Gehört von heute an das ganze Leben.

Don Cesar.

Entdeck' ich dir, was mich von hinnen ruft —   570

Don Manuel.

Laß mir dein Herz — dir bleibe dein Geheimnis.

Don Cesar.

Auch kein Geheimnis trenn' uns ferner mehr,
Bald soll die letzte dunkle Falte schwinden!

(Zu dem Chor gewendet.)

Euch künd' ich's an, damit ihr's alle wisset!
Der Streit ist abgeschlossen zwischen mir   575
Und dem geliebten Bruder! Den erklär' ich
Für meinen Todfeind und Beleidiger
Und werd' ihn hassen wie der Hölle Pforten,
Der den erloschnen Funken unsers Streits
Aufbläst zu neuen Flammen — Hoffe keiner   580
Mir zu gefallen oder Dank zu ernten,

Der von dem Bruder Böses mir berichtet,
Mit falscher Dienstbegier den bittern Pfeil
Des raschen Worts geschäftig weitersendet.
— Nicht Wurzeln auf der Lippe schlägt das Wort,   585
Das unbedacht dem schnellen Zorn entflohen,
Doch, von dem Ohr des Argwohns aufgefangen,
Kriecht es wie Schlingkraut endlos treibend fort
Und hängt ans Herz sich an mit tausend Ästen:
So trennen endlich in Verworrenheit   590
Unheilbar sich die Guten und die Besten!
(Er umarmt den Bruder noch einmal und geht ab, von dem zweiten
Chore begleitet.)

Siebenter Auftritt.

Don Manuel und der erste Chor.

Chor.

Verwundrungsvoll, o Herr, betracht' ich dich,
Und fast muß ich dich heute ganz verkennen.
Mit karger Rede kaum erwiderst du
Des Bruders Liebesworte, der gutmeinend   595
Mit offnem Herzen dir entgegenkommt.
Versunken in dich selber stehst du da,
Gleich einem Träumenden, als wäre nur
Dein Leib zugegen und die Seele fern.
Wer so dich sähe, möchte leicht der Kälte   600
Dich zeihn und stolz unfreundlichen Gemüts,
Ich aber will dich drum nicht fühllos schelten,
Denn heiter blickst du wie ein Glücklicher
Um dich, und Lächeln spielt um deine Wangen.

Don Manuel.

Was soll ich sagen? Was erwidern? Mag   605
Der Bruder Worte finden! Ihn ergreift
Ein überraschend neu Gefühl, er sieht
Den alten Haß aus seinem Busen schwinden,
Und wundernd fühlt er sein verwandelt Herz.
Ich — habe keinen Haß mehr mitgebracht,   610
Kaum weiß ich noch, warum wir blutig stritten.
Denn über allen ird'schen Dingen hoch
Schwebt mir auf Freudenfittichen die Seele,
Und in dem Glanzesmeer, das mich umfängt,
Sind alle Wolken mir und finstre Falten   615
Des Lebens ausgeglättet und verschwunden.
— Ich sehe diese Hallen, diese Säle
Und denke mir das freudige Erschrecken
Der überraschten, hocherstaunten Braut,
Wenn ich als Fürstin sie und Herrscherin   620
Durch dieses Hauses Pforten führen werde.
— Noch liebt sie nur den Liebenden! Dem Fremdling,
Dem Namenlosen hat sie sich gegeben.
Nicht ahnet sie, daß es Don Manuel,
Messinas Fürst ist, der die goldne Binde   625
Ihr um die schöne Stirne flechten wird.
Wie süß ist's, das Geliebte zu beglücken
Mit ungehoffter Größe Glanz und Schein!
Längst spart' ich mir dies höchste der Entzücken:
Wohl bleibt es stets sein höchster Schmuck allein,   630
Doch auch die Hoheit darf das Schöne schmücken,
Der goldne Reif erhebt den Edelstein.

Chor.

Ich höre dich, o Herr, vom langen Schweigen

Zum erstenmal den stummen Mund entsiegeln.
Mit Späheraugen folgt' ich dir schon längst,   635
Ein seltsam wunderbar Geheimnis ahnend,
Doch nicht erkühnt' ich mich, was du vor mir
In tiefes Dunkel hüllst, dir abzufragen.
Dich reizt nicht mehr der Jagden muntre Lust,
Der Rosse Wettlauf und des Falken Sieg.   640
Aus der Gefährten Aug' verschwindest du,
So oft die Sonne sinkt zum Himmelsrande,
Und keiner unsers Chors, die wir dich sonst
In jeder Kriegs= und Jagdgefahr begleiten,
Mag deines stillen Pfads Gefährte sein.   645
Warum verschleierst du bis diesen Tag
Dein Liebesglück mit dieser neid'schen Hülle?
Was zwingt den Mächtigen, daß er verhehle?
Denn Furcht ist fern von deiner großen Seele.

Don Manuel.

Geflügelt ist das Glück und schwer zu binden,   650
Nur in verschloßner Lade wird's bewahrt,
Das Schweigen ist zum Hüter ihm gesetzt,
Und rasch entfliegt es, wenn Geschwätzigkeit
Voreilig wagt, die Decke zu erheben.
Doch jetzt, dem Ziel so nahe, darf ich wohl   655
Das lange Schweigen brechen, und ich will's.
Denn mit der nächsten Morgensonne Strahl
Ist sie die Meine, und des Dämons Neid
Wird keine Macht mehr haben über mich.
Nicht mehr verstohlen werd' ich zu ihr schleichen,   660
Nicht rauben mehr der Liebe goldne Frucht,
Nicht mehr die Freude haschen auf der Flucht,
Das Morgen wird dem schönen Heute gleichen,

Nicht Blitzen gleich, die schnell vorüber schießen
Und plötzlich von der Nacht verschlungen sind,   665
Mein Glück wird sein gleichwie des Baches Fließen,
Gleichwie der Sand des Stundenglases rinnt!

Chor.

So nenne sie uns, Herr, die dich im stillen
Beglückt, daß wir dein Los beneidend rühmen
Und würdig ehren unsers Fürsten Braut.   670
Sag' an, wo du sie fandest, wo verbirgst,
In welches Orts verschwiegner Heimlichkeit?
Denn wir durchziehen schwärmend weit und breit
Die Insel auf der Jagd verschlungnen Pfaden,
Doch keine Spur hat uns dein Glück verraten,   675
So daß ich bald mich überreden möchte,
Es hülle sie ein Zaubernebel ein.

Don Manuel.

Den Zauber lös' ich auf, denn heute noch
Soll, was verborgen war, die Sonne schauen.
Vernehmet denn und hört, wie mir geschah.   680
Fünf Monde sind's, es herrschte noch im Lande
Des Vaters Macht und beugete gewaltsam
Der Jugend starren Nacken in das Joch —
Nichts kannt' ich als der Waffen wilde Freuden
Und als des Weidwerks kriegerische Lust.   685
— Wir hatten schon den ganzen Tag gejagt
Entlang des Waldgebirges — da geschah's,
Daß die Verfolgung einer weißen Hindin
Mich weit hinweg aus eurem Haufen riß.
Das scheue Tier floh durch des Tales Krümmen,   690
Durch Busch und Kluft und bahnenlos Gestrüpp,
Auf Wurfes Weite sah ich's stets vor mir,

Doch könnt' ich's nicht erreichen noch erzielen,
Bis es zuletzt an eines Gartens Pforte mir
Verschwand. Schnell von dem Roß herab mich werfend, 695
Dring' ich ihm nach, schon mit dem Speere zielend,
Da seh' ich wundernd das erschrockne Tier
Zu einer Nonne Füßen zitternd liegen,
Die es mit zarten Händen schmeichelnd kost.
Bewegungslos starr' ich das Wunder an, 700
Den Jagdspieß in der Hand, zum Wurf ausholend —
Sie aber blickt mit großen Augen flehend
Mich an, so stehn wir schweigend gegeneinander —
Wie lange Frist, das kann ich nicht ermessen,
Denn alles Maß der Zeiten war vergessen. 705
Tief in die Seele drückt sie mir den Blick,
Und umgewandelt schnell ist mir das Herz.
— Was ich nun sprach, was die Holdsel'ge mir
Erwidert, möge niemand mich befragen,
Denn wie ein Traumbild liegt es hinter mir 710
Aus früher Kindheit dämmerhellen Tagen;
An meiner Brust fühlt' ich die ihre schlagen,
Als die Besinnungskraft mir wieder kam.
Da hört' ich einer Glocke helles Läuten,
Den Ruf zur Hora schien es zu bedeuten, 715
Und schnell, wie Geister in die Luft verwehen,
Entschwand sie mir und ward nicht mehr gesehen.

Chor.

Mit Furcht, o Herr, erfüllt mich dein Bericht.
Raub hast du an dem Göttlichen begangen,
Des Himmels Braut berührt mit sündigem Verlangen, 720
Denn furchtbar heilig ist des Klosters Pflicht.

Don Manuel.

Jetzt hatt' ich eine Straße nur zu wandeln,

Das unstet schwanke Sehnen war gebunden,
Dem Leben war sein Inhalt ausgefunden.
Und wie der Pilger sich nach Osten wendet,   725
Wo ihm die Sonne der Verheißung glänzt,
So kehrte sich mein Hoffen und mein Sehnen
Dem einen hellen Himmelspunkte zu.
Kein Tag entstieg dem Meer und sank hinunter,
Der nicht zwei glücklich Liebende vereinte;   730
Geflochten still war unsrer Herzen Bund,
Nur der allsehnde Äther über uns
War des verschwiegnen Glücks vertrauter Zeuge,
Es brauchte weiter keines Menschen Dienst.
Das waren goldne Stunden, sel'ge Tage!   735
— Nicht Raub am Himmel war mein Glück, denn noch
Durch kein Gelübde war das Herz gefesselt,
Das sich auf ewig mir zu eigen gab.

Chor.
So war das Kloster eine Freistatt nur
Der zarten Jugend, nicht des Lebens Grab?   740

Don Manuel.
Ein heilig Pfand ward sie dem Gotteshaus
Vertraut, das man zurück einst werde fordern.

Chor.
Doch welches Blutes rühmt sie sich zu sein?
Denn nur vom Edeln kann das Edle stammen.

Don Manuel.
Sich selber ein Geheimnis wuchs sie auf,   745
Nicht kennt sie ihr Geschlecht noch Vaterland.

Chor.
Und leitet keine dunkle Spur zurück
Zu ihres Daseins unbekannten Quellen?

Don Manuel.

Daß sie von edelm Blut, gesteht der Mann,
Der einz'ge, der um ihre Herkunft weiß.   750

Chor.

Wer ist der Mann? Nichts halte mir zurück,
Denn wissend nur kann ich dir nützlich raten.

Don Manuel.

Ein alter Diener naht von Zeit zu Zeit,
Der einz'ge Bote zwischen Kind und Mutter.

Chor.

Von diesem Alten hast du nichts erforscht?   755
Feigherzig und geschwätzig ist das Alter.

Don Manuel.

Nie wagt' ich's, einer Neugier nachzugeben,
Die mein verschwiegnes Glück gefährden konnte.

Chor.

Was aber war der Inhalt seiner Worte,
Wenn er die Jungfrau zu besuchen kam?   760

Don Manuel.

Auf eine Zeit, die alles lösen werde,
Hat er von Jahr zu Jahren sie vertröstet.

Chor.

Und diese Zeit, die alles lösen soll,
Hat er sie näher deutend nicht bezeichnet?

Don Manuel.

Seit wenig Monden drohete der Greis   765
Mit einer nahen Änderung ihres Schicksals.

Chor.

Er drohte, sagst du? Also fürchtest du
Ein Licht zu schöpfen, das dich nicht erfreut?

Don Manuel.

Ein jeder Wechsel schreckt den Glücklichen,
Wo kein Gewinn zu hoffen, droht Verlust.   770

Chor.

Doch konnte die Entdeckung, die du fürchtest,
Auch deiner Liebe günst'ge Zeichen bringen.

Don Manuel.

Auch stürzen konnte sie mein Glück, drum wählt' ich
Das Sicherste, ihr schnell zuvorzukommen.

Chor.

Wie das, o Herr? Mit Furcht erfüllst du mich,   775
Und eine rasche Tat muß ich besorgen.

Don Manuel.

Schon seit den letzten Monden ließ der Greis
Geheimnisvolle Winke sich entfallen,
Daß nicht mehr ferne sei der Tag, der sie
Den Ihrigen zurücke geben werde.   780
Seit gestern aber sprach er's deutlich aus,
Daß mit der nächsten Morgensonne Strahl —
Dies aber ist der Tag, der heute leuchtet —
Ihr Schicksal sich entscheidend werde lösen.
Kein Augenblick war zu verlieren, schnell   785
War mein Entschluß gefaßt und schnell vollstreckt.
In dieser Nacht raubt' ich die Jungfrau weg
Und brachte sie verborgen nach Messina.

Chor.

Welch kühn verwegen-räuberische Tat!
— Verzeih, o Herr, die freie Tadelrede!   790
Doch solches ist des weisern Alters Recht,
Wenn sich die rasche Jugend kühn vergißt.

Don Manuel.

Unfern vom Kloster der Barmherzigen,
In eines Gartens abgeschiedner Stille,
Der von der Neugier nicht betreten wird,   795
Trennt' ich mich eben jetzt von ihr, hieher
Zu der Versöhnung mit dem Bruder eilend.
In banger Furcht ließ ich sie dort allein
Zurück, die sich nichts weniger erwartet,
Als in dem Glanz der Fürstin eingeholt   800
Und auf erhabnem Fußgestell des Ruhms
Vor ganz Messina ausgestellt zu werden.
Denn anders nicht soll sie mich wiedersehn
Als in der Größe Schmuck und Staat und festlich
Von eurem ritterlichen Chor umgeben.   805
Nicht will ich, daß Don Manuels Verlobte
Als eine Heimatlose, Flüchtige
Der Mutter nahen soll, die ich ihr gebe;
Als eine Fürstin fürstlich will ich sie
Einführen in die Hofburg meiner Väter.   810

Chor.

Gebiete, Herr! Wir harren deines Winks.

Don Manuel.

Ich habe mich aus ihrem Arm gerissen,
Doch nur mit ihr werd' ich beschäftigt sein.
Denn nach dem Bazar sollt ihr mich anjetzt
Begleiten, wo die Mohren zum Verkauf   815
Ausstellen, was das Morgenland erzeugt
An edelm Stoff und feinem Kunstgebild.
Erst wählet aus die zierlichen Sandalen,
Der zartgeformten Füße Schutz und Zier,
Dann zum Gewande wählt das Kunstgewebe   820

Des Indiers, hellglänzend wie der Schnee
Des Ätna, der der nächste ist dem Licht —
Und leicht umfließ' es, wie der Morgenduft,
Den zarten Bau der jugendlichen Glieder.
Von Purpur sei, mit zarten Fäden Goldes   825
Durchwirkt der Gürtel, der die Tunika
Unter dem zücht'gen Busen reizend knüpft.
Dazu den Mantel wählt, von glänzender
Seide gewebt, in bleichem Purpur schimmernd,
Über der Achsel heft' ihn eine goldne   830
Zikade — Auch die Spangen nicht vergeßt,
Die schönen Arme reizend zu umzirken,
Auch nicht der Perlen und Korallen Schmuck,
Der Meeresgöttin wundersame Gaben.

Um die Locken winde sich ein Diadem,   835
Gefüget aus dem köstlichsten Gestein,
Worin der feurig glühende Rubin
Mit dem Smaragd die Farbenblitze kreuze,
Oben im Haarschmuck sei der lange Schleier
Befestigt, der die glänzende Gestalt   840
Gleich einem hellen Lichtgewölk umfließe,
Und mit der Myrte jungfräulichem Kranze
Vollende krönend sich das schöne Ganze.

Chor.

Es soll geschehen, Herr! wie du gebietest,
Denn fertig und vollendet findet sich   845
Dies alles auf dem Bazar ausgestellt.

Don Manuel.

Den schönsten Zelter führet dann hervor
Aus meinen Ställen; seine Farbe sei
Lichtweiß, gleichwie des Sonnengottes Pferde,

Von Purpur sei die Decke, und Geschirr   850
Und Zügel reich besetzt mit edeln Steinen,
Denn tragen soll er meine Königin.
Ihr selber haltet euch bereit, im Glanz
Des Ritterstaates, unterm freud'gen Schall
Der Hörner eure Fürstin heimzuführen.   855
Dies alles zu besorgen geh' ich jetzt;
Zwei unter euch erwähl' ich zu Begleitern,
Ihr andern wartet mein — Was ihr vernahmt,
Bewahrt's in eures Busens tiefem Grunde,
Bis ich das Band gelöst von eurem Munde.   860
        (Er geht ab, von zweien aus dem Chor begleitet.)

Achter Auftritt.

Chor.
Sage, was werden wir jetzt beginnen,
Da die Fürsten ruhen vom Streit,
Auszufüllen die Leere der Stunden
Und die lange unendliche Zeit?
Etwas fürchten und hoffen und sorgen   865
Muß der Mensch für den kommenden Morgen,
Daß er die Schwere des Daseins ertrage
Und das ermüdende Gleichmaß der Tage,
Und mit erfrischendem Windesweben
Kräuselnd bewege das stockende Leben.   870
Einer aus dem Chor.
Schön ist der Friede! Ein lieblicher Knabe
Liegt er gelagert am ruhigen Bach,
Und die hüpfenden Lämmer grasen

Luftig um ihn auf dem fonnigten Rafen;
Süßes Tönen entlockt er der Flöte,　　　　　　　　　875
Und das Echo des Berges wird wach,
Oder im Schimmer der Abendröte
Wiegt ihn in Schlummer der murmelnde Bach —
Aber der Krieg auch hat feine Ehre,
Der Beweger des Menfchengefchicks;　　　　　　　880
Mir gefällt ein lebendiges Leben,
Mir ein ewiges Schwanken und Schwingen und Schweben
Auf der fteigenden, fallenden Welle des Glücks.

Denn der Menfch verkümmert im Frieden,
Müßige Ruh' ift das Grab des Muts.　　　　　　885
Das Gefetz ift der Freund des Schwachen,
Alles will es nur eben machen,
Möchte gern die Welt verflachen,
Aber der Krieg läßt die Kraft erfcheinen,
Alles erhebt er zum Ungemeinen,　　　　　　　890
Selber dem Feigen erzeugt er den Mut.

Ein zweiter.
Stehen nicht Amors Tempel offen?
Wallet nicht zu dem Schönen die Welt?
Da ift das Fürchten! Da ift das Hoffen!
König ift hier, wer den Augen gefällt!　　　　　895
Auch die Liebe beweget das Leben,
Daß fich die graulichten Farben erheben,
Reizend betrügt fie die glücklichen Jahre,
Die gefällige Tochter des Schaums,
In das Gemeine und Traurigwahre　　　　　　900
Webt fie die Bilder des goldenen Traums.

Ein dritter.
Bleibe die Blume dem blühenden Lenze,

Scheine das Schöne! Und flechte sich Kränze,
Wem die Locken noch jugendlich grünen,
Aber dem männlichen Alter ziemt's,   905
Einem ernsteren Gott zu dienen.

Erster.

Der strengen Diana, der Freundin der Jagden,
Lasset uns folgen ins wilde Gehölz,
Wo die Wälder am dunkelsten nachten,
Und den Springbock stürzen vom Fels.   910
Denn die Jagd ist ein Gleichnis der Schlachten,
Des ernsten Kriegsgotts lustige Braut —
Man ist auf mit dem Morgenstrahl,
Wenn die schmetternden Hörner laden
Lustig hinaus in das dampfende Tal,   915
Über Berge, über Klüfte,
Die ermatteten Glieder zu baden
In den erfrischenden Strömen der Lüfte!

Zweiter.

Oder wollen wir uns der blauen
Göttin, der ewig bewegten, vertrauen,   920
Die uns mit freundlicher Spiegelhelle
Ladet in ihren unendlichen Schoß?
Bauen wir auf der tanzenden Welle
Uns ein lustig schwimmendes Schloß?
Wer das grüne kristallene Feld   925
Pflügt mit des Schiffes eilendem Kiele,
Der vermählt sich das Glück, dem gehört die Welt,
Ohne die Saat erblüht ihm die Ernte!
Denn das Meer ist der Raum der Hoffnung
Und der Zufälle launisch Reich,   930
Hier wird der Reiche schnell zum Armen,

Und der Ärmſte dem Fürſten gleich.
Wie der Wind mit Gedankenſchnelle
Läuft um die ganze Windesroſe,
Wechſeln hier des Geſchickes Loſe,   935
Dreht das Glück ſeine Kugel um;
Auf den Wellen iſt alles Welle,
Auf dem Meer iſt kein Eigentum.

Dritter.

Aber nicht bloß im Wellenreiche,
Auf der wogenden Meeresflut,   940
Auch auf der Erde, ſo feſt ſie ruht
Auf den ewigen, alten Säulen,
Wanket das Glück und will nicht weilen.
— Sorge gibt mir dieſer neue Frieden,
Und nicht fröhlich mag ich ihm vertrauen,   945
Auf der Lava, die der Berg geſchieden,
Möcht' ich nimmer meine Hütte bauen.
Denn zu tief ſchon hat der Haß gefreſſen,
Und zu ſchwere Taten ſind geſchehn,
Die ſich nie vergeben und vergeſſen,   950
Noch hab' ich das Ende nicht geſehn,
Und mich ſchrecken ahnungsvolle Träume!
Nicht Wahrſagung reden ſoll mein Mund,
Aber ſehr mißfällt mir dies Geheime,
Dieſer Ehe ſegenloſer Bund,   955
Dieſe lichtſcheu krummen Liebespfade,
Dieſes Kloſterraubs verwegne Tat,
Denn das Gute liebt ſich das Gerade,
Böſe Früchte trägt die böſe Saat.

    Auch ein Raub war's, wie wir alle wiſſen,   960
Der des alten Fürſten ehliches Gemahl

In ein frevelnd Ehebett gerissen,
Denn sie war des Vaters Wahl.
Und der Ahnherr schüttete im Zorne
Grauenvoller Flüche schrecklichen Samen   965
Auf das sündige Ehebett aus.
Greueltaten ohne Namen,
Schwarze Verbrechen verbirgt dies Haus.

Chor.

Ja, es hat nicht gut begonnen,
Glaubt mir, und es endet nicht gut,   970
Denn gebüßt wird unter der Sonnen
Jede Tat der verblendeten Wut.
Es ist kein Zufall und blindes Los,
Daß die Brüder sich wütend selbst zerstören,
Denn verflucht ward der Mutter Schoß,   975
Sie sollte den Haß und den Streit gebären.
— Aber ich will es schweigend verhüllen,
Denn die Rachgötter schaffen im Stillen;
Zeit ist's, die Unfälle zu beweinen,
Wenn sie nahen und wirklich erscheinen.   980

(Der Chor geht ab.)

Zweiter Aufzug.

Erster Auftritt.

Die Szene verwandelt sich in einen Garten, der die Aussicht auf das Meer eröffnet. Aus einem anstoßenden Gartensaale tritt

Beatrice

(geht unruhig auf und nieder, nach allen Seiten umherspähend. Plötzlich steht sie still und horcht).

Er ist es nicht — Es war der Winde Spiel,
Die durch der Pinie Wipfel sausend streichen;
Schon neigt die Sonne sich zu ihrem Ziel,
Mit trägem Schritt seh' ich die Stunden schleichen,
Und mich ergreift ein schauderndes Gefühl,   985
Es schreckt mich selbst das wesenlose Schweigen.
Nichts zeigt sich mir, wie weit die Blicke tragen,
Er läßt mich hier in meiner Angst verzagen.

  Und nahe hör' ich wie ein rauschend Wehr
Die Stadt, die völkerwimmelnde, ertosen,   990
Ich höre fern das ungeheure Meer
An seine Ufer dumpferbrandend stoßen,
Es stürmen alle Schrecken auf mich her,
Klein fühl' ich mich in diesem Furchtbargroßen,
Und fortgeschleudert, wie das Blatt vom Baume,   995
Verlier' ich mich im grenzenlosen Raume.

Warum verließ ich meine stille Zelle?
Da lebt' ich ohne Sehnsucht, ohne Harm!
Das Herz war ruhig wie die Wiesenquelle,
An Wünschen leer, doch nicht an Freuden arm.   1000
Ergriffen jetzt hat mich des Lebens Welle,
Mich faßt die Welt in ihren Riesenarm,
Zerrissen hab' ich alle frühern Bande,
Vertrauend eines Schwures leichtem Pfande.

    Wo waren die Sinne?   1005
Was hab' ich getan?
Ergriff mich betörend
Ein rasender Wahn?

    Den Schleier zerriß ich
Jungfräulicher Zucht,   1010
Die Pforten durchbrach ich der heiligen Zelle —
Umstrickte mich blendend ein Zauber der Hölle?
Dem Manne folgt' ich,
Dem kühnen Entführer in sträflicher Flucht.

    O komm, mein Geliebter!   1015
Wo bleibst du und säumest? Befreie, befreie
Die kämpfende Seele! Mich naget die Reue,
Es faßt mich der Schmerz.
Mit liebender Nähe versichre mein Herz!

    Und sollt' ich mich dem Manne nicht ergeben,   1020
Der in der Welt allein sich an mich schloß?
Denn ausgesetzt ward ich ins fremde Leben,
Und frühe schon hat mich ein strenges Los
(Ich darf den dunkeln Schleier nicht erheben)
Gerissen von dem mütterlichen Schoß.   1025
Nur einmal sah ich sie, die mich geboren,
Doch wie ein Traum ging mir das Bild verloren.

Und so erwuchs ich still am stillen Orte,
In Lebens Glut den Schatten beigesellt,
— Da stand er plötzlich an des Klosters Pforte,　　1030
Schön wie ein Gott und männlich wie ein Held.
O mein Empfinden nennen keine Worte!
Fremd kam er mir aus einer fremden Welt,
Und schnell, als wär' es ewig so gewesen,
Schloß sich der Bund, den keine Menschen lösen.　　1035
　Vergib, du Herrliche, die mich geboren,
Daß ich, vorgreifend den verhängten Stunden,
Mir eigenmächtig mein Geschick erkoren —
Nicht frei erwählt' ich's, es hat mich gefunden;
Einbringt der Gott auch zu verschloßnen Toren,　　1040
Zu Perseus' Turm hat er den Weg gefunden,
Dem Dämon ist sein Opfer unverloren.
Wär' es an öde Klippen angebunden
Und an des Atlas himmeltragende Säulen,
So wird ein Flügelroß es dort ereilen.　　1045
　Nicht hinter mich begehr' ich mehr zu schauen,
In keine Heimat sehn' ich mich zurück,
Der Liebe will ich liebend mich vertrauen:
Gibt es ein schönres als der Liebe Glück?
Mit meinem Los will ich mich gern bescheiden,　　1050
Ich kenne nicht des Lebens andre Freuden.
　Nicht kenn' ich sie und will sie nimmer kennen,
Die sich die Stifter meiner Tage nennen,
Wenn sie von dir mich, mein Geliebter, trennen,
Ein ewig Rätsel bleiben will ich mir,　　1055
Ich weiß genug, ich lebe dir!
　　　　　　　　(Aufmerkend.)
Horch, der lieben Stimme Schall!

— Nein, es war der Widerhall
Und des Meeres dumpfes Brausen,
Das sich an den Ufern bricht,   1060
Der Geliebte ist es nicht!
Weh mir! Weh mir! Wo er weilet?
Mich umschlingt ein kaltes Grausen!
Immer tiefer
Sinkt die Sonne! Immer öder   1065
Wird die Öde! Immer schwerer
Wird das Herz — Wo zögert er?
                    (Sie geht unruhig umher.)

Aus des Gartens sichern Mauern
Wag' ich meinen Schritt nicht mehr.
Kalt ergriff mich das Entsetzen,   1070
Als ich in die nahe Kirche
Wagte meinen Fuß zu setzen,
Denn mich trieb's mit mächt'gem Drang,
Aus der Seele tiefsten Tiefen,
Als sie zu der Hora riefen,   1075
Hinzuknien an heil'ger Stätte,
Zu der Göttlichen zu flehn,
Nimmer konnt' ich widerstehn.
Wenn ein Lauscher mich erspähte?
Voll von Feinden ist die Welt,   1080
Arglist hat auf allen Pfaden,
Fromme Unschuld zu verraten,
Ihr betrüglich Netz gestellt.
Einmal hab' ich's schon erfahren,
Als ich aus des Klosters Hut   1085
In die fremden Menschenscharen
Mich gewagt mit frevelm Mut.

Dort bei jenes Festes Feier,
Da der Fürst begraben ward,
Mein Erkühnen büßt' ich teuer,   1090
Nur ein Gott hat mich bewahrt —
Da der Jüngling mir, der fremde,
Nahte, mit dem Flammenauge,
Und mit Blicken, die mich schreckten,
Mir das Innerste durchzuckten,   1095
In das tiefste Herz mir schaute —
Noch durchschauert kaltes Grauen,
Da ich's denke, mir die Brust!
Nimmer, nimmer kann ich schauen
In die Augen des Geliebten,   1100
Dieser stillen Schuld bewußt!

                    (Aufhorchend.)

Stimmen im Garten!
Er ist's, der Geliebte!
Er selber! Jetzt täuschte
Kein Blendwerk mein Ohr,   1105
Es naht, es vermehrt sich!
In seine Arme!
An seine Brust!

(Sie eilt mit ausgebreiteten Armen nach der Tiefe des Gartens, Don
          Cesar tritt ihr entgegen.)

Zweiter Auftritt.

Don Cesar. Beatrice. Der Chor.

Beatrice (mit Schrecken zurückfliehend).

Weh mir! Was seh' ich!

(In demselben Augenblick tritt auch der Chor ein.)

Don Cesar.

Holde Schönheit, fürchte nichts!

(Zu dem Chor.)

Der rauhe Anblick eurer Waffen schreckt   1110
Die zarte Jungfrau — Weicht zurück und bleibt
In ehrerbiet'ger Ferne!

(Zu Beatricen.)

Fürchte nichts!

Die holde Scham, die Schönheit ist mir heilig.

(Der Chor hat sich zurückgezogen. Er tritt ihr näher und ergreift ihre
Hand.)

Wo warst du? Welches Gottes Macht entrückte,
Verbarg dich diese lange Zeit? Dich hab' ich   1115
Gesucht, nach dir geforschet, wachend, träumend
Warst du des Herzens einziges Gefühl,
Seit ich bei jenem Leichenfest des Fürsten
Wie eines Engels Lichterscheinung dich
Zum erstenmal erblickte — Nicht verborgen   1120
Blieb dir die Macht, mit der du mich bezwangst.
Der Blicke Feuer und der Lippe Stammeln,
Die Hand, die in der deinen zitternd lag,
Verriet sie dir — ein kühneres Geständnis
Verbot des Ortes ernste Majestät.   1125
— Der Messe Hochamt rief mich zum Gebet,

Und da ich von den Knieen jetzt erstanden,
Die erften Blicke schnell auf dich sich heften,
Warst du aus meinen Augen weggerückt,
Doch nachgezogen mit allmächt'gen Zaubers Banden 1130
Hast du mein Herz mit allen seinen Kräften.
Seit diesem Tage such' ich rastlos dich
An aller Kirchen und Paläste Pforten,
An allen offnen und verborgnen Orten,
Wo sich die schöne Unschuld zeigen kann, 1135
Hab' ich das Netz der Späher ausgebreitet,
Doch meiner Mühe sah ich keine Frucht,
Bis endlich heut', von einem Gott geleitet,
Des Spähers glückbekrönte Wachsamkeit
In dieser nächsten Kirche dich entdeckte. 1140
(Hier macht Beatrice, welche in dieser ganzen Zeit zitternd und abgewandt
gestanden, eine Bewegung des Schreckens.)

Ich habe dich wieder, und der Geist verlasse
Eher die Glieder, eh' ich von dir scheide!
Und daß ich fest sogleich den Zufall fasse
Und mich verwahre vor des Dämons Neide,
So red' ich dich vor diesen Zeugen allen 1145
Als meine Gattin an und reiche dir
Zum Pfande des die ritterliche Rechte.
(Er stellt sie dem Chor dar.)

Nicht forschen will ich, wer du bist — Ich will
Nur dich von dir, nichts frag' ich nach dem andern.
Daß deine Seele wie dein Ursprung rein, 1150
Hat mir dein erster Blick verbürget und beschworen,
Und wärst du selbst die Niedrigste geboren,
Du müßtest dennoch meine Liebe sein,
Die Freiheit hab' ich und die Wahl verloren.

Und daß du wissen mögest, ob ich auch   1155
Herr meiner Taten sei und hoch genug
Gestellt auf dieser Welt, auch das Geliebte
Mit starkem Arm zu mir emporzuheben,
Bedarf's nur, meinen Namen dir zu nennen.
— Ich bin Don Cesar, und in dieser Stadt   1160
Messina ist kein Größrer über mir.

(Beatrice schaudert zurück; er bemerkt es und fährt nach einer kleinen
Weile fort.)

Dein Staunen lob' ich und dein sittsam Schweigen,
Schamhafte Demut ist der Reize Krone,
Denn ein Verborgenes ist sich das Schöne,
Und es erschrickt vor seiner eignen Macht.   1165
— Ich geh' und überlasse dich dir selbst,
Daß sich dein Geist von seinem Schrecken löse,
Denn jedes Neue, auch das Glück, erschreckt.

(Zu dem Chor.)

Gebt ihr — sie ist's von diesem Augenblick!
Die Ehre meiner Braut und eurer Fürstin.   1170
Belehret sie von ihres Standes Größe.
Bald kehr' ich selbst zurück, sie heimzuführen,
Wie's meiner würdig ist und ihr gebührt.

(Er geht ab.)

Dritter Auftritt.

Beatrice und der Chor.

Chor.

Heil dir, o Jungfrau,
Liebliche Herrscherin!   1175
Dein ist die Krone,
Dein ist der Sieg!
Als die Erhalterin

Dieſes Geſchlechtes,
Künftiger Helden   1180
Blühende Mutter begrüß' ich dich!
    Dreifaches Heil dir!
Mit glücklichen Zeichen,
Glückliche, trittſt du
In ein götterbegünſtiges, glückliches Haus,   1185
Wo die Kränze des Ruhmes hängen
Und das goldene Zepter in ſtetiger Reihe
Wandert vom Ahnherrn zum Enkel hinab.
    Deines lieblichen Eintritts
Werden ſich freuen   1190
Die Penaten des Hauſes,
Die hohen, die ernſten,
Verehrten Alten;
An der Schwelle empfangen
Wird dich die immer blühende Hebe   1195
Und die goldne Victoria,
Die geflügelte Göttin,
Die auf der Hand ſchwebt des ewigen Vaters,
Ewig die Schwingen zum Siege geſpannt.
    Nimmer entweicht   1200
Die Krone der Schönheit
Aus dieſem Geſchlechte,
Scheidend reicht
Eine Fürſtin der andern
Den Gürtel der Anmut   1205
Und den Schleier der züchtigen Scham.
Aber das Schönſte
Erlebt mein Auge,
Denn ich ſehe die Blume der Tochter,
Ehe die Blume der Mutter verblüht.   1210

Beatrice (aus ihrem Schrecken erwachend).

Wehe mir! In welche Hand
Hat das Unglück mich gegeben!
Unter allen,
Welche leben,
Nicht in diese sollt' ich fallen!   1215
  Jetzt versteh' ich das Entsetzen,
Das geheimnisvolle Grauen,
Das mich schaudernd stets gefaßt,
Wenn man mir den Namen nannte
Dieses furchtbaren Geschlechtes,   1220
Das sich selbst vertilgend haßt,
Gegen seine eignen Glieder
Wütend mit Erbitterung rast!
Schaudernd hört' ich oft und wieder
Von dem Schlangenhaß der Brüder,   1225
Und jetzt reißt mein Schreckenschicksal
Mich die Arme, Rettungslose
In den Strudel dieses Hasses,
Dieses Unglücks mich hinein!
            (Sie flieht in den Gartensaal.)

Vierter Auftritt.

Chor.

Den begünstigten Sohn der Götter beneid' ich,   1230
Den beglückten Besitzer der Macht!
Immer das Köstlichste ist sein Anteil,
Und von allem, was hoch und herrlich

B.   4

Von den Sterblichen wird gepriesen,
Bricht er die Blume sich ab.   1235

  Von den Perlen, welche der tauchende Fischer
Auffängt, wählt er die reinsten für sich.
Für den Herrscher legt man zurück das Beste,
Was gewonnen ward mit gemeinsamer Arbeit;
Wenn sich die Diener durchs Los vergleichen,   1240
Ihm ist das Schönste gewiß.

  Aber eines doch ist sein köstlichstes Kleinod,
Jeder andre Vorzug sei ihm gegönnt,
Dieses beneid' ich ihm unter allem:
Daß er heimführt die Blume der Frauen,   1245
Die das Entzücken ist aller Augen,
Daß er sie eigen besitzt.

  Mit dem Schwerte springt der Korsar an die Küste
In dem nächtlich ergreifenden Überfall;
Männer führt er davon und Frauen   1250
Und ersättigt die wilde Begierde,
Nur die schönste Gestalt darf er nicht berühren,
Die ist des Königes Gut.

  Aber jetzt folgt mir, zu bewachen den Eingang
Und die Schwelle des heiligen Raums,   1255
Daß kein Ungeweihter in dieses Geheimnis
Dringe und der Herrscher uns lobe,
Der das Köstlichste, was er besitzet,
Unsrer Bewahrung vertraut.

       (Der Chor entfernt sich nach dem Hintergrunde.)

Fünfter Auftritt.

Die Szene verwandelt sich in ein Zimmer im Innern des Palastes.

Donna Isabella steht zwischen Don Manuel und Don Cesar.

Isabella.

Nun endlich ist mir der erwünschte Tag,　　1260
Der langersehnte, festliche erschienen —
Vereint seh' ich die Herzen meiner Kinder,
Wie ich die Hände leicht zusammenfüge,
Und im vertrauten Kreis zum erstenmal
Kann sich das Herz der Mutter freudig öffnen.　　1265
Fern ist der fremden Zeugen rohe Schar,
Die zwischen uns sich kampfgerüstet stellte —
Der Waffen Klang erschreckt mein Ohr nicht mehr,
Und wie der Eulen nachtgewohnte Brut
Von der zerstörten Brandstatt, wo sie lang'　　1270
Mit altverjährtem Eigentum genistet,
Auffliegt in düsterm Schwarm, den Tag verdunkelnd,
Wenn sich die lang' vertriebenen Bewohner
Heimkehrend nahen mit der Freude Schall,
Den neuen Bau lebendig zu beginnen,　　1275
So flieht der alte Haß mit seinem nächtlichen
Gefolge, dem hohläugigten Verdacht,
Der scheelen Mißgunst und dem bleichen Neide,
Aus diesen Toren murrend zu der Hölle,
Und mit dem Frieden zieht geselliges　　1280
Vertraun und holde Eintracht lächelnd ein.

(Sie hält inne.)

— Doch nicht genug, daß dieser heut'ge Tag
Jedem von beiden einen Bruder schenkt,
Auch eine Schwester hat er euch geboren.

—Ihr staunt? Ihr seht mich mit Verwundrung an? 1285
Ja, meine Söhne! Es ist Zeit, daß ich
Mein Schweigen breche und das Siegel löse
Von einem lang' verschlossenen Geheimnis.
— Auch eine Tochter hab' ich eurem Vater
Geboren — eine jüngre Schwester lebt　　　　　　1290
Euch noch — Ihr sollt noch heute sie umarmen.

Don Cesar.

Was sagst du, Mutter? Eine Schwester lebt uns,
Und nie vernahmen wir von dieser Schwester!

Don Manuel.

Wohl hörten wir in früher Kinderzeit,
Daß eine Schwester uns geboren worden,　　　　　1295
Doch in der Wiege schon, so ging die Sage,
Nahm sie der Tod hinweg.

Isabella.
Die Sage lügt!
Sie lebt!

Don Cesar.
Sie lebt, und du verschwiegest uns?

Isabella.

Von meinem Schweigen geb' ich Rechenschaft.
Hört, was gesäet ward in früher Zeit　　　　　　1300
Und jetzt zur frohen Ernte reifen soll.
— Ihr wart noch zarte Knaben, aber schon
Entzweite euch der jammervolle Zwist,
Der ewig nie mehr wiederkehren möge,
Und häufte Gram auf eurer Eltern Herz,　　　　　1305
Da wurde eurem Vater eines Tages
Ein seltsam wunderbarer Traum. Ihm deuchte,
Er säh' aus seinem hochzeitlichen Bette

Zwei Lorbeerbäume wachsen, ihr Gezweig
Dicht ineinander flechtend — zwischen beiden　1310
Wuchs eine Lilie empor — Sie ward
Zur Flamme, die, der Bäume dicht Gezweig
Und das Gebälk ergreifend, prasselnd aufschlug
Und um sich wütend, schnell, das ganze Haus
In ungeheurer Feuerflut verschlang.　1315
　Erschreckt von diesem seltsamen Gesichte
Befragt' der Vater einen sternekundigen
Arabier, der sein Orakel war,
An dem sein Herz mehr hing, als mir gefiel,
Um die Bedeutung.　Der Arabier　1320
Erklärte: wenn mein Schoß von einer Tochter
Entbunden würde, töten würde sie ihm
Die beiden Söhne, und sein ganzer Stamm
Durch sie vergehn — Und ich ward Mutter einer Tochter.
Der Vater aber gab den grausamen　1325
Befehl, die Neugeborene alsbald
Ins Meer zu werfen.　Ich vereitelte
Den blut'gen Vorsatz und erhielt die Tochter
Durch eines treuen Knechts verschwiegnen Dienst.

Don Cesar.

Gesegnet sei er, der dir hilfreich war,　1330
O nicht an Rat gebricht's der Mutterliebe!

Isabella.

Der Mutterliebe mächt'ge Stimme nicht
Allein trieb mich, das Kindlein zu verschonen.
Auch mir ward eines Traumes seltsames
Orakel, als mein Schoß mit dieser Tochter　1335
Gesegnet war: Ein Kind, wie Liebesgötter schön,
Sah ich im Grase spielen, und ein Löwe

Kam aus dem Wald, der in dem blut'gen Rachen
Die frisch gejagte Beute trug, und ließ
Sie schmeichelnd in den Schoß des Kindes fallen.   1340
Und aus den Lüften schwang ein Adler sich
Herab, ein zitternd Reh in seinen Fängen,
Und legt' es schmeichelnd in den Schoß des Kindes,
Und beide, Löw' und Adler, legen fromm
Gepaart sich zu des Kindes Füßen nieder.   1345
— Des Traums Verständnis löste mir ein Mönch,
Ein gottgeliebter Mann, bei dem das Herz
Rat fand und Trost in jeder ird'schen Not.
Der sprach: „Genesen würd' ich einer Tochter,
Die mir der Söhne streitende Gemüter   1350
In heißer Liebesglut vereinen würde."
— Im Innersten bewahrt' ich mir dies Wort,
Dem Gott der Wahrheit mehr als dem der Lüge
Vertrauend, rettet' ich die Gottverheißne,
Des Segens Tochter, meiner Hoffnung Pfand,   1355
Die mir des Friedens Werkzeug sollte sein,
Als euer Haß sich wachsend stets vermehrte.

      Don Manuel (seinen Bruder umarmend).
Nicht mehr der Schwester braucht's, der Liebe Band
Zu flechten, aber fester soll sie's knüpfen.

                Isabella.
So ließ ich an verborgner Stätte sie,   1360
Von meinen Augen fern, geheimnisvoll,
Durch fremde Hand erziehn — den Anblick selbst
Des lieben Angesichts, den heißerflehten,
Versagt' ich mir, den strengen Vater scheuend,
Der, von des Argwohns ruheloser Pein   1365
Und finster grübelndem Verdacht genagt,

Auf allen Schritten mir die Späher pflanzte.

Don Cesar.

Drei Monde aber deckt den Vater schon
Das stille Grab — Was wehrte dir, o Mutter,
Die lang' Verborgne an das Licht hervor   1370
Zu ziehn und unsre Herzen zu erfreuen?

Isabella.

Was sonst als euer unglücksel'ger Streit,
Der, unauslöschlich wütend, auf dem Grab
Des kaum entseelten Vaters sich entflammte,
Nicht Raum noch Stätte der Versöhnung gab?   1375
Konnt' ich die Schwester zwischen eure wild
Entblößten Schwerter stellen? Konntet ihr
In diesem Sturm die Mutterstimme hören?
Und sollt' ich sie, des Friedens teures Pfand,
Den letzten heil'gen Anker meiner Hoffnung,   1380
An eures Hasses Wut unzeitig wagen?
— Erst mußtet ihr's ertragen, euch als Brüder
Zu sehn, eh' ich die Schwester zwischen euch
Als einen Friedensengel stellen konnte.
Jetzt kann ich's, und ich führe sie euch zu.   1385
Den alten Diener hab' ich ausgesendet,
Und stündlich harr' ich seiner Wiederkehr,
Der, ihrer stillen Zuflucht sie entreißend,
Zurück an meine mütterliche Brust
Sie führt und in die brüderlichen Arme.   1390

Don Manuel.

Und sie ist nicht die einz'ge, die du heut'
In deine Mutterarme schließen wirst.
Es zieht die Freude ein durch alle Pforten,
Es füllt sich der verödete Palast

Und wird der Sitz der blühnden Anmut werden.   1395
— Vernimm, o Mutter, jetzt auch mein Geheimnis.
Eine Schwester gibſt du mir — Ich will dafür
Dir eine zweite liebe Tochter ſchenken.
Ja, Mutter! Segne deinen Sohn! — Dies Herz,
Es hat gewählt; gefunden hab' ich ſie,   1400
Die mir durchs Leben ſoll Gefährtin ſein.
Eh' dieſes Tages Sonne ſinkt, führ' ich
Die Gattin dir Don Manuels zu Füßen.

Iſabella.

An meine Bruſt will ich ſie freudig ſchließen,
Die meinen Erſtgebornen mir beglückt,   1405
Auf ihren Pfaden ſoll die Freude ſprießen,
Und jede Blume, die das Leben ſchmückt,
Und jedes Glück ſoll mir den Sohn belohnen,
Der mir die ſchönſte reicht der Mutterkronen!

Don Ceſar.

Verſchwende, Mutter, deines Segens Fülle   1410
Nicht an den einen erſtgebornen Sohn!
Wenn Liebe Segen gibt, ſo bring' auch ich
Dir eine Tochter, ſolcher Mutter wert,
Die mich der Liebe neu Gefühl gelehrt.
Eh' dieſes Tages Sonne ſinkt, führt auch   1415
Don Ceſar ſeine Gattin dir entgegen.

Don Manuel.

Allmächt'ge Liebe! Göttliche! Wohl nennt
Man dich mit Recht die Königin der Seelen!
Dir unterwirft ſich jedes Element,
Du kannſt das feindlich Streitende vermählen,   1420
Nichts lebt, was deine Hoheit nicht erkennt,
Und auch des Bruders wilden Sinn haſt du

Besiegt, der unbezwungen stets geblieben.

(Don Cesar umarmend.)

Jetzt glaub' ich an dein Herz und schließe dich
Mit Hoffnung an die brüderliche Brust,   1425
Nicht zweifl' ich mehr an dir, denn du kannst lieben.

Isabella.

Dreimal gesegnet sei mir dieser Tag,
Der mir auf einmal jede bange Sorge
Vom schwerbeladnen Busen hebt — Gegründet
Auf festen Säulen seh' ich mein Geschlecht,   1430
Und in der Zeiten Unermeßlichkeit
Kann ich hinabsehn mit zufriednem Geist.
Noch gestern sah ich mich im Witwenschleier,
Gleich einer Abgeschiednen, kinderlos,
In diesen öden Sälen ganz allein,   1435
Und heute werden in der Jugend Glanz
Drei blühnde Töchter mir zur Seite stehen.
Die Mutter zeige sich, die glückliche,
Von allen Weibern, die geboren haben,
Die sich mit mir an Herrlichkeit vergleicht!   1440
— Doch welcher Fürsten königliche Töchter
Erblühen denn an dieses Landes Grenzen,
Davon ich Kunde nie vernahm? — denn nicht
Unwürdig wählen konnten meine Söhne!

Don Manuel.

Nur heute, Mutter, fordre nicht, den Schleier   1445
Hinwegzuheben, der mein Glück bedeckt.
Es kommt der Tag, der alles lösen wird;
Am besten mag die Braut sich selbst verkünden,
Des sei gewiß, du wirst sie würdig finden.

Isabella.

Des Vaters eignen Sinn und Geist erkenn' ich   1450
In meinem erstgebornen Sohn! Der liebte
Von jeher, sich verborgen in sich selbst
Zu spinnen und den Ratschluß zu bewahren
Im unzugangbar fest verschlossenen Gemüt!
Gern mag ich dir die kurze Frist vergönnen,   1455
Doch mein Sohn Cesar, des bin ich gewiß,
Wird jetzt mir eine Königstochter nennen.

Don Cesar.

Nicht meine Weise ist's, geheimnisvoll
Mich zu verhüllen, Mutter. Frei und offen
Wie meine Stirne trag' ich mein Gemüt;   1460
Doch was du jetzt von mir begehrst zu wissen,
Das, Mutter — laß mich's redlich dir gestehn,
Hab' ich mich selbst noch nicht gefragt. Fragt man,
Woher der Sonne Himmelsfeuer flamme?
Die alle Welt verklärt, erklärt sich selbst,   1465
Ihr Licht bezeugt, daß sie vom Lichte stamme.
Ins klare Auge sah ich meiner Braut,
Ins Herz des Herzens hab' ich ihr geschaut,
Am reinen Glanz will ich die Perle kennen,
Doch ihren Namen kann ich dir nicht nennen.   1470

Isabella.

Wie, mein Sohn Cesar? Kläre mir das auf.
Zu gern dem ersten mächtigen Gefühl
Vertrautest du, wie einer Götterstimme.
Auf rascher Jugendtat erwart' ich dich,
Doch nicht auf töricht kindischer — Laß hören,   1475
Was deine Wahl gelenkt.

Don Cesar.

Wahl, meine Mutter?
Ist's Wahl, wenn des Gestirnes Macht den Menschen
Ereilt in der verhängnisvollen Stunde?
Nicht eine Braut zu suchen, ging ich aus,
Nicht wahrlich solches Eitle konnte mir　　　　　1480
Zu Sinne kommen in dem Haus des Todes,
Denn dorten fand ich, die ich nicht gesucht.
Gleichgültig war und nichts bedeutend mir
Der Frauen leer geschwätziges Geschlecht,
Denn eine zweite sah ich nicht wie dich,　　　　1485
Die ich gleich wie ein Götterbild verehre.
Es war des Vaters ernste Totenfeier,
Im Volksgedräng verborgen wohnten wir
Ihr bei, du weißt's, in unbekannter Kleidung:
So hattest du's mit Weisheit angeordnet,　　　　1490
Daß unsers Haders wild ausbrechende
Gewalt des Festes Würde nicht verletze.
— Mit schwarzem Flor behangen war das Schiff
Der Kirche, zwanzig Genien umstanden
Mit Fackeln in den Händen den Altar,　　　　　1495
Vor dem der Totensarg erhaben ruhte,
Mit weißbekreuztem Grabestuch bedeckt.
Und auf dem Grabtuch sahe man den Stab
Der Herrschaft liegen und die Fürstenkrone,
Den ritterlichen Schmuck der goldnen Sporen,　　1500
Das Schwert mit diamantenem Gehäng.
— Und alles lag in stiller Andacht knieend,
Als ungesehen jetzt vom hohen Chor
Herab die Orgel anfing, sich zu regen,
Und hundertstimmig der Gesang begann —　　　　1505

Und als der Chor noch fortklang, stieg der Sarg
Mitsamt dem Boden, der ihn trug, allmählich
Versinkend in die Unterwelt hinab,
Das Grabtuch aber überschleierte
Weit ausgebreitet die verborgne Mündung, 1510
Und auf der Erde blieb der irb'sche Schmuck
Zurück, dem Niederfahrenden nicht folgend —
Doch auf den Seraphsflügeln des Gesangs
Schwang die befreite Seele sich nach oben,
Den Himmel suchend und den Schoß der Gnade. 1515
— Dies alles, Mutter, ruf' ich dir, genau
Beschreibend, ins Gedächtnis jetzt zurück,
Daß du erkennest, ob zu jener Stunde
Ein weltlich Wünschen mir im Herzen war.
Und diesen festlich ernsten Augenblick 1520
Erwählte sich der Lenker meines Lebens,
Mich zu berühren mit der Liebe Strahl —
Wie es geschah, frag' ich mich selbst vergebens.

Isabella.

Vollende dennoch! Laß mich alles hören.

Don Cesar.

Woher sie kam, und wie sie sich zu mir 1525
Gefunden, dieses frage nicht — Als ich
Die Augen wandte, stand sie mir zur Seite,
Und dunkel mächtig, wunderbar, ergriff
Im tiefsten Innersten mich ihre Nähe.
Nicht ihres Wesens schöner Außenschein, 1530
Nicht ihres Lächelns holder Zauber war's,
Die Reize nicht, die auf der Wange schweben,
Selbst nicht der Glanz der göttlichen Gestalt —
Es war ihr tiefstes und geheimstes Leben,

Was mich ergriff mit heiliger Gewalt; 1535
Wie Zaubers Kräfte unbegreiflich weben —
Die Seelen schienen ohne Worteslaut
Sich ohne Mittel geistig zu berühren,
Als sich mein Atem mischte mit dem ihren,
Fremd war sie mir und innig doch vertraut, 1540
Und klar auf einmal fühlt' ich's in mir werden,
Die ist es oder keine sonst auf Erden!

   Don Manuel (mit Feuer einfallend).

Das ist der Liebe heil'ger Götterstrahl,
Der in die Seele schlägt und trifft und zündet,
Wenn sich Verwandtes zum Verwandten findet, 1545
Da ist kein Widerstand und keine Wahl,
Es löst der Mensch nicht, was der Himmel bindet.
— Dem Bruder fall' ich bei, ich muß ihn loben,
Mein eigen Schicksal ist's, was er erzählt,
Den Schleier hat er glücklich aufgehoben 1550
Von dem Gefühl, das dunkel mich beseelt.

   Isabella.

Den eignen freien Weg, ich seh' es wohl,
Will das Verhängnis gehn mit meinen Kindern.
Vom Berge stürzt der ungeheure Strom,
Wühlt sich sein Bette selbst und bricht sich Bahn, 1555
Nicht des gemeßnen Pfades achtet er,
Den ihm die Klugheit vorbedächtig baut.
So unterwerf' ich mich — wie kann ich's ändern? —
Der unregiersam stärkern Götterhand,
Die meines Hauses Schicksal dunkel spinnt; 1560
Der Söhne Herz ist meiner Hoffnung Pfand,
Sie denken groß, wie sie geboren sind.

Sechster Auftritt.

Isabella. Don Manuel. Don Cesar. Diego zeigt sich an der Türe.

Isabella.

Doch sieh! Da kommt mein treuer Knecht zurück!
Nur näher, näher, redlicher Diego!
Wo ist mein Kind? — Sie wissen alles! Hier　　1565
Ist kein Geheimnis mehr — Wo ist sie? Sprich!
Verbirg sie länger nicht, wir sind gefaßt,
Die höchste Freude zu ertragen. Komm!
(Sie will mit ihm nach der Türe gehen.)
Was ist das? Wie? Du zögerst? Du verstummst?
Das ist kein Blick, der Gutes mir verkündet!　　1570
Was ist dir? Sprich! Ein Schauder faßt mich an.
Wo ist sie? Wo ist Beatrice? (Will hinaus.)

Don Manuel (für sich, betroffen).

Beatrice!

Diego (hält sie zurück).

Bleib!

Isabella.

Wo ist sie? Mich entseelt die Angst.

Diego.

Sie folgt
Mir nicht. Ich bringe dir die Tochter nicht.

Isabella.

Was ist geschehn? Bei allen Heil'gen, rede!　　1575

Don Cesar.

Wo ist die Schwester? Unglücksel'ger, rede!

Diego.

Sie ist geraubt! Gestohlen von Korsaren!
O hätt' ich nimmer diesen Tag gesehn!

Don Manuel.

Fass' dich, o Mutter!

Don Cesar.
Mutter, sei gefaßt!
Bezwinge dich, bis du ihn ganz vernommen!   1580

Diego.

Ich machte schnell mich auf, wie du befohlen,
Die oft betretne Straße nach dem Kloster
Zum letztenmal zu gehn — Die Freude trug mich
Auf leichten Flügeln fort.

Don Cesar.
Zur Sache!

Don Manuel.
Rede!

Diego.

Und da ich in die wohlbekannten Höfe   1585
Des Klosters trete, die ich oft betrat,
Nach deiner Tochter ungeduldig frage,
Seh' ich des Schreckens Bild in jedem Auge,
Entsetzt vernehm' ich das Entsetzliche.
(Isabella sinkt bleich und zitternd auf einen Sessel, Don Manuel ist
um sie beschäftigt.)

Don Cesar.

Und Mauren, sagst du, raubten sie hinweg?   1590
Sah man die Mauren? Wer bezeugte dies?

Diego.

Ein maurisch Räuberschiff gewahrte man
In einer Bucht, unfern dem Kloster ankernd.

Don Cesar.

Manch Segel rettet sich in diese Buchten
Vor des Orkanes Wut — Wo ist das Schiff?   1595

Diego.

Heut' frühe sah man es in hoher See
Mit voller Segel Kraft das Weite suchen.

Don Cesar.

Hört man von anderm Raub noch, der geschehn?
Dem Mauren gnügt einfache Beute nicht.

Diego.

Hinweggetrieben wurde mit Gewalt　　　　　　　1600
Die Rinderherde, die dort weidete.

Don Cesar.

Wie konnten Räuber aus des Klosters Mitte
Die Wohlverschloßne heimlich raubend stehlen?

Diego.

Des Klostergartens Mauern waren leicht
Auf hoher Leiter Sproffen überstiegen.　　　　　1605

Don Cesar.

Wie brachen sie ins Innerste der Zellen?
Denn fromme Nonnen hält der strenge Zwang.

Diego.

Die noch durch kein Gelübde sich gebunden,
Sie durfte frei im Freien sich ergehen.

Don Cesar.

Und pflegte sie des freien Rechtes oft　　　　　1610
Sich zu bedienen?　Dieses sage mir.

Diego.

Oft sah man sie des Gartens Stille suchen,
Der Wiederkehr vergaß sie heute nur.

Don Cesar (nachdem er sich eine Weile bedacht).

Raub sagst du?　War sie frei genug dem Räuber,
So konnte sie in Freiheit auch entfliehen.　　　1615

Jsabella (steht auf).

Es ist Gewalt! Es ist verwegner Raub!
Nicht pflichtvergessen konnte meine Tochter
Aus freier Neigung dem Entführer folgen!
— Don Manuel! Don Cesar! Eine Schwester
Dacht' ich euch zuzuführen, doch ich selbst   1620
Soll jetzt sie eurem Heldenarm verdanken!
In eurer Kraft erhebt euch, meine Söhne!
Nicht ruhig duldet es, daß eure Schwester
Des frechen Diebes Beute sei — Ergreift
Die Waffen! Rüstet Schiffe aus! Durchforscht   1625
Die ganze Küste! Durch alle Meere setzt
Dem Räuber nach! Erobert euch die Schwester!

Don Cesar.

Leb' wohl! Zur Rache flieg' ich, zur Entdeckung!
(Er geht ab. Don Manuel, aus einer tiefen Zerstreuung erwachend,
wendet sich beunruhigt zu Diego.)

Don Manuel.

Wann, sagst du, sei sie unsichtbar geworden?

Diego.

Seit diesem Morgen erst ward sie vermißt.   1630

Don Manuel (zu Donna Jsabella).

Und Beatrice nennt sich deine Tochter?

Jsabella.

Dies ist ihr Name! Eile! Frage nicht!

Don Manuel.

Nur eines noch, o Mutter, laß mich wissen —

Jsabella.

Fliege zur Tat! Des Bruders Beispiel folge!

Don Manuel.

In welcher Gegend, ich beschwöre dich —   1635

B.   5

Isabella (ihn forttreibend).

Sieh meine Tränen! Meine Todesangst!

Don Manuel.

In welcher Gegend hieltst du sie verborgen?

Isabella.

Verborgner nicht war sie im Schoß der Erde!

Diego.

O jetzt ergreift mich plötzlich bange Furcht.

Don Manuel.

Furcht, und worüber? Sage, was du weißt.   1640

Diego.

Daß ich des Raubs unschuldig Ursach' sei.

Isabella.

Unglücklicher, entdecke, was geschehn.

Diego.

Ich habe dir's verhehlt, Gebieterin,
Dein Mutterherz mit Sorge zu verschonen.
Am Tage, als der Fürst beerdigt ward   1645
Und alle Welt, begierig nach dem Neuen,
Der ernsten Feier sich entgegendrängte,
Lag deine Tochter — denn die Kunde war
Auch in des Klosters Mauern eingedrungen —
Lag sie mir an mit unabläss'gem Flehn,   1650
Ihr dieses Festes Anblick zu gewähren.
Ich Unglückseliger ließ mich bewegen,
Verhüllte sie in ernste Trauertracht,
Und also war sie Zeugin jenes Festes.
Und dort, befürcht' ich, in des Volks Gewühl,   1655
Das sich herbeigedrängt von allen Enden,
Ward sie vom Aug' des Räubers ausgespäht,
Denn ihrer Schönheit Glanz birgt keine Hülle.

Don Manuel (vor sich, erleichtert).

Glückſel'ges Wort, das mir das Herz befreit!

Das gleicht ihr nicht!   Dies Zeichen trifft nicht zu.   1660

Iſabella.

Wahnſinn'ger Alter!   So verrietſt du mich!

Diego.

Gebieterin, ich dacht' es gut zu machen.

Die Stimme der Natur, die Macht des Bluts

Glaubt' ich in dieſem Wunſche zu erkennen;

Ich hielt es für des Himmels eignes Werk,   1665

Der mit verborgen ahnungsvollem Zuge

Die Tochter hintrieb zu des Vaters Grab!

Der frommen Pflicht wollt' ich ihr Recht erzeigen,

Und ſo, aus guter Meinung, ſchafft' ich Böſes!

Don Manuel (vor ſich).

Was ſteh' ich hier in Furcht und Zweifels Qualen?   1670

Schnell will ich Licht mir ſchaffen und Gewißheit.

(Will gehen.)

Don Ceſar (der zurückkommt).

Verzieh, Don Manuel, gleich folg' ich dir.

Don Manuel.

Folge mir nicht, hinweg, mir folge niemand!

(Er geht ab.)

Don Ceſar (ſieht ihm verwundert nach).

Was iſt dem Bruder?   Mutter, ſage mir's.

Iſabella.

Ich kenn' ihn nicht mehr.   Ganz verkenn' ich ihn.   1675

Don Ceſar.

Du ſiehſt mich wiederkehren, meine Mutter,

Denn in des Eifers heftiger Begier

Vergaß ich, um ein Zeichen dich zu fragen,

Woran man die verlorne Schweſter kennt.

Wie find' ich ihre Spuren, eh' ich weiß,   1680
Aus welchem Ort die Räuber sie geriffen?
Das Kloster nenne mir, das sie verbarg.

Isabella.

Der heiligen Cäcilia ist's gewidmet,
Und hinterm Waldgebirge, das zum Ätna
Sich langsam steigend hebt, liegt es versteckt,   1685
Wie ein verschwiegner Aufenthalt der Seelen.

Don Cesar.

Sei gutes Muts. Vertraue deinen Söhnen.
Die Schwester bring' ich dir zurück, müßt' ich
Durch alle Länder sie und Meere suchen.
Doch eines, Mutter, ist es, was mich kümmert: 1690
Die Braut verließ ich unter fremdem Schutz —
Nur dir kann ich das teure Pfand vertrauen,
Ich sende sie dir her, du wirst sie schauen,
An ihrer Bruft, an ihrem lieben Herzen
Wirst du des Grams vergessen und der Schmerzen.   1695
(Er geht ab.)

Isabella.

Wann endlich wird der alte Fluch sich lösen,
Der über diesem Hause lastend ruht?
Mit meiner Hoffnung spielt ein tückisch Wesen,
Und nimmer stillt sich seines Neides Wut.
So nahe glaubt' ich mich dem sichern Hafen,   1700
So fest vertraut' ich auf des Glückes Pfand,
Und alle Stürme glaubt' ich eingeschlafen,
Und freudig winkend sah ich schon das Land
Im Abendglanz der Sonne sich erhellen —
Da kommt ein Sturm, aus heitrer Luft gesandt,   1705
Und reißt mich wieder in den Kampf der Wellen!
(Sie geht nach dem innern Hause, wohin ihr Diego folgt.)

Dritter Aufzug.

Erster Auftritt.

Die Szene verwandelt sich in den Garten.

Beide Chöre. Zuletzt Beatrice.

(Der Chor des Don Manuel kommt in festlichem Aufzug, mit Kränzen geschmückt und die oben beschriebnen Brautgeschenke begleitend; der Chor des Don Cesar will ihm den Eintritt verwehren.)

Erster Chor.
Du würdest wohl tun, diesen Platz zu leeren.

Zweiter Chor.
Ich will's, wenn beßre Männer es begehren.

Erster Chor.
Du könntest merken, daß du lästig bist.

Zweiter Chor.
Deswegen bleib' ich, weil es dich verdrießt.   1710

Erster Chor.
Hier ist mein Platz.   Wer darf zurück mich halten?

Zweiter Chor.
Ich darf es tun, ich habe hier zu walten.

Erster Chor.
Mein Herrscher sendet mich, Don Manuel!

Zweiter Chor.
Ich stehe hier auf meines Herrn Befehl.

Erster Chor.

Dem ältern Bruder muß der jüngre weichen.   1715

Zweiter Chor.

Dem Erstbesitzenden gehört die Welt.

Erster Chor.

Verhaßter, geh und räume mir das Feld.

Zweiter Chor.

Nicht, bis sich unsre Schwerter erst vergleichen.

Erster Chor.

Find' ich dich überall in meinen Wegen?

Zweiter Chor.

Wo mir's gefällt, da tret' ich dir entgegen.   1720

Erster Chor.

Was hast du hier zu horchen und zu hüten?

Zweiter Chor.

Was hast du hier zu fragen, zu verbieten?

Erster Chor.

Dir steh' ich nicht zu Red' und Antwort hier.

Zweiter Chor.

Und nicht des Wortes Ehre gönn' ich dir.

Erster Chor.

Ehrfurcht gebührt, o Jüngling, meinen Jahren.   1725

Zweiter Chor.

In Tapferkeit bin ich, wie du, erfahren!

Beatrice (stürzt heraus).

Weh mir, was wollen diese wilden Scharen?

Erster Chor (zum zweiten).

Nichts acht' ich dich und deine stolze Miene!

Zweiter Chor.

Ein beßrer ist der Herrscher, dem ich diene!

Beatrice.

O weh mir, weh mir, wenn er jetzt erschiene!   1730

Erster Chor.

Du lügst! Don Manuel besiegt ihn weit!

Zweiter Chor.

Den Preis gewinnt mein Herr in jedem Streit.

Beatrice.

Jetzt wird er kommen, dies ist seine Zeit!

Erster Chor.

Wäre nicht Friede, Recht verschafft' ich mir!

Zweiter Chor.

Wär's nicht die Furcht, kein Friede wehrte dir.　　1735

Beatrice.

O wär' er tausend Meilen weit von hier!

Erster Chor.

Das Gesetz fürcht' ich, nicht deiner Blicke Trutz.

Zweiter Chor.

Wohl tust du dran, es ist des Feigen Schutz.

Erster Chor.

Fang an, ich folge!

Zweiter Chor.

Mein Schwert ist heraus!

Beatrice (in der heftigsten Beängstigung).

Sie werden handgemein, die Degen blitzen!　　1740
Ihr Himmelsmächte, haltet ihn zurück!
Werft euch in seinen Weg, ihr Hindernisse,
Eine Schlinge legt, ein Netz um seine Füße,
Daß er verfehle diesen Augenblick!
Ihr Engel alle, die ich flehend bat,　　1745
Ihn herzuführen, täuschet meine Bitte,
Weit, weit von hier entfernet seine Schritte!
(Sie eilt hinein. Indem die Chöre einander anfallen, erscheint Don
Manuel.)

Zweiter Auftritt.

Don Manuel. Der Chor

Don Manuel.

Was seh' ich! Haltet ein!

Erster Chor (zum zweiten).

Komm an! Komm an!

Zweiter Chor.

Nieder mit ihnen! Nieder!

Don Manuel (tritt zwischen sie mit gezognem Schwert).

Haltet ein!

Erster Chor.

Es ist der Fürst.

Zweiter Chor.

Der Bruder! Haltet Friede!   1750

Don Manuel.

Den streck' ich tot auf dieses Rasens Grund,
Der mit gezuckter Augenwimper nur
Die Fehde fortsetzt und dem Gegner droht!
Rast ihr? Was für ein Dämon reizt euch an,
Des alten Zwistes Flammen aufzublasen,   1755
Der zwischen uns, den Fürsten, abgetan
Und ausgeglichen ist auf immerdar?
— Wer fing den Streit an? Redet! Ich will's wissen.

Erster Chor.

Sie standen hier —

Zweiter Chor (unterbrechend).

Sie kamen —

Don Manuel (zum ersten Chor).

Rede du!

Erster Chor.

Wir kamen her, mein Fürst, die Hochzeitgaben   1760
Zu überreichen, wie du uns befahlst.
Geschmückt zu einem Feste, keineswegs
Zum Krieg bereit, du siehst es, zogen wir
In Frieden unsern Weg, nichts Arges denkend
Und trauend dem beschworenen Vertrag,   1765
Da fanden wir sie feindlich hier gelagert
Und uns den Eingang sperrend mit Gewalt.

Don Manuel.

Unsinnige, ist keine Freistatt sicher
Genug vor eurer blinden, tollen Wut?
Auch in der Unschuld still verborgnen Sitz   1770
Bricht euer Haber friedestörend ein?
                    (Zum zweiten Chor.)
Weiche zurück!   Hier sind Geheimnisse,
Die deine kühne Gegenwart nicht dulden.
                    (Da derselbe zögert.)
Zurück!   Dein Herr gebietet dir's durch mich,
Denn wir sind jetzt ein Haupt und ein Gemüt,   1775
Und mein Befehl ist auch der seine.   Geh!
                    (Zum ersten Chor.)
Du bleibst und wahrst des Eingangs.

Zweiter Chor.

                              Was beginnen?
Die Fürsten sind versöhnt, das ist die Wahrheit,
Und in der hohen Häupter Span und Streit
Sich unberufen, vielgeschäftig drängen   1780
Bringt wenig Dank und öfterer Gefahr.
Denn wenn der Mächtige des Streits ermüdet,
Wirft er behend auf den geringen Mann,

Der arglos ihm gedient, den blut'gen Mantel
Der Schuld, und leicht gereinigt steht er da.   1785
Drum mögen sich die Fürsten selbst vergleichen,
Ich acht' es für geratner, wir gehorchen.

(Der zweite Chor geht ab, der erste zieht sich nach dem Hintergrund der
Szene zurück. In demselben Augenblicke stürzt Beatrice heraus und wirft
sich in Don Manuels Arme.)

Dritter Auftritt.

Beatrice. Don Manuel.

Beatrice.

Du bist's. Ich habe dich wieder — Grausamer!
Du hast mich lange, lange schmachten lassen,
Der Furcht und allen Schrecknissen zum Raub   1790
Dahin gegeben — Doch nichts mehr davon!
Ich habe dich — in deinen lieben Armen
Ist Schutz und Schirm vor jeglicher Gefahr.
Komm! Sie sind weg! Wir haben Raum zur Flucht,
Fort, laß uns keinen Augenblick verlieren.   1795

(Sie will ihn mit sich fortziehen und sieht ihn jetzt erst genauer an.)

Was ist dir? So verschlossen feierlich
Empfängst du mich — entziehst dich meinen Armen,
Als wolltest du mich lieber ganz verstoßen?
Ich kenne dich nicht mehr — Ist dies Don Manuel,
Mein Gatte, mein Geliebter?

Don Manuel.

                    Beatrice!   1800

Beatrice.

Nein, rede nicht! Jetzt ist nicht Zeit zu Worten!
Fort laß uns eilen, schnell, der Augenblick
Ist kostbar —

Don Manuel.

Bleib! Antworte mir!

Beatrice.

Fort! Fort!
Eh' diese wilden Männer wiederkehren!

Don Manuel.

Bleib! Jene Männer werden uns nicht schaden.   1805

Beatrice.

Doch, doch, du kennst sie nicht, o komm! Entfliehe!

Don Manuel.

Von meinem Arm beschützt, was kannst du fürchten?

Beatrice.

O glaube mir, es gibt hier mächt'ge Menschen!

Don Manuel.

Geliebte, keinen mächtigern als mich.

Beatrice.

Du gegen diese vielen ganz allein?   1810

Don Manuel.

Ich ganz allein! Die Männer, die du fürchtest —

Beatrice.

Du kennst sie nicht, du weißt nicht, wem sie dienen.

Don Manuel.

Mir dienen sie, und ich bin ihr Gebieter.

Beatrice.

Du bist — Ein Schrecken fliegt durch meine Seele!

Don Manuel.

Lerne mich endlich kennen, Beatrice!   1815

Ich bin nicht der, der ich dir schien zu sein,
Der arme Ritter nicht, der unbekannte,
Der liebend nur um deine Liebe warb.
Wer ich wahrhaftig bin, was ich vermag,
Woher ich stamme, hab' ich dir verborgen.   1820

Beatrice.
Du bist Don Manuel nicht! Weh mir, wer bist du?

Don Manuel.
Don Manuel heiß' ich — doch ich bin der Höchste,
Der diesen Namen führt in dieser Stadt,
Ich bin Don Manuel, Fürst von Messina.

Beatrice.
Du wärst Don Manuel, Don Cesars Bruder?   1825

Don Manuel.
Don Cesar ist mein Bruder.

Beatrice.
　　　　　Ist dein Bruder!

Don Manuel.
Wie? dies erschreckt dich? Kennst du den Don Cesar?
Kennst du noch sonsten jemand meines Bluts?

Beatrice.
Du bist Don Manuel, der mit dem Bruder
In Hasse lebt und unversöhnter Fehde?   1830

Don Manuel.
Wir sind versöhnt, seit heute sind wir Brüder,
Nicht von Geburt nur, nein von Herzen auch.

Beatrice.
Versöhnt, seit heute!

Don Manuel.
　　　　　Sage mir, was ist das?
Was bringt dich so in Aufruhr? Kennst du mehr

Als nur den Namen bloß von meinem Hause? 1835
Weiß ich dein ganz Geheimnis? Haft du nichts,
Nichts mir verschwiegen oder vorenthalten?

Beatrice.

Was denkst du? Wie? Was hätt' ich zu gestehen?

Don Manuel.

Von deiner Mutter hast du mir noch nichts
Gesagt. Wer ist sie? Würdeft du sie kennen, 1840
Wenn ich sie dir beschriebe — dir sie zeigte?

Beatrice.

Du kennst sie — kennst sie und verbargeft mir?

Don Manuel.

Weh dir und wehe mir, wenn ich sie kenne!

Beatrice.

O, sie ist gütig wie das Licht der Sonne!
Ich seh' sie vor mir, die Erinnerung 1845
Belebt sich wieder, aus der Seele Tiefen
Erhebt sich mir die göttliche Gestalt.
Der braunen Locken dunkle Ringe seh' ich
Des weißen Halses edle Form beschatten,
Ich seh' der Stirne rein gewölbten Bogen, 1850
Des großen Auges dunkelhellen Glanz,
Auch ihrer Stimme seelenvolle Töne
Erwachen mir —

Don Manuel.

Weh mir! Du schilderst sie!

Beatrice.

Und ich entfloh ihr! Konnte sie verlaffen,
Vielleicht am Morgen eben dieses Tags, 1855
Der mich auf ewig ihr vereinen sollte!
O selbst die Mutter gab ich hin für dich!

Don Manuel.

Messinas Fürstin wird dir Mutter sein,
Zu ihr bring' ich dich jetzt, sie wartet deiner.

Beatrice.

Was sagst du? Deine Mutter und Don Cesars?   1860
Zu ihr mich bringen? Nimmer, nimmermehr.

Don Manuel.

Du schauderst? Was bedeutet dies Entsetzen?
Ist meine Mutter keine Fremde dir?

Beatrice.

O unglückselig traurige Entdeckung,
O hätt' ich nimmer diesen Tag gesehn!   1865

Don Manuel.

Was kann dich ängstigen, nun du mich kennst,
Den Fürsten findest in dem Unbekannten?

Beatrice.

O gib mir diesen Unbekannten wieder,
Mit ihm auf ödem Eiland wär' ich selig!

Don Cesar (hinter der Szene).

Zurück! Welch vieles Volk ist hier versammelt?   1870

Beatrice.

Gott! Diese Stimme! Wo verberg' ich mich?

Don Manuel.

Erkennst du diese Stimme? Nein, du hast
Sie nie gehört und kannst sie nicht erkennen!

Beatrice.

O laß uns fliehen, komm und weile nicht.

Don Manuel.

Was fliehn? Es ist des Bruders Stimme, der   1875
Mich sucht; zwar wundert mich, wie er entdeckte —

Beatrice.

Bei allen Heiligen des Himmels, meid ihn!
Begegne nicht dem heftig Stürmenden,
Laß dich von ihm an diesem Ort nicht finden.

Don Manuel.

Geliebte Seele, dich verwirrt die Furcht!   1880
Du hörst mich nicht, wir sind versöhnte Brüder!

Beatrice.

O Himmel, rette mich aus dieser Stunde!

Don Manuel.

Was ahnet mir! Welch ein Gedanke faßt
Mich schaudernd? — Wär' es möglich — Wäre dir
Die Stimme keine fremde? — Beatrice!   1885
Du warst — Mir grauet, weiter fort zu fragen —
Du warst — bei meines Vaters Leichenfeier?

Beatrice.

Weh mir!

Don Manuel.

  Du warst zugegen?

Beatrice.

    Zürne nicht!

Don Manuel.

Unglückliche, du warst?

Beatrice.

  Ich war zugegen.

Don Manuel.

Entsetzen!

Beatrice.

  Die Begierde war zu mächtig!   1890
Vergib mir! Ich gestand dir meinen Wunsch,
Doch plötzlich ernst und finster ließest du

Die Bitte fallen, und so schwieg auch ich.
Doch weiß ich nicht, welch bösen Sternes Macht
Mich trieb mit unbezwinglichem Gelüsten.   1895
Des Herzens heißen Drang mußt' ich vergnügen,
Der alte Diener lieh mir seinen Beistand,
Ich war dir ungehorsam, und ich ging.
(Sie schmiegt sich an ihn; indem tritt Don Cesar herein, von dem
ganzen Chor begleitet.)

Vierter Auftritt.

Beide Brüder. Beide Chöre. Beatrice.

Zweiter Chor (zu Don Cesar).
Du glaubst uns nicht — Glaub' deinen eignen Augen.

Don Cesar
(tritt heftig ein und fährt beim Anblick seines Bruders mit Entsetzen
zurück.)
Blendwerk der Hölle! Was? In seinen Armen! 1900
(Näher tretend, zu Don Manuel.)
Giftvolle Schlange! Das ist deine Liebe!
Deswegen logst du tückisch mir Versöhnung!
O, eine Stimme Gottes war mein Haß!
Fahre zur Hölle, falsche Schlangenseele!
(Er ersticht ihn.)

Don Manuel.
Ich bin des Todes — Beatrice — Bruder!   1905
(Er sinkt und stirbt. Beatrice fällt neben ihm ohnmächtig nieder.)

Erster Chor.

Mord! Mord! Herbei! Greift zu den Waffen alle!
Mit Blut gerächet sei die blut'ge Tat!
(Alle ziehen die Degen.)

Zweiter Chor.

Heil uns! Der lange Zwiespalt ist geendigt.
Nur einem Herrscher jetzt gehorcht Messina.

Erster Chor.

Rache! Rache! Der Mörder falle! falle!   1910
Ein sühnend Opfer dem Gemordeten!

Zweiter Chor.

Herr, fürchte nichts, wir stehen treu zu dir.

Don Cesar (mit Ansehen zwischen sie tretend).

Zurück — Ich habe meinen Feind getötet,
Der mein vertrauend redlich Herz betrog,
Die Bruderliebe mir zum Fallstrick legte.   1915
Ein furchtbar gräßlich Ansehn hat die Tat,
Doch der gerechte Himmel hat gerichtet.

Erster Chor.

Weh dir, Messina! Wehe! Wehe! Wehe!
Das gräßlich Ungeheure ist geschehn
In deinen Mauern — Wehe deinen Müttern   1920
Und Kindern, deinen Jünglingen und Greisen,
Und wehe der noch ungebornen Frucht.

Don Cesar.

Die Klage kommt zu spät — Hier schaffet Hilfe!
(Auf Beatricen zeigend.)
Ruft sie ins Leben! Schnell entfernet sie
Von diesem Ort des Schreckens und des Todes.   1925
— Ich kann nicht länger weilen, denn mich ruft
Die Sorge fort um die geraubte Schwester.

— Bringt sie in meiner Mutter Schloß und sprecht,
Es sei ihr Sohn Don Cesar, der sie sende!

(Er geht ab; die ohnmächtige Beatrice wird von dem zweiten Chor auf
eine Bank gesetzt und so hinweggetragen; der erste Chor bleibt bei dem
Leichnam zurück, um welchen auch die Knaben, die die Brautgeschenke
tragen, in einem Halbkreis herumstehen.)

Fünfter Auftritt.

Chor.

Sagt mir! Ich kann's nicht fassen und deuten   1930
Wie es so schnell sich erfüllend genaht.
Längst wohl sah ich im Geist mit weiten
Schritten das Schreckensgespenst herschreiten
Dieser entsetzlichen, blutigen Tat.
Dennoch übergießt mich ein Grauen,   1935
Da sie vorhanden ist und geschehen,
Da ich erfüllt muß vor Augen schauen,
Was ich in ahnender Furcht nur gesehen;
All mein Blut in den Adern erstarrt
Vor der gräßlich entschiedenen Gegenwart.   1940

Einer aus dem Chor.

Lasset erschallen die Stimme der Klage!
Holder Jüngling,
Da liegt er entseelt,
Hingestreckt in der Blüte der Tage!
Schwer umfangen von Todesnacht,   1945
An der Schwelle der bräutlichen Kammer!
Aber über dem Stummen erwacht
Lauter, unermeßlicher Jammer.

Ein zweiter.

Wir kommen, wir kommen,

Mit festlichem Prangen   1950
Die Braut zu empfangen,
Es bringen die Knaben
Die reichen Gewande, die bräutlichen Gaben,
Das Fest ist bereitet, es warten die Zeugen;
Aber der Bräutigam höret nicht mehr,   1955
Nimmer erweckt ihn der fröhliche Reigen,
Denn der Schlummer der Toten ist schwer.

Ganzer Chor.

Schwer und tief ist der Schlummer der Toten,
Nimmer erweckt ihn die Stimme der Braut,
Nimmer des Hifthorns fröhlicher Laut,   1960
Starr und fühllos liegt er am Boden!

Ein dritter.

Was sind Hoffnungen, was sind Entwürfe,
Die der Mensch, der vergängliche, baut?
Heute umarmtet ihr euch als Brüder,
Einig gestimmt mit Herzen und Munde,   1965
Diese Sonne, die jetzo nieder
Geht, sie leuchtete eurem Bunde!
Und jetzt liegst du, dem Staube vermählt,
Von des Brudermords Händen entseelt,
In dem Busen die gräßliche Wunde!   1970
Was sind Hoffnungen, was sind Entwürfe,
Die der Mensch, der flüchtige Sohn der Stunde,
Aufbaut auf dem betrüglichen Grunde?

Chor.

Zu der Mutter will ich dich tragen,
Eine unbeglückende Last!   1975
Diese Zypresse laßt uns zerschlagen

Mit der mörderischen Schneide der Axt,
Eine Bahre zu flechten aus ihren Zweigen;
Nimmer soll sie Lebendiges zeugen,
Die die tödliche Frucht getragen,   1980
Nimmer in fröhlichem Wuchs sich erheben,
Keinem Wandrer mehr Schatten geben;
Die sich genährt auf des Mordes Boden,
Soll verflucht sein zum Dienst der Toten!

Erster.

Aber wehe dem Mörder, wehe,   1985
Der dahingeht in törichtem Mut!
Hinab, hinab in der Erde Ritzen
Rinnet, rinnet, rinnet dein Blut.
Drunten aber im Tiefen sitzen
Lichtlos, ohne Gesang und Sprache,   1990
Der Themis Töchter, die nie vergessen,
Die Untrüglichen, die mit Gerechtigkeit messen,
Fangen es auf in schwarzen Gefäßen,
Rühren und mengen die schreckliche Rache.

Zweiter.

Leicht verschwindet der Taten Spur   1995
Von der sonnenbeleuchteten Erde,
Wie aus dem Antlitz die leichte Gebärde —
Aber nichts ist verloren und verschwunden,
Was die geheimnisvoll waltenden Stunden
In den dunkel schaffenden Schoß aufnahmen —   2000
Die Zeit ist eine blühende Flur,
Ein großes Lebendiges ist die Natur,
Und alles ist Frucht, und alles ist Samen.

Dritter.

Wehe, wehe dem Mörder, wehe,

Der sich gesät die tödliche Saat!   2005
Ein andres Antlitz, eh' sie geschehen,
Ein anderes zeigt die vollbrachte Tat.
Mutvoll blickt sie und kühn dir entgegen,
Wenn der Rache Gefühle den Busen bewegen,
Aber ist sie geschehn und begangen,   2010
Blickt sie dich an mit erbleichenden Wangen.
Selber die schrecklichen Furien schwangen
Gegen Orestes die höllischen Schlangen,
Reizten den Sohn zu dem Muttermord an;
Mit der Gerechtigkeit heiligen Zügen   2015
Wußten sie listig sein Herz zu betrügen,
Bis er die tödliche Tat nun getan —
Aber, da er den Schoß jetzt geschlagen,
Der ihn empfangen und liebend getragen,
Siehe, da kehrten sie   2020
Gegen ihn selber
Schrecklich sich um —
Und er erkannte die furchtbaren Jungfraun,
Die den Mörder ergreifend fassen,
Die von jetzt an ihn nimmer lassen,   2025
Die ihn mit ewigem Schlangenbiß nagen,
Die von Meer zu Meer ihn ruhelos jagen
Bis in das Delphische Heiligtum.
(Der Chor geht ab, den Leichnam Don Manuels auf einer Bahre tragend.)

Vierter Aufzug.

Erster Auftritt.

Die Säulenhalle. — Es ist Nacht; die Szene ist von oben herab durch eine große Lampe erleuchtet.

Donna Isabella und Diego treten auf.

Isabella.

Noch keine Kunde kam von meinen Söhnen,
Ob eine Spur sich fand von der Verlornen? 2030

Diego.

Noch nichts, Gebieterin — doch hoffe alles
Von deiner Söhne Ernst und Emsigkeit.

Isabella.

Wie ist mein Herz geängstiget, Diego!
Es stand bei mir, dies Unglück zu verhüten.

Diego.

Drück' nicht des Vorwurfs Stachel in dein Herz: 2035
An welcher Vorsicht ließest du's ermangeln?

Isabella.

Hätt' ich sie früher an das Licht gezogen,
Wie mich des Herzens Stimme mächtig trieb!

Diego.

Die Klugheit wehrte dir's, du tatest weise,
Doch der Erfolg ruht in des Himmels Hand. 2040

Isabella.

Ach, so ist keine Freude rein! Mein Glück
Wär' ein vollkommnes ohne diesen Zufall!

Diego.

Dies Glück ist nur verzögert, nicht zerstört,
Genieße du jetzt deiner Söhne Frieden.

Isabella.

Ich habe sie einander Herz an Herz   2045
Umarmen sehn — ein nie erlebter Anblick!

Diego.

Und nicht ein Schauspiel bloß, es ging von Herzen,
Denn ihr Geradsinn haßt der Lüge Zwang.

Isabella.

Ich seh' auch, daß sie zärtlicher Gefühle,
Der schönen Neigung fähig sind; mit Wonne   2050
Entdeck' ich, daß sie ehren, was sie lieben.
Der ungebundnen Freiheit wollen sie
Entsagen, nicht dem Zügel des Gesetzes
Entzieht sich ihre brausend wilde Jugend,
Und sittlich selbst blieb ihre Leidenschaft.   2055
— Ich will dir's jetzo gern gestehn, Diego,
Daß ich mit Sorge diesem Augenblick,
Der aufgeschloßnen Blume des Gefühls
Mit banger Furcht entgegensah — Die Liebe
Wird leicht zur Wut in heftigen Naturen.   2060
Wenn in den aufgehäuften Feuerzunder
Des alten Hasses auch noch dieser Blitz,
Der Eifersucht feindsel'ge Flamme schlug —
Mir schaudert, es zu denken — ihr Gefühl,
Das niemals einig war, gerade hier   2065
Zum erstenmal unselig sich begegnet —

Wohl mir! Auch diese donnerschwere Wolke,
Die über mir schwarz drohend niederhing,
Sie führte mir ein Engel still vorüber,
Und leicht nun atmet die befreite Brust. 2070

Diego.

Ja, freue deines Werkes dich. Du hast
Mit zartem Sinn und ruhigem Verstand
Vollendet, was der Vater nicht vermochte
Mit aller seiner Herrschermacht — Dein ist
Der Ruhm, doch auch dein Glücksstern ist zu loben! 2075

Isabella.

Vieles gelang mir! Viel auch tat das Glück!
Nichts Kleines war es, solche Heimlichkeit
Verhüllt zu tragen diese langen Jahre,
Den Mann zu täuschen, den umsichtigsten
Der Menschen, und ins Herz zurückzudrängen 2080
Den Trieb des Bluts, der mächtig, wie des Feuers
Verschloßner Gott, aus seinen Banden strebte!

Diego.

Ein Pfand ist mir des Glückes lange Gunst,
Daß alles sich erfreulich lösen wird.

Isabella.

Ich will nicht eher meine Sterne loben, 2085
Bis ich das Ende dieser Taten sah.
Daß mir der böse Genius nicht schlummert,
Erinnert warnend mich der Tochter Flucht.
— Schilt oder lobe meine Tat, Diego!
Doch dem Getreuen will ich nichts verbergen. 2090
Nicht tragen konnt' ich's, hier in müß'ger Ruh
Zu harren des Erfolgs, indes die Söhne
Geschäftig forschen nach der Tochter Spur.

Gehandelt hab' auch ich — Wo Menschenkunst
Nicht zureicht, hat der Himmel oft geraten.   2095

Diego.

Entdecke mir, was mir zu wissen ziemt.

Isabella.

Einsiedelnd auf des Ätna Höhen haust
Ein frommer Klausner, von uralters her
Der Greis genannt des Berges, welcher, näher
Dem Himmel wohnend als der andern Menschen   2100
Tief wandelndes Geschlecht, den irdʼschen Sinn
In leichter, reiner Ätherluft geläutert,
Und von dem Berg der aufgewälzten Jahre
Hinabsieht in das aufgelöste Spiel
Des unverständlich krummgewundnen Lebens.   2105
Nicht fremd ist ihm das Schicksal meines Hauses,
Oft hat der heilʼge Mann für uns den Himmel
Gefragt und manchen Fluch hinweg gebetet.
Zu ihm hinauf gesandt habʼ ich alsbald
Des raschen Boten jugendliche Kraft,   2110
Daß er mir Kunde von der Tochter gebe,
Und stündlich harrʼ ich dessen Wiederkehr.

Diego.

Trügt mich mein Auge nicht, Gebieterin,
So istʼs derselbe, der dort eilend naht,
Und Lob fürwahr verdient der Emsige!   2115

Zweiter Auftritt.

Bote. Die Vorigen.

Isabella.

Sagʼ an und weder Schlimmes hehle mir

Noch Gutes, sondern schöpfe rein die Wahrheit.
Was gab der Greis des Bergs dir zum Bescheide?

Bote.

Ich soll mich schnell zurückbegeben, war
Die Antwort, die Verlorne sei gefunden.　　　　　　2120

Isabella.

Glückfel'ger Mund, erfreulich Himmelswort,
Stets hast du das Erwünschte mir verkündet!
Und welchem meiner Söhne war's verliehen,
Die Spur zu finden der Verlorenen?

Bote.

Die Tiefverborgne fand dein ältster Sohn.　　　　　2125

Isabella.

Don Manuel ist es, dem ich sie verdanke!
Ach, stets war dieser mir ein Kind des Segens!
— Hast du dem Greis auch die geweihte Kerze
Gebracht, die zum Geschenk ich ihm gesendet,
Sie anzuzünden seinem Heiligen?　　　　　　　　2130
Denn was von Gaben sonst der Menschen Herzen
Erfreut, verschmäht der fromme Gottesdiener.

Bote.

Die Kerze nahm er schweigend von mir an,
Und zum Altar hintretend, wo die Lampe
Dem Heil'gen brannte, zündet' er sie flugs　　　　　2135
Dort an, und schnell in Brand steckt' er die Hütte,
Worin er Gott verehrt seit neunzig Jahren.

Isabella.

Was sagst du? Welches Schrecknis nennst du mir?

Bote.

Und dreimal Wehe! Wehe! rufend, stieg er

Herab vom Berg, mir aber winkt' er schweigend,　　2140
Ihm nicht zu folgen noch zurückzuschauen.
Und so, gejagt von Grausen, eilt' ich her!

Isabella.

In neuer Zweifel wogende Bewegung
Und ängstlich schwankende Verworrenheit
Stürzt mich das Widersprechende zurück.　　2145
Gefunden sei mir die verlorne Tochter
Von meinem ältsten Sohn, Don Manuel?
Die gute Rede kann mir nicht gedeihen,
Begleitet von der unglücksel'gen Tat.

Bote.

Blick' hinter dich, Gebieterin! Du siehst　　2150
Des Klausners Wort erfüllt vor deinen Augen,
Denn alles müßt' mich trügen, oder dies
Ist die verlorne Tochter, die du suchst,
Von deiner Söhne Ritterschar begleitet.

(Beatrice wird von dem zweiten Halbchor auf einem Tragsessel gebracht
und auf der vordern Bühne niedergesetzt. Sie ist noch ohne Leben und
Bewegung.)

Dritter Auftritt.

Isabella. Diego. Bote. Beatrice. Chor.

Chor.

Des Herrn Geheiß erfüllend, setzen wir　　2155
Die Jungfrau hier zu deinen Füßen nieder,
Gebieterin — Also befahl er uns
Zu tun und dir zu melden dieses Wort:
Es sei dein Sohn Don Cesar, der sie sende!

Isabella

(ist mit ausgebreiteten Armen auf sie zugeeilt und tritt mit Schrecken zurück).

O Himmel! Sie ist bleich und ohne Leben!   2160

Chor.

Sie lebt! Sie wird erwachen! Gönn' ihr Zeit,
Von dem Erstaunlichen sich zu erholen,
Das ihre Geister noch gebunden hält.

Isabella.

Mein Kind! Kind meiner Schmerzen, meiner Sorgen!
So sehen wir uns wieder! So mußt du   2165
Den Einzug halten in des Vaters Haus!
O laß an meinem Leben mich das deinige
Anzünden! An die mütterliche Brust
Will ich dich pressen, bis, vom Todesfrost
Gelöst, die warmen Adern wieder schlagen!   2170
(Zum Chor.)
O sprich! Welch Schreckliches ist hier geschehn?
Wo fandst du sie? Wie kam das teure Kind
In diesen kläglich jammervollen Zustand?

Chor.

Erfahr es nicht von mir, mein Mund ist stumm.
Dein Sohn Don Cesar wird dir alles deutlich   2175
Verkündigen, denn er ist's, der sie sendet.

Isabella.

Mein Sohn Don Manuel, so willst du sagen?

Chor.

Dein Sohn Don Cesar sendet sie dir zu.

Isabella (zu dem Boten).

War's nicht Don Manuel, den der Seher nannte?

Bote.

So ist es, Herrin, das war seine Rede. 2180

Isabella.

Welcher es sei, er hat mein Herz erfreut,
Die Tochter dank' ich ihm, er sei gesegnet!
O muß ein neid'scher Dämon mir die Wonne
Des heiß erflehten Augenblicks verbittern!
Ankämpfen muß ich gegen mein Entzücken! 2185
Die Tochter seh' ich in des Vaters Haus,
Sie aber sieht nicht mich, vernimmt mich nicht,
Sie kann der Mutter Freude nicht erwidern.
O öffnet euch, ihr lieben Augenlichter!
Erwärmet euch, ihr Hände! Hebe dich, 2190
Lebloser Busen, und schlage der Lust!
Diego! Das ist meine Tochter — Das
Die lang' Verborgne, die Gerettete,
Vor aller Welt kann ich sie jetzt erkennen!

Chor.

Ein seltsam neues Schrecknis glaub' ich ahnend 2195
Vor mir zu sehn und stehe wundernd, wie
Das Irrsal sich entwirren soll und lösen.

Isabella
(zum Chor, der Bestürzung und Verlegenheit ausdrückt).

O, ihr seid undurchdringlich harte Herzen!
Vom ehrnen Harnisch eurer Brust, gleichwie
Von einem schroffen Meeresfelsen, schlägt 2200
Die Freude meines Herzens mir zurück!
Umsonst in diesem ganzen Kreis umher
Späh' ich nach einem Auge, das empfindet.
Wo weilen meine Söhne, daß ich Anteil
In einem Auge lese, denn mir ist, 2205

Als ob der Wüste unmitleid'ge Scharen,
Des Meeres Ungeheuer mich umständen.

Diego.

Sie schlägt die Augen auf! Sie regt sich, lebt!

Isabella.

Sie lebt! Ihr erster Blick sei auf die Mutter!

Diego.

Das Auge schließt sie schaudernd wieder zu.　　　2210

Isabella (zum Chor).

Weiche zurück! Sie schreckt der fremde Anblick.

Chor (tritt zurück).

Gern meid' ich's, ihrem Blicke zu begegnen.

Diego.

Mit großen Augen mißt sie staunend dich.

Beatrice.

Wo bin ich? Diese Züge sollt' ich kennen.

Isabella.

Langsam kehrt die Besinnung ihr zurück.　　　2215

Diego.

Was macht sie? Auf die Kniee senkt sie sich.

Beatrice.

O schönes Engelsantlitz meiner Mutter!

Isabella.

Kind meines Herzens! Komm in meine Arme!

Beatrice.

Zu deinen Füßen sieh die Schuldige.

Isabella.

Ich habe dich wieder! Alles sei vergessen!　　　2220

Diego.

Betracht' auch mich! Erkennst du meine Züge?

Beatrice.

Des redlichen Diego greises Haupt!

Isabella.

Der treue Wächter deiner Kinderjahre.

Beatrice.

So bin ich wieder in dem Schoß der Meinen?

Isabella.

Und nichts soll uns mehr scheiden als der Tod. 2225

Beatrice.

Du willst mich nicht mehr in die Fremde stoßen?

Isabella.

Nichts trennt uns mehr, das Schicksal ist befriedigt.

Beatrice (sinkt an ihre Brust).

Und sind' ich wirklich mich an deinem Herzen?
Und alles war ein Traum, was ich erlebte?
Ein schwerer, fürchterlicher Traum — O Mutter! 2230
Ich sah ihn tot zu meinen Füßen fallen!
— Wie komm' ich aber hieher? Ich besinne
Mich nicht — Ach, wohl mir, wohl, daß ich gerettet
In deinen Armen bin! Sie wollten mich
Zur Fürstin Mutter von Messina bringen. 2235
Eher ins Grab!

Isabella.

              Komm zu dir, meine Tochter!
Messinas Fürstin —

              Beatrice.

              Nenne sie nicht mehr!
Mir gießt sich bei dem unglücksel'gen Namen
Ein Frost des Todes durch die Glieder.

Isabella.

                              Höre mich.

Beatrice.

Sie hat zwei Söhne, die sich tödlich haſſen,   2240
Don Manuel, Don Ceſar nennt man ſie.

Iſabella.

Ich bin's ja ſelbſt! Erkenne deine Mutter!

Beatrice.

Was ſagſt du? Welches Wort haſt du geredet?

Iſabella.

Ich, deine Mutter, bin Meſſinas Fürſtin.

Beatrice.

Du biſt Don Manuels Mutter und Don Ceſars? 2245

Iſabella.

Und deine Mutter! Deine Brüder nennſt du!

Beatrice.

Weh, weh mir! O entſetzensvolles Licht!

Iſabella.

Was iſt dir? Was erſchüttert dich ſo ſeltſam?

Beatrice
(wild um ſich her ſchauend, erblickt den Chor).

Das ſind ſie, ja! Jetzt, jetzt erkenn' ich ſie.
Mich hat kein Traum getäuſcht — Die ſind's! Die waren
Zugegen — Es iſt fürchterliche Wahrheit!   2251
Unglückliche, wo habt ihr ihn verborgen?

(Sie geht mit heftigem Schritt auf den Chor zu, der ſich von ihr
abwendet. Ein Trauermarſch läßt ſich in der Ferne hören.)

Chor.

Weh! Wehe!

Iſabella.

Wen verborgen? Was iſt wahr?
Ihr ſchweigt beſtürzt — ihr ſcheint ſie zu verſtehen.
Ich leſ' in euren Augen, eurer Stimme   2255

Gebrochnen Tönen etwas Unglückſel'ges,
Das mir zurückgehalten wird — Was iſt's?
Ich will es wiſſen. Warum heftet ihr
So ſchreckenvolle Blicke nach der Türe?
Und was für Töne hör' ich da erſchallen?   2260

Chor.

Es naht ſich! Es wird ſich mit Schrecken erklären.
Sei ſtark, Gebieterin, ſtähle dein Herz.
Mit Faſſung ertrage, was dich erwartet,
Mit männlicher Seele den tödlichen Schmerz!

Iſabella.

Was naht ſich? Was erwartet mich? — Ich höre 2265
Der Totenklage fürchterlichen Ton
Das Haus durchdringen — Wo ſind meine Söhne?

(Der erſte Halbchor bringt den Leichnam Don Manuels auf einer Bahre
getragen, die er auf der leer gelaſſenen Seite der Szene niederſetzt. Ein
ſchwarzes Tuch iſt darüber gebreitet.)

Vierter Auftritt.

Iſabella. Beatrice. Diego. Beide Chöre.

Erſter Chor.

Durch die Straßen der Städte,
Vom Jammer gefolget,
Schreitet das Unglück —   2270
Lauernd umſchleicht es
Die Häuſer der Menſchen,
Heute an dieſer
Pforte pocht es,
Morgen an jener,   2275

B.   7

Aber noch keinen hat es verschont.
Die unerwünschte
Schmerzliche Botschaft
Früher oder später
Bestellt es an jeder   2280
Schwelle, wo ein Lebendiger wohnt.
    Wenn die Blätter fallen
In des Jahres Kreise,
Wenn zum Grabe wallen
Entnervte Greise,   2285
Da gehorcht die Natur
Ruhig nur
Ihrem alten Gesetze,
Ihrem ewigen Brauch,
Da ist nichts, was den Menschen entsetze!   2290
    Aber das Ungeheure auch
Lerne erwarten im irdischen Leben!
Mit gewaltsamer Hand
Löset der Mord auch das heiligste Band,
In sein stygisches Boot   2295
Raffet der Tod
Auch der Jugend blühendes Leben!
Wenn die Wolken getürmt den Himmel schwärzen,
Wenn dumpftosend der Donner hallt,
Da, da fühlen sich alle Herzen   2300
In des furchtbaren Schicksals Gewalt.
Aber auch aus entwölkter Höhe
Kann der zündende Donner schlagen,
Darum in deinen fröhlichen Tagen
Fürchte des Unglücks tückische Nähe.   2305
Nicht an die Güter hänge dein Herz,

Die das Leben vergänglich zieren,
Wer besitzt, der lerne verlieren,
Wer im Glück ist, der lerne den Schmerz.

Isabella.

Was soll ich hören? Was verhüllt dies Tuch?　　2310
(Sie macht einen Schritt gegen die Bahre, bleibt aber unschlüssig
zaudernd stehen.)
Es zieht mich grausend hin und zieht mich schaudernd
Mit dunkler kalter Schreckenshand zurück.
(Zu Beatricen, welche sich zwischen sie und die Bahre geworfen.)
Laß mich! Was es auch sei, ich will's enthüllen!
(Sie hebt das Tuch auf und entdeckt Don Manuels Leichnam.)
O himmlische Mächte, es ist mein Sohn!
(Sie bleibt mit starrem Entsetzen stehen — Beatrice sinkt mit einem
Schrei des Schmerzens neben der Bahre nieder.)

Chor.

Unglückliche Mutter! Es ist dein Sohn!　　2315
Du hast es gesprochen, das Wort des Jammers,
Nicht meinen Lippen ist es entflohn.

Isabella.

Mein Sohn! Mein Manuel! — O ewige
Erbarmung — So muß ich dich wiederfinden!
Mit deinem Leben mußtest du die Schwester　　2320
Erkaufen aus des Räubers Hand! — Wo war
Dein Bruder, daß sein Arm dich nicht beschützte?
— O Fluch der Hand, die diese Wunde grub!
Fluch ihr, die den Verderblichen geboren,
Der mir den Sohn erschlug! Fluch seinem ganzen　　2325
Geschlecht!

Chor.

Weh! Wehe! Wehe! Wehe!

Isabella.

So haltet ihr mir Wort, ihr Himmelsmächte?
Das, das ist eure Wahrheit? Wehe dem,
Der euch vertraut mit redlichem Gemüt!
Worauf hab' ich gehofft, wovor gezittert,   2330
Wenn dies der Ausgang ist — O, die ihr hier
Mich schreckenvoll umsteht, an meinem Schmerz
Die Blicke weidend, lernt die Lügen kennen,
Womit die Träume uns, die Seher täuschen!
Glaube noch einer an der Götter Mund!   2335
— Als ich mich Mutter fühlte dieser Tochter,
Da träumte ihrem Vater eines Tags,
Er säh' aus seinem hochzeitlichen Bette
Zwei Lorbeerbäume wachsen — Zwischen ihnen
Wuchs eine Lilie empor, sie ward   2340
Zur Flamme, die der Bäume dicht Gezweig ergriff
Und, um sich wütend, schnell das ganze Haus
In ungeheurer Feuerflut verschlang.
Erschreckt von diesem seltsamen Gesichte,
Befrug der Vater einen Vogelschauer   2345
Und schwarzen Magier um die Bedeutung.
Der Magier erklärte: wenn mein Schoß
Von einer Tochter sich entbinden würde,
So würde sie die beiden Söhne ihm
Ermorden und vertilgen seinen Stamm!   2350

Chor.

Gebieterin, was sagst du? Wehe! Wehe!

Isabella.

Darum befahl der Vater, sie zu töten,
Doch ich entrückte sie dem Jammerschicksal!
— Die arme Unglückselige! Verstoßen

Ward sie als Kind aus ihrer Mutter Schoß,　　2355
Daß sie, erwachsen, nicht die Brüder morde!
Und jetzt durch Räubershände fällt der Bruder,
Nicht die Unschuldige hat ihn getötet!

Chor.
Weh! Wehe! Wehe! Wehe!

Isabella.
　　　　　　　　Keinen Glauben
Verdiente mir des Götzendieners Spruch,　　2360
Ein beßres Hoffen stärkte meine Seele.
Denn mir verkündigte ein andrer Mund,
Den ich für wahrhaft hielt, von dieser Tochter:
„In heißer Liebe würde sie dereinst
Der Söhne Herzen mir vereinigen."　　2365
— So widersprachen die Orakel sich,
Den Fluch zugleich und Segen auf das Haupt
Der Tochter legend — Nicht den Fluch hat sie
Verschuldet, die Unglückliche! Nicht Zeit
Ward ihr gegönnt, den Segen zu vollziehen,　　2370
Ein Mund hat wie der andere gelogen!
Die Kunst der Seher ist ein eitles Nichts,
Betrüger sind sie, oder sind betrogen.
Nichts Wahres läßt sich von der Zukunft wissen,
Du schöpfest drunten an der Hölle Flüssen,　　2375
Du schöpfest droben an dem Quell des Lichts.

Erster Chor.
Weh! Wehe! Was sagt du? Halt ein, halt ein!
Bezähme der Zunge verwegenes Toben!
Die Orakel sehen und treffen ein,
Der Ausgang wird die Wahrhaftigen loben!　　2380

Isabella.

Nicht zähmen will ich meine Zunge, laut,
Wie mir das Herz gebietet, will ich reden.
Warum besuchen wir die heil'gen Häuser
Und heben zu dem Himmel fromme Hände?
Gutmüt'ge Toren, was gewinnen wir　　　　　　2385
Mit unserm Glauben?　So unmöglich ist's,
Die Götter, die hochwohnenden, zu treffen
Als in den Mond mit einem Pfeil zu schießen.
Vermauert ist dem Sterblichen die Zukunft,
Und kein Gebet durchbohrt den ehrnen Himmel.　2390
Ob rechts die Vögel fliegen oder links,
Die Sterne so sich oder anders fügen —
Nicht Sinn ist in dem Buche der Natur,
Die Traumkunst träumt, und alle Zeichen trügen.

Zweiter Chor.

Halt ein, Unglückliche!　Wehe!　Wehe!　　　　2395
Du leugnest der Sonne leuchtendes Licht
Mit blinden Augen!　Die Götter leben,
Erkenne sie, die dich furchtbar umgeben!

Beatrice.

O Mutter!　Mutter!　Warum hast du mich
Gerettet!　Warum warfst du mich nicht hin　　　2400
Dem Fluch, der, eh' ich war, mich schon verfolgte?
Blödsicht'ge Mutter!　Warum dünktest du
Dich weiser, als die alles Schauenden,
Die Nah und Fernes aneinanderknüpfen
Und in der Zukunft späte Saaten sehn?　　　　2405
Dir selbst und mir, uns allen zum Verderben
Hast du den Todesgöttern ihren Raub,
Den sie gefordert, frevelnd vorenthalten!

Jetzt nehmen sie ihn zweifach, dreifach selbst.
Nicht dank' ich dir das traurige Geschenk,   2410
Dem Schmerz, dem Jammer hast du mich erhalten!

Erster Chor
(in heftiger Bewegung nach der Türe sehend).

Brechet auf, ihr Wunden!
Fließet, fließet!
In schwarzen Güssen
Stürzet hervor, ihr Bäche des Bluts.   2415
    Eherner Füße
Rauschen vernehm' ich,
Höllischer Schlangen
Zischendes Tönen,
Ich erkenne der Furien Schritt!   2420
    Stürzet ein, ihr Wände!
Versink, o Schwelle,
Unter der schrecklichen Füße Tritt!
Schwarze Dämpfe, entsteiget, entsteiget
Qualmend dem Abgrund! Verschlinget des Tages   2425
Lieblichen Schein!
Schützende Götter des Hauses, entweichet,
Lasset die rächenden Göttinnen ein!

Fünfter Auftritt.

Don Cesar. Isabella. Beatrice. Der Chor.

Beim Eintritt des Don Cesar zerteilt sich der Chor in fliehender Bewegung
vor ihm, er bleibt allein in der Mitte der Szene stehen.

Beatrice.

Weh mir, er ist's!

Isabella (tritt ihm entgegen).

        O mein Sohn Cesar! Muß ich so

Dich wiederſehen — O blick' her und ſieh   2430
Den Frevel einer gottverfluchten Hand!
(Führt ihn zu dem Leichnam.)

Don Ceſar
(tritt mit Entſetzen zurück, das Geſicht verhüllend).

Erſter Chor.

Brechet auf, ihr Wunden!
Fließet, fließet!
In ſchwarzen Güſſen
Strömet hervor, ihr Bäche des Bluts!   2435

Iſabella.

Du ſchauderſt und erſtarrſt! — Ja, das iſt alles,
Was dir noch übrig iſt von deinem Bruder!
Da liegen meine Hoffnungen — Sie ſtirbt
Im Keim, die junge Blume eures Friedens,
Und keine ſchöne Früchte ſollt' ich ſchauen.   2440

Don Ceſar.

Tröſte dich, Mutter. Redlich wollten wir
Den Frieden, aber Blut beſchloß der Himmel.

Iſabella.

O ich weiß, du liebteſt ihn, ich ſah entzückt
Die ſchönen Bande zwiſchen euch ſich flechten!
An deinem Herzen wollteſt du ihn tragen,   2445
Ihm reich erſetzen die verlornen Jahre.
Der blut'ge Mord kam deiner ſchönen Liebe
Zuvor — jetzt kannſt du nichts mehr, als ihn rächen.

Don Ceſar.

Komm, Mutter, komm! hier iſt kein Ort für dich,
Entreiß dich dieſem unglückſel'gen Anblick!   2450
(Er will ſie fortziehen.)

Isabella (fällt ihm um den Hals).

Du lebst mir noch! Du jetzt mein einziger!

Beatrice.

Weh, Mutter! Was beginnst du?

Don Cesar.

Weine dich aus

An diesem treuen Busen. Unverloren
Ist dir der Sohn, denn seine Liebe lebt
Unsterblich fort in deines Cesars Brust.   2455

Erster Chor.

Brechet auf, ihr Wunden!
Redet, ihr stummen!
In schwarzen Fluten
Stürzet hervor, ihr Bäche des Bluts.

Isabella (beider Hände fassend).

O meine Kinder!

Don Cesar.

Wie entzückt es mich,   2460
In deinen Armen sie zu sehen, Mutter!
Ja, laß sie deine Tochter sein! die Schwester —

Isabella (unterbricht ihn).

Dir dank' ich die Gerettete, mein Sohn!
Du hieltest Wort, du hast sie mir gesendet.

Don Cesar (erstaunt).

Wen, Mutter, sagst du, hab' ich dir gesendet?   2465

Isabella.

Sie mein' ich, die du vor dir siehst, die Schwester.

Don Cesar.

Sie meine Schwester!

Isabella.

Welche andre sonst?

Don Cesar.
Meine Schwester?

Isabella.
Die du selber mir gesendet.

Don Cesar.
Und seine Schwester!

Chor.
Wehe! Wehe! Wehe!

Beatrice.
O meine Mutter!

Isabella.
Ich erstaune — Redet! 2470

Don Cesar.
So sei der Tag verflucht, der mich geboren!

Isabella.
Was ist dir? Gott!

Don Cesar.
Verflucht der Schoß, der mich
Getragen! — Und verflucht sei deine Heimlichkeit,
Die all dies Gräßliche verschuldet! Falle
Der Donner nieder, der dein Herz zerschmettert, 2475
Nicht länger halt' ich schonend ihn zurück —
Ich selber, wiss' es, ich erschlug den Bruder,
In ihren Armen überrascht' ich ihn,
Sie ist es, die ich liebe, die zur Braut
Ich mir gewählt — den Bruder aber fand ich 2480
In ihren Armen — alles weißt du nun!
— Ist sie wahrhaftig seine, meine Schwester,
So bin ich schuldig einer Greueltat,
Die keine Reu' und Büßung kann versöhnen!

Chor.
Es ist gesprochen, du hast es vernommen, 2485

Das Schlimmste weißt du, nichts ist mehr zurück!
Wie die Seher verkündet, so ist es gekommen,
Denn noch niemand entfloh dem verhängten Geschick.
Und wer sich vermißt, es klüglich zu wenden,
Der muß es selber erbauend vollenden.   2490

Isabella.

Was kümmert's mich noch, ob die Götter sich
Als Lügner zeigen, oder sich als wahr
Bestätigen? Mir haben sie das Ärgste
Getan — Trotz biet' ich ihnen, mich noch härter
Zu treffen, als sie trafen — Wer für nichts mehr   2495
Zu zittern hat, der fürchtet sie nicht mehr.
Ermordet liegt mir der geliebte Sohn,
Und von dem lebenden scheid' ich mich selbst.
Er ist mein Sohn nicht — Einen Basilisken
Hab' ich erzeugt, genährt an meiner Brust,   2500
Der mir den bessern Sohn zu Tode stach.
— Komm, meine Tochter! Hier ist unsers Bleibens
Nicht mehr — den Rachegeistern überlaß' ich
Dies Haus — Ein Frevel führte mich herein,
Ein Frevel treibt mich aus — Mit Widerwillen   2505
Hab' ich's betreten und mit Furcht bewohnt,
Und in Verzweiflung räum' ich's — Alles dies
Erleid' ich schuldlos — doch bei Ehren bleiben
Die Orakel, und gerettet sind die Götter.

(Sie geht ab. Diego folgt ihr.)

Sechster Auftritt.

Beatrice. Don Cesar. Der Chor.

Don Cesar (Beatricen zurückhaltend).

Bleib, Schwester! Scheide du nicht so von mir!   2510

Mag mir die Mutter fluchen, mag dies Blut
Anklagend gegen mich zum Himmel rufen,
Mich alle Welt verdammen! Aber du
Fluche mir nicht! Von dir kann ich's nicht tragen.

Beatrice
(zeigt mit abgewandtem Gesicht auf den Leichnam).

Don Cesar.
Nicht den Geliebten hab' ich dir getötet!   2515
Den Bruder hab' ich dir und hab' ihn mir
Gemordet — dir gehört der Abgeschiedne jetzt
Nicht näher an als ich, der Lebende,
Und ich bin mitleidswürdiger als er,
Denn er schied rein hinweg, und ich bin schuldig.   2520

Beatrice (bricht in heftige Tränen aus).

Don Cesar.
Weine um den Bruder, ich will mit dir weinen,
Und mehr noch — rächen will ich ihn! Doch nicht
Um den Geliebten weine! Diesen Vorzug,
Den du dem Toten gibst, ertrag' ich nicht.
Den einz'gen Trost, den letzten, laß mich schöpfen   2525
Aus unsers Jammers bodenloser Tiefe,
Daß er dir näher nicht gehört als ich —
Denn unser furchtbar aufgelöstes Schicksal
Macht unsre Rechte gleich, wie unser Unglück.
In einen Fall verstrickt, drei liebende   2530
Geschwister, gehen wir vereinigt unter
Und teilen gleich der Tränen traurig Recht.
Doch wenn ich denken muß, daß deine Trauer
Mehr dem Geliebten als dem Bruder gilt,
Dann mischt sich Wut und Neid in meinen Schmerz,   2535

Und mich verläßt der Wehmut letzter Trost.
Nicht freudig, wie ich gerne will, kann ich
Das letzte Opfer seinen Manen bringen,
Doch sanft nachsenden will ich ihm die Seele,
Weiß ich nur, daß du meinen Staub mit seinem   2540
In einem Aschenkruge sammeln wirst.

(Den Arm um sie schlingend, mit einer leidenschaftlich zärtlichen Heftigkeit.)

Dich liebt' ich, wie ich nichts zuvor geliebt,
Da du noch eine Fremde für mich warst.
Weil ich dich liebte über alle Grenzen,
Trag' ich den schweren Fluch des Brudermords,   2545
Liebe zu dir war meine ganze Schuld.
— Jetzt bist du meine Schwester, und dein Mitleid
Fordr' ich von dir als einen heil'gen Zoll.

(Er sieht sie mit ausforschenden Blicken und schmerzlicher Erwartung
an, dann wendet er sich mit Heftigkeit von ihr.)

Nein, nein, nicht sehen kann ich diese Tränen —
In dieses Toten Gegenwart verläßt   2550
Der Mut mich, und die Brust zerreißt der Zweifel —
— Laß mich im Irrtum! Weine im Verborgnen!
Sieh nie mich wieder — niemals mehr — Nicht dich,
Nicht deine Mutter will ich wieder sehen,
Sie hat mich nie geliebt! Verraten endlich   2555
Hat sich ihr Herz, der Schmerz hat es geöffnet.
Sie nannt' ihn ihren bessern Sohn! — So hat sie
Verstellung ausgeübt ihr ganzes Leben!
— Und du bist falsch wie sie! Zwinge dich nicht!
Zeig' deinen Abscheu! Mein verhaßtes Antlitz   2560
Sollst du nicht wieder sehn! Geh hin auf ewig!

(Er geht ab. Sie steht unschlüssig, im Kampf widersprechender Gefühle,
dann reißt sie sich los und geht.)

Siebenter Auftritt.

Chor.

———— ———— ———— ———— ———— ————

Wohl dem! Selig muß ich ihn preisen,
Der in der Stille der ländlichen Flur,
Fern von des Lebens verworrenen Kreisen,
Kindlich liegt an der Brust der Natur.   2565
Denn das Herz wird mir schwer in der Fürsten Palästen,
Wenn ich herab vom Gipfel des Glücks
Stürzen sehe die Höchsten, die Besten
In der Schnelle des Augenblicks!
    Und auch der hat sich wohl gebettet,   2570
Der aus der stürmischen Lebenswelle,
Zeitig gewarnt, sich heraus gerettet
In des Klosters friedliche Zelle.
Der die stachelnde Sucht der Ehren
Von sich warf und die eitle Lust,   2575
Und die Wünsche, die ewig begehren,
Eingeschläfert in ruhiger Brust,
Ihn ergreift in dem Lebensgewühle
Nicht der Leidenschaft wilde Gewalt,
Nimmer in seinem stillen Asyle   2580
Sieht er der Menschheit traur'ge Gestalt.
Nur in bestimmter Höhe ziehet
Das Verbrechen hin und das Ungemach,
Wie die Pest die erhabenen Orte fliehet,
Dem Qualm der Städte wälzt es sich nach.   2585
Auf den Bergen ist Freiheit! Der Hauch der Grüfte
Steigt nicht hinauf in die reinen Lüfte:
Die Welt ist vollkommen überall,
Wo der Mensch nicht hinkommt mit seiner Qual.

Achter Auftritt.

Don Cesar.　Der Chor.

Don Cesar (gefaßter).

Das Recht des Herrschers üb' ich aus zum letztenmal,　　2590
Dem Grab zu übergeben diesen teuren Leib,
Denn dieses ist der Toten letzte Herrlichkeit.
Vernehmt denn meines Willens ernstlichen Beschluß,
Und wie ich's euch gebiete, also übt es aus
Genau. — Euch ist in frischem Angedenken noch　　2595
Das ernste Amt, denn nicht von langen Zeiten ist's,
Daß ihr zur Gruft begleitet eures Fürsten Leib.
Die Totenklage ist in diesen Mauern kaum
Verhallt, und eine Leiche drängt die andre fort
Ins Grab, daß eine Fackel an der andern sich　　2600
Anzünden, auf der Treppe Stufen sich der Zug
Der Klagemänner fast begegnen mag.
So ordnet denn ein feierlich Begräbnisfest
In dieses Schlosses Kirche, die des Vaters Staub
Verwahrt, geräuschlos bei verschloßnen Pforten an,　　2605
Und alles werde, wie es damals war, vollbracht.

Chor.

Mit schnellen Händen soll dies Werk bereitet sein,
O Herr — denn aufgerichtet steht der Katafalk
Ein Denkmal jener ernsten Festlichkeit noch da,
Und an den Bau des Todes rührte keine Hand.　　2610

Don Cesar.

Das war kein glücklich Zeichen, daß des Grabes Mund
Geöffnet blieb im Hause der Lebendigen.
Wie kam's, daß man das unglückselige Gerüst
Nicht nach vollbrachtem Dienste alsobald zerbrach?

Chor.

Die Not der Zeiten und der jammervolle Zwist,   2615
Der gleich nachher, Messina feindlich teilend, sich
Entflammt, zog unsre Augen von den Toten ab,
Und öde blieb, verschlossen dieses Heiligtum.

Don Cesar.

Ans Werk denn eilet ungesäumt! Noch diese Nacht
Vollende sich das mitternächtliche Geschäft!   2620
Die nächste Sonne finde von Verbrechen rein
Das Haus und leuchte einem fröhlichern Geschlecht.

(Der zweite Chor entfernt sich mit Don Manuels Leichnam.)

Erster Chor.

Soll ich der Mönche fromme Brüderschaft hieher
Berufen, daß sie nach der Kirche altem Brauch
Das Seelenamt verwalte und mit heil'gem Lied   2625
Zur ew'gen Ruh einsegne den Begrabenen?

Don Cesar.

Ihr frommes Lied mag fort und fort an unserm Grab
Auf ew'ge Zeiten schallen bei der Kerze Schein,
Doch heute nicht bedarf es ihres reinen Amts:
Der blut'ge Mord verscheucht das Heilige.   2630

Chor.

Beschließe nichts gewaltsam Blutiges, o Herr,
Wider dich selber wütend mit Verzweiflungstat:
Denn auf der Welt lebt niemand, der dich strafen kann,
Und fromme Büßung kauft den Zorn des Himmels ab.

Don Cesar.

Nicht auf der Welt lebt, wer mich richtend strafen kann,
Drum muß ich selber an mir selber es vollziehn.   2636
Bußfert'ge Sühne, weiß ich, nimmt der Himmel an,
Doch nur mit Blute büßt sich ab der blut'ge Mord.

Chor.

Des Jammers Fluten, die auf dieses Haus gestürmt,
Ziemt dir zu brechen, nicht zu häufen Leid auf Leid.   2640

Don Cesar.

Den alten Fluch des Hauses lös' ich sterbend auf,
Der freie Tod nur bricht die Kette des Geschicks.

Chor.

Zum Herrn bist du dich schuldig dem verwaisten Land,
Weil du des andern Herrscherhauptes uns beraubt.

Don Cesar.

Zuerst den Todesgöttern zahl' ich meine Schuld,   2645
Ein andrer Gott mag sorgen für die Lebenden.

Chor.

So weit die Sonne leuchtet, ist die Hoffnung auch,
Nur von dem Tod gewinnt sich nichts!   Bedenk' es wohl.

Don Cesar.

Du selbst bedenke schweigend deine Dienerpflicht,
Mich laß dem Geist gehorchen, der mich furchtbar treibt,
Denn in das Innre kann kein Glücklicher mir schaun.   2651
Und ehrst du fürchtend auch den Herrscher nicht in mir,
Den Verbrecher fürchte, den der Flüche schwerster drückt,
Das Haupt verehre des Unglücklichen,
Das auch den Göttern heilig ist — Wer das erfuhr,   2655
Was ich erleide und im Busen fühle,
Gibt keinem Irdischen mehr Rechenschaft.

Neunter Auftritt.

Donna Isabella.　Don Cesar.　Der Chor.

Isabella

(kommt mit zögernden Schritten und wirft unschlüssige Blicke auf Don
Cesar.　Endlich tritt sie ihm näher und spricht mit gefaßtem Ton).

Dich sollten meine Augen nicht mehr schauen,
So hatt' ich mir's in meinem Schmerz gelobt,
Doch in die Luft verwehen die Entschlüsse, 2660
Die eine Mutter, unnatürlich wütend,
Wider des Herzens Stimme faßt — Mein Sohn!
Mich treibt ein unglückseliges Gerücht
Aus meines Schmerzens öden Wohnungen
Hervor — Soll ich ihm glauben? Ist es wahr, 2665
Daß mir ein Tag zwei Söhne rauben soll?

Chor.

Entschlossen siehst du ihn, festen Muts,
Hinabzugehen mit freiem Schritte
Zu des Todes traurigen Toren.
Erprobe du jetzt die Kraft des Bluts, 2670
Die Gewalt der rührenden Mutterbitte.
Meine Worte hab' ich umsonst verloren.

Isabella.

Ich rufe die Verwünschungen zurück,
Die ich im blinden Wahnsinn der Verzweiflung
Auf dein geliebtes Haupt herunter rief. 2675
Eine Mutter kann des eignen Busens Kind,
Das sie mit Schmerz geboren, nicht verfluchen.
Nicht hört der Himmel solche sündige
Gebete; schwer von Tränen, fallen sie
Zurück von seinem leuchtenden Gewölbe. 2680

— Lebe, mein Sohn! Ich will den Mörder lieber sehn
Des einen Kindes, als um beide weinen.

Don Cesar.

Nicht wohl bedenkst du, Mutter, was du wünschest
Dir selbst und mir — Mein Platz kann nicht mehr sein
Bei den Lebendigen — Ja, könntest du   2685
Des Mörders gottverhaßten Anblick auch
Ertragen, Mutter, ich ertrüge nicht
Den stummen Vorwurf deines ew'gen Grams.

Isabella.

Kein Vorwurf soll dich kränken, keine laute
Noch stumme Klage in das Herz dir schneiden.   2690
In milder Wehmut wird der Schmerz sich lösen,
Gemeinsam trauernd wollen wir das Unglück
Beweinen und bedecken das Verbrechen.

Don Cesar (faßt ihre Hand, mit sanfter Stimme).

Das wirst du, Mutter. Also wird's geschehn.
In milder Wehmut wird dein Schmerz sich lösen —   2695
Dann, Mutter, wenn ein Totenmal den Mörder
Zugleich mit dem Gemordeten umschließt,
Ein Stein sich wölbet über beider Staube,
Dann wird der Fluch entwaffnet sein — Dann wirst
Du deine Söhne nicht mehr unterscheiden,   2700
Die Tränen, die dein schönes Auge weint,
Sie werden einem wie dem andern gelten —
Ein mächtiger Vermittler ist der Tod.
Da löschen alle Zornesflammen aus,
Der Haß versöhnt sich, und das schöne Mitleid   2705
Neigt sich, ein weinend Schwesterbild, mit sanft
Anschmiegender Umarmung auf die Urne.

Drum, Mutter, wehre du mir nicht, daß ich
Hinuntersteige und den Fluch versöhne.

Isabella.

Reich ist die Christenheit an Gnadenbildern,   2710
Zu denen wallend ein gequältes Herz
Kann Ruhe finden.   Manche schwere Bürde
Ward abgeworfen in Lorettos Haus,
Und segensvolle Himmelskraft umweht
Das heil'ge Grab, das alle Welt entsündigt.   2715
Vielkräftig auch ist das Gebet der Frommen,
Sie haben reichen Vorrat an Verdienst,
Und auf der Stelle, wo ein Mord geschah,
Kann sich ein Tempel reinigend erheben.

Don Cesar.

Wohl läßt der Pfeil sich aus dem Herzen ziehn,   2720
Doch nie wird das verletzte mehr gesunden.
Lebe, wer's kann, ein Leben der Zerknirschung,
Mit strengen Bußkasteiungen allmählich
Abschöpfend eine ew'ge Schuld — Ich kann
Nicht leben, Mutter, mit gebrochnem Herzen.   2725
Aufblicken muß ich freudig zu den Frohen
Und in den Äther greifen über mir
Mit freiem Geist — Der Neid vergiftete mein Leben,
Da wir noch deine Liebe gleich geteilt.
Denkst du, daß ich den Vorzug werde tragen,   2730
Den ihm dein Schmerz gegeben über mich?
Der Tod hat eine reinigende Kraft,
In seinem unvergänglichen Palaste
Zu echter Tugend reinem Diamant
Das Sterbliche zu läutern und die Flecken   2735

Der mangelhaften Menschheit zu verzehren.
Weit, wie die Sterne abstehn von der Erde,
Wird er erhaben stehen über mir,
Und hat der alte Neid uns in dem Leben
Getrennt, da wir noch gleiche Brüder waren,   2740
So wird er rastlos mir das Herz zernagen,
Nun er das Ewige mir abgewann
Und jenseits alles Wettstreits wie ein Gott
In der Erinnerung der Menschen wandelt.

Isabella.

O hab' ich euch nur darum nach Messina   2745
Gerufen, um euch beide zu begraben!
Euch zu versöhnen, rief ich euch hieher,
Und ein verderblich Schicksal kehret all
Mein Hoffen in sein Gegenteil mir um!

Don Cesar.

Schilt nicht den Ausgang, Mutter! Es erfüllt   2750
Sich alles, was versprochen ward. Wir zogen ein
Mit Friedenshoffnungen in diese Tore,
Und friedlich werden wir zusammen ruhn,
Versöhnt auf ewig, in dem Haus des Todes.

Isabella.

Lebe, mein Sohn! Laß deine Mutter nicht   2755
Freundlos im Land der Fremblinge zurück,
Rohherziger Verhöhnung preisgegeben,
Weil sie der Söhne Kraft nicht mehr beschützt.

Don Cesar.

Wenn alle Welt dich herzlos kalt verhöhnt,
So flüchte du dich hin zu unserm Grabe   2760
Und rufe deiner Söhne Gottheit an,
Denn Götter sind wir dann, wir hören dich,

Und wie des Himmels Zwillinge dem Schiffer
Ein leuchtend Sternbild, wollen wir mit Trost
Dir nahe sein und deine Seele stärken.   2765

Isabella.

Lebe, mein Sohn! Für deine Mutter lebe!
Ich kann's nicht tragen, alles zu verlieren!
(Sie schlingt ihre Arme mit leidenschaftlicher Heftigkeit um ihn, er macht
sich sanft von ihr los und reicht ihr die Hand mit abgewandtem Gesicht.)

Don Cesar.

Leb' wohl!

Isabella.

Ach, wohl erfahr' ich's schmerzlich fühlend nun,
Daß nichts die Mutter über dich vermag!   2770
Gibt's keine andre Stimme, welche dir
Zum Herzen mächt'ger als die meine bringt?
(Sie geht nach dem Eingang der Szene.)
Komm, meine Tochter! Wenn der tote Bruder
Ihn so gewaltig nachzieht in die Gruft,
So mag vielleicht die Schwester, die geliebte,   2775
Mit schöner Lebenshoffnung Zauberschein
Zurück ihn locken in das Licht der Sonne.

Zehnter Auftritt.

Beatrice erscheint am Eingange der Szene. Donna Isabella.
Don Cesar und der Chor.

Don Cesar (bei ihrem Anblick heftig bewegt sich verhüllend).
O Mutter! Mutter! Was ersinnest du?

Isabella (führt sie vorwärts).

Die Mutter hat umsonst zu ihm gefleht,
Beschwöre du, erfleh' ihn, daß er lebe.   2780

Don Ceſar.

Argliſt'ge Mutter! Alſo prüfſt du mich!
In neuen Kampf willſt du zurück mich ſtürzen?
Das Licht der Sonne mir noch teuer machen
Auf meinem Wege zu der ew'gen Nacht?
— Da ſteht der holde Lebensengel mächtig　　　　　2785
Vor mir, und tauſend Blumen ſchüttet er
Und tauſend goldne Früchte lebenduftend
Aus reichem Füllhorn ſtrömend vor mir aus,
Das Herz geht auf im warmen Strahl der Sonne,
Und neu erwacht in der erſtorbnen Bruſt　　　　　2790
Die Hoffnung wieder und die Lebensluſt.

Iſabella.

Fleh' ihn, dich oder niemand wird er hören,
Daß er den Stab nicht raube dir und mir.

Beatrice.

Ein Opfer fordert der geliebte Tote,
Es ſoll ihm werden, Mutter — Aber mich　　　　　2795
Laß dieſes Opfer ſein! Dem Tode war ich
Geweiht, eh' ich das Leben ſah. Mich fordert
Der Fluch, der dieſes Haus verfolgt, und Raub
Am Himmel iſt das Leben, das ich lebe.
Ich bin's, die ihn gemordet, eures Streits　　　　　2800
Entſchlafne Furien gewecket — Mir
Gebührt es, ſeine Manen zu verſöhnen!

Chor.

O jammervolle Mutter! Hin zum Tod
Drängen ſich eifernd alle deine Kinder
Und laſſen dich allein, verlaſſen ſtehen　　　　　2805
Im freudlos öden, liebeleeren Leben.

Beatrice.

Du, Bruder, rette dein geliebtes Haupt,
Für deine Mutter lebe! ˙Sie bedarf
Des Sohns; erst heute fand sie eine Tochter,
Und leicht entbehrt sie, was sie nie besaß.   2810

Don Cesar (mit tief verwundeter Seele).

Wir mögen leben, Mutter, oder sterben,
Wenn sie nur dem Geliebten sich vereinigt!

Beatrice.

Beneidest du des Bruders toten Staub?

Don Cesar.

Er lebt in deinem Schmerz ein selig Leben,
Ich werde ewig tot sein bei den Toten.   2815

Beatrice.

O Bruder!

Don Cesar (mit dem Ausdruck der heftigsten Leidenschaft).

Schwester, weinest du um mich?

Beatrice.

Lebe für unsre Mutter!

Don Cesar (läßt ihre Hand los, zurücktretend).

Für die Mutter?

Beatrice (neigt sich an seine Brust).

Lebe für sie und tröste deine Schwester.

Chor.

Sie hat gesiegt! Dem rührenden Flehen
Der Schwester konnt' er nicht widerstehen.   2820
Trostlose Mutter! Gib Raum der Hoffnung,
Er erwählt das Leben, dir bleibt dein Sohn!

(In diesem Augenblick läßt sich ein Chorgesang hören, die Flügeltüre
wird geöffnet, man sieht in der Kirche den Katafalk aufgerichtet und den
Sarg von Kandelabern umgeben.)

Don Cesar (gegen den Sarg gewendet).

Nein, Bruder!   Nicht dein Opfer will ich dir
Entziehen — deine Stimme aus dem Sarg
Ruft mächt'ger dringend als der Mutter Tränen   2825
Und mächt'ger als der Liebe Flehn — Ich halte
In meinen Armen, was das ird'sche Leben
Zu einem Los der Götter machen kann —
Doch ich, der Mörder, sollte glücklich sein,
Und deine heil'ge Unschuld ungerächet   2830
Im tiefen Grabe liegen — das verhüte
Der allgerechte Lenker unsrer Tage,
Daß solche Teilung sei in seiner Welt —
— Die Tränen sah ich, die auch mir geflossen,
Befriedigt ist mein Herz, ich folge dir.   2835

(Er durchsticht sich mit einem Dolch und gleitet sterbend an seiner
Schwester nieder, die sich der Mutter in die Arme wirft.)

Chor (nach einem tiefen Schweigen).

Erschüttert steh' ich, weiß nicht, ob ich ihn
Bejammern oder preisen soll sein Los.
Dies eine fühl' ich und erkenn' es klar:
Das Leben ist der Güter höchstes nicht,
Der Übel größtes aber ist die Schuld.   2840

NOTES

ACT I.

In the original edition of Die Braut von Messina (1803) and in the subsequent reprints among Schiller's collected works which were brought out for Cotta by his friend Körner there was no division into acts and scenes. The division into four acts, which is now (since 1869) usually given in the German editions and which has been adopted here, was taken from the Hamburg acting-copy. There is no doubt that this division was made by Schiller himself in order to facilitate the production of his play on the stage, but in the printed editions he preferred to follow the classical Greek usage of not indicating any breaks. The scene of action is laid in three different localities and really changes but four times, viz. from the spacious hall supported on columns (ll. 1—980) to a garden (ll. 981—1259), from thence to a room in the interior of the palace (ll. 1260—1706), then back to the garden (ll. 1707—2028), and finally back to the hall supported on columns (ll. 2029—2840). Schiller added to the title the explanation Ein Trauerspiel mit Chören. The Hamburg acting-copy substitutes for this in vier Aufzügen.

The action of the First Act comprises the address by the Princess Mother Isabella to the Elders of the town of Messina; the dispatch of her faithful old servant Diego to fetch her daughter Beatrice from the place of hiding, a convent, where she had been brought up from infancy; the entry of the Chorus consisting of the retainers of the two Princes; the meeting of the brothers and their final reconciliation; Don Manuel's account of his first meeting with Beatrice and of her flight with him; the reflections of the Chorus. The scene of action during the whole of the First Act (ll. 1—980) is a spacious hall supported on pillars—a wide folding-door at the back (in der Tiefe) of the stage leads to a chapel.

The word Aufzug, m. is derived from aufziehen, 'to draw up,' 'to raise.' When the curtain is lifted up in the theatre an act begins, hence Aufzug comes to mean 'act.' Another meaning is 'parade,' 'procession,' and another is 'lift,' 'hoist.' The word often denotes a somewhat comical appearance. The term Uft, *m.* (fr. the French *acte*, Lat. *actus*) is also much used in German.

SCENE 1.

Auftritt, fr. auftreten, 'to step forth,' hence 'to appear on the stage.' As a new scene generally begins with the appearance of a new person on the stage, Uuftritt comes to mean 'scene.' The word Scene or Szene (pronounce *stse:nə*), *f.* is likewise used. It is borrowed fr. the Fr. *scène*, fr. Lat. *scena*, fr. Greek σκηνή, 'a booth,' 'a stage.'

This Scene corresponds to the 'Prologos' of the ancient Greek plays. The address of the Princess to the Elders of the town of Messina, who listen in humble silence, contains the main points of the *exposition* of the drama, i.e. those facts and circumstances which the hearer must know at the outset in order to understand the development of the dramatic plot. Isabella is in deep mourning, so are her sons throughout the whole play; only Beatrice appears in a white garment. Isabella speaks with great dignity and impressiveness, first as widow, subsequently as mother, and finally as ruler. The whole situation is analogous to that found in several ancient Greek tragedies. For instance, in the 'Persae' of Aeschylus Queen Atossa leaves her gold-resplendent mansions and addresses the Elders who are full of anxiety and grief. The 'Phoenissae' of Euripides likewise begins with a speech of the royal mother Iocasta, Queen of Thebes, who is waiting for a meeting of her two sons who are enemies and have been fighting one another. Not only are many situations in Schiller's drama either conscious imitations of situations met with in the masterpieces of the ancient Greek tragedians or conceived in the spirit of the Greek drama, but the language and style in the German drama were purposely modelled on classical patterns. See the Introduction.

1. This line has become a familiar quotation in German.

Not. The bitter necessity that has caused her to come forth from her seclusion is explained in ll. 47—97, especially ll. 62—74.

2. greifen Häupter, 'hoary fathers,' the Elders of the town. Isabella does not ask their opinion, she only informs them of what she has done and proposes to do, and dismisses the representatives of the people of Messina with a proud word of warning.

3. verschwiegenen, 'silent' in the meaning of 'secluded.' See l. 1686, ein verschwiegner Aufenthalt der Seelen.

4. Frauenſaals, 'woman's apartment.' Medieval women, like those of ancient Greece and the Mahommedan world, lived mostly in the seclusion of their own apartments. In the German poems of the 12th and 13th centuries this room exclusively inhabited by ladies was called *diu kemenâte* (from [*camera*] *caminata*), i.e. a room provided with a good fire-place.

7. Verloren, i.e. hat. This omission of the auxiliary is very frequent in poetry. See ll. 446, 459, 460, 586, etc.

8. Die ſchwarzumflorte Nachtgeſtalt, 'the gloomy figure enveloped in black,' i.e. herself in her widow's weeds.

11. Des Augenblicks Gebieterſtimme, 'the imperious voice of the present moment.' The Elders had given her the choice either to reconcile the brothers and thus to end the pernicious feud, or to abdicate for herself and her race (ll. 62—74). The language of this drama is very rich in personifications of abstract nouns, cp. also der Zukunft Schoß, l. 325; das Ohr des Argwohns, l. 587; die Hände des Brudermords, l. 1969, and others.

12. entwohnte, 'unwonted,' 'unaccustomed.' entwohnt is a word now no longer used, the opposite of the ordinary gewohnt. It is an old past partic. of entwohnen, 'to wean oneself from a thing.' Thus it means 'something of which one has lost the habit.' One would now say in prose das Licht, deſſen ich mich entwöhnt habe, an das ich nicht gewohnt bin, more rarely deſſen ich entwohnt bin. In Die Piccolomini, l. 326, Schiller says aller Zucht entwohnt. In Goethe's Fauſt we read mich faßt ein längſt entwohnter Schauer (l. 4405), while in the Zueignung zu Fauſt we have mich ergreift ein längſt entwöhntes Sehnen (l. 25). Cp. nachtgewohnt, l. 1269.

13. dreimal; some editions have zweimal which is obviously a mistake. See l. 1368.

Lichtgeſtalt, *f.* for lichte, helle, leuchtende Geſtalt, 'luminous orb,' 'orb of light.' Cp. Nachtgeſtalt, l. 8, and Lichterſcheinung, l. 1119.

14. den fürſtlichen Gemahl, 'my princely spouse,' 'my princely consort.' In l. 961 Gemahl is used as a neuter. See the note.

15. trug, 'bore,' 'consigned.' trug, a Latinism for tragen ließ. The action performed by others is ascribed to him who ordered it.

16. mächtigwaltend, 'with mighty sway.' He was powerful, but not beloved. See ll. 34 sqq. mächtigwaltend is formed in the Homeric way. See l. 992.

dieſer Statt gebot, poetical for über dieſe Stadt herrſchte.

17. gegen eine Welt, short for gegen eine ganze Welt. Similarly in ll. 99, 368. Compare also l. 65. Messina is looked upon as a separate state at war with the neighbouring states.

19. dahin, supply gegangen, 'gone,' 'departed.' Verbs of motion are not unfrequently suppressed in German, e.g. Woher des Wegs? Wo willst du hin?

lebt...fort (l. 20), 'lives on,' 'continues to live.'

20. Heldenpaare...glorreicher Söhne. The fort would in prose be placed after Söhne as the genitive should not be separated by any intervening words from the noun which it qualifies. But in poetry, more especially in poetry the style of which is influenced by the ancient classical languages, such constructions are not unfrequently found. See ll. 1009 —11, 1137, 1403, 1933, 2099.

24. unbekannt verhängnisvollem, 'unknown (and) fatal.' unbekannt is here not an adverb, but an uninflected adjective. This use of two adjectives, the former of which remains uninflected and is not joined by und to the latter, is characteristic of Schiller's poetic diction in his later dramas. In adopting this construction in Wallenstein and subsequent plays he seems to have been influenced by Goethe's use of the uninflected adjective in Iphigenie and Torquato Tasso. See my note to Iphigenie, l. 97 (tief geheimnisvolles Schicksal), and Otto Behaghel's exhaustive discussion and historical explanation of the use of the uninflected adjective in Schiller (in 'Wissenschaftliche Beihefte zur Zeitschrift des Allgemeinen Deutschen Sprachvereins,' Heft 26 (June 1905), especially pp. 196—198). For other instances of this construction in Die Braut von Messina see ll. 106, 201, 328, 349, 427, 507—508, 567, 601, 723, 789, 837, 956, etc. No one, not even the brothers themselves, knows the cause of this unnatural hatred.

26. Der Kindheit frohe Einigkeit, viz. that happy union which is natural and usual with children. It does not mean that these brothers were ever happily united during their childhood. See l. 28.

Instead of the lines 26 and 27 the Ratisbon MS. has only one line:

Und trennte früh die jugendlichen Herzen.

28. Eintracht, *f.* 'accord,' is not connected with either trachten or tragen, but with treffen, and originally refers to the hitting the same aim, aiming at the same goal. The opposite is Zwietracht or Zwist (l. 63).

31. kindlich mir geneigt, 'devoted to me with filial love.'

34. weil (which is short for dieweil, die Weile) has here preserved

its old temporal meaning 'while,' which is now as a rule expressed by
während or so lange. Other instances occur in ll. 110, 165, etc. In
Die Piccolomini, III. 2, l. 1377, Illo says: Das Eisen muß geschmiedet
werden weil es glüht.

    gefürchtet, 'inspiring awe,' ' by means of fear,' ' with stern control.'

    35. durch gleicher Strenge furchtbare Gerechtigkeit, 'with the awful
justice of even severity,' hence 'with the awful justice of impartial
severity.'

    36. This line has six accented syllables. See the Introduction,
p. lxxxiii.

    die Heftigbrausenden, 'the turbulent youths.' The adjective heftig-
brausend was formed by Schiller in imitation of classical usage. See
l. 16 n.

    37. Eisenschwere, *f.* 'iron weight.'

    38. vereinend, 'uniting them,' ' to unity.' They were not really
united in their hearts, but yoked together, like unwilling oxen, under
the same heavy yoke and thus forced to obey. Notice the glottal stop
in pronunciation of vereinend (pron. *fər"ainənt*).

    starren Sinn, 'stubborn mind.' The compound Starrsinn, *m.*
' obstinacy,' is equally common.

    41. Machtgebot, *n.* ' despotic command,' 'stern authority.'

    43. ungebessert, ' unimproved,' 'uncorrected,' i.e. ' unabated,' 'un-
appeased.'

    in der tiefen Brust, classical and poetic for tief in ihrer Brust.

    45. leise has here the meaning of ' tiny,' 'small.' die leise Quelle,
i.e. their hatred.

    46. Strome, ' mighty river,' refers to the violent outburst of their
hatred. Strom corresponds etymologically to the English *stream*, but
it is only used of large rivers, e.g. der Rheinstrom. A river of ordinary
size is always called ein Fluß, and the English *stream* must in most cases
be rendered in German by der Bach or das Flüßchen.

    49. bändigt, bricht...los (51). The use of the present tense vividly
expresses the suddenness of the outbreak. Nowhere in the play is it
said that der alte Groll has anything to do with a fight for the throne.
Either brother calls himself, even after their reconciliation has taken
place and when they honestly believe themselves to be friends for the
rest of their lives, den Höchsten in der Stadt (see ll. 1161 and 1822). In
ll. 70 and 92 they are called die Herrscher. Obviously the poet did not
wish to complicate matters by making the brothers rivals for the rulership.

50. eingepreßte, 'repressed,' 'smothered.' In his Lied von der Glocke (l. 23) Schiller also has the phrase die eingepreßte Flamme.

53. This line and the following show how the quarrel of the hostile brothers has been the cause of a general (l. 55) quarrel between the townspeople of Messina, some of whom sided with the elder and some with the younger brother. Even members of the same family took different sides and met in open fight, thus violating all the sacred bonds of nature.

55. Losung, *f.* 'watchword,' 'signal.'

58. ihr (fahet zerreißen) is strongly contrasted with mir (zerriß). zerreißen is here in both cases an intransitive verb, meaning ' to be rent,' ' to burst asunder,' ' to break.'

63. Bruderzwist, *m.* 'fraternal strife.' Zwist, ' quarrel,' originally ' disunion,' is connected with zwei. sich entzweien, 'to disunite,' 'to fall out,' 'to quarrel.'

64. bürgerlichem Streit, or Bürgerkrieg, 'civil war.'

65. umgarnt, 'ensnared.' umgarnen is derived fr. das Garn, 'thread,' 'net,' 'snare,' 'decoy.'

66. In prose nur would be placed before durch Eintracht.

67. siehe is obsolete and poetic for sieh. It was common in the 16th century and in Luther's Bible. In M.H.G. the imperative was *sich.*

71. sich befehden, more correctly einander befehden. See also ll. 178—179.

78. dieses Herz, for mein Herz, also in ll. 113, 295, 499, 1399.

80. das nicht zu Hoffende, 'that (the attainment of) which should or could not be hoped for,' i.e. 'the hopeless task,' of bringing about a reconciliation. In the phrase das...zu Hoffende we have really an old inflected infinitive, 'the (thing) to be hoped.' Constructions like this with the prefixed definite article are of rather recent date in the German language and are rare even in poetic diction. There occur a few instances in the Second Part of Goethe's Faust, e.g. ll. 6222—3: Kein Weg! Ins Unbetretene, nicht zu Betretende; ein Weg ans Unerbetene, nicht zu Erbittende; also in l. 8922 we find das zu Opfernde zeig' an. In ordinary prose such passive inflected infinitives assuming the force of a qualifying adjective before a noun are now quite common, e.g. der zu schreibende Brief, 'the letter to be written'; die nicht zu leugnende Tatsache, 'the fact not to be denied' (= unleugbare, 'undeniable').

83. Unabgeschreckt, ' unterrified,' 'undismayed.' The chief stress falls on the prefix un, and the rhythm of the beginning of the line is thus transposed. See Introd. p. lxxviii.

84. Beſchickt' ich ſie, 'I sent messengers to them,' is an old technical term that is now obsolete. We should in this sense now say Schickte ich nach ihnen or Schickte ich (Boten) zu ihnen. The word is still in common use in the phrase eine Verſammlung or Ausſtellung beſchicken = Vertreter zu einer V. or A. ſchicken, 'to send representatives to an assembly or an exhibition,' 'to be represented at....'

85. erhielt, 'obtained,' 'brought it about.' Usually erreichte.

86. ſie's = ſie es. Es is an old genitive (M.H.G. es) of es (M.H.G. ez) governed by zufrieden, 'content (with it).' Similar phrases are ich bin es müde, ' I am tired of it '; ich bin es ſatt, ' I have had enough of it '; ich wurde es gewahr, ' I became aware of it.' Cp. l. 517.

88. von Angeſicht is short for von Angeſicht zu Angeſicht, 'face to face.' It would be possible to say (einander) ins Angeſicht zu ſehen.

89. verſchieden, i.e. iſt, 'has died.' Verſcheiden or abſcheiden is high style and poetic for the ordinary aus dem Leben ſcheiden, 'to depart this life.' See note to l. 7.

91. Anzug, *m.* 'approach,' is less usual than Heranziehen.

95. uns andere, viz. myself and my sons who are the rulers.

gewähren, the same as Gewähr leiſten, Gewähr or Bürgſchaft übernehmen, 'be answerable,' 'give surety.' Schiller uses gewähren in the same sense in Wilhelm Tell, I. 4, l. 710: Ich muß für Eure Sicherheit gewähren; and in Maria Stuart, III. 4, l. 2357: Und welches Pfand gewährte mir für Euch? Another verb of the same meaning is bürgen (= Bürge ſein). The usual meaning of einen gewähren laſſen is 'to leave a person alone,' 'to leave a person undisturbed.'

98. gnug, instead of genug, is a contraction often found in poetry.

99. See l. 17 where the same was said of the old Prince.

100. gegen euch, with strong stress on euch (in case you should oppose their will), stands emphatically at the end of a very statesmanlike and impressive speech.

SCENE 2.

This Scene supplements the information given in Scene 1 by acquainting the hearers with the existence of a sister of the hostile brothers whom the mother only now thinks it safe to introduce to them.

101. Diego is a trisyllabic word. He is the old trusty family servant (l. 102), the θεράπων of the ancient Greek tragedy, to whom the proud

B.   9

Princess unbosoms herself and to whom she can allow herself to speak simply as the anxious mother.

102. Rebliĉ Herz, in ordinary prose Rebliĉes. Adjectives preceding nouns in older German were frequently uninflected. In modern German prose the adjective must always be inflected, but the old license still exists in poetry, especially before neuter nouns, in some idiomatic phrases such as bar Gelb, gut Heil, auf gut Glück, and in many compounds, e.g. Ebelstein, Jungfrau, Starrsinn, Eigensinn. See ll. 378, 459, 484, 519, 555, etc. Two uninflected adjectives before a noun occur in l. 636, ein seltsam wunderbar Geheimnis.

103. Schiller occasionally separates, as here, two substantives, which are not connected by unb, by means of some short words, verbs or other parts of speech. This produces a pleasant variety in the structure of the sentence. See also l. 2334.

104. bas Glück ber Glücklichen (genit. sing.). It is one of the characteristics of the poetic language of Schiller in his later poems and plays, and especially in this drama, that an idea is emphasised by placing side by side in the same sentence words belonging to the same stem. See l. 95, and l. 121, ben traur'gen Dienst ber Traurigen, and also ll. 622, 744, 809, 881, 937, 959, 1028, 1033, 1048, 1065—6, 1183—4, 1198—9, 1589, 1609. These so-called 'palillogies' are not uncommon in the ancient Greek plays, e.g. ἐν ξένᾳ ξένον in Sophocles (*Philoctetes*, l. 135), and also in Roman writers.

105. Verpfänbet, 'given in pledge,' (= als Pfanb) anvertraut, 'trusted.'

106. schmerzlich süßes is an effective oxymoron. Schiller is fond of using such. Some are common in every language, e.g. offenes Geheimnis, berebtes Schweigen.

110. weil, 'while.' See l. 34 n.

111. herrisch may mean 'tyrannically,' but may just as well only mean als Herr, her husband being her lord. herrisch waltete would in that case be 'did lord it.'

112. ihre refers to Natur (l. 109).

116. alterschweren, 'age-encumbered,' for von Alter schweren, 'heavy with age.' See l. 124. In his translation of Die Phönizierinnen of Euripides l. 274 Schiller makes the aged Iocasta say: (Ich wanke nun) mit alterschwerem Tritt. Compounds with Alter often show the noun in the genitive case, e.g. altersschwach, 'weak with age.'

119. mir, 'for me,' an expressive ethical dative.

120. auf beßre Tage, 'until better days.'

124. verjüngen, 'make young again,' hence 'quicken.'

130. Kraft und Zug, for starke Anziehung or anziehende Kraft, 'attractive power,' 'force of attraction,' 'strong attraction.'

A similar hendiadys, i.e. coordination of two nouns one of which stands instead of an adjective to form one idea, occurs in l. 1154, die Freiheit und die Wahl for die freie Wahl.

SCENE 3.

In this Scene, which corresponds to the 'parodos' of the Greek tragedies, the Chorus enters the stage for the first time; it is divided into two semi-choruses of twelve knights each. See the Introduction, pp. xlv sqq., and Schiller's own Essay printed on pp. 239—247. The Chorus consists of older and younger knights of Messina, the older men being followers of Don Manuel, the younger followers of Don Cesar. The former are calmer, more reflective and sober-minded, the younger hot-headed and passionate. The character of the two brothers is to some extent reflected in the frame of mind of their adherents. A similar affinity exists in Wallenstein between the temper of the generals and that of their men. In the songs of the Chorus of this Scene we have a supplement to the two preceding Scenes as we learn from them the mood of the men of Messina. The Elders had acted (ll. 62 sqq.), but at the end of the First Scene they had retired without speaking. While the idea of introducing a Chorus into this play was taken from the Greek drama, the treatment of the Chorus is very original and intentionally very different from the classical models. Goethe's Choruses in the Second Part of Faust (Act III. Helena Act), which were partly written before Schiller's Braut von Messina, are much more similar to the ancient Greek Choruses.

The structure of this Scene is most artistic. Towards the end of it Isabella appears in the background between her two sons, but during it only the Chorus speaks. It may be divided into five portions: *A* (ll. 132—154) being two short monologues of Chorus I (ll. 132—144) and Chorus II (ll. 145—154). From their utterances we gather their general attitude, which in the case of the first Chorus is quiet and peaceful, in that of the second Chorus is angry and aggressive. *B* (ll. 155—189) is a dialogue in which the peaceful overtures of Chorus I (ll. 155—180) are haughtily rejected by Chorus II (ll. 181—189). *C* (ll. 190—252) contains reflections of the older men, of whom three speakers come forward to comment on (*a*) (ll. 190—211) the folly of destroying one

another for the sake of a race of foreign rulers; (*b*) (ll. 212—227) the
necessity of obeying their protecting sway; (*c*) (ll. 228—252) the advantages of a lowly and subordinate position as contrasted with the dangers
to which the rulers are exposed.   At this moment Isabella and her sons
appear at the portal at the back of the stage, and in *D* (ll. 253—258)
both Choruses unite in a brief song of praise and homage.   This is
followed by *E* (ll. 259—292), two songs containing thoughts of the
semi-choruses on their rulers, in which Chorus I (ll. 259—276) brings
out the aesthetic point of view, while Chorus II (ll. 277—292) takes
the historic and practical point of view.   After their songs are
finished Isabella comes forward with her sons, all clad in deepest
mourning.

136. Säulengetragenes, 'upborne on pillars,' for von Säulen or auf
Säulen getragenes. See Säulenhalle, p. 1, and compare Mignon's song:
Kennst du das Haus? Auf Säulen ruht sein Dach; Es glänzt der Saal, es
schimmert das Gemach. The adj. säulengetragen is formed after the model
of Greek compounds; such compounds occur frequently in poetry,
e.g. himmelumwandelnd (l. 213), fluchbefreit (l. 534), völkerwimmelnd (l. 990),
glückbekrönt (l. 1139), götterbegünstigt (l. 1185), nachtgewohnt (l. 1269),
sonnenbeleuchtet (l. 1996), also grünumgebne Hütten, weinumrankte Lauben,
and the English compounds 'moss-grown,' 'weather-beaten,' etc.

140. des Streits schlangenhaarigtes Scheusal, 'the monster of Discord
with snaky locks,' viz. Eris, the Goddess of Discord, 'whose fury
wearieth not, sister and friend of murderous Ares' (Homer's *Iliad* IV.
440—441). She is graphically represented as serpent-haired, a repulsive Medusa-like creature. In Vergil's *Aeneid* VI. l. 280, she shakes
vipereum crinem, 'her viper-hair,' and at the end of his poem Kassandra
(ll. 125—126) Schiller says:

> Eris schüttelt ihre Schlangen,
> Alle Götter fliehn davon.

haarigt, now haarig. The suffix -igt or -icht is almost exclusively
appended to *names of material* to point out some resemblance to the
noun, e.g. steinicht. Only töricht, 'foolish,' is derived fr. a noun denoting
a person, der Tor, 'the fool.' Schiller is fond of using the suffix -icht or
-igt in many cases where modern usage demands -ig. Cp. felsigt (l. 462),
sonnigt (l. 874), hohläugigt. The suffix -ig denotes 'having,' 'containing,'
'possessing,' while -igt, -icht convey the idea of 'similarity,' 'resemblance.' Thus one ought to be able to distinguish between steinichte
Früchte and a steiniges Feld. With adjectives denoting colour Schiller also

likes the ending ⸱licht, where we now say ⸱lich, e.g. rötlicht (l. 207), graulicht (l. 897).

143. ber Eib, ber Erinnyen Sohn. The oath was personified by the Greek writer Hesiod as Horkos (Ὅρκος), the son of Strife, Eris, and was represented as a deity who punished the false and perjured. In a wider sense he is here called 'the Son of the Erinnyes,' the avenging deities. They are conceived as the guardians of sacred duties, and in this way the solemn oath is their offspring, as it is his special function to safeguard sacred obligations. They protect the houses in which the oath is kept sacred. If, however, the solemn promise is broken, or if other sacred duties are violated, the Erinnyen change into Avenging Deities, Furien or Rachegöttinnen. They were sometimes called by the euphemistic name Eumeniden, 'Eumenides,' 'the well-meaning' or 'gracious' goddesses, as if to propitiate them. The 'Eumenides' are usually spoken of collectively, but in l. 152 only one is mentioned. ber Eib refers to the solemn oath given by the two brothers to keep the peace, and also to the oath of vassals to their liege-lords to abstain from conflict. Erinnyen (pron. *Ē-rĭn-nü-ən*). The Greek name is, according to the best authorities, Ἐρῑνύς (not Ἐριννύς), the plural Ἐρῑνύες, Attic Ἐρῑνῦς. From Ἐρινύες, Latin *Ērīnyes*, *Ērinnyĕs*, Goethe took the form Erinnyen in his Iphigenie auf Tauris, and Schiller, probably following the example of Goethe, in this and other passages, e.g. Wallensteins Tod, III. 20, 2322; and Die Götter Griechenlands, l. 72. In his ballad Der Ring bes Polykrates, l. 76, Schiller uses the form Erinnen which is less correct than Erinnyen.

144. Hölle, 'Hell,' for the 'Nether World.' The Oath, Horkos, is looked upon as a Demon living in the Lower Regions, on the banks of the river Styx. Cp. *Iliad*, XV. 36. The Erinnyen too are represented as living in the Nether World, see l. 1989. The oath to refrain from strife keeps watch at the threshold of the Palace, and therefore strife and bloodshed cannot cross it. The rime Hölle with Schwelle is perfectly correct in Schiller's South German, Swabian, pronunciation. He said Helle without rounding the lips. See Introd. p. lxxxviii and the rimes ll. 178—179, befehben: töten. Bellermann has fitly compared the description of Peace within the precincts of a Prince's abode as given in Goethe's Torquato Tasso, II. 4, ll. 1495—1501:

> Die Majestät verbreitet ihren Schutz
> Auf jeden, der sich ihr wie einer Gottheit
> Und ihrer unverletzten Wohnung naht.

Wie an dem Fuße des Altars, bezähmt

Sich auf der Schwelle jede Leidenschaft.

Da blinkt kein Schwert, da fällt kein drohend Wort,

Da fordert selbst Beleid'gung keine Rache.

145. Zürnend ergrimmt, ' grows furious with rage,' ' is inflamed with rage and ire.'

147. Medusen is of course the weak genitive singular. We should now say der Medusa, but in the compound still Medusenhaupt. In older German many feminines had the weak forms in *-en* in the gen. and dat. sing. These have now been given up by form-association with the nom. and accus. sing. but the older forms survive in poetry, e.g. Sonnen (ll. 199 and 971), and also in compounds such as Sonnenschein, Erden- glück, Heidenröslein, and many others.

To the passionate minds of the younger men the sight of Don Manuel's followers is as hateful as the loathed head of the Gorgo Medusa. In Schiller's rendering of Die Phönizierinnen of Euripides (see the Introd. p. xi) in Act II. Sc. 4, ll. 459—461, Iocasta says to her son Eteocles:

Es ist kein abgerißnes

Medusenhaupt, was du betrachten sollst,

Dein Bruder ist's, der zu dir kam.

For another trace of the influence of ' The Phoenician Damsels' on Die Braut von Messina see l. 450 n.

150. Ehre des Worts, ' honour of addressing words to him,' ' honour of a parley.'

154. der waltende Gottesfriede, ' the prevailing truce of God,' is the medieval *treuga dei*, established by the Church which thus enforced the cessation of all feuds during certain days and at certain specified places. The forbidden days were the festival days of the Church and the days from Thursday to Sunday inclusive. The *treuga dei* was first proposed in the South of France, and was advocated by the monks of Cluny; it was introduced into Germany in the eleventh century under Henry III. Apparently the hostile brothers too are bound by it.

161. Brüderlich, ' like brothers,' as they are children of the same town.

163. Schützende Götter, viz. die Penaten (l. 1191) or Hausgötter (l. 445). Schiller took these, as well as Ceres and Aurora, from Roman conceptions.

165. Weil, see l. 34 n.

167. Harmlos, 'not inflicting harm,' 'without anger,' 'amicably.'

168. bas Wort, bas heilenbe. heilenb, 'healing,' has here the sense of 'appeasing,' 'conciliatory.' Adjectives are in Schiller's and Goethe's poetry not unfrequently placed with repetition of the definite article after the substantive, as if put in by an afterthought. The adjective thereby gains additional force. See l. 990, bie Stabt, bie völkerwimmelnbe ; l. 1438, bie Mutter zeige sich, bie glückliche; also ll. 1362, 2387, 2775; or in Schiller's ballad Die Bürgschaft, l. 84, ber Freunb, ber liebenbe; in Wilhelm Tell, IV. 3, l. 2577, bie armen Kinblein, bie unschulbigen.

170. erneuen rimes with Freien in Schiller's dialect. He pronounced erneien. See l. 144, and the Introd. p. lxxxix.

176. ja has here no stress and means 'after all.'

177. Jene, viz. bie Fürsten, 'our lords.' This is explained more fully in ll. 204 sqq. They are probably descendants of the Normans who conquered the island. See the Introduction, p. xxix.

180. Compare the parallel passage in Die Jungfrau von Orleans, I. 5, ll. 844—5 :

> Für seinen König muß bas Volk sich opfern,
>
> Das ist bas Schicksal unb Gesetz ber Welt.

bie Orbnung, 'the (natural) order,' 'the tradition,' 'the custom.'

181. Mögen sie's wissen, 'Let them see to it,' with a strong stress on sie.

183. Mich ficht es nicht an, lit. 'it does not militate against me,' hence 'it does not trouble me,' 'I do not mind.' It is a characteristic fact that none of the knights knows of any reason for their feud.

190. bei mir selbst erwogen, 'in my heart I (have) pondered.'

192. bes Korns hochwallenbe Gassen = burch bie hohen wallenben Gassen bes Korns, 'mid the alleys of corn that waved so high.' Sicily always was particularly rich in fruit and corn ; it was at the time of the Roman empire the granary of Italy. See l. 224. It would be pedantic to assume from this line that the time of action was the time imme-diately preceding the harvest.

195. uns...nicht beraten, 'not taken counsel among ourselves.'

196. bas brausenbe Blut, 'our surging blood.' The definite article or the demonstrative pronoun has often in Schiller's later poetry the sense of the possessive pronoun and must be rendered by it in English. See ll. 519, 683, 1347, 2070, and compare l. 78, bieses Herz.

197. sie...biese Saaten. In the poetical language of old and modern times pronouns are occasionally placed early in a sentence and only subsequently find their proper explanation by a noun. Thus more marked attention is drawn to the noun. Instances occur in the earliest German poetry that has come down to our times, and instances in Goethe's and Schiller's dramas are not rare. See also ll. 429, 630, 898, 2316, 2438.

198. The custom of training grape-vines upon elms is very common in Italy. Cp. the *ulmus* as contrasted with *platanus caelebs* (Horace, *Odes* II. 15, 4—5), and (*vitis*) *ulmo coniuncta marita* (Catullus LXII. 54). W. v. Humboldt wrote to Schiller from Italy: Welche Gegend am Trasimenischen See, welche Eichen, und Weinreben, die sich um Ulmen schlingen!

201. (Tage) spinnen, 'spin out,' ' pass,' 'live.'

202. leicht, viz. so that it becomes light and easy. Note the pleasing effect of the alliteration (l) in this line. Cp. ll. 871—872, 1721.

203. mit rasendem Beginnen, 'with mad emprise' for 'madly.'

207. The rulers were Norsemen from Scandinavia, usually called Norma'nnen (from No'rdmannen), who had come in their Viking ships from the West (der Sonne rötlichtem Untergang) through the Straits of Gibraltar into the Mediterranean. They "secured a foothold in southern Italy in the first part of the eleventh century, some little time before the conquest of England. Their superior fighting qualities had led to their services being sought after by the Christian rulers of that region in their constant feuds with each other, and particularly in their warfare against the Moslems, who at that time were in possession of the island of Sicily, and were constantly troubling the neighbouring shores of Italy. From the position of guests and mercenaries the Norman knights soon rose to that of masters and rulers. They got possession finally of all southern Italy and of Sicily, and built up in these southern lands a prosperous state which came to be known as the Kingdom of Naples or the Kingdom of Naples and Sicily, and which lasted, although with many changes of dynasties, until the political unification of Italy in our own day. The most celebrated of Norman leaders during this period of conquest and organisation was Robert Guiscard (d. 1085), a character only less celebrated than the renowned William the Conqueror. His entire career was one series of daring and adventurous exploits." (Philip Van Ness Myers, *Medieval and Modern History*. Boston. Ginn & Co. [No year.] Revised ed. p. 102.) See also ll. 253, 341 sqq. The retainers of the Princes are no longer Norman knights but natives of the town of Messina.

rötlichtem, usually rötlichem. See l. 140 n. and l. 897.

212. Wohl! 'True!' short for: Du haft wohl gefprochen.

213. himmelumwandelnde, 'heaven-encircling,' seems to be a word peculiar to Schiller. But the adjective himmelwandelnd, applied in one passage to the sun and in another to the moon, occurs in the poetry of Schiller's older contemporary, Friedrich von Stolberg, which Schiller very probably knew. Johann Heinrich Voss, the famous translator of Homer, also an older contemporary of Schiller, has the adjective erdumwandelnd, said of Menfchen (*Iliad* v. 442). In *Iliad* VIII. l. 68 we read of the sun: οὐρανὸν ἀμφιβέβηκε. See note to l. 136.

216. fperren und fchließen, for abfperren und einfchließen. Simple words are as a rule more poetic than compounds.

217. 'The bold Corsairs' means the Moorish pirates from whom the powerful sway of the bold Norman rulers was to protect the Sicilians. See ll. 1577, 1592.

218. Rorfár, fr. Ital. *corsaro*, fr. Medieval Latin *cursarius*, a privateering vessel or a privateer making a *cursus*, 'inroad,' 'cruise.' The German word for Rorfar is Seeräuber, his vessel is a Räuberfchiff, l. 1592.

219. durchfreuzt, 'cruises along.'

222. Sitzen, 'dwellings,' 'homesteads,' 'lands,' 'domain.'

224. die goldene Ceres lacht. Instead of das goldne Korn Schiller says, by a bold personification, die goldene Ceres, just as in his poem Klage der Ceres, l. 6, instead of der unbewölkte Himmel we find (lacht) der unbewölfte Zeus.

225. der friedliche Pan. Pan was the god of shepherds and flocks among the Greeks, hence 'the guardian of the fields.' As the name of Ceres is used metonymically for a rich harvest, so Pan stands for large flocks, and both together for rural prosperity and Arcadian happiness.

226. Wo refers back to Nicht, wo (l. 224). In prose it would be Nicht da, wo...fondern da, wo.

der Berge Schacht, 'shaft of the mountains,' 'mountain-shaft.' Schiller may have thought of Scandinavia, the home of the valiant Vikings. Ernst Moritz Arndt, who wrote many powerful songs when Germany rose against Napoleon, sings :

> Der Gott, der Eifen wachfen ließ,
>
> Der wollte keine Knechte;

while the old motto of the pine-clad Harz mountains is :

> Es grüne die Tanne, es wachfe das Erz!
>
> Gott fchenke uns allen ein fröhliches Herz!

229. flücht'gem, 'fleeting,' 'short-lived.'

230. ewig, 'everlastingly,' 'ever.'

231. bie Fülle, 'the abundance of natural resources.'

233. warb = warb gegeben, wurbe ju teil, 'was given,' 'fell to (their) share.' Cp. ll. 1306, 1334.

234. unjerbrechliche, 'that cannot be broken,' 'invincible.'

239. This is the first hint of a tragic end of the rulers. The idea of the bonnernbe Fall is fully worked out in ll. 242 sqq.

240. lob' ich mir, 'I am in favour of,' 'I wish for.' Cp. Goethe's Fauft, l. 2171 : Mein Leipjig lob' ich mir. Cp. also liebt fich, l. 958.

With the sentiments expressed in the following lines compare Paul Heyse's fine poem über ein Stünblein that begins Dulbe, gebulbe bich fein, and the principal idea of which is

> Höh' unb Tiefe hat Luft unb Leib.
>
> Sag ihm ab, bem törigen Neib :
>
> Anberer Gram birgt anbre Wonne.

242. Wetterbäche, *m. pl.* 'storm streams,' i.e. mountain streams swollen by hailstorms. The common word for 'torrents' is Gießbäche. A fine contrast to this passage is the sketch of the beneficent career of a genius and leader of men under the image of a mountain stream developing into a mighty river found in Goethe's poem Mahomets Gesang.

243. bes Hagels unenblichen Schloßen, lit. 'endless hailstones of hail,' say 'endless storms of hail.' The o in Schloßen is sounded long in the best German pronunciation, but in some parts of Germany it is short. It is intended to form a rime with the short o of gefloßen and geschoßen. See Wilhelm Viëtor, *Deutsches Ausprachewörterbuch*, Leipzig, 1911, p. 363, and Theodor Siebs, *Deutsche Bühnenaussprache*, Köln, [10]1912, pp. 48 and 171.

247. Wogengeschwemme, *n.* 'sweep of the waters,' 'swirling waves.' This is one of the many compound words coined by Schiller in this drama.

248. bie gewaltigen, viz. Wetterbäche.

hemme, subj. 'might stop,' 'can restrain.'

251. verrinnenb, as it runs away and is lost in the sand. Compare the fine description of high and low tide in Goethe's Fauft, Part II. Act IV. ll. 10212—21.

252. 'Havoc is all that makes them known,' i.e. all that bears witness of them is the destruction which they leave behind.

253. This line is especially true with regard to the rapid changes in the ruling dynasties. The Norman dynasty came to an end towards the end of the twelfth century when Constance, daughter of the Norman

King Roger II, and aunt and heir of the last Norman King William II, married (in 1186) Henry, the son of Frederic Barbarossa, who in this way won for the noble family of the Hohenstaufen the Kingdom of Naples and Sicily. The Hohenstaufen lost their Italian dominions in 1268 to Charles of Anjou, brother of King Louis IX of France, but only a few years later, in 1282, all the French living in Sicily were murdered on the same day (March 30) and Peter of Aragon was elected King of Sicily. Thus Sicily saw during two centuries four different races of rulers. Cp. the Introduction, pp. xxviii—xxix.

254. With this and the preceding lines compare the very similar lines in Schiller's Jungfrau von Orleans, Prologue, Scene 3, ll. 375 sqq.:

> Laſſen wir die Großen,
>
> Der Erde Fürſten, um die Erde loſen;
>
> Wir können ruhig die Zerſtörung ſchauen,
>
> Denn ſturmfeſt ſteht der Boden, den wir bauen.

Donna is the Italian for 'Lady' (fr. *domina*), and Don for 'Lord' (fr. *dominus*). Cesar is another form of the Italian name *Cesare*, while Cäſar is the ordinary German equivalent for the Roman Gaius Julius Caesar.

255. This line and the following bear a strong resemblance to the 'Persae' of Aeschylus which Schiller had read in the translation of Stolberg. See the Introd. p. xv. Here (p. 163) we find the Chorus addressing the approaching Queen:

> Siehe! dem Antlitz der Götter gleich
>
> Wallet ein Licht hervor,
>
> Unſers Königes Mutter!
>
> Unſre Königin! Wir fallen nieder,
>
> Wir müſſen alle
>
> Sie empfangen mit der Begrüßung Wort.

258. dein herrliches Haupt = dich Herrliche. Haupt stands here, like the Greek κάρα or κεφαλή, and the Latin *caput*, poetically for 'personality,' 'being.' Thus in l. 2222 we have des redlichen Diego greiſes Haupt, in l. 2807 dein geliebtes Haupt, in Die Phönizierinnen (l. 657) der Mutter heilig Haupt, and in Goethe's Iphigenie, l. 2016, we read des Königes verehrtes Haupt = der verehrte König. In a similar way the word *lîp* was used in old German, e.g. *mîn lîp* = myself, *Sîvrides lîp* = *Sîfrit*, *eines rehte guoten riters lîp* = *ein rehte guoter riter*. Cp. the English no*body*, any*body*. But these old German periphrastic terms were probably unknown to Schiller and have not influenced his poetic language.

259. In old German poetry beautiful women are frequently likened

to the bright moon.   In the 𝔑𝔦𝔟𝔢𝔩𝔲𝔫𝔤𝔢𝔫𝔩𝔦𝔢𝔟, Stanza 283 (B), the fair
Princess Kriemhilt stands out from her maidens as the bright moon
among the stars.   Here the mother is the moon and the sons are the stars.

260.   𝔐𝔦𝔩𝔟𝔢𝔯𝔢 = 𝔯𝔢𝔠𝔥𝔱 𝔪𝔦𝔩𝔟𝔢, 𝔣𝔢𝔥𝔯 𝔪𝔦𝔩𝔟𝔢 is a so-called Klopstockian
comparative, which merely denotes a very high degree but no actual
comparison.   This use of the comparative occurs in Latin poetry,
whence Klopstock introduced it into his 𝔐𝔢𝔣𝔣𝔦𝔞𝔰 and his 𝔒𝔟𝔢𝔫.
In the ode 𝔘𝔫 𝔪𝔢𝔦𝔫𝔢 𝔉𝔯𝔢𝔲𝔫𝔟𝔢 (57, 1) he says:

        𝔍𝔥𝔪 𝔩𝔞𝔲𝔣𝔠𝔥𝔱 𝔢𝔫𝔱𝔷ü𝔠𝔱 𝔡𝔦𝔢 𝔣𝔢𝔦𝔫𝔢𝔯𝔢 𝔖𝔠𝔥ä𝔣𝔢𝔯𝔦𝔫,

where 𝔣𝔢𝔦𝔫𝔢𝔯𝔢 means 𝔣𝔢𝔥𝔯 𝔣𝔢𝔦𝔫𝔢, 𝔣𝔢𝔥𝔯 𝔞𝔫𝔪𝔲𝔱𝔦𝔤𝔢.   In his religious epic 𝔇𝔢𝔯
𝔐𝔢𝔣𝔣𝔦𝔞𝔰 (Canto IV) Klopstock says of the Lord:

𝔗𝔯𝔞𝔱 𝔧𝔢𝔱𝔷𝔱 𝔦𝔫 𝔡𝔦𝔢 𝔣𝔱𝔦𝔩𝔩𝔢𝔯𝔢 𝔚𝔬𝔥𝔫𝔲𝔫𝔤 𝔈𝔦𝔫𝔢𝔰 𝔳𝔢𝔯𝔨𝔞𝔫𝔫𝔱𝔢𝔫 𝔯𝔢𝔡𝔩𝔦𝔠𝔥𝔢𝔫 𝔐𝔞𝔫𝔫𝔰.

Goethe imitated this peculiarity of Klopstock's, e.g. in his elegiac poem
𝔥𝔢𝔯𝔪𝔞𝔫𝔫 𝔲𝔫𝔟 𝔇𝔬𝔯𝔬𝔱𝔥𝔢𝔞, l. 33, where he says, in speaking of his
intended idyllic epic of the same name:

      𝔇𝔢𝔲𝔱𝔣𝔠𝔥𝔢𝔫 𝔣𝔢𝔩𝔟𝔢𝔯 𝔣ü𝔥𝔯' 𝔦𝔠𝔥 𝔢𝔲𝔠𝔥 𝔷𝔲 𝔦𝔫 𝔡𝔦𝔢 𝔣𝔱𝔦𝔩𝔩𝔢𝔯𝔢 𝔚𝔬𝔥𝔫𝔲𝔫𝔤.

This peculiarity of Klopstock, Goethe and Schiller is not found in
modern German poetry.

262.   𝔡𝔢𝔯 𝔐𝔲𝔱𝔱𝔢𝔯...𝔥𝔬𝔥𝔢𝔦𝔱 = 𝔡𝔦𝔢 𝔥𝔬𝔥𝔢 or 𝔥𝔬𝔥𝔢𝔦𝔱𝔰𝔳𝔬𝔩𝔩𝔢 𝔐𝔲𝔱𝔱𝔢𝔯.

264.   𝔡𝔢𝔯 𝔖ö𝔥𝔫𝔢...𝔎𝔯𝔞𝔣𝔱 = 𝔡𝔦𝔢 𝔨𝔯ä𝔣𝔱𝔦𝔤𝔢𝔫 𝔖ö𝔥𝔫𝔢.   This construction is
here and in many other passages in Schiller and Goethe an intentional imitation of the Homeric paraphrases with ἴς, βίη, σθένος,
μένος and the genit. of a proper name, e.g. κρατερὴ ἴς 'Οδυσῆος, ἱερὴ
ἴς Τηλεμάχοιο, etc.   The same construction is frequently met with in
the plays of Sophocles.   Milton's line, *where the might of Gabriel
fought, Par. Lost*, VI. 355, is likewise a classical reminiscence.   In
Schiller's poetry such constructions are very frequent.   We have in the
ballad 𝔇𝔢𝔯 𝔊𝔯𝔞𝔣 𝔳𝔬𝔫 𝔥𝔞𝔟𝔰𝔟𝔲𝔯𝔤, ll. 1 and 3:

      𝔘𝔲 𝔘𝔞𝔠𝔥𝔢𝔫 𝔦𝔫 𝔣𝔢𝔦𝔫𝔢𝔯 𝔎𝔞𝔦𝔣𝔢𝔯𝔭𝔯𝔞𝔠𝔥𝔱...
      𝔖𝔞ß 𝔎ö𝔫𝔦𝔤 𝔯𝔲𝔡𝔬𝔩𝔣𝔰 𝔥𝔢𝔦𝔩𝔦𝔤𝔢 𝔐𝔞𝔠𝔥𝔱.

These constructions are not even restricted to proper names or even
human beings, for in the ballad 𝔇𝔦𝔢 𝔎𝔯𝔞𝔫𝔦𝔠𝔥𝔢 𝔡𝔢𝔰 𝔍𝔟𝔶𝔨𝔲𝔰, l. 32,
Schiller says 𝔡𝔢𝔰 𝔅𝔬𝔤𝔢𝔫𝔰 𝔎𝔯𝔞𝔣𝔱 instead of 𝔇𝔢𝔯 𝔨𝔯ä𝔣𝔱𝔦𝔤𝔢 𝔅𝔬𝔤𝔢𝔫.   Similar instances
occur in Medieval German poetry, where a direct imitation of Homer
is not to be supposed.   In the M.H.G. popular epic *Kudrun*, Stanza
655, 2, we find *Daz Herwiges ellen* (*geliebte sich sint*), 'The strength of
Herwic,' i.e. 'Strong Herwic' ('showed himself then very pleasant').
In his rimed Gospel-harmony (written in the second half of the ninth
century) Otfrid von Weissenburg says of Christ (II. 11, 9): *thiu selben*

Kristes kraft, 'the strength of Christ himself'='the strong Christ himself.' See ll. 682, 2110, 2758.

265. Nicht...zu fepn, 'Her form and image hath not its like to be seen on earth.' It is a very characteristic peculiarity of Schiller's poetical diction that he often places an emphatic and almost impetuous nicht at the beginning of a sentence. There are many other instances of this in our drama, viz. ll. 472, 585, 1148, 1331, 1443, 2053, 2358, 2368, 2393, 2635, 2823.

267. This line and the following up to l. 276 (incl.) were, accord-to Schiller's intentions, not to be spoken on the stage. His probable reason was the fear that the comparison of Isabella with the Holy Virgin might give offence to many hearers.

Hoch auf des Lebens Gipfel gestellt does not specially refer to Isabella's august position as Princess, but is rather meant to give a general expression to the thought that a beautiful mother surrounded by her sons is the highest that life can show us—she is the highest in nature, in religion (272) and in art (275).

271. Render 'the world in its glorious perfection is crowned,' i.e. in the mother and her sons the gloriousness of the world is completed.

272. nicht Schöneres, 'nothing more beautiful.' This is unusual and poetic, but in conformity with the older usage in which nicht meant 'nought' and Schöneres was really a genitive. In ordinary prose one would now say nichts Schöneres. Schöneres and Höheres (l. 274) are nouns.

273. auf dem himmlischen Thron refers to the Mother of God, the Madonna, the subject of so many masterly productions by great painters and sculptors.

279. ewig qualifies erneut as well as sprossend.

281. wandeln wird, 'will (ever) move,' i.e. will last as long as the sun will move round the earth.

282. Great rulers give their names to whole periods of history, e.g. the age of Frederic Barbarossa, the age of Elizabeth, the age of Frederic the Great.

283. verrauschen, lit. 'cease to roar,' i.e. 'vanish rapidly' (like a roaring stream). This verb, like verklingen (l. 284), is mainly used with regard to sound. Here to the high sounding names of nations.

284. verklingen, 'sound no longer,' 'die away.'

286. dunkelnachtenden, 'shedding deep night.' The verb nachten is rare and poetic. It means 'to be night,' also 'to be steeped in night' (l. 909), or, as here, 'to spread night.' Render 'spreads its swart wings.'

288. Just as the highest peaks in a mountain range shine in solitary splendour in the early morning (𝔄urora, l. 291) and in the late evening when all the rest of the world is steeped in monotonous gray, so the names of great rulers stand out in history ' as the towering summits of existence,' when little is remembered of the great mass of their peoples. In writing these lines Schiller may have thought of a passage in a famous Storm and Stress drama which he knew well. See the Introd. In the domestic tragedy 𝔍uliu𝔰 von 𝔗arent by Joh. A. Leisewitz (Act III. Sc. 3) the hero is addressed by his father as follows: 𝔍n einem 𝔍ah𝔯h𝔲n𝔡ert bi𝔰t 𝔡u, 𝔡er 𝔉ür𝔰t, 𝔡er einzige von allen 𝔡einen 𝔗arentinern, 𝔡en man noch kennt, wie eine 𝔖ta𝔡t mit 𝔡er 𝔈ntfernung ver𝔰chwin𝔡et un𝔡 blo𝔰 noch 𝔡ie 𝔗ürme hervorragen. With the thought expressed in these lines cp. also Paul Heyse's fine poem 𝔇ul𝔡e, ge𝔡ul𝔡e 𝔡ich fein! See l. 240 n.

<h3 align="center">Scene 4.</h3>

In this Scene we see the endeavours of the Princess Mother to bring about a reconciliation of her sons. It may well be compared with analogous scenes in 𝔍uliu𝔰 von 𝔗arent (Act III. Sc. 3), Racine's *Les Frères Ennemis* (Act IV. Sc. 3), and the *Phoenissae* of Euripides (Act II. Sc. 4), part of which Schiller himself translated into German blank verse (in 1788) under the title 𝔇ie 𝔓höni𝔷ierinnen. This scene is the last scene of the Greek play which Schiller translated.

294. 𝔎önigin 𝔡e𝔰 𝔥immel𝔰, the Holy Virgin. See l. 273.

295. 𝔡ie𝔰e𝔰 𝔥erz, for mein 𝔥erz. See l. 78 n.

296. 𝔡er Übermut, 'arrogant pride,' the Greek ὕβρις. An allusion to the story of Niobe, the proud mother, whose inflated pride brought down upon herself and her children the wrath of the gods. See ll. 1438 ff.

297. vergäße sich, ' might forget itself.'

300. Lit. ' I quite embrace the fulness of my happiness,' i.e. ' I realise my happiness in its full extent.'

301. gewaltsam...teilen, ' constrainedly divide,' i.e. ' constrain myself to divide.'

302. fröhliche 𝔈rgießung, ' happy outpouring.'

304. 𝔡er 𝔑ähe (...freute), now usually an 𝔡er 𝔑ähe.

306. ewig zwei, ' ever two,' ' ever disunited.'

308. trunken, lit. 'drunk,' 'intoxicated,' is often used with regard to joy, delight, exultation. Render ' exultant.' The adjective freu𝔡etrunken, ' intoxicated with joy,' ' overjoyed,' is not unusual.

Don Manuel. Don (from *dominus*) is really more a Spanish than an Italian form of address. In Italy it is generally used of persons of high birth and also sometimes of priests. Manuel, in prose dissyllabic, is as a rule trisyllabic in Schiller's poetry. See the Introduction, p. lxxv.

Don Cesar. This proper name is used for the name of the supreme ruler in Germany and in Russia in the form of Kaiser and Zar.

311. das Herz an seinem Anblick weide, 'with heartfelt joy take pleasure in the sight of him.' die Augen weiden (an einem or einer S.), 'to feast one's eyes' (on a person or a thing), is a common expression, but das Herz weiden, lit. 'to pasture,' i.e. 'to feast one's heart,' is very unusual.

316. Mit welchem Herzen, 'with what (kind of a) heart,' 'with what disposition,' 'how disposed.'

321. War is here, as elsewhere, boldly likened to a steed that waits outside the ancestral hall furiously champing the iron bit, and is only restrained for the moment. For the conception of war as des Streits schlangenhaarigtes Scheusal see l. 140. The phrase in das eherne Gebiß knirschen, 'to champ its iron bit,' is rare and poetic, but compare Schiller's ballad Der Kampf mit dem Drachen, ll. 145—146:

> Ob auch das Roß sich grauend bäumt
> Und knirscht und in den Zügel schäumt.

These lines are rendered by E. P. Arnold-Forster (p. 197):

> My frightened steed might prance and rear
> And champ his bit in natural fear.

323. sich zu entfesseln, 'to set itself free.'

324. Frieden is the accusative, the nominative is Friede (l. 871). Hence the phrase is short for (gebt uns) Krieg oder Frieden!...wir sind gerüstet zu beiden (l. 327). The form Frieden is now occasionally found as a nominative but this should not be imitated.

Lose rimes with Schoße which was pronounced Schose by the Swabian poet. In the original edition Schiller had Loose : Schoose. See the note on his pronunciation to ll. 144 and 170 and the Introduction, p. lxxxix. A similar thought and the same rime occur in Schiller's Lied von der Glocke, ll. 53—54, where he says of the babe:

> Ihm ruhen noch im Zeitenschoße
> Die schwarzen und die heitern Lose.

The idea of the lots is Homeric, and the phrase im Schoße der Zukunft reminds one of the common Homeric phrase das ruht im Schoße der Götter (θεῶν ἐν γούνασι κεῖται).

328. furchtbar is not an adverb. See l. 106 n.

329. follen, viz. tun. 'What is the use of...?'

330. zubereitet is very unusual for vorbereitet. Zubereiten is almost exclusively said of food and of raw material. It occurs several times instead of bereiten in Goethe's Iphigenie the language of which exercised some influence on Schiller's diction in this drama.

331. fremde Schar, 'host of strangers.' See l. 346, fremde Herrschaft = Herrschaft der Fremden or von Fremden, and l. 496, fremder Leidenschaft = Leidenschaft fremder Menschen.

337. raschen Diener. Rasch has here not its usual meaning 'quick,' but is used in the sense of the English 'rash,' 'hasty.' Cp. des raschen Worts (l. 584), eine rasche Tat (l. 776), die rasche Jugend (l. 792), rasche Jugendtat (l. 1474). rasch is not unfrequently used in the poetry of Goethe and Schiller in a sense of blame. See Goethe's Iphigenie, ll. 472, 1824, 2031; Schiller's Die Piccolomini, v. 1, l. 2475; Wallensteins Tod, II. 2, l. 1090. In this passage Isabella shows herself to be a very shrewd observer.

340. von Herzen mit euch meinen stands for von Herzen gut or herzlich gut mit euch meinen.

341. See ll. 203—211.

343. Sich...der Herrschaft angemaßt, 'usurped sovereign power.' In earlier German sich anmaßen took either the genitive or the accusative case of the object. The genitive survives only in poetry, while the accusative is the only case that is now admitted in ordinary prose.

344. sich selbst zu leben, 'to live for himself and according to his own fancy,' 'to live independently.' Now usually für sich selbst zu leben. But cp. Goethe's Hermann und Dorothea, Canto VI. l. 11:

> Damals hoffte jeder sich selbst zu leben.

348. gern versagten, i.e. den sie gern versagen würden, der (euch) gern von ihnen versagt werden würde.

349. dies Geschlecht, contemptuously 'this race,' 'men of this stamp.' The same expression occurs several times in Wallensteins Tod, e.g. I. 7, l. 584, and v. 4, l. 3522, dies Geschlecht kann sich nicht anders freuen als bei Tisch. Dies Geschlecht is really a Biblical term (see Hebrews iii. 10, Darum ich entrüstet ward über dies Geschlecht) which seems to mean 'a bad sort of people.'

350. Schadenfreude, i.e. Freude am Schaden anderer, 'malice.'

352. Häupter. The Hamburg acting-copy reads Häuser. See ll. 238—239.

353. Such stories form the subjects of the great medieval heroic epics such as The Song of the Exiled Dietrich von Bern, The Song of the Death of Horny Siegfrid, The Fall of the Nibelungs, and others.

354. ſich...fort erzählt, 'is handed down in tales.' The reflexive in German must often be rendered by the English passive. Cp. l. 407.

358. los, for loſe, locker, leicht zu löſen.

359. das leichte Glück, 'capricious Fortune,' 'fickle Fortune.' leicht means here 'easily moved,' 'unstable,' 'inconstant,' 'fickle.' Cp. Heine's poem Das Glück iſt eine leichte Dirne. See l. 650 n.

360. Laune, f. 'humour.' Laune, M.H.G. lûne, comes originally from the Latin *luna*, 'moon.' In M.H.G. it means 'phases of the moon,' 'changeableness of fortune,' 'instability of humour,' 'whim.' Cp. in French *avoir des lunes*. Thus the word is an interesting illustration of the medieval belief in the influence of the moon on the disposition of the mind.

361. The general sense of the following lines is that in the changeableness of all human conditions and relations only blood relationship can be trusted; the ties of blood are reliable because they are inborn, while all others are formed by casual interest.

Nur die Natur iſt redlich. Compare with this passage Schiller's words in Der Spaziergang, ll. 193 sqq., and Goethe's elegy Euphroſyne, ll. 69 sqq. Cp. also l. 230.

362. Liegt...feſt, 'lies firmly attached,' 'clings fast.'

363. Wenn, for während. See l. 34 n.

364. treibt, 'is drifting.'

366. Wohl dem, dem die Geburt den Bruder gab. Cp. Legouvé's line (in his tragedy 'La mort d'Abel'):

> *Le frère est un ami donné par la nature.*

See the Introduction, p. lxix, and J. Imelmann, 'Anmerkungen zu deutschen Dichtern,' p. 17.

367. Anerſchaffen, 'given by creation,' 'given by birth.' Cp. l. 389.

369. zweifach, 'double,' i.e. his strength is doubled when his brother stands by his side.

370. The following lines of the Chorus reflect the impression produced on the bystanders by the powerful and wise speech of the mother. The Chorus is here not divided but simply gives utterance to what every listener must feel at this moment. This is one of the passages where the Chorus is not voicing the feelings of a party, but is what A. W. v. Schlegel called the Greek chorus generally, an 'ideal spectator.'

B.   IO

es ist etwas Großes...um, 'there is something great...in *or* about.'

372. Tun und Verkehren. In this phrase Verkehren may be taken in a twofold sense.   Either it may be a synonym of der Verkehr or das Treiben, Handeln, in which case the phrase should be rendered by 'doings and actions,' or Verkehren may have the sense of 'wrong actions,' 'foolish actions,' 'follies.' Etwas verkehren means 'to turn a thing the wrong way'; the adj. verkehrt means 'false,' 'perverted.'   Probably the former meaning was intended by Schiller.   Tun und Verkehren is called in l. 374 das verworrene Streben.

373. ruhiger Klarheit, 'calm clearness,' 'serene calm.'

374. das verworrene Streben, 'our confused aspirations' as opposed to the clear survey and purpose of the ruler.   See l. 2144 n.

377. Sieh dich umher, very unusual for Sieh umher or Sieh dich um, 'Look round.'

378. als deines Bruders, in prose als das deines Bruders.

381. Ein jeder, viz. von euch.

feines Alters, 'of his age,' 'for his years.'

382. weicht, 'gives way,' hence 'is inferior.'

383. euch, instead of the reciprocal einander.   See also ll. 452, 2240. Angesicht, instead of the ordinary Gesicht, is poetic.

390. Frevler an dem, 'offender against your (own blood).'

393. anzuschließen is intended to rime with Füßen (l. 391).   Rime is often used by Schiller at the end of passages in blank verse to mark strongly the conclusion of an important speech.   See the Introduction, pp. lxxxvi sqq.

394. Note the chiastic construction of this line by means of which the contrast is still further emphasised.

398. möchte has here still the old meaning, which is now obsolete and poetic, of vermöchte, könnte.

Bette is the older form of the modern Bett.   It is still sometimes used in prose and is frequent in poetry.

399. Schwefelstroms, 'sulphur stream,' refers to the liquid lava.   The simile is very appropriate in a town which is not far distant from Mount Etna.   Cp. also ll. 946 sqq.

401. Geburt, 'birth,' say 'product' (Erzeugnis).   Schiller is very fond of using the word Geburt in this sense.

Lavarinde, 'crust of lava.'

402. dem Gesunden, i.e. that which was before gesund, dem gesunden und bebauten Boden, the soil that was before cultivated and inhabited.

Now there reigns destruction which has befallen the healthy land like a disease. The idea is that the natural healthy brotherly love is covered beyond recognition by the pernicious stream of hatred.

The substitution of ben Gefilben for bem Gefunben proposed by some commentators is not justified in any way.

407. Vergibt fich, 'is forgiven,' 'can be forgiven.' See l. 950.

verföhnt fich, 'is to be atoned for,' 'can be expiated.'

409. Ratfchluß, *m.* 'resolution.'

wohlbefonnen, 'after full consideration,' 'with fixed purpose.'

410. fteigt hinauf, 'goes back to.' Cp. the French *remonter*.

411. unverftänb'ger, here 'unreasoning,' 'unreflecting,' 'thoughtless.'

412. ihn, viz. Euern Haber (l. 410).

414. aus, now usually heraus. herausfinben, 'to find out.'

417. fortgezeugt, 'propagated.'

unglückfel'ger, 'unfortunate.'

418. Die neufte Unbill, 'the most recent wrong,' viz. that even on this day, in the presence of their loving mother, they will not give up their deep-rooted hatred. In the Hamburg acting-copy there is a marginal note by Schiller himself in which he replaced the poetic Unbill by the more common word Feinbfchaft.

geboren, viz. hat. See l. 7 n.

With the whole passage cp. the words of Octavio in Schiller's Die Piccolomini, V. 1, ll. 2452—3:

> Das eben ift ber Fluch ber böfen Tat,
>
> Daß fie, fortzeugenb, immer Böfes muß gebären.

419. alle fchwere, now usually alle fchweren. After alle and feine the adjectives as a rule take the weak form in modern German, but Lessing and the Weimar classics frequently employ the strong forms. Cp. l. 615, alle finftre Falten, and l. 2440, feine fchöne Früchte. But l. 54, alle heil'gen Banbe, and l. 1003, alle frühern Banbe.

fchwere Taten instead of Greueltaten (compare Latin *facinora*). Schwer may either have a physical or a moral sense. See also l. 949. In his fine ballad Die Kraniche bes Jbyfus (XVI. 6) Schiller has bes Morbes fchwere Tat. In Goethe's Jphigenie, II. 2, l. 890, the murder of Agamemnon is called a fchwere Tat.

421. wolltet ihr is subj., 'do you really intend?'

422. fortkämpfen, 'fight on,' 'go on fighting,' 'continue.'

424. vertilgen, usually tilgen. vertilgen is commonly used in the sense of 'to destroy the life of some one,' 'to wipe some one out of existence.' In Schiller's 𝔐𝔞𝔯𝔦𝔞 𝔖𝔱𝔲𝔞𝔯𝔱, IV. 10, ll. 3245—6, Elizabeth says with regard to Mary:

> Der Zweifel meiner fürstlichen Geburt,
>
> Er ist getilgt, sobald ich dich vertilge.

426. schenkt, in the sense of erlaßt, 'remit.'

427. eine Schuld abtragen, 'to pay off a debt,' which is hoch aufgelaufen, has 'run up high' or 'mounted up high.' unabtragbare Schuld, a debt which cannot be cleared away *or* paid (off).

429. ihn, i.e. den alten Haß (l. 430). See l. 197 n.

431. sei, i.e. geweiht (l. 432).

433. In this and the following lines the twofold character of the Chorus is clearly noticeable. In ll. 433—435 they speak as the 'ideal spectator,' as a body of disinterested Messinians deeply impressed by the wise words of Isabella, while in ll. 436—439 they relapse into the warlike attitude of thoughtless partisan adherents of each of the two brothers.

437. gerecht, usually recht; perhaps under the influence of genehm.

440. Der Worte Köcher, 'the quiver of speech.' The words are likened to arrows. The idea occurs sometimes in ancient classical poetry. Cp. also the common Homeric phrase ἔπεα πτερόεντα, 'winged words,' geflügelte Worte. This line and the following have six strongly accented syllables. From here to the end the despairing mother speaks with ever increasing passionate emotion.

444. sinnlos wütend, 'with senseless fury.' sinnlos is here an adverb. But see l. 24 n.

445. des Hausgotts...Altar, the altar of the household god, one of the Penates who protected the family hearth. In many Greek households there was a domestic altar to Zeus the Hospitable. In other passages not one god but several Penates are mentioned. See ll. 163, 1191. On the mixture of heathen and Christian conceptions in this play see the Introd. pp. xxvi—xxvii.

447. Wechselmords, for wechselseitigen (or gegenseitigen) Mordes, 'mutual murder,' is poetic.

450. das thebanische Paar refers to Eteocles and Polynices, the sons of Oedipus and Iocasta, who fought against one another in deadly hatred and perished in single combat for the rulership of their native city, the one by the spear of the other. The famous feud and ruin of the hostile brothers of ancient Thebes is the subject of two fine Greek tragedies which were well known to Schiller. One is the play of

Aeschylus 'The Seven against Thebes' and the other the 'Phoenician Damsels' of Euripides. In contrasting them with Schiller's hostile brothers it should be noted that in the ancient drama the lyrical and romantic element of love is wholly absent from their conflict.

452. eherner Umarmung, lit. 'brazen embrace,' 'iron grasp.' The adjective ehern in the sense of feft, unwiberftehlich, unlöslich is here used after the analogy of the Homeric χάλκεος. It had often been used in this way by Goethe in his Sphigenie, and Schiller's poetical language in Die Braut von Messina shows in more than one instance the influence of Goethe's Hellenic drama.

455. Notice the rimes from here to the end of Isabella's speech (heile : Säule : teile ; hebt : gelebt) which give it an impressive conclusion. See the note to l. 591. Cp. ll. 2390, 2416.

457. hebt, in prose erhebt or emporhebt, emporfteigt.

458. zweigefpalten, for in zwei gefpalten, 'parting in two.' The Roman poet Statius relates that the flame rising from the common funeral pyre of the brothers had divided itself asunder in order to manifest that even in death the brothers kept their old feeling of hatred. On the other hand legends relate how roses and lilies growing on the tombs of lovers intertwine as a token of their affection lasting beyond the grave.

459. fchaubernd, for fchauberhaftes, 'abominable,' 'horrifying,' 'hideous.' Cp. l. 1884 n. and wunbernd for verwunbert, l. 609.

gestorben (feib) unb gelebt (habt). See l. 7 n. This line has again six accented syllables. See l. 36, and Introd. p. lxxxiii.

SCENE 5.

This Scene, the beginning and end of which are marked by short rimed utterances of the whole Chorus, brings before the spectator the effect of the mother's strong appeal. The brothers who are both devoted sons are deeply moved and ultimately become reconciled. With this Scene the exposition of the drama is completed.

463. Ich nicht vergoß. This line is somewhat obscure. So far, it seems, no blood of kindred has been spilt, and the hands of the knights are unstained (rein, l. 464). So the line seems to have the hypothetical sense: Wenn einmal verwanbtes Blut fließen follte, fo vergoß ich es nicht or ich will bas Bruberblut nicht vergoffen haben, by which utterance the knights forming the Chorus decline all responsibility for the actions of their masters. These words show how deeply the Chorus is moved by the idea of the fratricide suggested by the fate of the hostile brothers of Thebes.

It is characteristic of the brothers that Don Cesar in each case makes the first attempt at an approach, he speaks first, steps nearer (l. 482) and begins the lively *stichomythia* (l. 489), while Don Manuel is the first to acknowledge the good qualities of his brother (l. 472).

472. Gefarn. We should now say Gefar in the accusative too. Perhaps the poet was anxious to show clearly the grammatical relation of the name and therefore chose the obsolete ending. Cp. l. 147 n.

wer, for ber, welcher, 'he who.'

473. Fühlt' er is the subj. of the preterite: 'if he felt.'

476. edles has here still its original meaning of 'high born,' 'noble,' and not the usual modern moral sense. With edel is connected the noun ber Abel, 'nobility.'

482. fo gerecht (erfannt), unusual for für or als fo gerecht, 'known to be so just.' The acting-copies have gefannt.

484. bir...Gewußt, for in bir...Gewußt, is an imitation of the Greek dative construction which is quite unknown in ordinary German prose.

verföhnlich, 'placable,' 'forgiving,'

485. fpart' ich = hätte ich gefpart.

486. abgefchildert, now obsolete, is replaced by gefchildert, 'depicted,' 'described.' Abfchildern was quite common in the German classics of the eighteenth century. It originally meant 'to paint (one's arms) on a shield (ber Schild),' then simply 'to paint.' Subsequently 'to paint with words,' 'to depict,' 'to describe vividly and graphically.'

487. Don Manuel uses Isabella's argument in ll. 336 sqq. and his brother at once agrees with him. In the following lines, in fact throughout the whole of this Scene, the characteristic *stichomythia* should be noticed.

Stichomythia ($\sigma\tau\iota\chi o\mu\nu\theta\iota a$), 'talking in [alternate] lines,' is common in Greek tragic writers, in the classical French tragedians, in Shakespeare, and it was very successfully imitated by both Goethe and Schiller. By means of it the dialogue is carried on in short and often quite epigrammatic sentences by which it gains much in animation. The most frequent kinds of stichomythia are those in which each speaker has regularly either only one line (ll. 489 sqq.) or two lines (ll. 501 sqq.). At the beginning of this Scene (ll. 466—488) sometimes two, sometimes one, sometimes three lines are given to each speaker, but in each case the other brother has exactly the same number of lines allotted to him.

As a rule this parallelism is used to bring out strongly and pointedly diametrically opposed views of two speakers, accusation and retort, and thus consists of a number of antitheses. In other cases a string of questions and answers are given in the exactly corresponding lines of stichomythia, as in ll. 739—776. In this Scene, however, it is remarkable that each sentence of the one brother is confirmed or supplemented by a similar utterance of the other brother till in the end they are reconciled and all discord has vanished. The usual kind of stichomythia occurs later in the play in ll. 1707 sqq. with the peculiarity however, not found in the ancient classics, that each couple of antithetic lines are bound together into one metrical unit by means of rime. See the Introduction, pp. xc—xci.

496. frember Leibenſchaft. See l. 331 n.

497. This line refers to ll. 356 sqq.

499. The substitution of bir reichen for ergreifen, which has been proposed by some critics, is an unnecessary alteration of Schiller's text.

500. Beibe betrachten einanber. The brothers had so far studiously avoided looking at each other. Cp. l. 383 and the stage direction after l. 432.

504. noch wunberbarer rühret, 'touches my heart with even greater wonder.' He thinks of his beloved Beatrice. This is the first very faint hint that Beatrice may be a member of his family. Don Cesar apparently does not notice this observation.

507. freunblich ſanftgeſinnte, 'kind and tender-hearted.' See l. 24 n.

508. übelwollend mir gehäſſ'ge, 'malevolent and full of hatred towards me.' Gehäſſig has here clearly the meaning of haſſerfüllt (gegen mich), feinbſelig (mir or gegen mich), and not that of verhaßt, 'odious,' 'detested,' which it may also have. Note the contrast with l. 508.

509. The same motive occurs in Klinger's domestic drama Die Zwillinge in which the same subject of the hostile brothers had been treated before Schiller. In Klinger's play the object of discord is a neapolitaniſches Hengſtchen, later on Apfelſchimmel. Schiller knew the play well (see the Introd. p. lxxi) and may have taken the motive of the Pferbe von arab'ſcher Zucht from it.

nahmſt...In Anſpruch, 'thou claim'dst.'

511. ich's. Es refers to bas Geſuch or some similar word.

514. ich beſchwöre bich, 'I beseech thee.'

517. bin ich's wohl zufrieben. See the note on l. 86.

520. bie Herzen, for unſre Herzen. Cp. l. 196 n.

522. Instead of the strong jeber one would expect beibe in agreement with wir and werben.

524. 2Bas stands here, as sometimes, instead of für was, wesħalb, weswegen, warum.

The reconciliation of the attendants is analogous to the reconciliation of the hostile French and Burgundian knights in Schiller's drama Die Jungfrau von Orleans (Act III. Scene 3).

SCENE 6.

Schiller adopted from the Greek tragedians the practice of announcing the coming of a messenger by one of the persons on the stage by whom he is seen approaching in the distance and of conjecturing the nature of the message from the expression of his face. See also l. 1570. Bearers of good news in the ancient drama usually had wreaths on their heads or branches of green olive twigs fastened on their staves (l. 542). In medieval German poetry a bringer of joyful tidings made the character of his message known at once by claiming the messenger's reward. In M.H.G. he said, *gebet mir daz botenbrôt*, and this typical saying was adopted by Lessing in his drama Nathan ber 2Beife, where a Saracen at the time of the Crusades asks Sultan Saladin for his due reward on account of the good news he has brought. See also ll. 1563, 2113.

530. ausgefenbet, viz. ħaft or ħatteft. See l. 7 n.

532. ħarret bein, 'awaits thee.' See wartet mein, l. 858. This old genitive bein is poetic for ħarret beiner or wartet auf bich.

534. fluchbefreiten, a bold compound instead of vom Fluch befreiten. The curse from which the town is now freed is the threatening civil war; the reconciliation of the brothers has saved Messina from it.

540. neu verjüngten Phönir, a 'Phoenix in renewed youth.' The Phoenix, lit. 'the red one,' 'the shining one,' is a unique bird of Egyptian mythology, like an eagle in shape but with wings of mingled red and gold. It is said to have burnt itself by setting fire to its own nest at the expiration of a period of 500 years, and from the flames flew forth a new Phoenix youthful and beautiful. Hence it became the symbol of eternal rejuvenescence and also of a transition to a higher life. The legend of the Phoenix is told by several ancient authors, e.g. Ovid (*Metamorphoses* XV. 392—402); but it is worth mentioning that a particularly beautiful poem on the Phoenix exists also in Old English, written in all probability by the great Northumbrian poet Cynewulf.

542. See the note at the beginning of this Scene.

This line is to be taken in a metaphorical sense. It simply means 'I am the bearer of joyful tidings.'

544. verfammeln is as a rule only used of persons. But the consequence of the joyful tidings is that mother, brothers and the missing girl will be 'brought together' and 'united' in the same place.

549. Note the indirect way in which Don Cesar's joyful emotion is vividly brought before the spectator.

552. mitfreuend, 'rejoicing with (him).'

558. dein Anblick, 'the sight of you.'

mir ahnet, 'I anticipate.' The impersonal construction mir ahnet (and also in some of the older classics mich ahnet) occurs side by side with ich ahne, 'I have a presentiment,' and is especially frequent in poetry. Cp. l. 1883, was ahnet mir?

559. Herzensfreunde, or Busenfreunde, 'bosom friends.'

560. Der lang' gebundne Trieb, 'the shoot long kept back,' viz. the germ of brotherly love. Trieb means 'shoot' as well as 'impulse.' Don Manuel continues the meaning 'shoot' in l. 563 by speaking of Blüte and Frucht.

562. Nachholen, 'retrieve.' The fluctuating stress on Nach in Nachholen brings the word into special prominence and makes the statement all the more emphatic. See the Introd. pp. lxxvi—lxxvii.

das verlorne Leben, he has not enjoyed and consequently has lost his life on account of his hatred of his brother. See die verlornen Jahre, l. 2446.

563. This somewhat sententious line, characteristic of the elder brother, shows that his thoughts are busy with something else. This is made clear by Scene 7.

After **567.** Zerstreuung, 'absence of mind.'

568. Liebe. Manuel obviously thinks only of his own love for Beatrice. Don Cesar must understand the word Liebe to refer to the new brotherly love. The line is intentionally ambiguous.

570. Entdeckt' ich, the subjunctive of the imperfect, 'if I were to disclose' (I should be delayed too long). If he did, the play would probably soon be over. Don Manuel does not press his brother—he is himself not much given to disclosing his own feelings and secrets, and is at the present moment less anxious than ever to know of his brother's and to continue the conversation with him.

572. trenn', the present subjunctive trenne for möge or soll trennen.

578. der Hölle Pforten, 'the Gates of Hell' metaphorically for 'Hell' itself. The expression is at once Biblical and Homeric. In the New Testament we read (Matthew xvi. 18): bie Pforten ber Hölle follen fie nicht überwältigen. In Homeric language, which Schiller knew from J. H. Voss' famous translation, he met with the very phrase haffen wie bie Pforten bes Habes, e.g. *Iliad* IX. 312, verhaßt ift jener, fo fehr wie bes Aibes Pforten, and *Odyssey* XIV. 156, ber ift mir verhaßt wie bie Pforten ber unterften Tiefe. The modern phrase is verhaßt wie ber Tob. Cp. l. 2669, zu bes Tobes traurigen Toren.

584. rafchen. See l. 336 n.

585. Nicht Wurzeln...fchlägt, 'Does not take root.' The hasty word is soon forgotten by him who spoke it, but it is carefully preserved by a suspicious rival. The angry word is likened to a carelessly scattered seed from which a malignant weed will soon sprout forth.

588. Schlingfraut, 'twining plant,' 'rank weed'; more common are the words Schlinggewächs or Schlingpflanze.

enblos treibenb, 'sprouting endlessly,' 'in endless propagation.'

590. Verworrenheit, for Verwirrung bes Gefühls, 'confusion of feeling,' 'perversion of feeling,' 'morbid feeling.'

trennen fich unheilbar, 'separate in a breach that can never be healed,' 'are for ever lost to one another.' Unheilbar may also be taken in the sense of unverföhnlich, 'in irreconcilable hatred.'

591. bie Beften rimes with Äften. Rimes were employed by Schiller and other German dramatists, after the model of Shakespeare, at the close of a scene in order to provide an impressive ending. See the note to l. 455, and the Introduction, p. lxxxvi.

Scene 7.

In this Scene Don Manuel discloses his secret, viz. his love for Beatrice and her flight with him, to his faithful followers. His detailed account is called forth by the remarks of his men on his strange absence of mind during the important conversation with his brother. The Chorus voice here the natural feeling of the onlookers.

593. verfennen usually means falfch fennen, nicht fennen, *méconnaître*, 'to mistake,' 'misjudge.' But here it has the meaning of nicht wieber erfennen, 'not to recognise any more.' The speaker indicates that he was mistaken in his old conception of Don Manuel's character.

ich muß bich faft ganz verfennen, 'I almost fail to recognise thee,' seems to be a reminiscence of Goethe's Torquato Taffo, IV. 2, l. 2250: Mein teurer Freunb, faft ganz verfenn' ich bich. See also l. 1675: Ganz verfenn' ich ihn, 'I do not understand him at all,' 'I cannot make him out.'

595. gutmeinenb, 'well meaning.' The stress on gut is as strong as that on meinenb and brings gut into special prominence. For this and other cases of fluctuating stress see the Introduction, p. lxxviii.

602. füh[lo8, poetic for the usual gefühllo8. The acting-copies have lieblo8. In them certain poetic words have been replaced in a number of cases by more common expressions.

609. wunbernb, instead of which fich wunbernb', verwunbert, or ftaunenb are now usually employed. This use of this present participle occurs not unfrequently in Schiller's poetry, e.g. ll. 697, 2196, and also l. 116 of Der Spaziergang :

       Seltfamer Sprachen Gewirr brauft in ba8 wunbernbe Ohr;

and l. 137 of the same poem:

       Da zerrinnt vor bem wunbernben Blick ber Nebel be8 Wahne8.

In Wilhelm Tell, I. 2, l. 221, Schiller also writes:

       Vor biefem Haufe hielt er wunbernb an.

In modern German prose wunbern is only used impersonally or re-flexively: fich über eine Sache wunbern or verwunbern. In the personal intransitive sense wunbern is replaced by ftaunen. Cp. the analogous use of türmenb, 'towering,' for fich türmenb in Schiller's poetry, e.g. bie türmenbe Stabt in l. 67 of Der Spaziergang.

fein verwanbelt Herz, for fein Herz verwanbelt.

615. mir, ethical dative, 'for me.'

finftre after alle would now be finftern. But the strong form of the adj. after alle and feine is common in the classical writers of the eighteenth century.

Falten...au8geglättet unb verfchwunben. A similar metaphor is used by Wallenstein with regard to Max Piccolomini in Wallenftein8 Tob, V. 3, ll. 3423—5 :

                    Sein Leben

       Liegt faltenlo8 unb leuchtenb au8gebreitet,

       Kein bunfler Flecken blieb in ihm zurück.

618. benfe mir, 'picture to myself,' 'imagine.'

622. liebt...ben Liebenben. On this peculiarity of Schiller's poetic diction see l. 104 n. It is especially frequent in the case of Liebe and lieben. See also ll. 1048—9.

623. Dem Namenlofen does not mean that his beloved does not know his Christian name (see ll. 1799 and 1821), but is here equivalent to

bem Unbekannten (ll. 1867 and 1868), the unknown, the man of whose
high birth and princely position she is ignorant.

In calling himself ben Namenlosen Don Manuel may perhaps mean to
say, like young Rudenz in Wilhelm Tell, II. 2, 1. 1598: Mich hat ber
Ruhm noch nicht genannt, in which case namenlos would be equivalent to
unberühmt, one 'who has not yet made a name for himself.' But, to
judge from Don Manuel's character, it is hardly likely that he would
call himself in Sicily 'unrenowned.'

624. ahnet, in prose ahnt. The older and longer form is often used
in poetry. See Introduction, p. lxxiii.

625. bie golbne Binbe, 'the golden diadem,' a golden fillet set with
jewels (l. 632) as badge of sovereignty. See l. 835. In l. 632 the
diadem is called ber golbne Reif, 'the golden circlet.' Similarly Schiller
says in his poem Das Glück, ll. 27—29, of Zeus, the father of gods and
men:

> Unter bie Menge greift er mit Eigenwillen, unb welches
> Haupt ihm gefället, um bas flicht er mit liebenber Hanb
> Jetzt ben Lorbeer, unb jetzt bie herrschaftgebenbe Binbe.

In this passage we have the same phrase: bie Binbe einem um bas Haupt
(or bie Stirne) flechten, viz. einen zum Fürsten zu erheben. An exact parallel
to this line occurs in Die Piccolomini, II. 3, ll. 752—753, where Wallenstein hopes to change his warlike laurels into a royal diadem for his
daughter Thekla. The exact words are:

> ben Kranz bes kriegerischen Lebens...
> In einen königlichen Schmuck verwanbelt
> Um biese schöne Stirne flechten.

626. Ihr um, in prose (and in the acting-copies) um ihre.

627. bas Geliebte, here and in l. 1157 for bas geliebte Wesen, as in
Latin and Greek. In older German we commonly find *daz liep*, bas Lieb.
In modern German prose one now generally uses two words : ber
Geliebte and bie Geliebte.

628. In prose: Mit bem Glanz unb Schein ungehoffter Größe.

630. es refers proleptically to bas Schöne (l. 631). Cp. l. 197 n.

632. erhebt, 'sets off.' See ll. 835—838. In Medieval German
poetry the idea of gold studded with precious stones and each in its
turn ornamented by the other is very frequent.

ben Edelstein refers to bas Schöne. The beautiful girl will be still more
beautiful wearing the golden circlet of the Princess.

Don Manuel is so much carried away by his feeling that the end of this passage is full of lyric pathos and the lines 627—632 are adorned with rime. Cp. also ll. 660 ff.

635. Späheraugen, say 'spying eyes,' 'curious eyes.'

638. dir abzufragen, lit. 'obtain from thee by questioning,' hence 'question thee (closely) about.'

639. der Jagden, the plural on account of the various kinds of hunting. Cp. l. 907.

640. des Falken Sieg, viz. over other falcons in catching the heron. It does not mean the victory of the gerfalcon over the hunted heron. Thus des Falken Sieg in the Wettfliegen is a parallel of der Rosse Wettlauf, but it really stands for Falkenjagd (Jagd mit Falken) or Reiherbeize (Beizen auf Reiher), 'falcon's flight,' 'falconry,' 'hawking,' 'heron-hunting.'

643. unsres Chors, 'of our train.' Chor has here, and in l. 805, as often in Schiller's poetry, not the usual meaning of 'chorus,' but of a 'band of men,' 'followers.' In his ballad Die Bürgschaft, l. 124, a man forces his way through a large crowd and this is expressed:

> Da zertrennt er gewaltig den dichten Chor;

and in another fine ballad Der Taucher, l. 21, the poet speaks of

> der Knappen zagendem Chor.

It is a little awkward that just here the 'Chorus' of the older knights uses Chor in a different sense.

sonst, 'formerly,' 'once.'

645. Mag, in the old German sense of 'may,' 'is allowed.' This use of mag is now obsolete and poetic, in ordinary German it has been replaced sometimes by darf and sometimes by kann. Cp. l. 676.

647. neid'schen Hülle, 'envious veil.' The covering is not really envious, but Don Manuel's happiness is to be screened from the eye of envy. Render 'jealous veil.'

648. Note the rime of verhehle and Seele (l. 649) and cp. the Introd. p. lxxxviii.

650. 'Fortuna is a winged and very fickle deity.' See l. 359 n.

zu binden, 'to be chained,' 'to be fettered.' Cp. the lines of Heinrich Heine:

> Das Glück ist eine leichte Dirne,
> Die weilt nicht gern am selben Ort,
> Sie streicht das Haar dir aus der Stirne
> Und küßt dich schnell und flattert fort.

651. In this line and the following Don Manuel refers to the well-known myth of Pandora. This beautiful 'all-gifted' woman brought to Epimetheus, the brother of Prometheus, a casket in which, according to a late Greek tradition, all the blessings of the gods were enclosed. When Epimetheus rashly opened the box the winged blessings escaped and were lost for the human race, Hope alone remaining at the bottom of the vessel. According to an older tradition all the ills were enclosed in the box and, on its being opened, escaped and spread all over the earth. The first-mentioned (younger) tradition suits the sense of this passage better.

In many passages in his poetry Schiller has expressed the view that happiness, above all happiness in love, is a gift from the gods which must not be disclosed to the gossiping crowd. Cp. his poem Das Geheimniß; Die Piccolomini, III. 5, ll. 1729—35; Wallensteins Tod, III. 18, ll. 2050—4; Maria Stuart, II. 5, ll. 1629—31, and other passages. The medieval Minnesingers were of the same opinion and praised the happiness of *tougen minne*, 'secret love.'

654. die Decke, 'the covering,' more usual den Deckel, 'the lid' (of the box).

658. des Dämons Neid, 'the envy of the evil spirit' who, like the gods, as conceived by the ancients, grudged mortals any pure and lasting happiness. Dämon has here the modern sense of 'demon,' 'evil spirit'; in Greek the word δαίμων only means 'supernatural being,' 'spirit,' 'ghost.' The evil spirit was called by Goethe in Faust II a Widerdämon. The belief in the envy of the gods and the instability of Fortune is illustrated by the story of the ring of Polycrates which furnished the subject of one of Schiller's finest ballads.

661. goldne. Schiller and Goethe are in the habit of calling anything beautiful and desirable golden. Cp. goldner Traum (l. 901). In his ballad Hero und Leander, ll. 19—20, Schiller says similarly:

Und die süße Frucht der Liebe
Hing am Abgrund der Gefahr.

Happiness in love is in several passages of Schiller's poetry looked upon as 'a sacred spoil.' Cp. Die Piccolomini, III. 6, l. 1732.

663. Das Morgen. The words heute and morgen if used substantively are neuters, and thus das Morgen, 'the to-morrow,' is distinguished from der Morgen, 'the morning.'

666. In this line and the following the even and uninterrupted flow of his hoped for happiness by the side of his beloved is likened to the running of a brook and of the sand in the hour-glass. Instead of Stundenglas one often says Sanduhr.

669. dein Los beneidend rühmen, 'envy and praise thy lot.'

673. schwärmend, 'roving,' generally said of bees and birds.

674. Die Insel, viz. Sicily, of which Messina is the chief town. verschlungnen, lit. 'entwined,' 'labyrinthine.'

676. mich überreden möchte, 'might persuade myself.' Mögen has here again the older sense of können, the English 'may.'

677. Zaubernebel, *m.* 'magic mist.'

680. Vernehmet denn und hört. Such tautologies occur sometimes in impressive diction. Cp. l. 266.

682. Des Vaters Macht, for der mächtige Vater. See l. 264 n.

683. Der Jugend, for meiner Jugend. See l. 196 n.

das Joch. See ll. 37, 38.

685. des Weidwerks is a poetic term instead of der Jagd. Weidwerk usually means the 'art of hunting,' and the term Weidmann denotes a 'skilled huntsman.' Die Weide means 'the pasture,' 'the place where animals go for food,' and in older German it also took the meaning of 'hunting,' 'fishing.'

686. Don Manuel's first meeting with Beatrice is very similar to that of the Indian King Dushanta with Śakuntalá in the famous Indian romantic love drama by Kalidasa. Schiller knew it very well and he, as well as Goethe, had a very high opinion of it. He had published part of it (in Forster's translation) in 1790 in the tenth part of his Thalia, and he read the whole (published in 1791) probably at the beginning of 1792. *Śakuntalá* (after the name of the heroine of the play) is held to be perhaps the most beautiful specimen of the classical Indian drama and Schiller himself had at one time the design of adapting it for the Weimar stage. Thus it is not impossible that in the description of the first meeting of the lovers he may have been influenced by the charming opening scene of Kalidasa's play. The following of a hind leading to the discovery of a woman in a remote place occurs also in medieval legends, e.g. in the story of Genoveva.

687. Entlang des Waldgebirgs, 'along the wooded hills.' The use of entlang with the genitive case after it is very rare. The usual construction is to place entlang *after* an accusative, as in Goethe's poem An den Mond, l. 21:

> Rausche, Fluß, das Tal entlang!

688. Hindin was formed by means of the suffix -in (through form-association with Hündin, Füchsin, etc.) from the older word die Hinde, 'hind.' The modern prose word is Hirschkuh. A *white* hind is especially uncommon, and for that reason often found in poetry. The chase of a *milk white* stag is a favourite enterprise of huntsmen in legends and popular poetry.

690. Krümmen, fr. Krümme, *f.* (also Krumme), 'bend,' 'winding,' instead of which Krümmung would be used in ordinary prose. The subst. Krümme is derived fr. the adj. frumm, 'bent,' 'crooked,' as die Güte, fr. gut, Glätte, fr. glatt, etc. It is a common word in older German and often used by poets of the 18th century, especially by Schiller. Cp. Die Piccolomini, I. 4, l. 468; Wallensteins Tod, III. 15, l. 1927 (Schlangenkrümme).

692. Auf Wurfes Weite, 'within the throw (of a javelin).' One can also say auf Wurfweite, as auf Schußweite, lit. 'within the distance of a throw,' 'within the distance of a shot.'

693. erzielen is a rare word meaning either durch (gutes) Zielen treffen, 'to hit (with a well aimed throw),' say 'hit it with my spear,' or merely aufs Ziel nehmen, 'to aim at.' Zielen, 'to take aim.'

697. wundernd. See l. 609 n.

698. Nonne. Beatrice was brought up by the nuns and wore the garments of a nun, but she was not a nun and had not taken any religious vows (ll. 737 ff.).

699. es...kost, 'pets it,' 'caresses it.' Kosen no longer takes a direct object, but is as a rule only used intransitively, meaning 'to talk fondly' or 'to make love.' Compare Heine's lines:

Die Veilchen kichern und kosen

Und schaun zu den Sternen empor.

But Schiller says in Die Räuber, II. 2:

er streichelte und koste den Nacken.

The compound liebkosen is generally used in the sense of 'to pet,' 'to fondle,' 'to caress.'

701. ausholend, 'lifting up the arm (for a throw),' ausholen (zu einer S. always denotes the stretching or lifting of an arm for striking, throwing, etc.). The strong accent on aus is very expressive. See the paragraph on fluctuating stress in the Introd. pp. lxxvi—lxxviii.

The situation depicted in ll. 696—703 has been made the subject of a capital sketch by C. Jäger which is easily accessible in the volume called 'Schiller-Galerie' (cartoons by W. v. Kaulbach, C. Jäger, and four other artists). München, Verlagsanstalt für Kunst und Wissenschaft. No year. It has justly been called (by E. Förster): „ein Bild von Anmut und Lebensfrische aus diesem sonst so düstern Trauerspiele. Anmutig

und voll hohen weiblichen Adels ist Beatrice, lebensfrisch, in jugendlichem Übermut
steht Don Manuel vor ihr, dessen bisher ungezügeltem Willen eine Erscheinung
Schranken setzt, die er seither nicht kannte; so bilden diese beiden Figuren einen
wirksamen Gegensatz, der sich selbst in der flehenten Hirschkuh und dem beute=
lustigen Jagdhund fortsetzt."

703. gegen einander, usually einander gegenüber.

704. Most lines between ll. 704 and 724 are connected by means of
rime which gives them a specially elevated and lyric character. See the
Introd. pp. lxxxvi sqq. and also xlv.

707. umgewandelt schnell. Schiller is fond of putting the emphatic
past participle, followed by an enclitic adverb, at the beginning of the
sentence and of placing the noun which it qualifies later in the sentence.
This is much stronger and more poetic than the ordinary mein Herz ist
schnell umgewandelt. Cp. ll. 731, 1001, 2555. Cp. also l. 303 where
an infinitive is used in the same way.

711. dämmerhellen Tagen, 'twilight days.' Dämmerhell is a compound
of the obsolete noun der Dämmer, 'twilight,' instead of which we now
usually say die Dämmerung and the adjective hell. Dämmer still occurs
frequently in compounds, e.g. Dämmerlicht, Dämmerschein, Dämmerstunde,
dämmergrau, dämmervoll. The meaning of dämmerhell is, like the French
clair-obscur, finsterhell, halbdunkel, verschwommen, unbestimmt.

713. Besinnungskraft, *f.* lit. 'power of collecting myself,' for 'consciousness.' Say 'when I regained consciousness,' 'when the power of
recollection returned to me.'

715. Hora, *f.* is the 'hour (for prayer),' Betstunde. Cp. l. 1075.
Hora (canonica and *regularis*) is the appointed hour at which monks
and nuns sing and pray together. The prayers are also sometimes
called Die Horen. In Julius von Tarent (see the Introd. p. lxxi), II. 2,
the nun Blanca says to Julius in order to make him leave her: Hören
Sie! die Glocke zur Hora läutet.

717. und ward nicht mehr gesehen is also the last line of Goethe's
famous ballad Der Fischer.

721. des Klosters Pflicht, 'the duties of the convent,' 'the cloister's
vows.' furchtbar heilig, 'awful and sacred.' See l. 24 n. The modern
adverb furchtbar in colloquial phrases such as furchtbar schwer, furchtbar
froh, etc. does not yet occur in the language of Schiller and
Goethe.

722. It is noteworthy that at first Don Manuel, carried away by his
feelings, does not heed the grave warning of the Chorus. But when at

last in ll. 736 and foll. he answers the objections of his knights he begins with a strong denial of their charge (l. 719).

723. unſtet ſchwanfe. See l. 24 n. In prose Das unſtete und ſchwanfende Sehnen, 'my restless and vague longings.'

724. Dem Leben, for meinem Leben. See l. 196 n.

Inhalt, 'contents,' i.e. 'purpose,' 'aim,' 'meaning.'

ausgefunden, unusual for gefunden. Ausfinden or herausfinden means 'to find out with much seeking and exertion.'

726. die Sonne der Verheißung is by some commentators referred to the Holy Sepulchre at Jerusalem which promises absolution from his sins to the faithful pilgrim. See l. 2715.

728. Himmelspunfte=Punft am Himmel, 'heavenly point,' 'the load star of my heaven.'

732. der allſehnde Äther über uns. Cp. Schiller's grand ballad Die Kraniche des Ibyfus, ll. 71—72:

> Nur Helios vermag's zu ſagen,
> Der alles Irdiſche beſcheint.

734 probably means that no priest was required to give their union a formal blessing. Cp. ll. 955, 1800. It may, however, merely mean that no messenger or other go-between was employed by the lovers, not even Diego.

735. goldne Stunden. Cp. l. 661 n. and Das Lied von der Glocke, l. 75:

> Der erſten Liebe goldne Zeit,

where the lines 69—79 form a good parallel to Don Manuel's words in this account of the happy five months of his love.

736. Nicht Raub am Himmel. A strong accent falls on Nicht. See ll. 719 and 1609, and also cp. ll. 2798—9. In Julius von Tarent (see Introd. p. lxxi) the situation was worse, as Blanca had actually taken the veil.

739. Notice the skilful use made of *stichomythia* in the rapid exchange of question and answer. Cp. l. 487 n.

Freiſtatt, freie Statt, freie Stätte, 'asylum,' 'place of refuge.' Cp. l. 1768.

740. des Lebens Grab, because the nun renounces the joys of life and remains in the nunnery until her death.

741. The spectator, remembering the words of Isabella to Diego (ll. 117 ff.), will here be struck by the first suspicion that Don Manuel's beloved may be his sister. The more probable this becomes in the course of the action, the more will the spectator conceive fear of the inevitable and pity for the unsuspecting lovers. This ever intensified feeling of fear and pity in the heart of the spectator as the play goes on and the secrets are unravelled before him brings about the deep tragic effect which the drama never fails to exercise.

742. werbe, the subjunctive because it is understood: 'she was entrusted...(*with the intention that*) she would be recalled.'

743. rühmt fie fich ju fein is an imitation of the well-known and common Homeric phrase εὔχομαι εἶναι, 'I proudly call myself.' It does not here imply any kind of actual boasting on the part of Beatrice. Schiller took this Homeric phrase from the famous translation of Homer by Johann Heinrich Voss, and he used it again in his next drama, Wilhelm Tell, where Gertrud, Stauffacher's clever and brave wife, says, with more fitness, to her husband, I. 2, l. 240 (with the suppression of ju fein):

Des ebeln Iberg8 Tochter rühm' ich mich.

744. vom Ebeln, 'of a noble race.' Ebel in older German only referred to high birth which was considered to be indispensable for a noble disposition. Here ebel is used in this older sense. Cp. l. 476 n., and the compounds Ebelmann, 'nobleman,' and Ebelfiß, 'nobleman's castle.'

746. Nicht...noch stands often in the great classical plays in verse where in prose weber...noch would be required. Cp. ll. 1375, 2141.

752. wiffend nur, 'only if I am fully informed.'

762. von Jahr ju Jahren is poetic instead of von Jahr ju Jahr. Goethe is especially fond of this way of putting the plural of the noun in the second part of such phrases. Cp. the first scene of the Second Part of Fauft: Wunsch um Wünsche (l. 4658: einen Wunsch um den andern), von Sturz ju Sturzen (l. 4718: von Sturz ju Sturz), Schaum an Schäume (l. 4720). In his Zueignung to Fauft, l. 29: Träne folgt den Tränen. fie vertröstet, 'held out hopes to her,' say 'put her off.'

764. näher belongs not to deutend but to bezeichnet.

765. wenig Monden, poetic for wenigen Monaten. See l. 777, feit den letzten Monden. Mond instead of Monat is very common in poetry. Probably since the death of the old Prince three months ago. Cp. ll. 1368 sqq.

768. schöpfen, 'to draw,' here 'to obtain,' is very uncommon in connexion with Licht, but Schiller is fond of this expressive metaphor. Cp. Troft schöpfen, l. 2525, and ll. 2375—6.

769. This line has become a familiar quotation.

777. ließ...ſich entfallen (l. 778), usually ließ...fallen.

780. zurücke is the older form of zurück which still occurs frequently in Goethe's and Schiller's poetry. Cp. the Introd. p. lxxiii, and A. W. Schlegel's ballad Arion, ll. 159—160:

> Wir ließen recht im Glücke
> Ihn zu Corinth zurücke.

787. The motif of abduction from the convent occurs also in Julius von Tarent, IV. 6. See Introd. p. lxxi.

788. nach Meſſina. From Act II. Sc. I it is clear that the secret garden (l. 794) to which Don Manuel had conveyed Beatrice was not in the town itself but near Messina. Cp. ll. 989—990.

793. ber Barmherzigen, probably short for ber barmherzigen Brüder (*fratelli di misericordia*), an order mainly devoted to the nursing of the sick. This order was really established much later (in 1540, the corresponding order of the barmh. Schweſtern not till 1634), but the anachronism does not matter in a play in which historical accuracy in such details was in no case aimed at by the poet. Six barmherzige Brüber were introduced by him into his next play, Wilhelm Tell, with good effect, but again not in accordance with strict chronology. See my note to Wilhelm Tell, IV. 3, l. 2831. Others explain ber Barmherzigen as ber barmherzigen Jungfrau, the Holy Virgin, the Mother of Mercy.

794. abgeſchiebner, 'secluded,' 'lone.' But cp. l. 1434.

796. hieher, instead of which the less euphonic hierher is now more usual. In older German, especially in South German, hier had become hie, and compounds with hie of which the second part begins with a consonant are common in the language of the German classics, e.g. hiebei, hiemit, hievon, etc. In modern German prose, especially in North German, the form hier is used almost exclusively whether the second part begins with a vowel (hieran, hierin, etc.) or a consonant (hierburch, hiermit, etc.). But in the word hienieben, 'here below,' which is only used in the high style, the shorter form hie is exclusively used. Cp. l. 2747.

799. ſich...erwartet. Erwarten with the dative of the personal pronoun is very rare, but occurs also in other passages in Schiller, e.g.

> Nichts ſchont er ſelber und erwartet ſich nicht Schonung.

nichts weniger, 'nothing less,' 'anything but.'

800. eingeholt is a technical term and means 'brought (into the town) in great state.' It refers to the official reception of a prince or a princess

outside the walls of a town into which the distinguished visitor is then
led in great state.

801. Fußgestell, pedestal. Fußgestell des Ruhms is der Thron.

802. ausgestellt, 'set forth,' 'exhibited.'

806. Verlobte, 'bride.' The terms Verlobte, Braut (l. 619) and
Gattin (l. 1403), also Geliebter and Gatte (l. 1800), and Ehe (l. 955) are
used indiscriminately by Don Manuel and Beatrice. They were not
actually united by any formal bond (l. 734) but looked upon one another
as united for ever. See l. 955 n.

810. Hofburg, *f.* 'princely castle.' The Imperial Palace of Vienna,
the ancestral seat of the Kings and Emperors of Austria, is still called
die Hofburg.

814. Bazar, the oriental 'trade-hall,' 'stores.' Schiller evidently
laid the stress on the first syllable (see also l. 846), but now the pronunciation is always Basa'r, and the usual spelling Basar, not Bazar.
See Theodor Siebs, *Deutsche Bühnenaussprache*, 10th ed. Bonn, 1912,
p. 68, and Wilhelm Viëtor, *Deutsches Aussprachewörterbuch*, Leipzig,
1912, p. 37ᵃ. The word ultimately goes back to the Persian *bāzar*,
'market place.' Carl August Böttiger, for a long time headmaster of
the Weimar Grammar School, uses the same pronunciation (Ba'sar) in a
line occurring in an elegiac poem to Schiller, in which he says of
himself:

> Hörte die Braut von Messina dich lesen, den Chortakt bemessend,
> Half—so war dein Gebot—ordnen im Basar den Schmuck;

and Goethe uses the word with the stress on the first syllable in des
Goldschmieds Ba'zärlä'bchen in the Buch Suleika of his West-östlicher
Divan (see Jubilee Edition, Vol. v. 76, l. 25, ed. Konrad Burdach).
German words for Bazar are Kaufhalle, Markthalle, or Kaufhaus.

anjetzt, an enlarged form of jetzt, is really a word belonging to the
stiff and artificial chancery language, and is now no longer used.

815. Mohren are here Mauren, Mahommedan Moors, the North
African merchants whose oriental wares were exhibited at the Bazar
(l. 816). The word der Mohr is used for any black-skinned man and
has often the sense of 'negro,' while der Maure designates a Mahommedan Moor only. Mohr, old German *môr*, is really derived from the
Latin *Maurus*.

817. Kunstgebild, *n.* 'artistic creations,' obviously referring to fine
embroidery, Kunststickerei; das Gebilde is alles, was gebildet ist.

818. Erst. In this and the following lines (818–843 and 847–855) a very detailed and really quite epic description is given of the costly garments and ornaments with which Don Manuel proposes to adorn his intended bride as Princess of Messina.   In these lines, which add one touch to another, from the sandals to the crowning myrtle-wreath, Schiller conveys a very lively picture of Beatrice dressed as a princess. He has changed mere description into action after the precept of Lessing in his Laofoon (Chapter XVI).   Lessing himself had referred to Homer's fine description (*Iliad* II. 42 sqq.) of the toilet of King Agamemnon in his tent, with which Schiller was certainly familiar.

820.   Kunſtgewebe, *n.* 'artistic webs,' 'fine fabrics.'

821.   Indiers is trisyllabic. See the Introd. p. lxxv.   The more usual form is now Inders.   The finest cotton materials were formerly manufactured in India.

822.   Ätna, the comparison is specially apt in the mouth of a Sicilian.

824.   Bau, *m.* 'build,' 'structure.'

829.   It has been proposed by a French critic (H. Weil) to read Veilchenpurpur instead of bleichem (Koerner: gleichem).

830.   heft' ihn, 'shall fix it.'

831.   Zikade, *f.* a clasp in the form of a 'cicada.'   Thus Schiller imagines the mantle over the tunic to be kept together over the right shoulder by a precious golden brooch in the familiar shape of a *cicada*, a cricket-like insect.

Spangen, *f. pl.* 'bracelets.'

832.   umzirken, 'encircle,' 'span,' is very rare for umſchließen.

834.   Meeresgöttin, viz. Amphitrite who in l. 919 is called die blaue Göttin, the goddess of the blue deep.   She was an Oceanid, the wife of Neptune and the mother of Triton.

835.   Um die Locken.   Notice the double anacrusis and cp. Introd. p. lxxxii.

Diade'm, *n.* 'diadem,' a fillet studded with jewels.   From this fillet 'wound' round the locks the metal crown was subsequently developed.

838.   die Farbenblitze kreuze, 'shall mingle its coloured lightnings,' 'mingle its flashes of colours.'   die stands for ſeine, see l. 196 n.

841.   hellen Lichtgewölk, 'clouds of bright light,' say 'a bright fleecy cloud.'   Lichtgewölk and also Farbenblitz are words of Schiller's own coining.

umfließe, 'shall float around,' 'shall play about.'

843.   Vollende krönend ſich, for Vollende ſich und kröne ſich, 'let...be completed and crowned.'

847. 3elter, *m.* is a horse that has been trained to a quiet pace (im 3elt ju gehen; jelten is 'to pace quietly,' 'to amble,' a 3eltgänger or Paßgänger is an 'ambler' or 'pacer'). Hence the word came to denote a specially quiet horse, a lady's horse, a 'palfrey.' Thus Julius Wolff writes in Till Eulenspiegel:

> Das Edelfräulein trug der 3elter.

849. This reference to the steeds of the Sun-god in the mouth of a Christian is not surprising in this play. See the Introduction, p. xxvii. Apollo was fond of white steeds.

853. im Glanz des Ritterstaates, 'in the splendour of knightly array.' It is characteristic of the proud and punctilious Don Manuel that he has most carefully thought out every detail of the dress of his beloved in order to introduce her arrayed in suitable splendour to his mother. Don Cesar considers these things trifles and does not trouble about ceremony in the least (ll. 1148—50).

855. heimzuführen. Einzuholen (l. 800 n.) would really be more appropriate. Die Braut heimführen, 'to take one's bride to one's home,' is usually only said of the bridegroom himself (see l. 1172).

857. 3wei unter euch. In l. 814 it seemed as if all his knights were to follow him to the Bazar, but apparently Don Manuel did not wish to appear there with his full retinue. Thus the remainder of the Chorus have an opportunity to conclude—after the model of the Greek plays— the first portion of the drama with their reflections in lyrical form.

858. wartet mein, poetic for wartet auf mich. See l. 532 n.

860. Don Manuel is still very anxious that his secret should be kept most scrupulously till he himself thinks fit to disclose it (II. 5, ll. 1391 sqq.). Don Cesar on the other hand has spread out a network of spies to find the girl he loved (ll. 1136—40).

SCENE 8.

The songs of the Chorus, corresponding to a Greek *stasimon*, i.e. songs of the Chorus between two scenes, clearly fall into two main divisions. The first (ll. 861—938) deals with the Chorus itself, setting forth the various medieval pastimes of knights in time of peace and thus answering the question of l. 861 : 'Prithee, to what shall we now betake us?' The second portion (ll. 943—980) refers to the Princes and contains anxious reflections on the future, gloomy forebodings and, incidentally, some important information as to the ancestors of the race, a deed of violence and a terrible curse. This second portion is most skilfully connected with the first (ll. 939—943).

Most lines have four strong accents between which there are some-times one and sometimes two unaccented syllables. The rhythm of the stanzas of the first portion is descending and mixed, viz. trochaic-dactylic, which gives to the metre a certain ease and liveliness. The second portion begins with purely trochaic verses without any admixture of dactyls. This changes the rhythm at once very markedly, and makes it grave and solemn (ll. 944—963). The end of the Scene is again more animated, having trochaic-dactylic rhythm. See the Introduction, p. lxxxi.

865. forgen (or Fürforge treffen), 'to make provision,' is the result of the fürchten and hoffen, and gives to life a purpose.

868. Gleichmaß, *n.* 'equal measure,' 'sameness,' 'monotonous round.'

869. Windesweben, *n.* 'blowing of the wind,' 'blast of the wind,' hence 'breeze.'

weben, 'to weave,' often means 'to move about.' Cp. the common riming phrase leben und weben. Weben means here the same as the ordinary wehen, and the Chorus insists that man must, like a strong and refresh-ing blast, agitate the stagnant water of life. In Wallensteins Lager, ll. 308—310, we read:

> Und der Geist, der im ganzen Korps tut leben,
> Reißet gewaltig, wie Windesweben,
> Auch den untersten Reiter mit.

In both passages Windesweben rimes with leben.

870. Kräuselnd bewege, 'may stir and ripple.'

871. Lines 871—891. These lines refer to Peace and War.

871—2. lieblicher...liegt...gelagert. Note the pleasing effect of the alliteration here and elsewhere (ll. 882, 902, 903) in this Scene and compare l. 202 n. With the thoughts so well expressed in the following lines on idyllic Arcadian life some passages from Das Lied von der Glocke may be compared, e.g. the passage on Peace and Concord in ll. 274—333; also Der Spaziergang, ll. 47—48:

> Vielfach ertönt der Herden Geläut' im belebten Gefilde,
> Und den Widerhall weckt einsam des Hirten Gesang.

872. gelagert (am), 'reposing *or* couched (by).'

874. sonnigten, now sonnigen. See l. 140 n.

882. Note the double anacrusis in this and the following line which makes the rhythm particularly brisk and lively.

884. verkümmert, 'becomes stunted,' i.e. 'degenerates,' 'deteriorates.'

887. eben, 'level'; eben machen, 'equalise.'

888. verflachen (= flach machen), 'bring down to the same level.'

889. erscheinen really means 'shine forth,' hence 'manifest itself.'

890. zum Ungemeinen, 'to the extraordinary,' 'to a loftier level.'

891. dem Feigen, 'for the coward,' i.e. 'in the coward.'

892. Lines 892—901 refer to Love and Beauty.

893. Wallet. Wallen really means 'to move on slowly' and is etymologically connected with (die) Welle, 'wave.' Hence it comes to mean 'to move on solemnly,' 'to move in procession,' and is especially used with reference to pilgrims journeying to a sanctuary. A 'pilgrim' is often called Waller, and a pilgrimage Wallfahrt, *f.* (or Pilgerfahrt, *f.*). Hence in this passage wallet refers to a pilgrimage to Amors Tempel (l. 892), and to the worship of Beauty. Cp. l. 2284.

896. beweget, 'stirs up,' 'brings motion into.'

897. graulichten, quite unusual for graulich or grau. See l. 140 n. 'Grayish,' 'wan' colours are 'dull' or 'gloomy' colours.

sich...erheben, 'rise up in brightness,' 'glow and brighten.' Compare with this and the following lines the fine passage in Wallensteins Tod, v. 3, ll. 3442—51, where Wallenstein laments the death of his high-minded friend Max Piccolomini:

> Doch fühl' ich's wohl, was ich in ihm verlor.
> Die Blume ist hinweg aus meinem Leben,
> Und kalt und farblos seh' ich's vor mir liegen.
> Denn er stand neben mir, wie meine Jugend,
> Er machte mir das Wirkliche zum Traum,
> Um die gemeine Deutlichkeit der Dinge
> Den goldnen Duft der Morgenröte webend —
> Im Feuer seines liebenden Gefühls
> Erhoben sich, mir selber zum Erstaunen,
> Des Lebens flach alltägliche Gestalten.

898. sie, viz. die gefällige Tochter des Schaums. Cp. l. 197 n. die glücklichen Jahre, viz. the time of youth.

899. gefällige has here still the older meaning of gefallende (die gefällt), anmutige, reizende, 'pleasing,' 'charming.' This meaning is quite common in the poetry of Goethe and Schiller. Goethe writes of a great Weimar actress (Corona Schrœter) in his poem Auf Miedings Tod, l. 173 and l. 181:

> Ihr kennt sie wohl; sie ist's, die stets gefällt....
> Sie tritt herbei. Seht sie gefällig stehn.

In modern German prose gefällig only means 'obliging,' 'ready to oblige' (die gern einen Gefallen tut).

Tochter des Schaums. Venus (Aphrodite) is often called die Schaumge-borene (aus dem Schaum geborene), 'she that is sprung from the foam (of the sea),' Greek Ἀφροδίτη, Ἀναδυομένη.

900. das Gemeine, 'the commonplace.' Cp. the fine passage on das Gemeine in Wallensteins Tod, I. 4, ll. 207—212. The opposite is das Ungemeine (l. 890).

das Traurigwahre, 'the sad reality (of life).'

902. dem blühenden Lenze, viz. des Lebens, i.e. Youth.

903. Scheine, viz. ihm, dem...Lenze.

flechte sich, viz. der, welchem die Locken, etc. The der is to be understood from the wem of l. 904.

904. grünen or grün sind. This is metaphorical for youthful strength and beauty, as *virere* is used by Latin poets (e.g. *dum virent genua* in Horace (*Epod.* 13, l. 4); or *donec virenti canities abest morosa*, Horace (*Odes* I. 9, l. 17); or Vergil in his *Aeneid*, Canto v. l. 295, *forma insignis viridique iuventa*).

906. Gott, here, as a general term, 'deity.'

907. strengen is opposed to gefälligen (l. 899), the stern to the charming maiden. Diana is a personification of the strenuous Chase as is Venus of the dalliance of Love.

909. am dunkelsten nachten, 'are steeped in deepest night,' 'spread their thickest shading.' On nachten see l. 286 n.

910. Springbock, *m.* is really an antelope, but there are no antelopes in Sicily. So the word must be taken to represent a kind of Steinbock. In this, as well as in other places in his poetry, Schiller is not very particular about his zoological terms.

911. Gleichnis, for Ebenbild, 'image.'

914. schmetternden Hörner, 'crashing horns,' 'echoing horns,' 'shrilling bugles.' Cp. the lyrical outbreak of the captive Queen of Scots (Maria Stuart, III. I, ll. 2134—42):

> Hörst du das Hifthorn? Hörst du's klingen,
> Mächtigen Rufes, durch Feld und Hain?
> Ach, auf das mutige Roß mich zu schwingen,
> An den fröhlichen Zug mich zu reihn!
> Noch mehr! O, die bekannte Stimme,

Schmerzlich süßer Erinnerung voll.
Oft vernahm sie mein Ohr mit Freuden
Auf des Hochlands bergigten Heiden,
Wenn die tobende Jagd erscholl.

916. The *one* unaccented syllable between *two* accented well expresses the difficulties of the chase : ǘber Bérge, ǘber Klǘfte.

919. After the pleasures of hunting the varied fortunes of the sailor are described (ll. 919—938).

der blauen Göttin, Amphitrite, the goddess of the blue sea. See l. 834 n. The blue sea is here personified, and die blaue Göttin stands metonymically for das blaue Meer. With the Latin poets *caeruleus* was a common epithet for Neptune. Similarly Schiller writes in his great elegy Der Spaziergang, l. 102 :

Aus dem Schilfe des Stroms winket der bläulichte Gott.

922. Ladet in...Schoß, 'invites upon her bosom.' The o in Schoß is long. See Introduction, p. lxxxviii, under (*a*).

923. Bauen wir, 'shall we build us ?'

924. lustig is an adjective and not an adverb. See l. 24 n.

925. das grüne kristallene Feld seems to be also a reminiscence from Vergil, two Cantos of whose *Aeneid* (II and IV) Schiller had translated in noble *ottave rime*. We are reminded of *campi liquentes* in Canto VI. l. 724. The idea of 'ploughing' the fields of the sea is a favourite one with the ancient classical writers, cp. Vergil, *Aeneid*, Canto II. l. 780, *aequor arandum*.

927. sich is the dative. He weds Fortune (to himself).

929. der Raum der Hoffnung, 'the field for Hope,' 'Hope's dominion.'

934. Windesrose, an expanded form, in order to make the word trisyllabic, instead of Windrose. The rose of the compass is divided up by many lines in all directions in order to indicate the different winds. Thus the word means 'wind-rose of the compass,' hence 'compass.'

937. The line expresses the thought that on the sea everything is for ever in motion, unstable and changeable.

939. This line and the following (till 943) lead on in a very natural way to the second portion of the utterances of the Chorus. The grave Cajetan who, according to the Hamburg acting-copy, was to speak the next passage is led from the idea of the changeable fortunes of the sailor to the sudden changes of Fortune on the land, and expresses a gloomy foreboding as to the stability of the reconciliation that has just been arrived at between the brothers.

940. wogenden Meeresflut, 'surging billows of the sea.'

941. fo feft, 'however firmly.' According to the ancients the earth was fixed and did not move. Cp. Goethe's ode Grenzen der Menschheit, ll. 23—24, auf der wohlbegründeten, dauernden Erde.

942. Säulen, a poetic idea, nowhere else expressed in this way. The image may perhaps be due to a confusion with the conception of the sky resting upon pillars firmly based upon the earth. For the rime Säulen : weilen (and Träume : Geheime, ll. 952 : 954) see the Introduction.

944. The trochaic metre of this and the following lines is heavy and gloomy, and thus well adapted to the fears and forebodings expressed in it. See the note before l. 865. The descending metre of five beats occurs frequently in Goethe's poetry and is often called serbisches Versmaß, as it occurs especially in Servian popular poetry from which it was frequently imitated by Goethe.

944. Frieden, for Friede. See l. 324 n.

946. geschieden, for ausgeschieden, ausgesondert or ausgeworfen (hat), 'has secreted,' 'has poured forth.' The mention of the crust of lava is very natural to the dwellers on the slopes of Mount Etna (l. 823). See ll. 399 sqq.

949. schwere Taten, for Greueltaten, l. 967. See l. 419 n.

950. sich...vergeben (and sich)...vergeffen, 'are forgiven and forgotten,' 'can be forgiven and forgotten.' The German reflexive, like the French, must often be rendered by the English passive voice. See the notes to ll. 354, 407, 2638.

953. On the transposed rhythm see Introd. p. lxxvii. The meaning is: I do not wish to be a prophet, may my forebodings prove untrue!

955. Ehe. The engagement and union of the lovers is here called Ehe, 'marriage,' just as Don Manuel's love is sometimes called Braut and sometimes Gattin. The Bund is called segenlos, as it was neither blessed by a priest nor by the parents and had been brought about by what the Chorus considers to be a crime. See l. 806 n.

956. lichtscheu krummen, 'crooked paths shunning light,' 'love-mazes hid from the light of day.'

958. liebt sich, usually only liebt. Sich is an ethical dative and gives to the verb lieben the idea 'to like especially,' 'to prefer,' e.g. Goethe's poem Stelknabe und Müllerin, l. 32:

Ich liebe mir den Müllerknecht;

or Fauſt, Part I. l. 320 (Prologue in Heaven) :

> Am meiſten lieb' ich mir die vollen, friſchen Wangen.

960. Auch ein Raub. The thought of the Kloſterraub of Don Manuel naturally suggests an older Raub by Don Manuel's father, who did not scruple to carry off his own father's intended bride, and thus brought down upon himself and his whole family the paternal curse.

961. ehliches Gemahl, now eheliche Gemahlin. In Middle High German *daz gemahel* usually means the 'wife.' Only in modern German is the distinction made between der Gemahl, 'husband,' and die Gemahlin, 'wife.' See l. 14, den fürſtlichen Gemahl. But the old neuter das Gemahl, 'wife,' is still found in Luther's Bible (Matthew i. 20), Maria, dein Gemahl, and also occasionally in German classical poetry, e.g. in Uhland's ballad Des Sängers Fluch, l. 18:

> Und auf dem Throne ſitzen der König und ſein Gemahl.

963. ſie, viz. Isabella.

des Vaters Wahl. In Schiller's Don Carlos just the opposite is the case. The King, Don Philip of Spain, had married Elisabeth of Valois who had been destined for his son Don Carlos and was loved by him. Cp. the Introduction, p. lxxi.

964. Ahnherr, 'ancestor.' The ancestress is called Ahnfrau. Grillparzer's first tragedy of an ancestress who cannot find rest in her grave till an old family curse has been fulfilled and the last descendant of her race killed is called Die Ahnfrau. This ancestral curse seems to have been suggested by a passage in Homer's *Iliad* (IX. 454—457). See the Introd. p. xxxiii. Such old curses are, however, quite common in the Bible, in popular traditions, and also in the Greek legend of Hippolytus and Theseus.

967. ohne Namen, i.e. unnennbare, unausſprechliche.

968. Schwarze Verbrechen. They are nowhere mentioned in the following Acts, and we may well assume that the common gossip and report greatly exaggerated.

971. Sonnen. See the note on Meduſen, l. 147.

973. The Chorus believe that they know the reason for the natred of the brothers, while Isabella (l. 24) says that she is ignorant of its origin.

974. ſich, better einander.

978. Rachgötter, usually Rachegötter, 'avenging deities.' A general term instead of Die Furien or Erinnyen.

ſchaffen. In Schiller's Swabian dialect ſchaffen has the meaning of wirken, 'operate,' 'work.'

The conception of a moral order of the world, in which guilt and punishment are indissolubly connected, is here mixed up with the conception of an old family curse which is bound to cause misfortune and bring about the ruin of the race. Very different are the noble and hopeful words of Goethe's Pylades (in ℑᵖһigenie, II. 1, l. *(17)*: Es erbt der Eltern Segen, nicht ihr Fluch.

ACT II.

Scene 1.

Monologue of Beatrice in a secluded garden near Messina, where she is waiting for the return of Don Manuel. The time of sunset is near (l. 983). She is consumed with fear and longing. Her varying emotions are well expressed by the changes of metre. A retrospective glance is cast over her life up to the present moment. She does not regret having sacrificed everything to her love. She remembers with fear meeting a youth with flaming eyes at the old Prince's funeral, which she had attended secretly against the wish of Don Manuel. This monologue was set to music by Franz Holstein (opus 38) under the title Beatrice, Scene aus der Braut von Messina, Leipzig, 1877. Zelter thought that the actress representing Beatrice should be a singer.

In many classical plays the hero or heroine is only introduced, as here, at the beginning of the Second Act: in Lessing's Minna von Barnhelm (Minna), Goethe's ℑᵖһigenie (Orest), Schiller's Maria Stuart (Elisabeth), and in Molière's *Tartufe* (Tartufe).

Similar lyrical monologues in plays preceding his Braut von Messina are found in Schiller's Maria Stuart (III. 1) and Die Jungfrau von Orleans (IV. 1), but not in Wallenstein.

In each case the high state of excitement causes the lyrical outburst. Schiller introduced this new kind of monologue for the first time into Maria Stuart. A similar, but yet different, case occurs in Goethe's ℑᵖһigenie, where (I. 4) the heroine pours out her feelings in passionate verse, but without any change of rhythm and without rime.

An analogous situation is developed with the greatest skill in varying metres in Schiller's fine lyrical poem Die Erwartung (written in 1796). Here a youthful lover is waiting for his beloved in a secret bower, and his excitement, disappointment, and reflections are well expressed by means of the changing rhythm. It has been compared in detail with our Scene in Hoffmeister's *Life of Schiller*, III. 265—266.

Several expressions in both poems are the same, but they are naturally called forth by the identical situation.

The monologue is made up of five different portions which are clearly distinguished from each other by the metre and by the sense. The metrical form is in each case wonderfully expressive of Beatrice's change of mood. The five portions are: *a* (ll. 981—1004), *b* (1005—19), *c* (1020—56), *d* (1057—1101), *e* (1102—9).

Beatrice. The name should be pronounced in the Italian way, viz. Beatrĭ'tſche (*be·a·' tri:tfə*).

981. The metre of ll. 981—1004 is the so-called *ottave rime*, (three) stanzas of eight lines each and the arrangement of rimes a b a b a b c c. Each line has five accents and the rhythm is ascending (iambic). This metre is characteristic of the great Italian epics of Tasso and Bojardo, and had been used with considerable freedom by Wieland in his Dberon, and by Schiller himself in his renderings of Cantos II and IV of Vergil's *Aeneid*. In a stricter form it had been employed by Goethe in various fine poems and also by Schiller himself in Die Erwartung, Die Begegnung, and in part of the lyrical monologue of Die Jungfrau von Orleans (IV. 1, ll. 2518—41). In German poetry the Italian epic metre changes its character and is especially well suited for lyrical poems of a lofty character (such as Goethe's fine Epilog zu Schillers Glocke) or lyrical passages in dramatic monologues. The character of the metre is lyric and exalted.

982. Pinie is a dissyllabic word. See the Introd. p. lxxv.

985. ein schauberndes Gefühl. Goethe's Iphigenie also steps forth from her sanctuary mit schauberndem Gefühl (I. 1, l. 4).

986. wefenloſe Schweigen, lit. 'unsubstantial silence,' 'intangible silence,' 'hollow silence.' The silence is called wefenlos because no living being (Wefen) is near. Cp. Vergil's *Aeneid*, Canto II. l. 755, *simul ipsa silentia terrent*, which Schiller himself had rendered: Es ſchreckt mich ſelbſt das Schweigen. For the rime Schweigen: ſchleichen see Introd. p. lxxxix, under (*c*).

987. wie weit, for wie weit auch, 'however far.'

989. ein rauſchend Wehr, 'a roaring weir.' On the uninflected form see l. 102 n.

990. Die Stabt, die völkerwimmelnbe, 'the town teeming with people.' With regard to the style see l. 168 n. and l. 213 n. On the hiatus of völkerwimmelnbe ertoſen cp. the Introd. p. lxxix.

992. bumpferbrauſenb, 'heavily surging up,' 'with a dull heavy surge.'

176   *DIE BRAUT VON MESSINA*   [ACT II.

Dumpferbrantenb, like bunfelnachtenb (l. 286) or völkerwimmelnb, is an adjective formed on the model Schiller found in Homeric diction and also in Goethe's Jphigenie. Cp. the note to mächtigwaltenb, l. 16, and to Säulengetragenes, l. 136.

stoßen. On the rime with ertofen see the Introd. p. lxxxix.

994. in biefem Furchtbargroßen, 'in this fearful immensity.' To a maiden accustomed to the quiet of a secluded religious house both the noise of the populous town and the dull roar of the sea are overwhelmingly great and terrible. Her fear is increased by her solitude. She feels herself small and helpless, and this arouses her suspicion of a danger coming to her from this great and harsh world which is stretching out its giant arm (l. 1002) to grasp her and to ruin her life.

1004. leichtem, 'light,' here 'slight,' 'frail.'

1005. Here begins the second portion of Beatrice's monologue. The short dactylic lines of two accents paint her great agitation.

bie Sinne, 'my senses.' See l. 196 n.

1009. Den Schleier zerriß ich jungfräulicher Zucht. On the separation of a genitive from the noun which it qualifies, after the manner of the ancient classical languages, see l. 20 n.

1011. This is a perhaps natural exaggeration. Beatrice, in this respect different from Blanca in Julius von Tarent, had not taken any vows. See l. 737.

1019. verfichre, i.e. mache ficher (unb ruhig), beruhige, 'make sure,' 'reassure.' She wishes her former assurance (Sicherheit) to be restored and her doubts and qualms of conscience to be banished.

1026. Obviously Isabella had only once been able to risk an interview with her daughter of which Beatrice has but a very vague recollection. At this moment the only impression of her noble mother that remains in her mind is that she was 'glorious' (herrlich, l. 1036).

1028. still am stillen Orte. See l. 104 n. and ll. 1033, 1048.

1029. In Lebens Glut, usually in bes Lebens Glut (or in ber Glut bes Lebens). This construction occurs very frequently in Schiller's poetry and is a peculiarity of his poetic style. By omitting the definite article before a genitive included between a preposition and another noun qualified by the genitive he almost changes the noun in the genitive (in our case Lebens) into a proper name. This is less striking in the case of Lebens as there is only one Leben, but in Schiller's poetry we also read mit Nordes Hauch, mit Schwärmers Ernst, mit Feuers Hülfe, an Ufers Rand, aus Ofens Rachen, aus Herzens Tiefen, etc.

With the hot blood of her race running in her veins the young and impulsive maiden felt her life in the convent among the nuns (who were dead to the world) to be like a dreary existence among the departed souls whom, using classical terminology, she likens to the 'shades' in the nether world. In l. 1686 the convent is called ein verſchwiegner Aufenthalt der Seelen. In a similar way, in Goethe's Iphigenie, I. 2, ll. 107—109, the Greek maiden says of her lonely existence in the sanctuary of Diana:

> Welch Leben iſt's, das an der heil'gen Stätte,
> Gleich einem Schatten um ſein eigen Grab,
> Ich nur vertrauern muß?

1030. The situation and feelings of Beatrice depicted in this and the following lines resemble very much those of Wallenstein's daughter Thekla, who had been brought up in a secluded convent when she made the acquaintance of gallant Max Piccolomini, who was to lead her to her father's camp and out into life. See Wallenſteins Tod, IV. 12, ll. 3169 sqq.

1035. löſen, for löſen werden or löſen können.

1037. den verhängten Stunden. The verb verhängen and the noun das Verhängniß are as a rule used with regard to the decrees of Fate or Providence. In this case it refers to the time of her release from the convent that was fore-ordained by her mother.

1038. So does Thekla in Wallenſteins Tod, Act IV. Sc. 11—12.

1040. Eindringt. The fluctuating stress (ei'ndrin'gt) brings the ein out very strongly. For this and similar cases see the Introd. p. lxxviii.

1041. Perſeus' Turm, viz. the brazen tower in which Danae was confined by her father Acrisios of Argos because an oracle had declared that she would give birth to a son who would kill his grandfather. But Zeus visited her in a shower of gold and thus frustrated the precautions of the king. Perseus was born in the tower. It would have been more correct to say Danae's tower. Perseus, grown to manhood, mounted on the winged steed Pegasus, saved Andromeda, the daughter of the King of Aethiopia, from a sea-monster and married her. In order to save the country from the ravages of the sea-monster the king's daughter had been given up as a victim and chained to a rock on the sea-shore. Here she was found and delivered by Perseus.

1042. Dämon is here used in a general way to denote a being armed with supernatural powers—a god or a demi-god or hero. It does not mean in this passage a malignant or destructive being, a cruel 'demon.'

B.   12

She thinks that ordinary mortals have no chance against the will of the 'demon'—however far removed or hidden away, her 'demon' will find her and her fate will be accomplished.

Opfer has not the sense of 'unhappy victim' but only means her whom the god or hero has selected for himself.

1044. Unb for Unb fogar.

Atlas was the Titan who was condemned to bear heaven on his shoulders. According to another story Perseus changed him into Mount Atlas. In this passage Mount Atlas is referred to and the idea is that, though the maiden had been bound to its summit, yet the winged horse would have taken her bold rescuer thither.

Two instances are given of a maiden in absolute solitude being thus overtaken by her fate: Danae (Perfeus' Turm) and Andromeda (öbe Klippen). What seemed impossible to men was effected by the shower of gold and by the winged horse.

From these allusions it appears that Beatrice had in the convent found opportunity to acquaint herself with Greek legendary lore.

1048. will ich. This is repeated in ll. 1050, 1052 and 1055, and it is thus quite clear that Beatrice's actions spring from her own character and free-will. She is responsible for them and accepts the full responsibility.

1050. mich...befcheiben, 'limit myself,' 'be content with.' She is content with her lot by the side of Don Manuel whom she loves but of whose high position she is ignorant.

1057. Here begins the fourth portion of the monologue (to l. 1101). It is written in descending rhythm of four beats. Many of the lines are devoid of rime; rimeless and rimed lines interchange without any fixed system. The trochees of four beats occur especially in Spanish epic and dramatic poetry and are therefore often called Spanifche Trochäen. In the Spanish dramas they are invariably rimed, but unrimed lines are found in the Cid Romances and in Herder's German rendering Der Cib. The plays of Calderon by which Schiller seems to have been influenced, perhaps unconsciously, became known to him in 1802 just when he was at work on Die Braut von Meffina. In the same year (1802) Schiller and Goethe produced on the Weimar stage Friedrich Schlegel's Alarcos, a play which bears throughout traces of Calderon's influence. Schiller's metre in this passage was subsequently imitated by Grillparzer in his Ahnfrau and by several writers of Fate-tragedies. The short monotonous descending lines produce a solemn and even somewhat gloomy effect. Schiller used the same (rimed) metre with the same effect in the year in which he wrote this Scene (1802), in his poem Κ a ſ ſ a n b r a.

1063. kaltes Graufen, usually kaltes Grauen, l. 1097. It is called kalt because it makes cold. See l. 1070.

1064. Immer tiefer...Immer öder...Immer ſchwerer. The threefold repetition is most impressive. Compare the fine lines in Bürger's ballad Das Lied vom braven Mann, ll. 66—69:

> Und immer höher ſchwoll die Flut,
> Und immer lauter ſchnob der Wind,
> Und immer tiefer ſank der Mut.

1077. der Göttlichen, viz. the Holy Virgin. Here she was seen by Don Cesar's spies. Cp. l. 1140.

1078. Nimmer is used here in the South German colloquial manner with the sense of nicht mehr, 'no more,' 'no longer.' Its usual meaning is nie, 'never,' as in Die Jungfrau von Orleans: Johanna geht, und nimmer kehrt ſie wieder. But in Schiller's poetry nimmer has often, as in l. 1099, the sense of nie mehr, 'no more,' 'no longer.'

1079. erſpähte, for either erſpähen würde or erſpäht hätte, erſpäht haben ſollte. This happened really. See ll. 546, 1140.

1081—2. Pfaden : verraten. On the rime see the Introd. p. lxxxix.

1084. Einmal. See ll. 1118 sqq., 1645 sqq. Einmal is an alteration made by Schiller's own hand in the Hamburg acting-copies and adopted in the latest Cotta Centenary Edition. Most editions have grauend (for mit Grauen, or ſchaudernd) which Schiller had originally written. This venture of Beatrice, undertaken against the expressed wish (ll. 1890 sqq.) of Don Manuel and never confessed to him, brings about her ruin and that of her brothers. Her guilt is twofold, she went to the funeral, and she kept her meeting with the strange youth secret from her lover.

1087. gewagt, viz. habe. See l. 7 n.

frevelm is archaic and poetic for frevelhaftem, 'wicked,' 'sinful.' The old adjective frevel, 'overbold,' 'presumptuous,' 'violating the law,' survives now only in compounds, Frevelmut, Freveltat, etc. from der frevel Mut, die frevel Tat, formed like Edelmut (der edel Mut), Großtat (die groß Tat), and many others in which the first part is an uninflected adjective. The old adjective frevel is now replaced by the compound frevelhaft, in which frevel is not an adjective but the noun der Frevel.

1088. jenes Feſtes Feier. See l. 1118, Leichenfeſt, l. 1887, Leichenfeier.

1090. Erkühnen, *n.* is an infinitive used as a noun, lit. 'bold act,' 'boldness.'

1091. ein Gott is merely a typical (Homeric) phrase which occurs often in Schiller's poetry even in the mouth of Christian speakers. Cp. ll. 1114 and 1138.

1092. Compare with this ll. 1525 sqq.

1101. ſtillen, 'silent,' viz. geheimen, 'secret,' 'not confessed.'

Schuld, viz. that she went against her lover's wish and kept the fact secret from him. She may have done the latter all the more as she was deeply impressed by the meeting with Don Cesar. Of course she does not in the least experience a feeling of love for him, but she cannot forget his impressive personality, perhaps the tie of blood may also be mysteriously asserting itself.

1102. In the concluding part of the monologue the metre becomes again more agitated in short rimeless trochaic-dactylic lines of two beats. Exactly the same contrast between the last seven lines and the preceding portion is found in Goethe's poem Meeres Stille und glück- liche Fahrt.

1105. Blendwerk, *n.* 'false show,' 'illusion,' is a word of which Schiller is very fond. Cp. l. 1900. Werk as the second part of some compounds, the first part of which is a verb, denotes a thing that is destined to carry out, or in other cases to undergo, the action of the verb. Blendwerk, 'a thing that dazzles' (from blenden), but Schnitzwerk, 'a thing that is carved,' 'carving.'

1106. Es naht, es vermehrt sich! Es is often used in German to denote that the subject of the action is vague, mysterious, or dreadful. Cp. in Schiller's ballad Der Taucher:

> Es riß mich hinunter blitzesschnell (l. 99),
>
> da kroch's heran, regte hundert Gelenke zugleich (ll. 129—130).

SCENE 2.

Don Cesar enters, addresses Beatrice in passionate words, tells her his name and position, and declares her to be his fiancée. She is struck with horror and unable to utter a single word as long as he is in the garden, except Weh mir! when she first sees him enter.

1110. Der rauhe Anblick, 'the rugged aspect,' 'the rude appearance.' She is not afraid of his men but of him.

1116. wachend, träumend belongs grammatically to du (1117), but of course refers to Don Cesar.

1117. des Herzens = meines Herzens. See l. 196 n. and ll. 1122—3.

1118. Leichenfest, *n*. is a less happy term than Leichenfeier (l. 1887), Totenfeier (l. 1487). In l. 2603 it is called Begräbnisfest. All these terms refer to the solemn funeral service, the feierliche Beisetzung as it would now be called in official language.

The meeting of Beatrice with Don Cesar in the church is in some respects similar to the meeting of Emilia with the Prince of Guastalla in Lessing's tragedy Emilia Galotti (Act II. Scene 6). This similarity has been remarked upon by several critics, and no doubt Lessing's well-known scene may have influenced Schiller. But the younger poet may also very well have hit upon the idea of a similar scene with similar disastrous consequences without being in any way directly dependent on Lessing. Some features which the two scenes have in common, and the important fact that in neither case does the girl inform her lover of the meeting with the strange man, are natural consequences of the assumed situation. The death of Don Manuel and the ruin of Beatrice are the result of the same want of openness towards her betrothed which causes the death of Emilia and her lover, Count Appiani.

1126. Der Messe Hochamt. Here Messe is redundant. Das Hochamt is a 'High Mass' or 'Grand Mass.' Cp. Seelenamt, l. 2625 n.

1128. heften, scil. wollten.

1139. glückbekrönte, 'crowned with success.' See l. 136 n.

1144. des Dämons Neide. In this case (but see l. 1042 n.) the Dämon must be a malicious spirit who loves to destroy the happiness of mortals. The ancients believed that too much success or happiness aroused the retributive wrath of the gods, the envy of the Olympians. This idea has been discussed by Ulrich von Wilamowitz-Möllendorff in his *Griechische Tragödien*, v. 21—24. The conception of the envy of the gods occurs in an early poem of Schiller's (Das Geheimnis der Reminiszenz, in a stanza that was subsequently rejected, written in 1781), but the best-known passage where it is found is in his ballad Der Ring des Polykrates, ll. 52—54, where the King of Egypt says:

> Mir grauet vor der Götter Neide;
> Des Lebens ungemischte Freude
> Ward keinem Irdischen zu teil.

See also ll. 2183—4.

1146. Gattin; in ll. 1170 and 1467 Braut. See note to ll. 806, 955.

1147. Zum Pfande des, 'in pledge of this.' Des has here the force of a demonstrative. Des is the old form of the genitive of das instead of which now the lengthened dessen is generally used. But in formal phrases such as zum Zeugniß des, in the compounds deswegen, deshalb, also in indeß, unterdeß, etc., and in archaic proverbs such as Wes das Herz voll ist des gehet der Mund über, the old des is still commonly found. It is also still found in Luther's translation of the Bible. Cp. l. 1449.

It never occurs to Don Cesar to ask Beatrice if she loves him. He feels sure that she was aware of his love when he first spoke to her (ll. 1120 sqq.) and he does not doubt for a moment that, although she is naturally at first surprised, she will soon be glad to become his wife. In his heart of hearts he considers it only natural and right that he, the Prince, should obtain the fairest of women. His men are of the same opinion. See ll. 1230—53.

1149. dem andern, e.g. her parentage, rank, wealth, etc.

1151. This line is an alexandrine. See the Introd. p. lxxxiii.

Hat...verbürget und beschworen, lit. 'has given bail for and has assured by oath,' i.e. 'has proved and attested,' 'proved beyond all doubt.' Cp. ll. 1467—8.

1153. meine Liebe, for meine Geliebte, in older German mein Lieb. The same expression occurs in Die Jungfrau von Orleans, I. 4, l. 620:

　　　　Nur meine Liebe will sie sein und heißen.

1154. Die Freiheit...und die Wahl, hendiadys for die freie Wahl. See l. 130 n.

1157. das Geliebte. See l. 627 n.

After **1161.** schaudert zurück, 'shrinks back in horror,' because she is in his hands and fears that he is much more powerful than Don Manuel and will prevent her union with him. She also shudders because she realises that she has to do with that ruthless Prince who is carrying on a disastrous feud with his own brother. Don Cesar again (l. 1110) misunderstands her horror and stupefaction and thinks it due to Staunen (l. 1162) at his high rank.

1163. der Reize Krone, i.e. the highest of charms.

1164. In prose das Schöne ist sich ein Verborgenes or sich selbst verborgen. Sich is the dative.

1165. erschrickt, 'is frightened,' is a strong and intransitive verb, but erschreckt (l. 1168), 'frightens,' is weak and transitive.

Don Cesar's views are identical with those of the impetuous and self-confident Guido in Julius von Tarent, who also does not brook any opposition and says (Act I. Sc. 3): Schönheit ist der natürliche Preis der Tapferkeit; und dabei haben die Weiber keine Stimme. Fragt man die Rose, ob sie dem, der Geruch hat, duften will?

SCENE 3.

The Chorus welcome Beatrice as the bride elect of their Prince. She expresses her horror at the fate which awaits her. The praise of the Chorus comes first and the despairing words of Beatrice afterwards. There is no dialogue between them and the maiden. The words of the Chorus are in free rhythm, Beatrice speaks in the trochaic metre of ll. 1057 sqq. See the note.

1174. $\mathfrak{H}$eil bir! contrasts strangely with $\mathfrak{W}$ebe mir! (l. 1211).

1177. ber $\mathfrak{S}$ieg, viz. over Don Cesar's heart.

1182. $\mathfrak{D}$reifaches $\mathfrak{H}$eil bir! 'Hail to thee thrice!' Notice the three-fold repetition of the word glüdlich in the following lines.

1183. $\mathfrak{M}$it glüdlichen $\mathfrak{Z}$eichen (or $\mathfrak{V}$orzeichen), 'under lucky auspices,' referring to the reconciliation of the brothers which has just taken place. She is called glüdlich as she is beautiful and is destined to become a princess. The family ($\mathfrak{H}$aus) is called glüdlich in this passage because it is famous and long established (ll. 1187—8). It does not matter for Schiller's play that a long succession of rulers in the Norman dynasty is not in accordance with the facts of history. In these matters the poet may freely deviate from history if it suits his purpose. The Chorus may well be optimistic at this auspicious moment, but the hearer does not forget the more gloomy view taken of the future of the Princes in ll. 944—980.

1191. $\mathfrak{D}$ie $\mathfrak{P}$enaten, 'the Penates,' the solemn household gods of the Romans. Cp. ll. 162—163, biejes $\mathfrak{P}$alaftes fchüßenbe $\mathfrak{G}$ötter, and l. 445.

1195. $\mathfrak{H}$ebe, the Goddess of Youth. If Hebe and Victoria are to receive her the meaning of the Chorus clearly is that her youthful beauty will secure for her the victory over all hearts.

1196. $\mathfrak{V}$ictoria. The description given of the Goddess of Victory is the typical representation of her by all the ancient artists since the time of Phidias. In the great statue of the Olympian Zeus made by this famous sculptor Victoria (the Greek Νίκη) was thus seen poised with outstretched wings on the hand of the 'eternal father.' In his poem $\mathfrak{P}$ompeji unb $\mathfrak{H}$erfulanum, l. 54, Schiller says:

$\mathfrak{U}$nb bie $\mathfrak{V}$ictoria fliegt leicht aus ber $\mathfrak{h}$altenben $\mathfrak{H}$anb.

1203. The lines 1203—5 seem to be inspired by the ancient representations of the seasons' linked dance. In the same way in which with the men the sceptre passes on from prince to prince, so in the case of the women charm and modesty are transmitted.

1205. Gürtel der Anmut, 'the girdle of charm.' This is a reference to the magic girdle of charm possessed, according to Greek mythology, by the goddess Aphrodite. Whoever wore it became immediately an object of love and desire. Schiller made excellent use of this idea in the introduction to his fine philosophical and aesthetic treatise on Anmut und Würde, 'Grace and Dignity.'

1206. Scham stands for Schamhaftigkeit, 'modesty.'

1208. Erlebt, 'lives to see,' hence 'witnesses,' 'beholds.'

1221. sich belongs to both vertilgend and haßt, and is short for das sich haßt und (in seinem Haß) sich selbst vertilgt.

1225. Schlangenhaß, *m.* 'serpent-like hatred,' is a compound coined by Schiller.

1226. Schreckensschicksal, *n.* 'fearful fate.'

Scene 4.

This Scene concludes the first portion of the Second Act by a song of the Chorus in the manner of the Greek 'stasimon.' It consists of five stanzas of the same structure, each consisting of six rimeless lines. The rhythm is mixed, trochaic-dactylic. The first five lines have four, the concluding lines of each stanza only three accents. The song extols the privileges of an exalted position, the enviable lot of rulers for whom always the very best and the most beautiful are reserved. The song is intended to produce a calming effect after the passionate utterances of Beatrice and Don Cesar. This song on the good fortune of princes may in some respects be compared with Schiller's fine philosophical poem in elegiac metre called Das Glück.

1230. Sohn der Götter, viz. the King. In Greek tradition, as well as in old Germanic, and also in Japanese tradition, the members of the ruling houses are supposed to be directly descended from the gods of supernatural beings.

1235. die Blume (like die Krone) is the best, the most valuable.

1240. sich...vergleichen, 'come to an agreement,' 'settle the matter' by lot, i.e. by chance, while the ruler is certain to get the best.

1244. beneid' ich ihm is a Latinism (*invideo illi*) instead of the usual um dies (or darum) beneide ich ihn.

1245. heimführt, 'leads home as his bride.' See the note to l. 855.

1247. eigen, short for zu eigen, als fein Eigen, 'for his own,' in which fuller form eigen is a noun.

1248. This line and the following are very true of the conditions prevailing in medieval Sicily. They also prepare for lines 1577 sqq. In Schiller's $\mathfrak{H}$iftorifche Memoires, Friebrich I we read: Mit bem Schwert in ber Hand hatten arabifche Korfaren fich Wohnfige in Apulien errungen (Säkular Ausgabe, XIII. 150, 13).

1256. Ungeweihter, probably for Uneingeweihter, 'uninitiated' into the secret.

SCENE 5.

With this Scene begins a new set. Important revelations are made in it, and it is the brightest in the play. There is a distinct break between Scenes 4 and 5, and it has even been suggested that in Schiller's original plan this Scene was to open the Third Act. This, however, is not convincing and it would certainly make Act II too short.

The scene is the third to which we are introduced in this play, a room in the interior of the Palace. The time of action must be the later part of the afternoon as it must fall after the first Scene of this Act (ll. 1064—5).

In this Scene the brothers are informed by their mother of the existence of a grown up sister who is expected to arrive every moment from her place of concealment, and the sons announce to Isabella that they will presently each bring to her a beautiful daughter-in-law. The Princess is overjoyed and defies any mother to declare herself happier than she (ll. 1438—40).

1261. feftliche erfchienen. On the hiatus see l. 990 n.

1269. wie is taken up by So in l. 1276.

ber Eulen nachtgewohnte Brut, 'brood of owls accustomed to the night.' The simile is fully developed. The brood of night owls signifies the secret hatred, the mouldering dwellings refer to the ancestral halls laid desolate by the feud of the brothers, while the long exiled inhabitants are Confidence and Concord who now joyfully return.

nachtgewohnt, for ber Nacht (genit.) or bie Nacht (acc.) gewohnt, usually an bie Nacht gewöhnt. This is a word of Schiller's own coining. See the notes to l. 136 and l. 12 (entwohnt).

1271. Mit altverjährtem Eigentum. Instead of Eigentum one would expect Eigentumsrecht or Befigrecht, 'right of possession,' 'right of ownership,' the ownership established by undisputed use during many years. Altverjährtes Eigentum is a possession held many years (alt) and to which time has given an indisputable claim (verjährt), hence 'a prescriptive property.' Altverjährtes has thus the sense of längst verjährtes. Render 'with prescriptive right of ownership.' The phrase seems to be a reminiscence of Goethe's Iphigenie, v. 2, ll. 1802—3, where King Thoas says of Iphigenie:

meine Güte
Scheint ihr ein altverjährtes Eigentum.

This is all the more likely as Schiller helped to stage Goethe's drama just during the time he wrote Die Braut von Messina. In Wallensteins Tod, I. 4, l. 195 the Duke of Friedland speaks of

verjährt geheiligtem Besitz.

In modern usage verjährt no longer means a right hallowed by age, but is exclusively used with regard to rights that have fallen into disuse and are no longer valid.

1298. verschwiegest. Verschweigen usually takes a direct object, hence we should expect das or es or ihr Dasein.

1304. ewig nie mehr, for auf ewig nie mehr.

1306. wurde eurem Vater. See l. 232 n.

1307. Ein seltsam wunderbarer Traum. See l. 24 n.

The oracle of the ancients is here to some extent replaced by dreams. The dream of the father is in some respects modelled on the oracle given to Laios (the father of Oedipus) and on the dream of Hecuba (the wife of King Priamus of Troy before the birth of her son Paris, which was to the effect that a torch would be born to the King that would set fire to the town of Troy). Schiller may also have thought of Hecuba's dream in the lost tragedy *Alexandros* of Sophocles, the outlines of which he knew from a story in the collection made by Hyginus. See Appendix IV. In the Nibelungenlied fair Kriem-hilt has three significant dreams, viz. that a pet falcon of hers was torn to pieces by two eagles, that her husband was chased and killed by two wild boars, that two hills came crashing down upon him and hid him for ever from her sight. Ancient peoples saw in such dreams hints given to mortals by some deity, and were consequently very anxious to note them and to have them explained. Schiller introduced some harassing dreams of the Countess Terzky with excellent effect in the concluding portion of Wallensteins Tod, v. 3, ll. 3467—3510. On the dramatic use of dreams see Introd. p. lxii.

Ihm leuchte. The accusative Ihn is more common and also older, but the dative is occasionally found in good authors, especially towards

the middle of the eighteenth century.   Goethe has both mid bünft and
mir bünft.   The dative seems to have been used on the model of such
expressions as mir ſcheint, kommt es vor, ſchwant, ahnt, and in the sense
of the Latin *mihi videtur*.   The accusative, however, is still regarded
as the more correct construction.

1318. Ara'bier, now usually A'raber.   On the pronunciation see
Introd. p. lxxv.   The Arabian was a Mahommedan astrologer whom
the Christian Isabella, who did not like him, in a later passage
contemptuously calls Bogelſchauer (2345), ſchwarzer Magier (2346) and
Gößendiener (2360).

1321. wenn mein Schoß von einer Tochter Entbunden würde, lit. 'if my
womb should be delivered of a daughter,' 'if I should be delivered of
a daughter.'

1322. töten würde ſie.   The oracle says *what* is to happen, but not
in what way it is to be brought about.

ihm, and mir (l. 1350) are expressive ethical datives.

1328. erhielt die Tochter.   In all the many ancient stories on the
pattern of which Schiller has modelled his dream and its consequences
the same thing occurs.   The oracle or dream is that a child will be born
who, when grown up, will perform certain momentous things; the King
orders the child to be destroyed; it is secretly saved for some reason or
other, grows up, and eventually performs the deed which the ruler had
been anxious to prevent by ordering its instant death.

1331. Rat, *m.* 'counsel,' 'expedient.'

der Mutterliebe is the dative after es gebricht (*dat.*)...an (*with
dat.*).

1333. das Kindlein zu verſchonen, 'to spare the babe.'   Verſchonen
originally took (like ſchonen) the genitive, e.g. in Luther's translation
of the Bible (Romans viii. 32):

welcher auch ſeines eigenen Sohnes nicht hat verſchonet.

This construction still survives in elevated diction.   But in l. 1644, as
here, it takes the accusative.

1334. Auch mir ward, etc.   Probably *after* her husband had dreamt
and related his dream to her.   It is only natural that the minds of both
parents should be exercised by the thought how the birth of another
child, perhaps of a daughter, would influence the relation of the
brothers.

1336. Liebesgötter, *m. pl.* 'cupids,' 'amourettes.'

1339. friſch has here the meaning of eben, ſoeben.

1344. fromm Gepaart, 'in peaceful harmony,' 'in gentle fellowship.'
The usual meaning of fromm is now 'pious,' but in older German it
meant 'doughty,' 'good,' 'harmless,' 'gentle.'

1346. Verständnis löste is unusual. Lösen is usually said of riddles or
puzzles, das Rätsel lösen. With Verständnis one would expect erschließen,
'open,' or vermitteln. Hence das Rätsel dieses Traumes löste or das Verständnis dieses Traumes vermittelte or erschloß mir. Say '(a monk) explained
to me the purport of my dream.'

With regard to the *two* dreams, one may find an illustration in the
double oracle that was given to Hercules. At the end of the *Trachiniae*
of Sophocles, the dying Hercules informs his faithful son Hyllus that he
had received two oracles, one that he should perish by no creature that
had the breath of life, but by one that had passed to the dwelling of
Hades; the other that, at the time 'which liveth and now is,' his
release from the toils laid upon him would be accomplished. The oracles
are both fulfilled as he passes away from all the troubles of the world
by the baneful gift of the dead centaur Nessus. Schiller knew this
drama well.

1347. das Herz, for mein Herz. See l. 196 n. and l. 519 n.

1349. Genesen würd' ich, 'I should give birth to.'

1353. Gott der Wahrheit refers to the Christian faith as opposed to
the Mahommedan (der Lüge).

1354. die Gottverheißne, for die von Gott verheißene, 'the (daughter) pro-
mised by God.' Die Gottverheißene was perhaps inspired by Goethe's die
Gottgegebene (Iphigenie, I. 2, l. 99), which was formed after the model
of the Greek θεόδοτος, θεόσδοτος. Cp. also l. 136 n.

1358. der Schwester braucht's, the genitive with the impers. es braucht
or es bedarf, 'there is need of.'

1360. Isabella does not say where, which is important for the continuation of the play. Don Manuel must not know.

1362. den Anblick...den heißerflehten. See l. 168 n.
selbst, 'even,' usually selbst den Anblick.

1388. Zuflucht, for Zufluchtsort, 'place of refuge.'

1399. Dies Herz, again for Mein Herz. See l. 78 n.

1404. Notice the use of rime in many passages of this Scene so full
of love and joyful emotion.

1405 and **1408.** mir is an expressive ethical dative.

1409. die schönste der Mütterkronen, viz. to see her beloved son happy
in his love by the side of a noble wife.

1427. The following passage (1427—40) is the climax of the tragedy, the point at which everything seems to be going well, when all sorrows have passed and for a time no cares and apprehensions remain.

1429. Gegründet Auf festen Säulen seh' ich mein Geschlecht. Isabella is carried away by her feeling of delight after her many years of fear and trembling, and in her delight oversteps, very naturally, the bounds of prudence and calm reflection. She thinks that in the future she will be surrounded by five children and that her race will henceforth be firmly established. With her words compare those of the proud father of the family in Schiller's Lied von der Glocke, ll. 133 sqq.:

> Und der Vater mit frohem Blick
> Von des Hauses weitschauendem Giebel
> Überzählet sein blühend Glück....
> Rühmt sich mit stolzem Mund:
> „Fest wie der Erde Grund,
> Gegen des Unglücks Macht
> Steht mir des Hauses Pracht!"

But Schiller adds the lines at this climax of the first part of the *Song of the Bell*, which are just as suitable with regard to Isabella and her boast in ll. 1438 sqq.:

> Doch mit des Geschickes Mächten
> Ist kein ew'ger Bund zu flechten,
> Und das Unglück schreitet schnell.

1432. hinabsehn, 'look down,' as one looks down a long alley or a long corridor. Longfellow speaks of the 'corridors of time.'

1434. Abgeschiednen, i.e. vom Leben A., 'departed spirit.' Cp. l. 794.

1438. This line and the following contain her boastful challenge to all women who ever were mothers asking if any one can compare with her in glory. This momentary exultation, this spirit of over-bearing pride which the Greeks called ὕβρις, reminds us of the boast of Niobe—and the punishment falls upon her, as it fell upon Niobe, almost at once. Her punishment and suffering are very much harder than she has deserved.

1443. Davon, probably instead of von denen, 'of whom.' But it may also refer to the fact of their existence, 'of which fact.'

Kunde, f. 'information,' 'news.' This noun belongs to kennen and its meaning is similar to Kenntnis, f. 'knowledge.' Kunde vernehmen is rare, but one often says Kunde bringen. Cp. l. 2029.

1445. From a dramatic point of view it is fitting that Don Manuel does not here repeat the full account which he gave to his knights, ll. 686 sqq.

1452. fich verborgen in fich felbst 3u fpinnen or einzufpinnen, 'to wrap himself up in mystery.'

1453. den Ratfchluß zu bewahren, 'to keep his counsel.' Cp. l. 409.

1454. unzugangbar, for the usual unzugänglichen, 'inaccessible.' The line is an alexandrine.

1455. die furze Frist, see ll. 1447—8 and l. 1402.

1458. The different characters of the brothers are very well marked by Schiller throughout the whole play, but nowhere better than in this Scene.

1464. Himmelsfeuer, 'heavenly fire,' 'celestial fire.'

1465. Die stands here for Diejenige, welche, referring to the sun. In German the gender of the sun is feminine, and this makes the comparison between Beatrice and the sun easier in German than in English.

verflärt, erflärt, 'glorifies,' 'explains.'

1468. Ins Herz des Herzens, for Ins Innerste des Herzens, 'into her innermost heart.' Schiller was fond of this expression, which he borrowed from Shakespeare. Cp. *Hamlet*, III. 2, ll. 78 sqq. :

> Give me the man
> That is not passion's slave and I will wear him
> In my heart's core, ay in my heart of heart.

As early as 1788 Schiller says, in his fourth letter on his play Don Carlos, of the Marquis of Posa and his princely friend : Im Herzen feines Herzens würde er ihn getragen haben wie Hamlet feinen Horatio (Goedeke, VI. 49), and in Wallensteins Tod, III. 18, ll. 2116—18, the Duke of Friedland says, commenting on the treachery of his false friend Octavio Piccolomini :

> Am Sternenhimmel fuchten meine Augen,
> Im weiten Weltenraum den Feind, den ich
> Im Herzen meines Herzens eingefchloffen.

A similar idea, but somewhat differently expressed, occurs in Goethe's poetry (cp. his song An Mignon, IV. 4, Herz im Herzen, and Iphigenie, III. 1, l. 947, das innre Herz).

1473. Götterstimme. The use of the term Götter seems rather strange in the mouth of the Christian Princess and it may be translated here by 'a voice from heaven.' But it should be noted that in the poetic language of Schiller and Goethe the plural die Götter, alone or in compounds, is of very frequent occurrence. (Cp. L. Bellermann, *Schillers Dramen*,

Beiträge zu ihrem Verständnis, II. 219—220, Berlin, 1891.) In Die Braut von Meſſina, where there is an intentional mixture of Christian and classical Greek conceptions and expressions (see the Introd. p. xxvii), the use of the term Götterſtimme and Götterhand (l. 1559) by Isabella is less surprising than the phrase Es leben Götter, die den Hochmut rächen in the mouth of Mary Stuart (III. 4, l. 2262).

1474. erwart' ich dich, viz. zu finden.

1476. meine Mutter in such phrases is not usual in German. One either says Mutter only, or liebe Mutter. Meine Mutter is a Gallicism (French *ma mère*). It occurs again in Don Cesar's mouth, l. 1676. Cp. also meine Tochter, l. 2773.

1477. des Geſtirnes Macht, 'the power of some star,' viz. fate directed by some predominating star. The belief in the supreme influence of the stars on the destiny of men is shared by all the persons of this drama who invariably seek for some outside influence shaping their lives, while in reality it is their own actions which bring about their ruin. The conception of predestination in love is so common that it easily appeals to all hearers.

1480. Nicht wahrlich ſolches Eitle. By means of wahrlich the emphatic nicht is separated from what follows and thus made still more impressive. This construction, which reminds one of ancient classical models, occurs only in Schiller's later dramas, e.g. Wallenſteins Tod, I. 7, ll. 569—570:

> Nicht wahrlich guter Wille ſtellte dich
>
> An dieſen Platz...;

and Demetrius, I. ll. 74—75:

> Nicht wahrlich Euer Anſtand widerſpricht
>
> Noch Eure Rede dieſem ſtolzen Anſpruch.

Compare the note on Nicht at the beginning of sentences, l. 265.

ſolches Eitle, 'such a vain thought.'

1481. Zu Sinne, in ordinary prose In den Sinn (kommen).

1482. dorten, for the usual dort, is an enlarged form of dort which is occasionally found since the sixteenth century and is not uncommon in Schiller's poetry, e.g. Wallenſteins Lager, l. 142, and Der Pilgrim, ll. 13—16:

> Bis zu einer goldnen Pforten
>
> Du gelangſt; da gehſt du ein;
>
> Denn das Irdiſche wird dorten
>
> Himmliſch, unvergänglich ſein.

1486. ein Götterbild, 'a divine image.' See l. 1473 n.

1487. See l. 1088 n., l. 1118 n., and also ll. 1887—98.

1488. wir, viz. the brothers.

1493. Many details in the following description were suggested by the impressive funeral of Duke Karl Eugen of Würtemberg (at Ludwigsburg) which Schiller attended in October, 1793, when he was on a visit to his native Swabian country.

1494. Genien, *m. pl.* 'genii,' for 'guardian angels,' 'cherubs.' Death was represented by the ancients as a genius with an inverted (i.e. extinguished) torch. On the trisyllabic pronunciation of the word cp. Introd. p. lxxv.

1496. Totenfarg, *m.* redundant for Sarg, *m.* 'coffin.'

1497. weißbekreuztem, 'with a white cross.' For Grabestuch and Grabtuch, 'pall,' see Introd. p. lxxv.

1498. fahe instead of fah is old fashioned and ceremonious. In the sixteenth century fahe (probably formed by form-association with the present fehe and the imperfect subj. fähe, and the many weak imperfects in -e) was common and occurs also in Luther's Bible, e.g. Und Gott fahe, daß es gut war (Genesis i. 10). These extended forms survived till late in the eighteenth century. Schiller uses fahe in several cases. See the Introd. p. lxxiii, and the note on fiehe, l. 67.

Stab der Herrschaft. The 'rod of authority' is das Zepter.

1501. Gehäng, or Wehrgehäng(e), *n.* is the diamond-studded 'belt.'

1502. alles, the neuter collective used idiomatically in a general way to comprise all who can be thought of; alle, 'all people,' 'everyone.' Cp. Das Lied von der Glocke, l. 191:

> Alles rennet, rettet, flüchtet.

1503. vom hohen Chor, 'from the lofty choir.' But cp. l. 643 n.

1504. fich zu regen, lit. 'to bestir itself,' 'to sound.'

1506. fortflung, an archaic form instead of fortflang. Such archaic forms occur first in the sixteenth century (Luther) and are occasionally even found in writers of the eighteenth century. The principal forms of flingen (fingen, fpringen, finfen, finden, binden, etc.) were, in Middle High German, *klinge, klanc, klungen, geklungen.* The difference between the radical vowel in the imperfect sing. and plur. (a—u) was subsequently levelled out, and as a rule the a of the singular was introduced into the plural. Hence instead of fie flungen it was said fie flangen. But occasionally, and quite exceptionally, the u (which is characteristic of the plural) entered into the singular and replaced the characteristic a. Hence flung instead of flang. Such forms have now quite died out. In ich warb, wir wurben the old state of things is still preserved, but by the side of the older warb (which is now used in high style and poetry) the younger wurbe (never wurb) has come in by form-association. The old u plurals survive in a few proverbial phrases, such as:

Unb wie bie Alten fungen,
So zwitfcherten bie Jungen.

1509. überfchleierte, 'spread a veil over,' is a word coined by Schiller.

1512. bem Nieberfahrenben, 'him who was descending' seems to be more appropriate than 'that which was descending,' which is grammatically also possible.

1513. auf Seraphsflügeln bes Gefangs, 'on seraphic wings of song.' The phrase auf Flügeln bes Gefanges occurs also in Heine's poetry, and Geibel sings in his Spielmanns Lieb:

Das Lieb hat Flügel.

1530. This line occurs only in the Hamburg and Regensburg acting-copies.

1536. weben, 'move,' 'act.' Cp. Winbesweben, 1. 869.

1538. fchienen Sich ohne Mittel geiftig zu berühren, 'seemed brought into direct spiritual contact.' ohne Mittel, in prose unmittelbar, 'without any medium,' 'directly.'

1540. Some critics think that the voice of kindred asserted itself. Beatrice (l. 1094), however, speaks of Bliden, bie mich fchredten.

1542. This line has become a familiar quotation. King Frederic William III of Prussia once spoke to a confidential friend of his late dearly beloved spouse, Queen Luise, and told him that his feelings when he met her for the first time had been exactly described by Schiller in a passage of one of his plays, but that he could not remember where it occurred. When he was shown ll. 1527—42 of Die Braut von Meffina the King, who as a rule was extremely reserved, was seized with deep emotion and said that this was the passage he had had in his mind.

1543. The quiet Don Manuel is deeply moved by his brother's words which eloquently express what he, too, felt but was not so well able to utter. His whole speech is in rimed lines. But cp. also ll. 704—717.

1545. Verwanbtes zu Verwanbtem, 'kindred to kindred,' 'when like meets like.' Cp. Das Lieb von ber Glode, l. 92:

ob fich bas Herz zum Herzen finbet.

In his novel 𝔇𝔦𝔢 𝔚𝔞𝔥𝔩𝔳𝔢𝔯𝔴𝔞𝔫𝔡𝔱𝔰𝔠𝔥𝔞𝔣𝔱𝔢𝔫, 'the elective affinities,' Goethe treats the subject of kindred (wahlverwandte) souls. The term wahlverwandt (= durch Wahl verwandt) is really a term used in chemistry and applied to the irresistible attraction of certain elements for others.

1547. löst, for kann lösen. Cp. l. 1658, birgt = kann bergen.

1548. fall' ich bei, 'I agree with,' is not unusual in the classics of the eighteenth century, but now exceedingly rare. The impersonal es fällt mir bei, which is likewise common in the eighteenth century, but now replaced by es fällt mir ein, 'it occurs to me,' must be kept apart from ich falle ihm bei (ich zolle or gebe ihm Beifall).

1551. dunkel mich beseelt, 'animates my soul darkly (or mysteriously).'

1559. unregierfam stärkern, for unregierfamen und stärkeren, 'ungovernable and stronger than my own.' Unregierfam is a word coined by Schiller and denotes something das sich nicht regieren läßt. It may have been formed on the pattern of lenkfam, 'guidable,' and unbeugfam, 'inflexible.'

Götterhand, 'divine hand.' See the note to l. 1473.

1560. dunkel, for im Dunkeln, im Verborgenen.

fpinnt, 'spins.' The idea is taken from the Parcae, the goddesses of Destiny, one of whom spins the thread of life.

1562. groß, 'highly,' 'nobly.'

SCENE 6.

The first blow is dealt to Isabella's feeling of happiness and security by the news brought by Diego of the sudden disappearance of Beatrice. He believes that she has been carried off by pirates. Isabella entreats her sons to rescue their sister, and they start, one after the other, Don Manuel with very scanty, Don Cesar with full information furnished by Isabella, in order to organise the pursuit. Isabella remains alone in gloomy meditation:

1563. The arrival of the messenger is again specially announced. See the note on Act I. Scene 6, on p. 152.

1564. He is apparently quite unknown to Don Manuel. Cp. ll. 757 sqq.

1568. Die höchste Freude. This is a fine touch of tragic irony. What is waiting for her is der höchste Schmerz.

1572. Beatrice is a word of four syllables. On the pronunciation see p. 175. Don Manuel is struck (betroffen) by the familiar name.

This line has seven accented syllables. As in it there is twice a change of speaker, its unusual length is not very noticeable. It is the only line with two syllables in excess that occurs in this play. See the Introd. p. lxxxiii.

1573. Mich entfeelt, high style for mich tötet. The active verb entfeelen is not often used in German poetry, but the past participle entfeelt occurs more frequently (see l. 1943). In Platen we find:

Und der Freude soll ich leben,
Und das Herz entfeelt der Gram.

1575. Bei allen Heil'gen, 'by all Heaven's saints.' This and many other utterances of Isabella show that she is a devout Roman Catholic, and that such terms as Götterstimme (l. 1473) and Götterhand (l. 1559) are only forms of speech with her. See l. 1473 n.

1579. Faff' dich refers to Isabella's mute action.

1583. Die Freude trug mich.... In the ancient drama messengers are often represented as garrulous and their way of relating facts as somewhat comical. But in Schiller's drama there is no room for the smallest comical effect. Diego is promptly stopped by Don Cesar.

1589. Entfeßt...das Entfeßliche. See l. 104 n.

Don Manuel ist um sie beschäftigt. It is essential for dramatic purposes that Don Manuel should not hear part of the information elicited by Don Cesar, for if he did he would soon perceive the identity of his lost sister Beatrice with his bride Beatrice whom he had just carried off from a place of concealment. For this reason he is represented as being busy with his mother and deaf to Diego's account. In l. 1629, after Don Cesar has rushed away, he begins to put his own questions.

1590. From here to l. 1615 the dialogue is carried on briskly by means of question and answer, each speaker having two lines allotted to him. On the *stichomythia* see Introd. p. xc and l. 487 n.

Mauren, Moorish pirates. See l. 815 n.

1594. rettet sich, 'takes refuge,' 'seeks shelter.'

1599. gnügt, for genügt. See the Introd. p. lxxiv.

1603. Die Wohlverschloßne, lit. 'the well locked-up one,' i.e. 'the well-guarded one.'

1605. Auf hoher Leiter Sproffen. Notice the omission of the indefinite article. This omission as well as that of the definite article with an attributive genitive is frequent in Schiller's poetry. Cp. l. 1029 n. and l. 1670.

1608. Die...Sie, in prose Sie, die.... The relative clause precedes the principal clause.

gebunden, viz. hatte. See l. 7 n. and l. 737 n.

1613. Der Wiederkehr vergaß sie. The genit. with vergeffen is now given up in favour of the accus. The old construction survives in Vergißmeinnicht.

1614. frei genug dem Räuber, i.e. sufficiently free of access for pirates to carry her off.

1615. Don Cesar hits the nail on the head. Don Manuel apparently does not notice it, as he is still plunged in thought on hearing the name Beatrice. Isabella, however, who has collected herself again, is indignant at the suggestion.

1617. pflichtvergeffen, 'forgetting her duty,' 'forgetful of her duty.' Pflichtvergeffen is a person who seine Pflicht vergeffen hat.

1626. Notice the two unaccented syllables between the second and third accented syllables, well marking Isabella's excitement. See the Introd. p. lxxxii, § 5, d.

1628. Don Cesar rushes away, for dramatic reasons, because he must not hear Diego's account, ll. 1643—69. If he had, he would have found out the truth at once, and the tragic end intended by the poet could not have been brought about.

1629. Don Manuel who, for special reasons of the poet's own, has so far not heard anything of Diego's story, goes back to Diego's words, l. 1577. Everything must be clear to him if three things are fully established, viz. (1) the time of her disappearance; (2) her name; and (3) the place from which she was taken. The first point is cleared up in l. 1630, the second in l. 1632. When he asks for information on the third point Isabella does not give him a direct answer. If she had done so, Don Manuel would have realised that Beatrice was his sister and the play would soon have come to a different end. In order to avoid this the poet makes Isabella urge him to leave at once (l. 1636) and put him off with an evasive answer (l. 1638). When it seems impossible that she can any longer avoid answering his straightforward question, Diego interposes, and his account gives Don Manuel a momentary relief (l. 1659), as he feels sure that his Beatrice has not attended his father's funeral. Still he does not wish to ask his mother any more questions but will now learn the truth about the funeral from Beatrice's own lips (ll. 1670—1). No sooner is he gone than Don Cesar, returning, easily obtains from Isabella all the necessary information about the convent where Beatrice was hidden. All this has been very cleverly thought out by Schiller and is as a rule not noticed by the spectators in the excitement caused by the stirring scene; it is, moreover, absolutely necessary for the continuation of the dramatic action; still in several places in this Scene the dramatic probability is but small and the action is balanced, as it were, on the edge of a knife. The whole somewhat complicated structure of this Scene was probably due to Schiller's desire to introduce as little shifting of scenes as possible into this drama.

1648. Lag beine Tochter...mir an (l. 1650), 'thy daughter entreated me,' 'solicited me,' 'urged me.'

1660. That is not like her; he feels sure that Beatrice would not have attended the funeral against his express wish. Cp. ll. 1088 sqq. and ll. 1887 sqq.

1661. Isabella had obviously given him strict orders never to allow Beatrice to leave the precincts of the convent. Nevertheless it is rather strange that, after what she has heard of Don Cesar's meeting the unknown beautiful maiden at the funeral of the Prince, Isabella does not for a moment suspect that this maiden might have been his sister Beatrice.

1662. ich bacht' es gut zu machen, 'I thought I acted for the best.'

1666. ahnungsvollem Zuge, 'attraction full of presage.'

1670. in...Zweifels Qualen. See l. 1028 n. and l. 1605 n.

1671. He decides to ask Beatrice if she has been present at the funeral service. He does this, putting the question off again and again on account of his dread of an affirmative answer, in Act III. 3, ll. 1886 sqq.

1672. Verzieh, 'tarry,' 'wait.'

1675. Ganz verfenn' ich ihn, 'I do not understand him at all,' 'I cannot make him out.' See l. 593 n.

1678. ein Zeichen, 'a sign,' he means a clue to her place of abode from which she has disappeared.

1683. This is, of course, a purely imaginary place.

1686. verschwiegner. See l. 3 n.

Seelen, 'souls'; in the mouth of Isabella it does not mean 'departed spirits' (Schatten). Cp. l. 1029 n.

1687. gutes Muts, now usually guten Mutes for euphonic reasons. The older strong inflexion is still usual in the phrase feineswegs, but allenfalls is now much more common than allesfalls.

1693. This makes the meeting of the brothers in the garden before the town unavoidable.

1696. Compare with this line and the following the words of Iphigenie in Goethe's drama, IV. 5, ll. 1694—6 :

> Soll biefer Fluch benn ewig walten? Soll
> Nie bies Geschlecht mit einem neuen Segen
> Sich wieber heben? — Nimmt boch alles ab!
> Das befte Glück, bes Lebens schönste Kraft
> Ermattet endlich, warum nicht ber Fluch?

Compare ll. 965 and 975.

1705. In some respect Thekla's monologue in Wallensteins Tod, IV. 12, ll. 3169 sqq. may be compared with this. After having described her short happiness in the consciousness of Max Piccolomini's love, she suddenly shudders and says, also beginning with Da kommt :

> — Da kommt bas Schicksal — roh und kalt
> Faßt es bes Freundes zärtliche Gestalt
> Und wirft ihn unter ten Hufschlag feiner Pferbe —
> — Das ist bas Los bes Schönen auf ber Erbe!

ein Sturm aus heitrer Luft, 'a storm in a clear sky.' One always says ein Donnerkeil aus heitrer Luft, 'a bolt from the blue,' but usually ein Sturm aus heiterm Himmel. These words prepare the hearer for the tragic crisis which is now fast approaching.

ACT III.

The scene of action during the whole of this Act which follows immediately on the Second is laid in the garden near Messina. The time of action is still the late afternoon of the first day. Beatrice, anxiously waiting for Don Manuel, is guarded by the knights of Don Cesar. The retainers of Don Manuel are approaching with the bridal gifts. Don Manuel himself is hurrying to the garden in order to ask Beatrice if she had really attended the funeral, in which case he cannot doubt that she is his sister. Don Cesar is also on his way to the garden, in order to send his declared bride to his mother, before starting in search of his sister. Thus the spectator knows that before long the brothers must meet in the garden. Before the meeting of the brothers takes place the knights of Don Manuel arrive and the old antagonistic spirit of the two Choruses suddenly flames up in its old force.

SCENE I.

The knights of Don Manuel arrive with their lord's presents for his bride. On finding the access to the house occupied by Don Cesar's followers they haughtily ask for admission, which is just as haughtily refused. Taunting words fly like winged arrows from host to host, and at the end of the Scene, unmindful of the anguish of Beatrice, the enraged men are just about to come to blows when they are stopped by Don Manuel.

The greater part of the Scene is carried on in a vivid *stichomyti̇̀ia* of single lines which, in this case, are moreover bound together by means of rime. See the Introd. pp. xc—xci.

The excited opening of this Scene is a good preparation for what is to come.

1716. This line about the *jus primi possessoris* reminds us of the proverb 'Possession is nine-tenths of the Law' and of the Latin *Beati possidentes*, 'happy are those who are in possession.'

1718. fich...vergleichen, lit. 'are compared,' hence 'have crossed,' 'have met.' But see l. 1786.

1719. in meinen Wegen, usually in or auf meinem Wege, mir im Wege.

1721. Note the alliteration. See l. 202 n. 'Listen and watch.' Render 'listen and lurk' or 'hearken and hide.'

1723. fteh'...zu Red'. The modern phrase einem Rede ftehen arose from the older einem zu or zur Rede ftehen, 'to stand to or for a speech,' 'to be prepared to answer,' 'to give an account.' Cp. the English 'to *stand* fire.' A similar common phrase in which the preposition is still kept in ordinary prose is einen zur Rede ftellen, 'to call someone to account.'

1725. From here the stichomythic dialogue is carried on in units of three rimed lines. The frightened Beatrice has in each case a line after the two Choruses have spoken theirs. The effect is that of an impassionate Terzetto in an opera.

1730. er refers not to Herrfcher (l. 1729) but to Don Manuel.

1731. befiegt ihn weit, 'is far superior to him.'

1733. dies ift feine Zeit, viz. the late afternoon. In l. 642 it is said that Don Manuel usually disappeared at sunset. Beatrice obviously thinks that he is always engaged during the day.

1737. The excited mood is well depicted by the transposed rhythm.

1740. Sie werden handgemein, 'they are coming to blows.' Handgemein really means 'hands together.' Hence the phrase originally means 'they are getting their hands together.'

1744. verfehle biefen Augenblick, 'may miss this moment' for 'may not arrive at this moment.'

1746. täufchet meine Bitte! One would expect erhöret nicht, läßt unerfüllt, verfagt! Täufchen is generally used with regard to eine Erwartung, eine Hoffnung. But as Beatrice's request included a hope, täufchen, although uncommon, is very expressive.

A similar situation occurs in Schiller's ballad Hero und Leander, where, when the storm in the night breaks forth, the unfortunate Hero, whose lover is swimming to her across the Hellespont, regrets her entreaties to the gods to bring Leander to her on that day. She calls out despairingly (ll. 162—165):

> Ach, was wagt' ich zu erflehn!
> Wenn bie Götter mich erhören!
> Wenn er fich ben falfchen Meeren
> Preis gab in bes Sturmes Wehn!

SCENE 2.

Don Manuel peremptorily bids the knights to desist from fighting, learns the cause, and bids Don Cesar's men to retire forthwith. They obey.

1752. mit gezuckter Augenwimper nur, 'with even so much as a quivering eyelash,' the least possible sign of anger and provocation. The phrase nicht mit ber Wimper zucken, lit. 'not to twitch an eyelash,' 'not to turn a hair,' is quite common, but gezuckte Wimper is unusual.

1754. Dämon is here of course an 'evil spirit.' See l. 658 n.

1757. auf immerbar, 'for ever,' a fine touch of tragic irony.

1768. Unfinnige refers to both Choruses. After l. 1771 he addresses his brother's retainers only.

1775. ein Haupt unb ein Gemüt, colloquially ein Herz unb eine Seele.

1777. wahrft bes Einganges, poetic for bewahrft ben Eingang.

beginnen has here again the sense of tun. See l. 861 n.

1779. Span, *m.* is a dialectic term peculiar to South Germany and found especially in Swabian writers. It means Zank, Streit, 'quarrel,' 'squabble.' Einen Span mit einem haben is our colloquial 'to have a spar with a person.' Span belongs to fpannen, 'to strain.' Cp. mit einem über ben Fuß gefpannt fein, 'to be on bad terms with a person,' gefpannteß Verhältniß, 'strained relations,' also widerfpenftig (sometimes widerfpenig), 'obstinate,' 'quarrelsome' (belonging to an old German compound der Widerfpan, 'quarrel').

1780. vielgefchäftig, 'officiously.' Cp. our '*busy*body.'

1781. öfterer, 'more often,' 'frequently.' Öfterer is really a comparative with the suffix twice repeated. Cp. mehrere. This comparative occurs occasionally in writers of the sixteenth to the eighteenth centuries. It is not unusual with Lessing, e.g. defto öfterer in Minna von Barnhelm, II. I. A superlative am öfteften is found in Goethe and Grillparzer. But öfterer and am öfteften are impossible in modern German.

1782. deß Streitß ermüdet, for deß Streiteß müde wird.

1783. dehend, 'adroitly.' geringen, 'common,' 'low.' The knights well remember ll. 336 sqq. and ll. 489 sqq.

1786. fich...vergleichen, 'come to terms.' But see l. 1718 n.

1787. acht' eß, usually erachte eß, 'consider it.'

It is somewhat astonishing that the men of Don Cesar do not with a single word explain the reason of their presence in the garden. This is strange from a psychological point of view, but it is necessary from the dramatic point of view that Don Manuel should not yet be informed that Don Cesar has seen Beatrice and has claimed her as his bride.

SCENE 3.

Don Manuel informs Beatrice of his high position. She gives him a description of Isabella from a very faint recollection and at last confesses to him with deep emotion that in spite of his express wish she did attend the funeral of the late Prince.

1793. Schutz und Schirm, 'shelter and protection,' is a common alliterative phrase.

1796. So verfchloffen feierlich, 'so reservedly and solemnly,' 'with such solemn reserve.' Don Manuel is solemn and reserved as he is about to ask her the great question which is to decide at once his own and her future happiness. Beatrice who is ignorant of his purpose and of his harassing anxiety does not understand his behaviour.

1800. Gatte...Geliebter. Cp. the note to l. 806.

1814. She does not suspect that he may be related to her, but she knows that a terrible conflict will ensue if he should be the brother of Don Cesar.

1825. Du wärft, the subjunctive to denote 'is it possible that you are,' 'are you then really?'

1826. This is the first 'anagnorisis,' the first of the many revelations that are now to follow, blow upon blow. This Scene contains no less than three revelations, viz. (1) Beatrice learns that Don Manuel is Don Cesar's brother, (2) Don Manuel is convinced that Beatrice is his sister, and (3) that she is loved by Don Cesar.

1828. The enlarged form ſonſten occurs sometimes in the eighteenth century instead of the usual ſonſt. ſonſten jemand, lit. 'otherwise anybody,' i.e. 'anyone else.' He thinks of course of Isabella. Cp. dorten, l. 1482 n.

1837. He thinks of her relation to his mother, but she thinks of her secret attendance at the funeral. Her anguish momentarily delays the recognition. He has not the heart to ask directly if she had been at the funeral and puts this dreaded question off by first asking her about her mother.

1844. In this line and the following the hazy recollection of Beatrice takes a more definite shape. She had seen her mother consciously only once (l. 1026) and her recollection had much faded, but suddenly it becomes vivid. She knows neither her mother's name nor that she is the Princess of Messina, only that she is of noble blood (l. 749).

1848. This line and the following contain a very good description of Schiller's noble and devoted wife Lotte.

1850. rein gewölbten Bogen, 'finely moulded arch.'

1851. dunkelhellen Glanz, 'dark bright lustre.' Cp. l. 711 n.

1854. ich entfloh ihr. Cp. ll. 1014 and 787.

1861. nimmermehr has here, as sometimes in Schiller's poetry, only the sense of nimmer or nie. Cp. l. 1078 n. It is very emphatic. She is afraid of meeting Don Cesar there and of having her secret divulged, and also of causing in the palace a renewal of the deadly strife between the brothers who both love her.

1869. auf ödem Eiland, 'on a desolate island,' away from the pomp and the strife of the princely dwelling.

1870. Welch vieles Volk is very unusual and probably a mixture of Welch großes Volk and Wie viel Volk.

1884. faßt Mich schaudernd, 'seizes me and makes me shudder,' 'what thought of horror assails me?' The thought does not shudder, but *makes* a person shudder. At the end of his elegy Der Spaziergang, ll. 186—187, Schiller says:

> ach! und es war nur ein Traum,
> Der mich schaudernd ergriff.

In this and several other instances in Schiller's poetry ſchaudernd is used for Schauder erregend or ſchaurig, and in the same way grauſend for Grauſen erregend, grauſig. See ll. 459 and 2311; also Wallenſteins Tod, III. 18, ll. 2101 and 2134.

1886. Du warſt—he must ask four times till the frightened girl gives the answer in the affirmative.

1890. Entſetzen! He is speechless till the end of the Scene. His worst suspicions have come true. Now he knows for certain that Beatrice is his sister and is beloved by his brother. He is overcome with horror and struck dumb. Beatrice, after having made her much dreaded confession, tells him how it came that she disobeyed him.

1892. ließeſt du Die Bitte fallen, lit. ' you let my request drop,' ' you turned a deaf ear to my supplication,' ' you did not pay any attention to my request.'

1894. welch böſen Sternes Macht. She is anxious to put the blame of her inconsiderate action on the fatal power of some evil star. It was, however, only the strong impulse of her heart which she was unable to control and thus she proves the truth of Thekla's words (in Die Piccolomini, III. 8, l. 1840):

Der Zug des Herzens iſt des Schickſals Stimme.

1896. vergnügen (acc.) means here and in other passages of Schiller's poetry Genüge leiſten (dat.), befriedigen (acc.), ' satisfy.' In his ballad Der Graf von Habsburg, ll. 85—86, Schiller says of Rudolf:

Und er ſelber auf ſeines Knappen Tier

Vergnüget noch weiter des Jagens Begier.

In the same way in Schiller's poetry the past part. vergnügt often means ' satisfied,' ' contented.'

1897. See ll. 1648 sqq. No possibility of a doubt is left in his mind. The help of Diego seems to her some slight excuse.

Sie ſchmiegt ſich an ihn, ' she clings to him imploringly,' hoping to be forgiven. In this attitude she is seen by Don Cesar.

SCENE 4.

Don Manuel, stunned by what he has just heard, speechless and defenceless, is killed by his brother. Beatrice swoons. No explanation as to her identity is given to the unsuspecting Don Cesar. He believes that he has done right.

1900. Blendwerk der Hölle! has become a familiar quotation. For a moment Don Cesar cannot believe what he sees to be true, his love for his brother prompts him to believe that he sees before him a delusion of hell. On Blendwerk see l. 1105 n. In Die Jungfrau von Orleans, II. 9, ll. 1689—90, the Black Knight says to Johanna:

> Verderblich Blendwerk! Fahre zu der Hölle
> Zurück, aus der du aufgestiegen bist.

1904. Fahre has here still its old meaning, 'go.'

1905. Ich bin des Todes, 'I am a dead man.' This is a common idiom and occurs often in Schiller. Very often we find the more complete phrase Ich bin ein Mann des Todes, which has the same meaning.

1909. This is the only line in the whole play which seems to refer to a rivalry of the brothers for the rulership of Messina.

1910. Rache! Rache!...falle! falle! These repetitions of words (cp. also 1985, 1987) are imitations of a peculiarity of style in the classical Greek dramas. Note the transposed accent (two trochees) at the beginning of this line.

1911. sühnend Opfer, usually Sühnopfer.

1913. mit Ansehen, 'with authority.'

1918. Weh dir, Messina! According to the conception of the ancient Greeks, as we meet it at the beginning of the *Oedipus Rex*, a murder (Blutschuld) perpetrated within the boundaries of a town called down the wrath of the avenging deities on the whole town and all its inhabitants till it was properly atoned for.

1919. Das gräßlich Ungeheure, 'the horrible monstrous deed.'

1924. Ruft sie ins Leben, viz. zurück, 'recall her to life.'

SCENE 5.

The reflections of the Chorus consist of portions of unequal length. Most lines have four accents and are rimed with a more or less free arrangement of rimes.

The Chorus which at the beginning of the Act was an angry partisan, rises in this Scene to the heights of dispassionate reflection. Its first thoughts are given to the sad fate of the murdered brother (ll. 1941—84); the second portion of the song deals with the murderer (ll. 1985—2028).

1931. genaht, viz. ift. Sich belongs to erfüllenb. Lit. 'how it has come upon us so quickly accomplishing itself,' i.e. 'how the accomplishment came with such speed.'

1933. Note the alliteration. In prose herschreiten would stand after Tat (l. 1934) and not separate the gen. biefer...Tat from bas Schreckens. gefpenft. But cp. l. 20 n. Note the level stress in he'rschrei'ten. Das Schreckensgefpenft is the terrible presentiment of the tragic end of the brothers' feud.

1935. übergießt mich...Grauen, 'horror is poured over my soul.'

1938. ahnenber Furcht, 'foreboding fear,' is strongly contrasted with the entschiebenen Gegenwart (l. 1940), 'realised present,' i.e. 'present reality.' The Chorus has really only had a very vague foreboding of approaching disaster (cp. ll. 969—980), while the spectator may well have had a distinct and ever growing feeling of the impending tragic issue.

1941. In Stolberg's translation of *The Persians* of Aeschylus one of the choruses begins:

> Laffet erschallen
> Traurige Töne,
> Jammernben Laut!

Klage, which in ll. 2266 and 2598 is called Totenklage, i.e. Klage um ben Toten.

1954. bie Zeugen, 'the witnesses' of the wedding ceremony, but here probably not in the Church sense (Trauzeugen) but in the general sense of Hochzeitsgäfte, 'wedding guests.'

1956. Reigen (by the side of Reihen), *m.* is a poetic word for Tanz. In older German *der reie* or *reige* was a sort of lively out-door dance while *tanz* was more quiet and stately. In old German ber Reie was gefprungen, ber Tanz was getreten. In modern poetry, however, as in this passage, ber Reigen is merely a poetic equivalent of ber Tanz. In Schiller's grandest ballad Die Kraniche bes Jbykus the Eumenides themselves (as in the play of Aeschylus) appear on the stage, singing and solemnly dancing, as the Chorus did in the plays of the ancients. In l. 137 Schiller says of this solemn dance:

> So fingenb, tanzen fie ben Reigen.

See the Appendix III, p. 261.

1957. See l. 1945, and l. 1958 where l. 1957 is repeated by the whole Chorus with a slight re-arrangement of the words. In many of the later stanzas of Schiller's poem Das Siegesfeft, written almost immediately after Die Braut von Meſſina, the four concluding lines (a sort of Chorus) are but a slight variation of the four lines which precede them.

1960. Hifthorns, *n.* 'bugle.' A somewhat older form is Hiefhorn. Hief or Hift is the 'sound of the bugle' and seems to belong to the O.H.G. verb *hiufan*, 'to call with a howling noise,' 'to howl.' One now often hears Hüfthorn as if it were a compound of Hüfte, *f.* 'hip,' and meant 'a horn hanging down from a girdle at the side of the hunter.'

1965. Einig geſtimmt...Munde, 'in cordial union with heart and speech,' 'of one accord in heart and voice.'

1966. jetzo, 'now' (also l. 2056), is an old-fashioned form (fr. the M.H.G. *ie zuo*) which occurs especially in poetry, while jetzt (fr. *ie-ze-t*) is now exclusively used in ordinary prose.

nieder Geht. The end of this Act is at sunset.

1969. Von des Brudermords Händen, instead of Von den Händen des Brudermörders or des mordenden Bruders, the abstract for the concrete. For the order of words see l. 11 n.

1971. Lines 1971—3 are an enlarged repetition of ll. 1962—3. See l. 1957 n.

1974. With this line the Chorus leaves the part of the reflecting spectator and assumes again the part of an active partisan.

1975. unbeglückende is not usual, but expressive.

1976. Zypreſſe, *f.*, pronounce *tsǖpré'sse* (in the phonetic script of the Association Phonétique Internationale: *tsy'presə*). The Hamburg acting-copy has a note to l. 1905, Er ſinkt unter einen Zypreſſenbaum. In Roman times the cypress was sacred to the god of the nether world and was often planted near graves.

1980. The murderous deed is looked upon as the produce of the tree near which and under whose shadow it was perpetrated. The murder is thus called 'the deadly fruit.'

1985. wehe dem Mörder, wehe. From here the Chorus utters maledictions against the murderer and predicts his downfall. With the following passages should be compared the grand chorus of the Eumenides in Schiller's Die Kraniche des Ibykus and the words of Orestes in Goethe's Iphigenie, III. 1, ll. 1051—70. In order to facilitate the comparison both passages are given in Appendix III, pp. 260—261.

1988. Rinnet, rinnet, rinnet paints very graphically the incessant trickling of the blood. A similar emphatic and graphic repetition of the verb (in this case preceded by unb) occurs in Schiller's Das Jbeal und das Leben, ll. 145—146:

des Erbenlebens

Schweres Traumbild finkt und finkt und finkt.

1990. Lichtlos, 'deprived of light,' 'where light is none.'

1991. der Themis Töchter, here apparently the Erinnyes (Furies), the avengers of murder. Themis is the Goddess of Justice, and the Erinnyes punish the criminal and give him what is due to him. In most cases, however, the Parcae (Fates) or the Horae (Hours) are called the daughters of Themis. Usually the Erinnyes are called the daughters of Night. Hence Schiller calls them lichtlos, and in Goethe's Jphigenie, Act III. Scene 1, l. 1054, they are called der Nacht uralte Töchter.

1992. Die Untrüglichen, for Die nicht trügen, 'those who do not deceive,' 'the upright ones.' It may also mean die sich nicht trügen können, 'those who cannot be deceived,' 'the infallible ones.' Untrüglich is used in German in the active as well as in the passive sense, but the active (der or das nicht trügt) is more common.

1994. Rühren und mengen, very drastic instead of bereiten. Here the vengeance is brewed from the blood of the murdered man. The idea, unfamiliar to the ancients, may have been suggested to Schiller by his translation of Shakespeare's *Macbeth* (in 1800). In Act IV. Sc. 3, ll. 1470 sqq. Schiller had given a spirited rendering of the song sung by the witches as they dance round their cauldron and stir its terrible broth.

1997. die leichte Gebärde, 'a fleeting expression.'

2000. In den bunkel schaffenben Schoß, 'into their mysteriously creative womb.'

2003. In this line and the preceding ones the Chorus insists on the great law of cause and effect. In this world all things are intimately connected, nothing is lost; there is no result without a cause, hence we are morally responsible for all our actions. The last line means that everything is the outcome (Frucht) of some cause, and every action in its turn is the cause (Samen) of some new development. Hence in Die Braut von Messina (which is no Fate-tragedy in the ordinary sense) Schiller insists, throughout this Chorus, on the general recognition of the law of causality and consequent responsibility. He sees in human life a well-ordered connection of act and consequence and not the inevitable results of the decrees of a cruel inexplicable Fate.

2004. Wehe, wehe..., wehe. See Appendix III, p. 260, l. 125.

2005. fid), ethical dative, for himself, i.e. for his own ruin.

2007. Ein anberes, another, i.e. a different one.   bie vollbradhte Σat = bie Σat, nachdem fie vollbradht ift.

2012. Selber would in prose be placed after Furien, 'the Furies themselves.'

2014. This is an allusion to the grand tragedy *The Eumenides* of Aeschylus. Clytemnestra had murdered her husband, King Agamemnon, on his victorious return from Troy, and she was in her turn killed in later years by her own son Orestes who had thought he was bound to avenge his father's death even on his mother. According to this passage the avenging goddesses assumed the sacred appearance of justice (l. 2015) to instigate the son to his horrible deed, and as soon as it had been accomplished pursued him relentlessly. This heart-stirring theme was the subject of many Greek tragedies and also enters into Goethe's Jphigenie.

2018. ben Schoß...geschlagen, 'had stricken the womb.'

2023. furchtbaren Jungfraun, viz. schrecklichen Furien (l. 2012).

2024. ergreifenb faffen, 'clutch in their grasp.'

2026. Die ihn...nagen, say 'whose serpent tooth ever gnaws him.' With the term nagen cp. the German Gewiffensbiffe, ber Gewiffenswurm, and the old English *Ayenbite of Inwit*.

2028. Bis in bas Delphische Heiligtum, 'even to the sacred Delphic shrine,' where, according to Apollo's promise, he was to find relief. The opening scene of *The Eumenides* is in fact laid at Delphi, in the temple of Apollo. Here Orestes is seen seated at the centre-stone, the Furies surrounding him are asleep, and Apollo himself comes to the rescue of the unhappy man. According to Greek tradition it was not the Furies who had urged Orestes to kill his mother, but the God of Light himself had charged him with the avenging of his father's death. It was therefore natural that, when once the command had been carried out, Apollo helped him in his troubles and, at the end of the Aeschylean drama, actually procured his acquittal when prosecuted by the Furies at Athens. It is worthy of note that while in the ancient play Orestes obtains his pardon by divine grace, in Goethe's Jphigenie he feels (at the end of Act III) that the Furies have left him owing to the gentle words of encouragement and forgiveness spoken to him by his pure and noble sister.

ACT IV.

The time of action is the night of the first day and the scene is laid in the Hall of Pillars of the First Act. This Act contains perhaps the most heart-stirring series of Scenes that Schiller ever wrote.

SCENE I.

This Scene is similar to the second Scene of the First Act. Isabella is confidentially discussing the new situation with her faithful Diego. She is still hopeful as to the future. She is happy to think that her sons have now become united and that there does not seem to be any danger that some sudden love-passion and jealousy may fan the old enmity into a new flame. She also informs Diego that she has sent a messenger to an aged hermit on Mount Etna to ask him for information about her lost daughter. This is a Scene of comparative calm before the out-break of a destructive storm.

2034. Es stand bei mir, 'it stood in my power.'

dies Unglück refers to the abduction of Beatrice. Isabella torments herself with the thought that, if she had not been so very cautious and had recalled her daughter sooner, the misfortune would not have happened (ll. 2037—8). This, however, is doubtful. If Don Manuel had known before that Beatrice would be claimed by her mother, he would very probably have persuaded her before to follow him (ll. 1052 sqq.).

2036. ermangeln, usually mangeln or fehlen, 'in what (kind of) pre-caution were you wanting?'

2040. Erfolg, *m.* means here not 'success' but 'result,' 'outcome' (Ausgang, l. 2380). See also l. 2092.

2048. Gerabsinn, usually gerader Sinn, 'upright mind,' 'uprightness,' 'frankness.' Gerabsinn is formed like Edelsinn, Scharfsinn, etc.

2050. schönen Neigung is love.

2051. was, 'her whom' or 'those whom'; ehren, because they wish to make the beloved maidens their wives.

2054. brausend wilde, 'wild impetuous,' 'wild and turbulent.'

2061. aufgehäuften Feuerzunder, 'accumulated (inflammable) material.' Feuerzunder, instead of the ordinary Zunder, used here metaphorically for 'the old hatred,' occurs also in Das Lied von der Glocke, ll. 354—355, with regard to the stored up, smouldering discontent of the people before the outbreak of the French revolution :

> Weh, wenn sich in dem Schoß der Städte
> Der Feuerzunder still gehäuft.

2063. schlug, instead of geschlagen hätte or wäre. The use of the indicative is much more drastic than the usual subjunctive.

2064. ihr Gefühl, supply wenn from l. 2061. wenn ihr Gefühl...sich begegnet (wäre). Another fine case of tragic irony. What Isabella here joyfully regards as averted is just what has happened, and the spectator cannot but deeply sympathise with the unhappy mother who must soon be rudely awakened from her dream.

2067. Wohl mir! tragic irony—Don Manuel's men will soon arrive with the corpse of her son killed by the jealousy of his brother.

donnerschwere, for von Donner schwere, 'big with thunder,' 'heavy with thunderbolts.' See l. *136* n.

2069. Sie, acc. referring to Wolfe. mir, ethic dative.

2070. die befreite Brust. See l. *196* n.

2081. Trieb des Bluts, 'impulse of the blood,' viz. her motherly love, is here compared to a shut-up fire. Fire, coming from heaven, is called a god.

2086. Bis ich...sah, usually Bis ich gesehen habe or haben werde. Cp. the common proverb Man soll den Tag nicht vor dem Abend loben. Isabella is now more cautious than before. Cp. ll. *1438* sqq.

2087. mir, a *dativus incommodi*. mir der...Genius = mein...Genius.

2088. Flucht must here be taken quite generally for 'disappearance.' It does not imply any sense of blame. Isabella does not believe that her daughter can have fled of her own free will. See ll. *1616* sqq. Still unwittingly she uses the right word.

2094. Menschenkunst, for menschliches Können, 'man's powers.'

2095. Nicht zureicht or ausreicht, 'is not sufficient.'

2097. Einsiedelnd, a bold participle instead of als Einsiedler. The verb einsiedeln, 'to lead the life of a hermit,' has been formed by Schiller from the noun der Einsiedler, 'the hermit' (on the pattern of lehren—Lehrer, sehen—Seher, etc.), while in all other cases the nouns (Lehrer, Seher) have been formed from the verbs (lehren, sehen). The form Einsiedler itself is of comparatively recent origin ; in older German the word was der Einsiedel (still surviving in the place Einsiedeln and in family names), M.H.G. *einsidel(e)*, O.H.G. *einsidilo*. The verb (sich) ansiedeln, 'to settle,' 'to colonise,' is common, also the noun der Ansiedler, 'the colonist,' and Einſiedler (for Einſiedel) obviously arose by form-association with Anſiedler.

auf des Ätna Höhen cannot mean on the summit, but simply high up on Mount Etna. The distance of Mount Etna from Messina is considerable, but in this drama time and place are treated with great freedom as far as unimportant incidents are concerned. It would be foolish to take pains to show that the messenger sent out in the afternoon cannot possibly be back in the evening, or even to think that this should be laid as a fault at the poet's door.

hauſt, 'dwells.' Hauſen is poetic and as a rule used of monsters or of beasts of prey, as in Der Kampf mit dem Drachen, ll. 185—186:

Hier hauſete der Wurm und lag
Den Raub erſpähend, Nacht und Tag.

But Schiller uses the word also in the general sense for 'to stay,' 'to dwell.' In Der Ring des Polykrates, l. 92, Amasis, the King of Egypt, says to his host Polykrates:

So kann ich hier nicht ferner hauſen.

2098. Ein frommer Klausner, probably the Mönch who explained Isabella's dream. See ll. 1346 and 2107. He is a figure similar to that of the aged Greek seer Tiresias in the plays of Sophocles.

von uralters her, usually either von alters her or von uralter Zeit. Render 'from time out of mind.'

2099. Der Greis genannt des Berges. On the separation of the genitive see l. 20 n. In Der Alpenjäger, l. 42, Schiller has the term der Bergesalte, but it there denotes not a hermit, but a mountain sprite.

2100. der Menſchen Tief wandelndes Geſchlecht, 'the race of men that wander below.' In Voss' translation of Homer's *Iliad*, v. 442, Schiller found erdumwandelnde Menſchen.

2102. In...reiner Ätherluft. Cp. ll. 2586—7, and Wilhelm Tell, II. 2, ll. 1444—6:

Bei dieſem Licht, das uns zuerſt begrüßt
Von allen Völkern, die tief unter uns
Schwer atmend wohnen in dem Qualm der Städte.

2103. Berg der aufgewälzten Jahre. The years are like rocks piled up to form a high mountain from which the old man looks down upon life and its many intertwined paths. They lie plain and without entanglement before his glance, he sees whence they come and whither they lead.

2104. das aufgelöſte Spiel, supply ihm, 'for him.' To his eye the

14—2

crooked windings of human life lie disentangled, the riddles of life are solved.

2105. unverſtåndlich, viz. to others.   Unverſtåndlich is an adjective. krummgewunonen, 'crooked and twisted,' 'labyrinthine.'

2108. hinweg gebetet, 'prayed away,' 'averted by his prayer.'

2110. Des raſchen Boten jugendliche Kraft, for Den raſchen, jugendlich kråftigen Boten.   Cp. der Söhne Kraft, l. 264 n. and des Vaters Macht, l. 682 n.

SCENE 2.

The messenger informs Isabella that the hermit sent word that her daughter had been found by Don Manuel, but adds that the old man had then set fire to his hut and had left it with exclamations of woe.

From this Scene up to the Fifth each Scene brings a new and terrible disclosure, until at the end of the Fifth nothing remains to be revealed to anyone, and the last Scenes of the drama are merely the tragic results of all that has preceded them.

2117. ſchöpfe...die Wahrheit.   The idea is that of a deep pure well from which the truth may be drawn.   Cp. der tiefverſteckte Born der Wahrheit in Das Ideal und das Leben.   In the same way das Recht ſchöpfen is an old German legal term which occurs in Schiller's Wilhelm Tell, II. 2, l. 1218.   The term der Schöffe, 'judge,' is connected with ſchöpfen in this sense.   Cp. also ll. 2375—6.

2121. Glückſel'ger Mund refers to the mouth of the hermit.

2130. ſeinem Heiligen or ſeinem Schutzheiligen, his patron saint, the saint to whom his devotion is given.   See l. 2135, dem Heil'gen.

2144. Verworrenheit, *f.* usually Verwirrung, 'perplexity.'   The frequent use of verworren and similar words is characteristic of our play. See ll. 374, 2197, 2564.

ångſtlich ſchwankende Verworrenheit, 'fluctuating sad perplexity.'

2145. das Widerſprechende, 'this contradiction.'   Cp. 2148—9.

2148. mir...gedeihen, 'be of advantage to me' (mir frommen).

2152. alles müßte mich trügen, oder, 'unless everything deceives me.'

The sentence alles müßte mich trügen might have been continued wenn dies nicht die verlorene Tochter iſt.   Instead of this the sentence simply runs on oder dies iſt, etc.

The same phrase occurs in Wallenſteins Tod, v. 4, l. 3527.

2154. deiner Söhne.   The messenger is under the impression that the retainers of both brothers are approaching.

SCENE 3.

Beatrice is brought by Don Cesar's knights, the zweite Halbchor. After she has recovered from her swoon she learns that Isabella, the Princess of Messina, is her mother, and that therefore Don Manuel and Don Cesar are her brothers. Don Cesar's men also learn the relation of their lord to Beatrice of which he himself is still ignorant.

2156. Die Jungfrau, 'the maiden.' The knights see in her only their lord's love, Isabella only her lost daughter. The term is thus purposely ambiguous.

2157. Also, 'thus.'

2160. bleich und ohne Leben. The same phrase occurs in Wilhelm Tell, IV. 3, l. 2801.

2162. Von dem Erstaunlichen. The Chorus does not dare to call the thing by the right name, which would be von dem Entsetzlichen. Cp. Schreckliches, l. 2171.

2163. Geister, rare for Lebensgeister or Sinne. The sing. Geist is more usual.

2165. So, 'thus,' is strongly accented. Cp. Die Kraniche des Ibykus, l. 53:

Und muß ich so so dich wieder finden!

when the corpse of the murdered singer is brought to his friend at Corinth. Cp. also ll. 2319, 2429.

2179. The hermit said fand (l. 2125), not fendet (ll. 2159, 2176).

2183. ein neid'scher Dämon. See l. 658 n.

2189. Augenlichter stands for Augen. This poetic use is not infrequent with older writers, but is now impossible. Die Lichter is still a hunter's term for the eyes of game. Das Augenlicht is now only used in the singular for die Sehkraft, 'eye-sight.'

2191. This whole line is written in a very free metre, which well brings out the excitement of the speaker. See the Introd. p. lxxxii. der Lust is probably an adverbial genitive, 'with delight.'

2194. erkennen has the sense of anerkennen, 'recognise.'

2195. Ein seltsam neues Schrecknis. The Chorus is not yet in the possession of the full truth.

2196. wundernd. See l. 609 n.

2197. Das Irrsal, 'the imbroglio,' 'this confusion.' Irrsal is now only poetic and but rarely used. It denotes the state of affairs when nobody knows what is going to happen and everything seems to be hopelessly entangled.   It is a stronger equivalent of bie Verwirrung. Another rare and poetic term for the same state of things is bas Wirrfal.

fich belongs to löfen as well as to entwirren.

2203.   Auge, bas empfinbet, 'eye that betrays signs of feeling,' 'look of sympathy.'   Another fine touch of tragic irony, as Isabella cannot understand the consternation and embarrassment of the Chorus.   einem has a special stress.

2204.   weilen, poetic for finb.   See l. 2267.

2205.   einem, with a special stress, 'some.'

mir ift for mir ift zu Mute or zu Sinne, 'I feel.'

2206.   unmitleib'ge, a rare word for mitleiblofe.   For the poetic use of compounds with un= see l. 1975 n.

2208.   From here to l. 2227 and from l. 2240 to l. 2248 the dialogue is again carried on in lively one line stichomythia.

2217.   Engelsantlit, *n.* 'angelic face.'   Cp. ll. 1844—53.   Before this line the Hamburg acting-copy has the stage-direction Nachbem fie fie lange angefehen, mit bem Ausbruck bes innigften Gefühls.

2218.   Kinb meines Herzens!   in prose mein Herzenskinb!

2219.   This line forms a strong contrast to the preceding line, viz. Füßen is contrasted with Arme, Schulbige with Herzenskinb.   Beatrice thinks only of her guilt in leaving the convent without her mother's permission.

2220.   Alles fei vergeffen.   Isabella does not understand what Beatrice is alluding to.

2224.   So, 'then.'   in bem Schoß ber Meinen, 'among those I love.'

2227.   Isabella believes that her dream-oracle has now been fulfilled and that Fate will no longer harass her.

2228.   With this and the following line compare the almost identical words of the philosopher in Der Spaziergang, ll. 185—187:

Bin ich wirflich allein?   In beinen Armen, an beinem
   Herzen wieber, Natur, ach! unb es war nur ein Traum,
Der mich fchaubernb ergriff?

2235.   Fürftin Mutter, 'Princess Mother,' say 'Queen Mother.'   Cp. ll. 1858—60.

2240.   fich...haffen, in ordinary prose einanber...haffen.   Cp. l. 383 n.

2247.   entfetensvolles Licht.   Cp. Don Manuel's Entfetzen! (l. 1890) when he makes the same terrible discovery.   Isabella, however, is not yet to be fully enlightened in this Scene—things are to be revealed to her by degrees.

2254. beſtürzt, 'in consternation.'

2255. eurer Stimme Gebrochnen Tönen, for in den gebrochenen Tönen eurer Stimme, 'in the broken sounds of your voices,' i.e. in your murmurings.

2257. mir zurückgehalten, now usually mir vorenthalten, 'is kept back from me.'

2259. nach der Türe. Usually heftet ihr auf die Tür or blickt nach der Tür. In Goethe's Fauſt, l. 686, Faust says, Doch warum heftet ſich mein Blick auf jene Stelle? Both Türe and Tür are used in modern German, but the latter form is more common.

2261. Es naht ſich!...Was? (l. 2265), i.e. ...das Unglück (l. 2270).

2266. Totenklage = Klage um einen Toten. Cp. l. 2598 and l. 1941 n.

2267. Wo ſind meine Söhne? Isabella in the utmost excitement and anguish repeats her call for her sons (l. 2204), from whom she expects help and comfort. It is another touch of tragic irony. When at the first representation of the drama at Weimar the first semi-chorus brought in the corpse of Don Manuel placed on a bier with a black pall spread over it, Schiller, who witnessed the impressive performance, exclaimed: Das iſt doch nun wirklich ein Trauerſpiel!

SCENE 4.

The purpose of the impressive song of Don Manuel's knights is to prepare Isabella for the terrible sight which she is to behold when the song is over. The knights then step back and the bier, which before the end of the song should not be visible, becomes exposed to the view of the unhappy mother. Isabella does not in this Scene realise the whole truth. She learns that her son is slain, but she does not know by whom. She thinks that Don Manuel has been killed by the pirates in the gallant attempt to save his sister's life. In her grief she mocks the oracles. She informs Beatrice and the Chorus of her husband's dream and the two conflicting explanations neither of which she thinks has come true. The Chorus who know better than she warn her to refrain from ridiculing the oracles, and Beatrice bitterly reproaches her mother for having spared her life. The knights of Don Manuel, seeing Don Cesar approach, break out into wild maledictions.

2268. Lines 2269—2309 form one of the most impressive songs in a drama which is rich in heart-stirring songs. It was early translated into English by William Taylor (of Norwich), and was set to music by G. Schumann, Z. Fibich, and by C. Berneker. Baumgart observes very

rightly : Schauer der Verehrung vor der Majestät der ewigen göttlichen
Weltordnung durchziehen diese Rede; in prachtvoller Steigerung schreitet der
Gedankengang von der Schilderung des Traurigen zur Schilderung des Tragischen
vor und warnt am Schluß vor der Unbeständigkeit des Glückes.

The song of the Chorus consists of three parts. The first part
(ll. 2268—81) speaks in a general way of misfortune which spares
no human being. In the second (ll. 2282—97) the misfortune is more
clearly defined as the sudden destruction of a youthful life. The third
part (ll. 2298—2309) contains the warning, introduced by a striking
antithesis, to be at all times prepared in the midst of happiness for
a sudden and terrible blow.

The first two portions consist mostly of short lines of two stresses,
the last portion has longer lines of four accents. The rhythm is, as
usual, mixed, viz. trochaic-dactylic. There is sometimes an anacrusis of
either one or two syllables. Towards the end of the first portion
and in the second and third most lines are connected by a free arrangement of rimes.

2270. das Unglück, stalking through the streets of the cities, is here
personified in the same way in which at the end of the Second Part of
Goethe's Faust (v. ll. 11384 sqq.) four gray women (Mangel, Schuld,
Sorge, Not) approach the dwelling of the aged Faust and try to enter.
In the distance they are followed by their brother—der Tod. 'Dame
Care' effects an entrance. In Das Lied von der Glocke, l. 146, Schiller
uses the same verb: das Unglück schreitet schnell.

2273—4. Heute an dieser Pforte pocht es. An interesting parallel to
these lines occurs in Horace (*Odes* I. 4, ll. 13—14) :

> (*Pallida Mors*) *aequo pulsat pede pauperum tabernas*
> *regumque turris.*

2280. Bestellt es, 'she delivers.'

2282. Wenn die Blätter fallen, etc. Cp. Homer's *Iliad* VI. 146—148 :
Gleich wie die Blätter im Walde, so sind die Geschlechter der Menschen;
Einige streuet der Wind auf die Erd' hin, andere wieder
Treibt der knospende Wald, erzeugt in des Frühlinges Wärme.

2285. Entnervte, 'nerveless,' 'feeble,' 'with strength shattered.'

2286. Da gehorcht die Natur...Ihrem alten Gesetze. With the thoughts
here expressed the exquisite passage in Goethe's elegy Euphrosyne,
ll. 69 sqq. should be compared:

> Ach Natur, wie sicher und groß in allem erscheinst du!
> Himmel und Erde befolgt ewiges, festes Gesetz......

Alles entsteht und vergeht nach Gesetz; doch über des Menschen
Leben, dem köstlichen Schatz, herrschet ein schwankendes Los.
Nicht dem blühenden nicht der willig scheidende Vater,
Seinem trefflichen Sohn, freundlich vom Rande der Gruft;
Nicht der Jüngere schließt dem Älteren immer das Auge,
Das sich willig gesenkt, kräftig dem Schwächeren zu.
Öfter, ach! verkehrt das Geschick die Ordnung der Tage:
Hülflos klaget ein Greis Kinder und Enkel umsonst,
Steht, ein beschädigter Stamm, dem rings zerschmetterte Zweige
Um die Seiten umher strömende Schloßen gestreckt.

2290. entsetze, subj. expressing possibility, entsetzen könnte.

2295. stygisches Boot, the Greek conception of the boat of the hoary ferryman Charon, who was supposed to take the souls of the departed spirits across the river Styx to the realms of Hades in the nether world.

2298. ' When black in the heavens the storm-clouds tower.'

2299. dumpftosend, 'with a dull roar.' Cp. dumpferbrandend, l. 992. On the occasion of one of the performances of his drama, at Lauchstädt, on July 3, 1803, a heavy thunderstorm broke over the theatre. Schiller wrote to his wife (on July 4) giving an interesting account of the performance under these great difficulties: „Lustig und fürchterlich zugleich war der Effekt, wenn bei den gewaltsamen Verwünschungen des Himmels, welche die Isabella im letzten Akt ausspricht, der Donner einfiel, und gerade bei den Worten des Chors: Wenn die Wolken getürmt...Schicksals Gewalt fiel der wirkliche Donner mit fürchterlichem Knallen ein, so daß Graff (who acted Cajetan, the leader of the first semi-chorus) eine Geste dabei machte, die das ganze Publicum ergriff." See also the Introd. p. xviii.

2302. entwölkter, 'cloudless,' is poetic for the ordinary prose word wolkenlos. It is formed as a contrast to bewölkt or umwölkt, 'clouded.'

2307. vergänglich zieren, 'adorn with a fleeting gloss.'

2309. Cp. also the lines 238—239.
lerne den Schmerz, viz. kennen or tragen.

2310. Only now is the bier with the pall spread over it exposed to the eyes of the Princess. With this situation is connected a fine poem, full of thought, by Feodor Loewe, at one time an actor at the Royal Theatre of Stuttgart, called Ein Stück Bühnenleben. Its opening stanzas run thus:

Braut von Messina! — Auf der Bahre lag
Don Manuel, vom Trauertuch umflossen;

Bleich war fein Antlik, wie ein Wintertag,
Sein Auge, scheingebrochen, fest geschlossen.
An seine Brust warf sich ein jammernd Weib
Und schrie zum Himmel so gewalt'ge Klagen,
So wahre, als ob wirklich einst ihr Leib
Den da Erschlagnen muttertreu getragen.

Dazwischen klang der Chor. Die Kränze sind
Auf seinen Häuptern welk schon und zerrissen;
Düstere Fackeln flatterten im Wind,
Der frostig hinschlich hinter den Kulissen.
Dem scheinbar Toten rann durch Kopf und Brust
Ein tiefer Schauer, seiner Seele graute;
Er dachte an den Bruder von Sankt Just,
Der, so wie er, sich selbst als Leiche schaute.

2312. Mit dunkler, kalter Schreckenshand. This expression seems to be a reminiscence of Goethe's Iphigenie, I. 3, l. 278, where we read of Elend, das jeden Schweifenden...mit kalter, fremder Schreckenshand erwartet. This expression was subsequently first used by Schiller in Wallensteins Tod, III. 2, ll. 1345—6, where Thekla says:

Jetzt ist sie da, die kalte Schreckenshand,
Die in mein fröhlich Hoffen schaudernd greift.

Beatricen, the old weak accus., now only Beatrice.

2314. This line has the same metrical form as the following lines of the Chorus.

des Schmerzens is common with Schiller. This older genitive Schmerzens (still older des Schmerzen, weak genit. of der Schmerze, now Schmerz) survives in compounds, e.g. Schmerzenskind. The form des Schmerzes, which is now commonly used, is of recent origin after the analogy of Scherz, Scherzes.

2316. Du...Nicht meinen Lippen occurs often in older tragic writers. In the *Hippolytus* of Euripides, l. 352, Phaedra says, 'By you, not me, that name was uttered.' In Racine's *Phèdre*, I. 3, Phèdre says, 'C'est toi qui l'as nommé'; in Schiller's translation of this play: Du nanntest ihn, nicht ich. The Chorus do not wish themselves to utter the evil news.

2323. O Fluch der Hand. The following terrible curses are very similar to those pronounced by King Oedipus against the murderer of Laios of whose identity with himself he is still ignorant. Isabella unwittingly curses herself and her whole race.

grub is very significant instead of the usual ſchlug.

2326. This line has only four accented syllables. It is otherwise quite regular, and, as it is the only instance of its kind in the play, it may perhaps be emended by adding another 𝔚ehe.

2330. This line refers to the two dreams and their explanations.

2331. die ihr, 'ye who.'

2333. 𝔇ie 𝔅licke weibend is as unjust as ll. 2198 sqq.

2335. This line is spoken in bitter irony and scorn. 'Let anyone continue to believe,' i.e. 'let who will still believe !'

2336. In order to prove the emptiness of dreams and oracles Isabella informs the Chorus and Beatrice of her husband's dream, omitting her own, and of the two explanations received of the two dreams. She thinks that neither has come true, while the others, knowing the whole truth, are deeply moved to see that the oracles have actually been fulfilled. The story of her husband's dream and of its explanation is given in nearly the same terms as before (ll. 1306 sqq.). It has been urged that, in this excited scene, a shorter account would be sufficient and more natural. But ll. 2336—66 produce the effect of a short lull in the stormy scenes before and after, and Schiller has probably for this reason strictly adhered to the somewhat stately epic style of the ancient Greek drama, in which such repetitions of stories and messages are not uncommon.

2345. 𝔅efrug. 𝔉rug is a recent form of the preterite of fragen formed after the analogy of trug and ſchlug. The original form of the pret. is weak: O.H.G. *fragēta*, N.H.G. fragte. The past participle has never been anything but weak: gefragt. The strong form frug is now very frequently used, even by the best authors, but, although frug can no longer be called unusual, fragte should be preferred. 𝔉rug occurs more than once in Schiller's poetry, but in l. 1317 we read befragt'.

𝔙ogelſchauer, *m.* 'augur,' a general term for a man explaining the future. The black magician who was a Mahommedan is here contemptuously called by a Roman name.

2346. ſchwarzen 𝔐agier, 'dark-hued magician.' The magic art was chiefly practised by Persians, here it must, however, refer to an Arabian necromancer; but all the terms used in this drama must be taken quite generally. The term is also contemptuous.

2349. ihm, *dativus incommodi.* Cp. l. 2087 n. and l. 2365.

2353. entrückte ſie, 'removed her,' 'saved her from.'

𝔍ammerſchickſal, *n.* for jammervollen 𝔖chickſal, 'woeful fate.'

2360. Verbiente mir, 'gained with me.' mir, for bei mir, für mich, or it is simply an ethical dative. Render ' deserved in my eyes (no credence).'

Gößenbieners, 'worshipper of idols,' another contemptuous designation in the mouth of a Christian woman. It usually refers to pagans and strictly speaking a Mahommedan should not be called idolater.

2375. Du schöpfest brunten...Du schöpfest broben for Ob du nun brunten... ober ob du troben...schöpfest, referring (*a*) to the Mahommedan or (*b*) to the Christian explanation of the two dreams. On schöpfen see l. 2117 n. The parallelism of ll. 2375 and 2376 enhances the bitter sarcasm.

2379. treffen ein, 'come true,' 'are fulfilled,' but one after the other, the mother's dream first (ll. 1336 sqq.), and not simultaneously.

2380. loben has here the meaning of (ihnen) Recht geben, (sie) als wahrhaft erweisen. 'The truthful ones will receive the praise that is due to them.'

2386. So unmöglich ist's, 'it is just as impossible.'

2387. Die Götter, die hochwohnenben. Isabella does not deny the existence of 'the gods dwelling on high,' but she denies their moral nature. Compare l. 2403, and 'The Song of the Parcae,' in Goethe's Iphigenie, IV. 5, and the fine (later) poem by Hölderlin, Hyperions Schicksalslied. See *The Oxford Book of German Verse* (Oxford, 1911), pp. 214—215.

2390. ben ehrnen Himmel, 'the brazen sky,' 'the iron heaven.' Ehern is here used, probably under the influence of the frequent occurrence of the word in Goethe's Iphigenie, in the sense of fest, unwiberstehlich, unburchbringlich. It is thus used by the German classical writers on the analogy of the Homeric χάλκεος. Cp. l. 2416, eherne Füße. But it occurs also in the Bible, e.g. Deuteronomy xxviii. 23: ber Himmel, ber über beinem Haupte ist, wirb ehern sein unb bie Erbe unter bir eisern; in Leviticus xxvi. 19 we read similarly: ich will euern Himmel wie Eisen unb eure Erbe wie Erz machen. Cp. l. 452 n.

2391. rechts...fliegen ober links, a good or bad omen in the view of the Vogelschauer (l. 2345).

2394. Die Traumkunst träumt. See l. 104 n.

2396. Note the effective alliteration in this line.

2398. In the Hamburg and Regensburg acting-copies this line is followed by the following two lines:

Alle Ritter (nach einanber):

      Die Götter leben, bie Götter leben,

      Erkenne sie, bie bich furchtbar umgeben!

The later Cotta editions which include these lines in their text are from this line to l. 2589 behind the numbering of the first editions, while in the latest critical 'Säkular Ausgabe,' the Cotta edition has returned to the original numbering. After l. 2589 another line is thus repeated, so that after l. 2590 the numbering of this and some other editions which repeat and count that line differs to the extent of three lines.

2400. warfst du mich nicht hin Dem Fluch, 'didst thou not throw me away a prey to the curse,' 'abandon me to the curse.'

2402. Blödsicht'ge, 'dimsighted,' say 'shortsighted.' Blödsichtig is a rare and obsolete, but expressive word. In old German blöde often means 'weakly,' 'feeble,' 'deficient.' The expression blöde Augen for 'weak eyes' is still sometimes heard, and in Luther's Bible, Genesis xxix. 17 we read (Lea hatte) ein blödes Gesicht, 'a weak eye-sight.' From this the adj. blödsichtig is formed like weitsichtig, kurzsichtig, hellsichtig; blödsinnig, 'mad' (from Blödsinn, *m.* 'madness'), is very common.

2403. die alles Schauenden, 'those who see everything,' viz. the omniscient gods. This does not refer to die Seher who had explained the dreams, but to die Todesgötter, l. 2407.

2404. Nah und Fernes, in prose Nahes und Fernes. In poetry it sometimes happens that the first of two adjectives connected by und is left without inflexion if the two may be taken to form one phrase (e.g. nah und fern, groß und klein, jung und alt, etc.), and if it is felt that the inflexion of the second adjective is sufficient for the group. Cp. Goethe's Faust, l. 203: das groß und kleine Himmelslicht; Goethe's Sonett, 17, 5: in jung und alten Tagen. In Wilhelm Tell, III. 3, l. 2006, Tell says, mein überschwellend und empörtes Herz.

2407. ihren Raub, viz. one child, myself.

2409. zweifach, dreifach. She foresees the death of Don Cesar and perhaps also her own.

2410. dank' ich dir das...Geschenk, in prose ich danke dir für das...Geschenk. The sad gift is the gift of her life.

2411. in heftiger Bewegung, as Don Manuel's men see Don Cesar approaching.

2412. Brechet auf, ihr Wunden! There was a medieval tradition in old French and German poetry that the wounds of a man slain in fight or murdered began to bleed afresh when the slayer approached the bier on which he lay stretched out. In this way the bier was supposed to accuse the murderer and it was thought that secret murder could thus be found out.   An early instance occurs in the famous old French Romance by Chrétien de Troyes, *Le Chevalier au lion,* which was adapted in a masterly way for a courtly German public by Hartman von Ouwe (*Iwein*, ll. 1355 sqq.). Very soon afterwards we meet with an analogous scene in the greatest German popular epic *Der Nibelunge Nôt* ('the Lay of the Nibelungs'), where fierce Hagen is made by Kriemhilt to approach the bier of her husband whom he has treacherously murdered.   In Stanza 1044 we read :

> *Daz ist ein michel wunder : vil dicke ez noch geschiht,*
> *swā man den mortmeilen bī dem tōten siht,*
> *sō bluotent im die wunden : als ouch dā geschach.*
> *dā von man die schulde dā ze Hagenen gesach.*
> *Die wunden vluzzen sēre alsam si tāten ē.*

This has been rendered by Arthur S. Way ('The Lay of the Nibelung Men,' Cambridge, 1911, p. 142):

> A marvel it is past telling, oft we have known it betide :
> When the slayer murder-polluted is seen by the dead man's side,
> The wounds bleed in witness against him : so did it now befall,
> And thereby was the guilt of Hagen made manifest unto all.
> For the wound brake forth into bleeding, as freely as at the first.

This so-called *bārreht,* 'right of the bier,' had also a place in old German jurisprudence.   The same belief is alluded to in an impressive scene (Act I. Scene 2) of Shakespeare's *King Richard III,* where the unfortunate Anne says :

> O gentlemen, see, see ! dead Henry's wounds
> Open their congeal'd mouths, and bleed afresh.

2414. Jn ſchwarzen Güſſen. Blut is called ſchwarz by Schiller in conformity with Homeric usage where μέλαν αἷμα means swart, dark blood, but had been translated by Voss as ſchwarzes Blut. The gloomy lines 2412—15 are from time to time ominously repeated by Don Manuel's knights, viz. ll. 2432—5, and, with one important modification, ll. 2456—9.

2416. Eherner Füße Rauſchen. The feet of the Furies are called ehern (in imitation of the term χαλκόπους 'Ερινύς, 'the brazen-footed Fury,' cp. Sophocles' *Electra*, l. 490), because they are never wearied. Schiller probably borrowed the expression from Goethe's Jphigenie, l. 1129. For this whole passage see Appendix III, pp. 258—261.

2425. des Tages, for the sake of contrast. It is now really night. See before l. 2029.

Don Cesar only now learns (l. 2467) that Beatrice is his sister. He curses his mother and her secret ways and pronounces the severest judgment upon himself. He informs Isabella (l. 2477) that he slew his brother and is cursed by the despairing mother. Now all secrets have been revealed and the very worst prophecies have been fulfilled.

This Scene is one of the grandest in all dramatic literature. On the oil-painting representing it which is in the Grand Ducal Library at Weimar, see the Introd. p. xxiii.

2431. gottverfluchten, for von Gott verfluchten. Cp. l. 136 n.

2446. die verlornen Jahre. See l. 562 n.

2448. A fine touch of tragic irony. Don Cesar really avenges Don Manuel but in another way than Isabella imagines. Cp. also l. 2451 and l. 2522.

2451. Similarly moving is the moment when Wallenstein embraces Butler in Wallensteins Tod, III. 10, l. 1689.

2452. Was beginnst du? See l. 861 n. Beatrice cannot bear to see Isabella embrace the murderer.

Weine dich aus an diesem treuen Busen. In the Hamburg acting-copy we read for ll. 2453—4 the following :

> An dieser treuen Brust. So lang dies Herz
>
> Noch schlägt, ist dir der Bruder unverloren.

So here the lines are addressed to Beatrice and not to Isabella.

2454. feine Liebe, 'his love for you (his mother).'

2457. Redet ihr stummen, viz. to accuse the murderer. This line is not found in the previous corresponding passages.

2462. die Schwester—habe ich nicht gefunden he was going to say, as he does not know that Beatrice is she, but he is interrupted by his mother.

2471. So, 'then,' if that is the case, 'let the day be cursed !'

2472. Verflucht der Schoß. Curse against curse, see ll. 2324 sqq.

2473. deine Heimlichkeit. It is not unnatural that Don Cesar, who is beside himself with grief and horror, should impute all the blame to his mother's secrecy. Certainly she is not the only one to blame, in fact she is probably less to blame than any of her children. Whatever she did, she did for the best and with good reason, after careful consideration. It is very doubtful whether she would have improved matters if she had sent for Beatrice immediately after her husband's death, although, if she had, Don Cesar would not have seen and fallen in love with Beatrice at the funeral.   On the whole, one may well agree with Diego's view expressed in ll. 2035—40.

2474. Falle der Donner nieder, i.e. the truth about the murder. The use of Donner and donnern is frequent in the poetry of Klopstock, who, not to mention several passages in his Meſſias, has in his Ode an Ebert:

Finſtrer Gedanke laß ab!   Laß ab in die Seele zu donnern.

It has been suggested that in Schiller's drama there are several reminiscences (if indeed they are reminiscences) of Gessner's well-known prose epic Der Tod Abels.   In the Fifth Canto of this work and in a parallel situation we find the following passage:

Mehala rief: Donnre es ganz über mich aus, Mutter, ganz über mich das Ungewitter! Ha! Schon ſtürmt er in meinem Buſen, der donnernde Gedanke! Vater! Mutter! O ſchonet nicht!   See Imelmann's essay quoted on p. 271.

2484. Büßung, *f.* 'expiation,' 'penitence,' is somewhat stronger than the ordinary term Buße, *f.* 'penance.'   Reue und Buße is a common phrase.

verſöhnen, usually fühnen, 'atone for,' 'expiate.'

2488. dem verhängten Geſchick, viz. dem ihm von den höheren Mächten beſtimmten or verhängten Schickſal.   This fatalistic idea of the Chorus is not that of the poet.   In his view it is the characters who make their fate.   See the Introd. p. xli.

2490. erbauend vollenden, for erbauen und vollenden, 'build it up and complete it.'

2497. der geliebte Sohn is calculated to wound Don Cesar, and l. 2501, den beſſern Sohn, to wound him still more deeply.   But Isabella is beside herself with grief and has lost for a time all moderation, fairness and self-control.

2499. Baſili'sken, 'cockatrice.'   It was a fabulous animal having the body of a cock and the tail of a serpent.   It was supposed to have the power of killing by its look anyone on whom it fixed its eyes.   It was represented with a mitre-shaped crest and hence is called in Greek βασιλίσκος, 'little king.'   This Baſilist is several times mentioned in the Old Testament (e.g. Is. lix. 5, xi. 8 ; Jer. viii. 17), and it is known to the medieval 'bestiaries.'   There is a lizard known by the name of Baſilist which has of course none of the fabulous qualities ascribed to the monster of this name.   Schiller several times in his poetry alludes to the Basilisk and Basiliskenblick, e.g. in Maria Stuart, III. 4, l. 2441, and in his ballad Der Kampf mit dem Drachen, l. 227. In this case, however, as also in Wallensteins Tod, III. 18, l. 2110, der Basilisk seems to denote something even worse than a serpent, the phrase eine Schlange am Busen hegen or nähren being proverbial. Cp. Aesop's well-known fable.

2502. Hier ist unsres Bleibens Nicht mehr, lit. 'there is no longer any abiding for us here,' 'we cannot stay here any longer.' The genit. unsres Bleibens depends on Nicht which in this phrase has still its old meaning of 'not a whit,' 'nothing.' See l. 272 n.

2503. den Rachegeistern, viz. the Furies. The term Rachegeister (or Rachgötter, l. 978, rächende Göttinnen, l. 2428) was probably taken from Goethe's Iphigenie (II. 1, l. 564). The ancients avoided as much as possible calling them by their name. Schiller imitates this here and in other passages.

2504. Ein Frevel. See ll. 960 sqq.

2509. These words are spoken with the bitterest scorn. The despairing mother who feels herself 'free from guilt,' as she has acted throughout with the best intentions and with the greatest care, is at last ready to acknowledge, but with bitter sarcasm, the infallibility of the oracles and the supreme power of the gods who have asserted their superior authority, but have ruined her life.

Scene 6.

After the mother has left Don Cesar with curses and words of utter despair, Beatrice leaves him without looking at him and without a word of love or comfort. Don Cesar implores her for a word of sympathy, his envy of the dead brother and his jealousy are still tormenting him. At last he vows that neither mother nor sister shall see him again.

2522. rächen will ich ihn. This is the first hint at his resolution of killing himself. Cp. l. 2448.

2523. It is a fine touch of the poet that Don Cesar is not at once able to free himself from his envy and jealousy, he has still to fight a tremendous battle within his own heart, till at last he conquers and is free from all petty feelings in the last Scene of the drama.

2528. unser furchtbar aufgelöstes Schicksal, i.e. unser Schicksal, das sich so furchtbar aufgelöst hat or das so furchtbar aufgelöst (worden) ist. Their fate was wrapt in mystery. It is now 'unfolded,' 'explained.' Fate's 'knot' (ber Sdhidfjalsfnoten) is now 'untied,' 'unravelled,' Fate's 'riddle' (Räthel) is 'solved' ((auf)gelöft). Their terrible destiny, now so painfully plain, was that they both should love their own sister and that this love was to ruin them and their house.

2529. Macht...Unglüd. He means that Don Manuel had as little rightful claim on Beatrice as he himself and was as unhappy as himself in his love.

2530. In einen Fall, 'in one and the same downfall.'

2532. ber Tränen...Recht, for Recht auf Tränen.

2538. feinen Manen. This is a pagan idea. 'Manes' was the name which the Romans gave to the souls of the departed who were worshipped as gods. Seinen Manen consequently signifies 'to his departed soul.' Cp. also l. 2802, and Die Kraniche des Ibykus, ll. 63—64, where the people, enraged by the murder of the singer, demands:

> Zu rächen bes Erfchlag'nen Manen,
> Zu fühnen mit bes Mörbers Blut.

2539. bie Seele, 'my soul.' See l. 196.

2541. in einem Afchenfruge, 'in one funeral urn.' This idea is again quite classical and heathen, and moreover not in harmony with the mode of burying the late Prince, in whose case instead of an Afchenfrug a Sarg is mentioned (l. 1506). The custom of burning the dead is not medieval, but Greek and Roman. In Homer's *Iliad* XXIII. 91—92, the spirit of Patroclus requests his bosom friend Achilles:

> So auch unfer Gebein umfchließ' ein gleiches Behältnis,
> Jenes golbne Gefäß, bas bie göttliche Mutter bir fchenfte.

Don Cesar means to say that he will be ready to die if only he knows that she cares for him no less than for his brother and will not make a distinction between his remains and those of Don Manuel but will weep for both of them alike as her brothers.

2548. Zoll, lit. 'toll,' say 'tribute.'
ausforfchenben, usually only forfchenben.

2551. ber Zweifel, viz. for whom you are weeping.

2561. Geh hin auf ewig! Don Cesar with these angry words renounces her for ever. Thus he seems to have lost both his mother and his sister. He is tormented, beside his feeling of guilt, by envy and jealousy. He is resolved to die, but he cannot yet leave this world in peace with himself and his family. Beatrice 'stands irresolute in the struggle of conflicting feelings.' This allows us to hope that—ultimately—she may find the strength to forgive.

SCENE 7.

The reflections of the whole Chorus on the misery of human existence fitly conclude the series of heart-stirring Scenes in this Act. They are intended to produce a calming effect and to prepare the spectator's mind for the fine concluding Scenes. In this Scene the Chorus speak not as partisans but voice the feelings of the sympathetic onlooker. After having witnessed all the horrors brought about by human short-sightedness and lack of self-control, the Chorus may well sing the praises of simple Nature and a retired and peaceful life under simple conditions.

The dashes before l. 2562 are probably meant to indicate that, after Don Cesar has left the stage, the retainers of both brothers stand for a while in profound silence, overcome by their feeling for the unhappy family and overawed by the pitiful destruction that has so suddenly come upon the princely house of Messina. Cp. also nach einem tiefen Schweigen, l. 2836. It has been very fitly suggested (by Bellermann) that the most natural way of marking a pause would be by the introduction of some appropriate music. The spectator, whose feelings are stirred to their depths, would be relieved by some soft melody, some inspiring strains of music, but is not at once prepared for the ordinary sound of the human voice. In his next drama, Wilhelm Tell, when after the grand Rütli scene (Act II. Sc. 2) chosen men of the three Swiss cantons have in the stillness of the night solemnly taken the oath of their covenant, Schiller gives a similar and very characteristic stage-direction : Indem sie zu drei verschiedenen Seiten in größter Ruhe abgehen, fällt das Orchester mit einem prachtvollen Schwung ein; die leere Szene bleibt noch eine Zeit lang offen und zeigt das Schauspiel der aufgehenden Sonne über den Eisbergen.

2562. Selig muß ich ihn preisen, 'I must call his lot happy.' This line and the following remind us of the well-known lines of Horace (*Epodes* II. 1—3):

> *Beatus ille qui procul negotiis,*
> *Ut prisca gens mortalium,*
> *Paterna rura bobus exercet suis.*

2564. verworrenen Kreisen, 'confused circles,' say 'sore confusion.'

2565. With the conception of this and the preceding lines compare also the end of the grand elegy Der Spaziergang, ll. 171—190, especially lines such as the following :

> O, so öffnet euch, Mauern, und gebt den Gefangenen ledig!
> Zu der verlassenen Flur kehr' er gerettet zurück !...

Bin ich wirklich allein? In deinen Armen, an deinem
    Herzen wieder, Natur, ach! und es war nur ein Traum,
Der mich schaudernd ergriff mit des Lebens furchtbarem Bilde,
    Mit dem stürzenden Tal stürzte der finstre hinab.
Keiner nehm' ich mein Leben von deinem reinen Altare,
    Nehme den fröhlichen Mut hoffender Jugend zurück....

2568. die Besten means here 'the noblest,' 'the rulers.' The word is used as an equivalent of the Greek οἱ ἄριστοι and the Latin *optimates.*

2574. die stachelnde Sucht der Ehren, 'the goad of ambition.' Sucht originally denotes 'illness,' hence any inordinate and uncontrolled desire. It is not connected with suchen, 'to seek,' but with siech, 'sick.' Sucht der Ehren is a Latinism and stands for Sucht nach Ehren or nach Ehre (in case Ehren is taken to be a weak genit. sing.), hence for the common compound Ehrsucht.

2575. die eitle Lust, 'vain pleasures.' Several medieval princes gave up their high position and retired into monasteries. Even the great Emperor Charles V ended his life in voluntary retirement among the monks of the Spanish monastery St Just.

2577. Eingeschläfert, viz. hat, 'has lulled to sleep.'

2578. In prose the order of words would be Die wilde Gewalt der Leidenschaft in dem Lebensgewühle ('tumult of life') ergreift ihn nicht.

2581. der Menschheit traur'ge Gestalt, lit. 'the sad shape of humanity,' i.e. 'mankind's pitiful forms and fashions.' In Das Ideal und das Leben, l. 91, the poet speaks of der Menschheit* traur'ge Blöße.

2582. in bestimmter Höhe, 'at a certain fixed height.' This refers to a certain medium *niveau* of morality, a middle state of human life and pursuit, which is the sphere of passion, crime and misfortune. The contented minds, who in their simple wishes and expectations are either remote from or lifted above des Lebens verworrene Kreise (l. 2564) and the Lebensgewühl (l. 2578), who have kept themselves free from sordid ambitions and selfish passions, may safely look down, as from the pure heights of mountains, on the ambitions, crimes and miseries of the towns. These moral diseases—as formidable as pestilence—which are rampant in the populous town where selfishness, jealousy and hatred assert themselves and cause constant feud and ruin, do not touch their heights. The minds of the monk and of the free son of the hills have risen above the low level of human passion.

2585. Qualm der Städte, 'vapour of the cities.' Schiller used the same expression again in Wilhelm Tell, II. 2, ll. 1445—6:

> alle Völker, die tief unter uns
> Schwer atmend wohnen in dem Qualm der Städte.

2586. Auf den Bergen ist Freiheit. This has become a familiar quotation. In Wilhelm Tell, I. 3, l. 389, Tell points to the high mountains and says:

> Das Haus der Freiheit hat uns Gott gegründet.

Der Hauch der Grüfte, viz. sin, guilt, and remorse.

2588—9. Die Welt ist vollkommen...Qual. This idea entered through the teaching of Rousseau into many German writings of the eighteenth century. Works such as Haller's Die Alpen, E. v. Kleist's Der Frühling, many idyllic poems, or odes such as Hölty's Wunderseliger Mann, welcher der Stadt entfloh, reflect the great influence of Rousseau's gospel of 'Return to Nature' on his contemporaries. The ideas expressed in this song were also those of the youthful Schiller, but no longer those of the mature poet who wrote Die Braut von Messina, whose studies had convinced him of the exaggerations contained in Rousseau's early views. The French writer had said in his *Émile*: *Tout est bien sortant des mains de l'auteur des choses: tout dégénère entre les mains de l'homme*, which reminds us of these lines.

Qual, for innere Qual, Seelenqual, the torments of his unruly heart, the violent passions, his feeling of sin and remorse, which he takes with him wherever he goes. Nature, however, as Goethe well knew and depicted in several grand Scenes of his Faust, has the power of calming, soothing and healing the wounded human heart.

2589. The later Cotta editions repeat line 2586 as Auf den Bergen ist Freiheit, adding 'etc.,' by which means the divergence from the usual counting is increased to three lines. See l. 2398 n.

SCENE 8.

There is clearly a short break between this Scene and the preceding ones. The last three Scenes, of which this is the first, contain the catastrophe and are really a kind of short Fifth Act. See the Introd. p. xxx. They show Don Cesar with much composure making all the preparations for his brother's funeral and his own, and at the same time heroically conquering his envy and jealousy so that ultimately he is able to leave the world in peace with himself and those around him. Three attempts are made to persuade him to desist from his purpose, viz. by the Chorus (Sc. 8), his mother (Sc. 9), and, the most difficult of all to resist, by Beatrice (Sc. 10).

The metre of this Scene differs from that of almost all other scenes in blank verse. In it Schiller makes a very effective use of the stern and stately trimeters of the ancient Greek tragedy. See the Introd. p. lxxxiv.

In this Scene Don Cesar gives the necessary instructions for his brother's funeral, hints at his own resolution, and refuses to pay any attention to the various reasons of the Chorus for sparing his own life.

2592. tiefes, viz. the suitable funeral.

Herrlichkeit, *f.* 'splendour,' 'pomp,' 'honour.'

2596. von langen Zeiten, unusual and poetic for lange (Zeit) her. It was apparently formed on the analogy of vor langen Zeiten, 'a long time ago.'

2598. Totenklage, *f.* 'funeral dirge.' See l. 2266 n.

2602. Klagemänner, 'mourners.' The unusual word Klagemänner seems to have been formed on the model of the common Klageweiber, the professional female mourners (*praeficae*) of the Romans. In this case we have to think of torch-bearing men (l. 2600) who accompany the coffin with their gloomy songs of lamentation (ll. 1941 and 2266). der Zug der Klagemänner, one train returning from the funeral of the old Prince, another starting for the funeral of Don Manuel, 'almost meet.' This is, of course, an exaggeration, as three months had elapsed (l. 1368) since the funeral of Don Manuel's father.

2608. der Katafalk, 'the catafalque,' is a decorated raised stage on which at state funerals the coffin is placed during the solemn obsequies. The term is borrowed from the Italian *catafalco*, the etymology of which is doubtful. In l. 2610 the Katafalk is called Bau des Todes, 'structure of death,' and in l. 2613 das unglückselige Gerüst, 'the melancholy structure.'

2611. Zeichen, 'sign,' for Vorzeichen, 'omen.' Medieval men, no less than the ancient Greeks and Romans, paid much attention to what they considered to be good or bad omens.

2614. alsobald, poetic and high style for alsbald, 'at once.'

2616. Notice the *enjambement* and see the Introd. p. xc.

2620. das mitternächtliche Geschäft, viz. the solemn obsequies at midnight. In Schiller's time all funerals at Weimar took place at midnight, and Schiller himself was buried at that hour. Hence Goethe wrote in his Epilog zu Schillers Glocke, ll. 9—10:

Da hör' ich schreckhaft mitternächt'ges Läuten,

Das dumpf und schwer die Trauertöne schwellt.

There is little difference between mitternächtlich and mitternächtig.

After 2622. Der zweite Chor. Note that Don Cesar sends his own men to attend to everything connected with his brother's funeral, and that Don Manuel's knights, the older men, remain with him and that *these* subsequently entreat him not to kill himself.

2625. Das Seelenamt verwalte, 'may perform the requiem.' Seelenamt stands for Amt für die Seele eines Verstorbenen, Totenamt. A 'mass for the dead' ('a requiem') is really not held at night. Cp. l. 1126, Hochamt.

2627. an unserm Grab. This is a clear intimation that Don Cesar intends to atone for his deed by taking his own life. This purpose, from which the Chorus endeavours to dissuade him, forms the centre of interest during the last Scenes of the play. Will the entreaties of Don Manuel's men, of his mother, and even of Beatrice finally prevail upon him and save his life? In this way the interest is kept up to the very last and the hero's final decision is all the more impressive.

2635. Don Cesar answers both arguments, opposing l. 2635 to l. 2633, and ll. 2637—8 to l. 2634. In the following dialogue (a short stichomythia) each argument of the knights is refuted by Don Cesar.

2636. es, viz. die Rache or die Sühne.

2638. büßt sich ab, 'is atoned for,' 'can be atoned for.' The German reflexive must often be rendered by the English passive. See l. 354 n.

2641. lös' ich sterbend auf, 'I shall dissolve by my death.' What is dissolved vanishes and is no more. The curse is looked upon as a dark cloud hovering over his house. Cp. l. 2709, den Fluch versöhne.

2642. Der freie Tod. freie, for freiwillige, frei gewählte, 'voluntary.' Cp. mit freiem Schritte, l. 2668.

die Kette des Geschicks, 'the chain of fate,' in which from each rash action some fresh disastrous result must necessarily ensue as link is indissolubly connected with link in a heavy chain. Cp. Wallensteins Tod, III. 18, ll. 2132—4.

These words contain the leading thought by which Don Cesar's action is henceforth inspired.

2643. With the considerations here urged by the Chorus compare the fine passage in Hebbel's Agnes Bernauer (Act V. Scene 10).

2648. Nur...nichts, i.e. Death puts an end to all hopes.

2651. Glücklicher, i.e. a man free from heavy moral guilt, a man whose soul is not weighed down by a curse.

2654. This line and ll. 2656—7 are again written in the usual metre and thus lead over to the following scenes in blank verse.

2657. keinem Irdischen does not mean 'to no mortal man,' but 'to nothing that is human.' The idea is that a man in Don Cesar's present position no longer gives heed to human affairs.

In Schiller's youthful tragedy Fiesco, III. 1, the stern old republican Verrina says : Es gibt Taten, die sich keinem Menschenurteil mehr unterwerfen.

Scene 9.

Isabella endeavours in vain to dissuade Don Cesar.

2659. gelobt, 'vowed,' past partic. of geloben.

2661. unnatürlich wütend, for in unnatürlicher Wut. Wütend is the present participle 'raging,' not the adjective 'enraged,' and unnatürlich an adverb.

2673. rufe...zurück, 'revoke,' usually nehme...zurück, 'take back'; but rufe is here used on account of die ich...herunter rief, 'that I called down upon.'

2678. solche sündige, now either solch sündige or solche sündigen.

2689. keine laute Noch stumme, in prose weder eine laute noch eine stumme or keine laute oder stumme.

2691. sich lösen, 'dissolve itself' and pass away. Cp. l. 2641 n.

2694. Das wirst du, Mutter. Du is strongly accented as it is contrasted with wir (l. 2692).

2696. Totenmal, n. unusual for Grabmal, n. 'tomb.'

2698. Ein Stein, 'one sepulchral stone.' In l. 2541, Don Cesar did not speak of a stone which was to overarch the dust of both of them but of an urn which was to contain the ashes of both. The former conception is Christian and medieval, the latter pagan and Greek. The Urne occurs again in l. 2707.

2703. Vermittler, m. 'intercessor.' The Hamburg acting-copy, revised by the poet, has Versöhner, 'atoner.'

2705. versöhnt sich, 'becomes reconciled.' Cp. l. 2638 n.

2706. ein weinend Schwesterbild, 'the figure of a weeping sister.' Schwesterbild may also simply mean 'sister,' just as Frauenbild, Mannsbild, in older German meant 'woman,' 'man.' The expression is metaphorical but at the same time we fancy we see a beautiful figure, a mourning maiden bending compassionately over an urn, at the head of

the tomb. 'Beautiful Pity' is here conceived under the form of a
weeping and loving sister—obviously Don Cesar's imagination is
influenced by his thoughts of Beatrice whom he pictures to himself as
full of compassion for him too.

2707. mit fanft Anſchmiegender Umarmung, 'with a gently clinging
embrace.' In Die Geſchlechter, l. 27, Schiller says of the maiden :

    Ach, ſie ſuchet umfonſt, was ſie ſanft anſchmiegend umfaſſe.

The Hamburg acting-copy has instead of ll. 2706—7 the following,
which are easier to recite :

    Steht wie ein weinend Schweſterbild mit ſanfter
    Umarmung auf die Urne hingebückt.

2709. Hinunterſteige, viz. in das Haus des Todes (l. 2754). Cp. also
ll. 2668—9.

2710. Gnadenbildern, for Gnade ſpendenden (or wirkenden) Bildern,
is a term of the Roman Catholic Church for images, the veneration
of which procures grace. Say 'miraculous images,' ' wonder-working
images.' Isabella mentions four different ways of seeking forgiveness
for his sin.

2713. in Lorettos Haus. Loretto is the most famous place of
pilgrimage in Central Italy. The Haus is the *Casa Santa*, the ' Holy
Dwelling,' viz. two rooms of the dwelling of St Mary and the
Holy Family, which, according to the legend, was carried by the
angels from Nazareth to Loretto (near Ancona on the Adriatic), and
is preserved under the dome of an imposing church for pilgrims.

2715. das alle Welt entſündigt, 'that redeems all comers,' i.e. if
penitent pilgrims visit the Holy Land and pray at the Holy Sepulchre,
Christ will pardon them. entſündigt = von Sünde befreit. Cp. l. 726.

2717. Vorrat an Verdienſt, ' store of meritorious deeds.' According
to the Roman Catholic doctrine the Church administers the large
treasure of good works that has been accumulated, over and above
what God requires of men, by the meritorious lives of Christ, the
Virgin Mary and the Saints, and the Church can dispense grace to
all repentant sinners out of this so-called 'supererogatory store of merit '
(Gnadenhort).

2719. ein Tempel, the pagan term, not very surprising in this play,
instead of which one would expect Gotteshaus, Votivkirche. The erection
of expiatory churches (Sühnekapellen) in the place where a crime has
been committed is even now not unusual in Roman Catholic countries.

2721. gefunden, poetic for geſund werden.

2723. Bußkasteiungen, 'penitent mortifications,' 'penance and mortification.' Kasteien, older German *kastîen*, goes back to Lat. *castigare*, 'to chastise,' 'to mortify' (the flesh), das Fleisch züchtigen.

2724. Abschöpfend, 'drawing out,' i.e. 'wiping off,' 'atoning for.' The idea seems to be that of a large amount of guilt being enclosed in a cask like water that may be drawn out little by little.

2729. Da, 'when.' geteilt, viz. haben, instead of teilten.

2735. läutern, 'purify,' say 'refine.'

2736. mangelhaften, 'imperfect,' say 'frail,' 'faulty.' Menschheit, *f.* 'humanity,' for 'human nature.'

verzehren, 'destroy,' 'consume,' 'eradicate,' 'blot out.'

2737. abstehn, 'stand away from,' 'are distant from.'

2741. er, viz. der Neid.

2742. Nun er...abgewann, lit. 'now that he (Don Manuel) has won from me everlasting bliss,' i.e. 'now that he enjoys before me (has anticipated me in obtaining) immortality.'

2743. jenseits alles Wettstreits, 'beyond all competition,' 'beyond all rivalry.'

wie ein Gott, i.e. free from all human imperfections. Don Cesar is not yet free from his jealousy.

2744. wandelt, 'moves,' 'lives,' in the recollection of mankind, especially of Isabella and Beatrice.

2753. zusammen ruhn. Cp. l. 1345 (fromm gepaart).

2754. Haus des Todes. Cp. l. 1481. Schiller is very fond of the metaphorical use of Haus. In Die Ideale, l. 76, he asks: Wer...folgt mir bis zum finstern Haus? In Die Jungfrau von Orleans, IV. 1, l. 2600, the Maid speaks of the pure spirits, i.e. the angels, in deinem ew'gen Haus.

2757. Rohherziger is a rare word, formed on the pattern of hartherziger, kaltherziger, warmherziger, leichtherziger, etc. rohherzig, lit. 'coarse-minded,' say 'cold-hearted,' 'unfeeling.' Cp. l. 2759, herzlos kalt.

preisgegeben, 'exposed to,' 'given up to.' Preisgeben orig. means 'to give up as a booty,' 'to give over entirely'; preis, fr. the French *prise*, means 'what has been taken,' 'booty.' It is not connected with Preis, *m.* 'price,' or with Preis, *m.* 'praise,' which are both borrowed from the French *prix* (old Fr. *pris*, Latin *pretium*).

2758. sie, accus. der Söhne Kraft. See l. 264 n.

2761. deiner Söhne Gottheit. The conception expressed in this and the following lines is the pagan idea of apotheosis or deification. In

Greek legendary lore eminent men, e.g. Hercules, were raised to the rank of gods, also the heroic brothers Castor and Pollux, the brothers of fair Helen of Troy. Don Cesar intimates that he and Don Manuel will soon be similarly united.

2763. des Himmels Zwillinge, 'the Twins of Heaven,' or 'the Gemini,' the Dioscuri, Castor and Pollux. They were the protectors of mariners and indicated their presence by means of the sparks of St Elmo's fire on the mastheads of ships.

2764. Ein...Sternbild, supply nahe sind. Ein leuchtend Sternbild reminds us of the epithet *lucida sidera* given to *fratres Helenae* by Horace (*Odes* I. 3, l. 2). Don Cesar imagines for himself, now re-united with his brother, the noble task of watching over and protecting their mother.

2768. This line is a unique instance in our drama of a line of but one beat. It has been suggested (by Zarncke) that it might be taken together with the following and looked upon as a line of six accents. See the Introd. p. lxxxv. But Schiller probably intended a pause to come in after the quiet but determined Leb' wohl! and indicated this by leaving the line incomplete.

2776. Zauberschein, *m.* 'magic radiance,' is a dative qualified by the preceding genitive.

The 'beautiful hope' is that Don Cesar may look upon his life as useful and necessary to his nearest and dearest, that he may consent to live for his mother and to comfort his sister, and leave it to time and their affection to make life endurable to him.

SCENE 10.

Beatrice in her turn tries to persuade Don Cesar to live. She has herself with a great effort overcome her horror of him and now pities him with all her heart. Yet he falters but one short moment. When he sees that mother and sister no longer hate him and are ready to live with him and to lighten his heavy lot, he still abides by his first decision and takes his life. The Chorus concludes the play with a few lines which express the conviction that the events of the tragedy must inspire in any open-minded onlooker.

2778. Was ersannest du? 'what hast thou contrived?' 'what is it that thou hast planned?' He feels that the hardest trial is still to come.

2780. erfleh' ihn, 'move him by thy entreaties,' 'implore him.' This is a very strange use of the verb erflehen, which usually means 'to obtain by entreating,' e.g. ich habe das Leben des Bruders von dem König erfleht, 'I have obtained my brother's life from the King by my entreaties.' The absolute phrase Laß dich erflehen! means lit. 'allow thyself to be won over by my entreaties,' hence 'listen to my entreaties and grant them.'

But erfleh' ihn, daß er lebe, 'win him over by entreaties that he may live,' is very unusual.

2781. Also, here poetic for So, 'thus.'

2785. Lebensengel, 'Angel of Life,' calling him back into life. Hence the appropriate adj. lebenduftend (l. 2787).

2786. Blumen...und...Früchte. We are reminded of Schiller's charming poem Das Mädchen aus der Fremde, who brought flowers and fruit in abundance.

2787. lebenduftend, 'exhaling life,' 'emitting a sweet scent of life.' In Goethe's Faust, II. 3, ll. 9045—6, we hear of youthful Teutons : goldgelockte, frische Bubenschar. Die duften Jugend.

2793. den Stab, for die Stütze, 'the support,' viz. himself.

2795. Es soll ihm werden, 'He shall have it.' See l. 232 n.

2798. Raub am Himmel, 'robbery from heaven.' Cp. l. 736.

2800. gemordet...gewecket, viz. hat.

2804. eifernd, for wetteifernd, 'in emulation.'

2806. liebeleeren is used proleptically, in a life which becomes thus (or will then be) leer an Liebe, 'void of love.'

2807. dein geliebtes Haupt. dein...Haupt stands for dich. See l. 258 n. Beatrice uses here for the first time a word of endearment : geliebtes.

2812. Wenn...nur, 'if...only,' 'provided that.'

2816. O Bruder. By this sob of deepest compassion with her unhappy brother Beatrice at last shows that her heart is full of forgiving love.

2817. unsre Mutter. In l. 2808 she had only said deine. This difference is of the greatest significance. And yet Don Cesar is not content that Beatrice wishes him to live only for the sake of their mother. So she further yields by reclining on his breast and adding softly 'and console thy sister.'

2819. Sie hat gesiegt. The Chorus have kept up their hope to the last and joyfully proclaim that Beatrice has gained the victory. Most spectators will have shared this feeling. Don Cesar, however, has wavered but for a single moment. The moral spirit in him rises triumphant over all the inducements to live. He strongly feels that he must not live and enjoy life while the brother whom he has slain lies in his coffin. He sees before him the solemn catafalque and hears the strains of the dirge—the spectators must see and hear them also in order to understand what is powerfully working in his mind—and with supreme courage he resolutely gives up what might be a life of usefulness in order to do what he feels is his stern duty. Like Max Piccolomini in 𝕎𝔞𝔩𝔩𝔢𝔫𝔣𝔱𝔢𝔦𝔫, Don Cesar heroically rises superior to all the allurements of life and becomes what Schiller used to call a 'sublime character.' The triumph of the moral spirit over the sensuous nature of man, even to the sacrifice of life itself, is called by Schiller 𝔇𝔞𝔰 𝔈𝔯𝔥𝔞𝔟𝔢𝔫𝔢. It is consequently wrong to see in the sudden appearance of Don Manuel's coffin a stage trick which is intended to decide the struggle in Don Cesar's mind. This would have been unworthy of Schiller. That struggle is decided already : Don Cesar is resolved not to live in any case. The catafalque with the coffin placed on it only brings home to the spectator what was all the time before Don Cesar's inner eye, but what was not so fully realised by the Chorus, i.e. Don Cesar's strong sense of guilt and the need of expiation.

2830. 𝔡𝔢𝔦𝔫𝔢...𝔘𝔫𝔰𝔠𝔥𝔲𝔩𝔡, for 𝔡𝔲 𝔘𝔫𝔰𝔠𝔥𝔲𝔩𝔡𝔦𝔤𝔢𝔯. Cp. l. 1969 n. Don Cesar's deep love of justice is the real reason for his suicide (see l. 2635)—he also feels that he must not and cannot enjoy a happy life while his brother has been deprived of life by him, and he clearly sees that death is less of an evil than a life spoilt by the stings of guilt and re-morse of conscience.

2835. 𝔅𝔢𝔣𝔯𝔦𝔢𝔡𝔦𝔤𝔱 𝔦𝔰𝔱 𝔪𝔢𝔦𝔫 ℌ𝔢𝔯𝔷, 'my heart is satisfied,' at last he is at peace with himself.

2836. After a profound silence the Chorus conclude with a short song. This corresponds to the exodus of the Greek Chorus which usually gives the outcome and the final impression of the tragedy in a few terse lines. The Chorus feel with regard to Don Cesar's end the terrible weight of guilt and the sublimity of a moral victory. There are cases in which life is not the most valuable of human posses-sions, viz. when it is ruined by a deep consciousness of guilt.

2839—40. These lines have become a familiar quotation. The second line which clearly proves that Schiller's drama was not intended by the poet to be a mere 'fate-tragedy,' in the bad sense of the word, expresses the same idea that is found in Cicero (*ad familiares*, VI. 4, 2):

nec esse ullum malum praeter culpam.   We are also reminded of the song of the Erinnyes in Die Kraniche des Jbykus (ll. 121 sqq.): Wohl dem, der frei von Schuld und Fehle, etc. (see Appendix III, p. 260), and of the words of Rustan in Grillparzer's Der Traum ein Leben (IV. ll. 2653—5), that are so characteristic of Grillparzer's own views of life:

> Eines nur ist Glück hienieden,
> Eins: des Innern stiller Frieden
> Und die schuldbefreite Brust!

APPENDICES

APPENDIX I

Über den Gebrauch des Chors in der Tragödie.

Ein poetisches Werk muß sich selbst rechtfertigen, und wo die Tat nicht spricht, da wird das Wort nicht viel helfen. Man könnte es also gar wohl dem Chor überlassen, sein eigener Sprecher zu sein, wenn er nur erst selbst auf die gehörige Art zur Darstellung gebracht wäre. Aber das tragische Dichterwerk wird erst durch die theatralische Vorstellung zu 5 einem Ganzen; nur die Worte gibt der Dichter, Musik und Tanz müssen hinzukommen, sie zu beleben. Solange also dem Chor diese sinnlich mächtige Begleitung fehlt, solange wird er in der Ökonomie des Trauer= spiels als ein Außending, als ein fremdartiger Körper und als ein Aufenthalt erscheinen, der nur den Gang der Handlung unterbricht, der 10 die Täuschung stört, der den Zuschauer erkältet. Um dem Chor sein Recht anzutun, muß man sich also von der wirklichen Bühne auf eine mögliche versetzen; aber das muß man überall, wo man zu etwas Höherem gelangen will. Was die Kunst noch nicht hat, das soll sie erwerben; der zufällige Mangel an Hilfsmitteln darf die schaffende Ein= 15 bildungskraft des Dichters nicht beschränken. Das Würdigste setzt er sich zum Ziel, einem Ideale strebt er nach, die ausübende Kunst mag sich nach den Umständen bequemen.

Es ist nicht wahr, was man gewöhnlich behaupten hört, daß das Publikum die Kunst herabzieht; der Künstler zieht das Publikum herab, 20 und zu allen Zeiten, wo die Kunst verfiel, ist sie durch die Künstler gefallen. Das Publikum braucht nichts als Empfänglichkeit, und diese besitzt es. Es tritt vor den Vorhang mit einem unbestimmten Verlangen, mit einem vielseitigen Vermögen. Zu dem Höchsten bringt es eine Fähigkeit mit; es erfreut sich an dem Verständigen und Rechten, und 25 wenn es damit angefangen hat, sich mit dem Schlechten zu begnügen, so wird es zuverlässig damit aufhören, das Vortreffliche zu fordern, wenn man es ihm erst gegeben hat.

Der Dichter, hört man einwenden, hat gut nach einem Ideal arbeiten, der Kunstrichter hat gut nach Ideen urteilen; die bedingte, beschränkte, 30

ausübende Kunst ruht auf dem Bedürfnis. Der Unternehmer will
bestehen, der Schauspieler will sich zeigen, der Zuschauer will unterhalten
und in Bewegung gesetzt sein. Das Vergnügen sucht er und ist unzu-
frieden, wenn man ihm da eine Anstrengung zumutet, wo er ein Spiel und
5 eine Erholung erwartet.

Aber, indem man das Theater ernsthafter behandelt, will man das
Vergnügen des Zuschauers nicht aufheben, sondern veredeln. Es soll ein
Spiel bleiben, aber ein poetisches. Alle Kunst ist der Freude gewidmet,
und es gibt keine höhere und keine ernsthaftere Aufgabe, als die Menschen
10 zu beglücken. Die rechte Kunst ist nur diese, welche den höchsten Genuß
verschafft. Der höchste Genuß aber ist die Freiheit des Gemütes in dem
lebendigen Spiel aller seiner Kräfte.

Jeder Mensch zwar erwartet von den Künsten der Einbildungskraft
eine gewisse Befreiung von den Schranken des Wirklichen; er will sich an
15 dem Möglichen ergötzen und seiner Phantasie Raum geben. Der am
wenigsten erwartet, will doch sein Geschäft, sein gemeines Leben, sein
Individuum vergessen, er will sich in außerordentlichen Lagen fühlen, sich
an den seltsamen Kombinationen des Zufalls weiden; er will, wenn er
von ernsthafterer Natur ist, die moralische Weltregierung, die er im
20 wirklichen Leben vermißt, auf der Schaubühne finden. Aber er weiß
selbst recht gut, daß er nur ein leeres Spiel treibt, daß er im eigentlichen
Sinn sich nur an Träumen weidet, und wenn er von dem Schauplatz
wieder in die wirkliche Welt zurückkehrt, so umgibt ihn diese wieder mit
ihrer ganzen drückenden Enge, er ist ihr Raub, wie vorher; denn sie selbst
25 ist geblieben, was sie war, und an ihm ist nichts verändert worden.
Dadurch ist also nichts gewonnen, als ein gefälliger Wahn des Augenblicks, der beim Erwachen verschwindet.

Und eben darum, weil es hier nur auf eine vorübergehende Täuschung
abgesehen ist, so ist auch nur ein Schein der Wahrheit oder die beliebte
30 Wahrscheinlichkeit nötig, die man so gern an die Stelle der Wahrheit
setzt.

Die wahre Kunst aber hat es nicht bloß auf ein vorübergehendes Spiel
abgesehen; es ist ihr ernst damit, den Menschen nicht bloß in einen
augenblicklichen Traum von Freiheit zu versetzen, sondern ihn wirklich und
35 in der Tat frei zu machen, und dieses dadurch, daß sie eine Kraft in ihm
erweckt, übt und ausbildet, die sinnliche Welt, die sonst nur als ein roher
Stoff auf uns lastet, als eine blinde Macht auf uns drückt, in eine

objektive Ferne zu rücken, in ein freies Werk unseres Geistes zu
verwandeln und das Materielle durch Ideen zu beherrschen.

Und eben darum, weil die wahre Kunst etwas Reelles und Objektives
will, so kann sie sich nicht bloß mit dem Scheine der Wahrheit begnügen;
auf der Wahrheit selbst, auf dem festen und tiefen Grunde der Natur 5
errichtet sie ihr ideales Gebäude.

Wie aber nun die Kunst zugleich ganz ideell und doch im tiefsten
Sinne reell sein — wie sie das Wirkliche ganz verlassen und doch aufs
genaueste mit der Natur übereinstimmen soll und kann, das ist's, was
wenige fassen, was die Ansicht poetischer und plastischer Werke so schielend 10
macht, weil beide Forderungen einander im gemeinen Urteil geradezu
aufzuheben scheinen.

Auch begegnet es gewöhnlich, daß man das eine mit Aufopferung des
andern zu erreichen sucht und eben deswegen beides verfehlt. Wem die
Natur zwar einen treuen Sinn und eine Innigkeit des Gefühls verliehen, 15
aber die schaffende Einbildungskraft versagte, der wird ein treuer Maler
des Wirklichen sein, er wird die zufälligen Erscheinungen, aber nie
den Geist der Natur ergreifen. Nur den Stoff der Welt wird er uns
wiederbringen; aber es wird eben darum nicht unser Werk, nicht das freie
Produkt unseres bildenden Geistes sein und kann also auch die wohltätige 20
Wirkung der Kunst, welche in der Freiheit besteht, nicht haben. Ernst
zwar, doch unerfreulich ist die Stimmung, mit der uns ein solcher
Künstler und Dichter entläßt, und wir sehen uns durch die Kunst selbst,
die uns befreien sollte, in die gemeine enge Wirklichkeit peinlich zurück=
versetzt. Wem hingegen zwar eine rege Phantasie, aber ohne Gemüt und 25
Charakter, zu teil geworden, der wird sich um keine Wahrheit bekümmern,
sondern mit dem Weltstoff nur spielen, nur durch phantastische und bizarre
Kombinationen zu überraschen suchen, und wie sein ganzes Tun nur
Schaum und Schein ist, so wird er zwar für den Augenblick unterhalten,
aber im Gemüt nichts erbauen und begründen. Sein Spiel ist, so wie 30
der Ernst des anderen, kein poetisches. Phantastische Gebilde willkürlich
aneinander reihen, heißt nicht ins Ideale gehen, und das Wirkliche
nachahmend wieder bringen, heißt nicht die Natur darstellen. Beide
Forderungen stehen so wenig im Widerspruch miteinander, daß sie viel=
mehr — eine und dieselbe sind; daß die Kunst nur dadurch wahr ist, daß 35
sie das Wirkliche ganz verläßt und rein ideell wird. Die Natur selbst ist
nur eine Idee des Geistes, die nie in die Sinne fällt. Unter der Decke

B. 16

der Erscheinungen liegt sie, aber sie selbst kommt niemals zur Erscheinung.
Bloß der Kunst des Ideals ist es verliehen, oder vielmehr, es ist ihr
aufgegeben, diesen Geist des Alls zu ergreifen und in einer körperlichen
Form zu binden. Auch sie selbst kann ihn zwar nie vor die Sinne, aber
5 doch durch ihre schaffende Gewalt vor die Einbildungskraft bringen und
dadurch wahrer sein, als alle Wirklichkeit, und realer, als alle Erfahrung.
Es ergibt sich daraus von selbst, daß der Künstler kein einziges Element
aus der Wirklichkeit brauchen kann, wie er es findet, daß sein Werk in
allen seinen Teilen ideell sein muß, wenn es als ein Ganzes Realität
10 haben und mit der Natur übereinstimmen soll.

Was von Poesie und Kunst im ganzen wahr ist, gilt auch von allen
Gattungen derselben, und es läßt sich ohne Mühe von dem jetzt Gesagten
auf die Tragödie die Anwendung machen. Auch hier hatte man lange
und hat noch jetzt mit dem gemeinen Begriff des Natürlichen zu
15 kämpfen, welcher alle Poesie und Kunst geradezu aufhebt und vernichtet.
Der bildenden Kunst gibt man zwar notdürftig, doch mehr aus konven=
tionellen als aus inneren Gründen, eine gewisse Idealität zu; aber von
der Poesie und von der dramatischen insbesondere verlangt man Illusion,
die, wenn sie auch wirklich zu leisten wäre, immer nur ein armseliger
20 Gauklerbetrug sein würde. Alles Äußere bei einer dramatischen Vor=
stellung steht diesem Begriff entgegen — alles ist nur ein Symbol des
Wirklichen. Der Tag selbst auf dem Theater ist nur ein künstlicher, die
Architektur ist nur eine symbolische, die metrische Sprache selbst ist ideal;
aber die Handlung soll nun einmal real sein und der Teil das Ganze
25 zerstören. So haben die Franzosen, die den Geist der Alten zuerst ganz
mißverstanden, eine Einheit des Orts und der Zeit nach dem gemeinsten
empirischen Sinn auf der Schaubühne eingeführt, als ob hier ein anderer
Ort wäre, als der bloß ideale Raum, und eine andere Zeit, als bloß die
stetige Folge der Handlung.

30 Durch Einführung einer metrischen Sprache ist man indes der poetischen
Tragödie schon um einen großen Schritt näher gekommen. Es sind einige
lyrische Versuche auf der Schaubühne glücklich durchgegangen, und die
Poesie hat sich durch ihre eigene lebendige Kraft im einzelnen manchen
Sieg über das herrschende Vorurteil errungen. Aber mit den Einzelnen
35 ist wenig gewonnen, wenn nicht der Irrtum im Ganzen fällt, und es ist
nicht genug, daß man das nur als eine poetische Freiheit duldet, was doch
das Wesen aller Poesie ist. Die Einführung des Chors wäre der letzte,

der entscheidende Schritt — und wenn derselbe auch nur dazu diente, dem Naturalism in der Kunst offen und ehrlich den Krieg zu erklären, so sollte er uns eine lebendige Mauer sein, die die Tragödie um sich herumzieht, um sich von der wirklichen Welt rein abzuschließen und sich ihren idealen Boden, ihre poetische Freiheit zu bewahren. 5

Die Tragödie der Griechen ist, wie man weiß, aus dem Chor entsprungen. Aber sowie sie sich historisch und der Zeitfolge nach daraus loswand, so kann man auch sagen, daß sie poetisch und dem Geiste nach aus demselben entstanden, und daß ohne diesen beharrlichen Zeugen und Träger der Handlung eine ganz andere Dichtung aus ihr geworden wäre. 10 Die Abschaffung des Chors und die Zusammenziehung dieses sinnlich mächtigen Organs in die charakterlose langweilig wiederkehrende Figur eines ärmlichen Vertrauten war also keine so große Verbesserung der Tragödie, als die Franzosen und ihre Nachbeter sich eingebildet haben.

Die alte Tragödie, welche sich ursprünglich nur mit Göttern, Helden 15 und Königen abgab, brauchte den Chor als eine notwendige Begleitung; sie fand ihn in der Natur und brauchte ihn, weil sie ihn fand. Die Handlungen und Schicksale der Helden und Könige sind schon an sich selbst öffentlich und waren es in der einfachen Urzeit noch mehr. Der Chor war folglich in der alten Tragödie mehr ein natürliches Organ, er 20 folgte schon aus der poetischen Gestalt des wirklichen Lebens. In der neuen Tragödie wird er zu einem Kunstorgan; er hilft die Poesie hervorbringen. Der neuere Dichter findet den Chor nicht mehr in der Natur, er muß ihn poetisch erschaffen und einführen, das ist, er muß mit der Fabel, die er behandelt, eine solche Veränderung vornehmen, wodurch 25 sie in jene kindliche Zeit und in jene einfache Form des Lebens zurückversetzt wird.

Der Chor leistet daher dem neuern Tragiker noch weit wesentlichere Dienste, als dem alten Dichter, eben deswegen, weil er die moderne gemeine Welt in die alte poetische verwandelt, weil er ihm alles das unbrauchbar 30 macht, was der Poesie widerstrebt, und ihn auf die einfachsten, ursprünglichsten und naivsten Motive hinauftreibt. Der Palast der Könige ist jetzt geschlossen, die Gerichte haben sich von den Toren der Städte in das Innere der Häuser zurückgezogen, die Schrift hat das lebendige Wort verdrängt, das Volk selbst, die sinnlich lebendige Masse, ist, wo sie nicht 35 als rohe Gewalt wirkt, zum Staat, folglich zu einem abgezogenen Begriff geworden, die Götter sind in die Brust des Menschen zurückgekehrt. Der

Dichter muß die Paläste wieder auftun, er muß die Gerichte unter freiem
Himmel herausführen, er muß die Götter wieder aufstellen, er muß alles
Unmittelbare, das durch die künstliche Einrichtung des wirklichen Lebens
aufgehoben ist, wieder herstellen und alles künstliche Machwerk an dem
5 Menschen und um denselben, das die Erscheinung seiner inneren Natur
und seines ursprünglichen Charakters hindert, wie der Bildhauer
die modernen Gewänder, abwerfen und von allen äußern Umgebungen
desselben nichts aufnehmen, als was die höchste der Formen, die
menschliche, sichtbar macht.

10   Aber eben so, wie der bildende Künstler die faltige Fülle der Gewänder
um seine Figuren breitet, um die Räume seines Bildes reich und anmutig
auszufüllen, um die getrennten Partien desselben in ruhigen Massen stetig
zu verbinden, um der Farbe, die das Auge reizt und erquickt, einen
Spielraum zu geben, um die menschlichen Formen zugleich geistreich
15 zu verhüllen und sichtbar zu machen, ebenso durchflicht und umgibt der
tragische Dichter seine streng abgemessene Handlung und die festen Umrisse
seiner handelnden Figuren mit einem lyrischen Prachtgewebe, in welchem
sich, als wie in einem weit gefalteten Purpurgewand, die handelnden
Personen frei und edel mit einer gehaltenen Würde und hoher Ruhe bewegen.

20   In einer höhern Organisation darf der Stoff oder das Elementarische
nicht mehr sichtbar sein; die chemische Farbe verschwindet in der feinen
Karnation des Lebendigen. Aber auch der Stoff hat seine Herrlichkeit
und kann als solcher in einem Kunstkörper aufgenommen werden. Dann
aber muß er sich durch Leben und Fülle und durch Harmonie seinen Platz
25 verdienen und die Formen, die er umgibt, geltend machen, anstatt sie durch
seine Schwere zu erdrücken.

    In Werken der bildenden Kunst ist dieses jedem leicht verständlich, aber
auch in der Poesie und in der tragischen, von der hier die Rede ist, findet
dasselbe statt. Alles, was der Verstand sich im allgemeinen ausspricht,
30 ist ebenso wie das, was bloß die Sinne reizt, nur Stoff und rohes
Element in einem Dichterwerk und wird da, wo es vorherrscht, unaus-
bleiblich das Poetische zerstören; denn dieses liegt gerade in dem In-
differenzpunkt des Ideellen und Sinnlichen. Nun ist aber der Mensch so
gebildet, daß er immer von dem Besondern ins Allgemeine gehen will, und
35 die Reflexion muß also auch in der Tragödie ihren Platz erhalten. Soll
sie aber diesen Platz verdienen, so muß sie das, was ihr an sinnlichem
Leben fehlt, durch den Vortrag wieder gewinnen; denn wenn die zwei

Elemente der Poesie, das Ideale und Sinnliche, nicht innig verbunden zusammen wirken, so müssen sie nebeneinander wirken, oder die Poesie ist aufgehoben. Wenn die Wage nicht vollkommen inne steht, da kann das Gleichgewicht nur durch eine Schwankung der beiden Schalen hergestellt werden. 5

Und dieses leistet nun der Chor in der Tragödie. Der Chor ist selbst kein Individuum, sondern ein allgemeiner Begriff; aber dieser Begriff repräsentiert sich durch eine sinnlich mächtige Masse, welche durch ihre ausfüllende Gegenwart den Sinnen imponiert. Der Chor verläßt den engen Kreis der Handlung, um sich über Vergangenes und Künftiges, 10 über ferne Zeiten und Völker, über das Menschliche überhaupt zu verbreiten, um die großen Resultate des Lebens zu ziehen und die Lehren der Weisheit auszusprechen. Aber er tut dieses mit der vollen Macht der Phantasie, mit einer kühnen lyrischen Freiheit, welche auf den hohen Gipfeln der menschlichen Dinge, wie mit Schritten der Götter, ein= 15 hergeht — und er tut es, von der ganzen sinnlichen Macht des Rhythmus und der Musik in Tönen und Bewegungen begleitet.

Der Chor reinigt also das tragische Gedicht, indem er die Reflexion von der Handlung absondert und eben durch diese Absonderung sie selbst mit poetischer Kraft ausrüstet; ebenso, wie der bildende Künstler die 20 gemeine Notdurft der Bekleidung durch eine reiche Draperie in einen Reiz und in eine Schönheit verwandelt.

Aber ebenso, wie sich der Maler gezwungen sieht, den Farbenton des Lebendigen zu verstärken, um den mächtigen Stoffen das Gleichgewicht zu halten, so legt die lyrische Sprache des Chors dem Dichter auf, 25 verhältnismäßig die ganze Sprache des Gedichts zu erheben und dadurch die sinnliche Gewalt des Ausdrucks überhaupt zu verstärken. Nur der Chor berechtigt den tragischen Dichter zu dieser Erhebung des Tons, die das Ohr ausfüllt, die den Geist anspannt, die das ganze Gemüt erweitert. Diese eine Riesengestalt in seinem Bilde nötigt ihn, alle seine Figuren auf 30 den Kothurn zu stellen und seinem Gemälde dadurch die tragische Größe zu geben. Nimmt man den Chor hinweg, so muß die Sprache der Tragödie im ganzen sinken, oder was jetzt groß und mächtig ist, wird gezwungen und überspannt erscheinen. Der alte Chor, in das französische Trauerspiel eingeführt, würde es in seiner ganzen Dürftigkeit darstellen 35 und zunichte machen: eben derselbe würde ohne Zweifel Shakespeares Tragödie erst ihre wahre Bedeutung geben.

So wie der Chor in die Sprache Leben bringt, so bringt er Ruhe in die Handlung — aber die schöne und hohe Ruhe, die der Charakter eines edeln Kunstwerkes sein muß. Denn das Gemüt des Zuschauers soll auch in der heftigsten Passion seine Freiheit behalten; es soll kein Raub der
5 Eindrücke sein, sondern sich immer klar und heiter von den Rührungen scheiden, die es erleidet. Was das gemeine Urteil an dem Chor zu tadeln pflegt, daß er die Täuschung aufhebe, daß er die Gewalt der Affekte breche, das gereicht ihm zu seiner höchsten Empfehlung; denn eben diese blinde Gewalt der Affekte ist es, die der wahre Künstler vermeidet, diese Täuschung
10 ist es, die er zu erregen verschmäht. Wenn die Schläge, womit die Tragödie unser Herz trifft, ohne Unterbrechung aufeinander folgten, so würde das Leiden über die Tätigkeit siegen. Wir würden uns mit dem Stoffe vermengen und nicht mehr über demselben schweben. Dadurch, daß der Chor die Teile auseinander hält und zwischen die Passionen mit
15 seiner beruhigenden Betrachtung tritt, gibt er uns unsere Freiheit zurück, die im Sturm der Affekte verloren gehen würde. Auch die tragischen Personen selbst bedürfen dieses Anhalts, dieser Ruhe, um sich zu sammeln; denn sie sind keine wirklichen Wesen, die bloß der Gewalt des Moments gehorchen und bloß ein Individuum darstellen, sondern ideale Personen
20 und Repräsentanten ihrer Gattung, die das Tiefe der Menschheit aus= sprechen. Die Gegenwart des Chors, der als ein richtender Zeuge sie vernimmt und die ersten Ausbrüche ihrer Leidenschaft durch seine Dazwischenkunft bändigt, motiviert die Besonnenheit, mit der sie handeln, und die Würde, mit der sie reden. Sie stehen gewissermaßen schon auf
25 einem natürlichen Theater, weil sie vor Zuschauern sprechen und handeln, und werden eben deswegen desto tauglicher, von dem Kunsttheater zu einem Publikum zu reden.

Soviel über meine Befugnis, den alten Chor auf die tragische Bühne zurückzuführen. Chöre kennt man zwar auch schon in der modernen
30 Tragödie; aber der Chor des griechischen Trauerspiels, so wie ich ihn hier gebraucht habe, der Chor als eine einzige ideale Person, die die ganze Handlung trägt und begleitet, dieser ist von jenen opernhaften Chören wesentlich verschieden, und wenn ich bei Gelegenheit der griechischen Tragödie von Chören anstatt von einem Chor sprechen höre, so entsteht
35 mir der Verdacht, daß man nicht recht wisse, wovon man rede. Der Chor der alten Tragödie ist meines Wissens seit dem Verfall derselben nie wieder auf der Bühne erschienen.

Ich habe den Chor zwar in zwei Teile getrennt und im Streit mit sich selbst dargestellt; aber dies ist nur dann der Fall, wo er als wirkliche Person und als blinde Menge mithandelt. Als Chor und als ideale Person ist er immer eins mit sich selbst. Ich habe den Ort verändert und den Chor mehrmal abgehen lassen; aber auch Aeschylus, der Schöpfer der 5 Tragödie, und Sophokles, der größte Meister in dieser Kunst, haben sich dieser Freiheit bedient.

Eine andere Freiheit, die ich mir erlaubt, möchte schwerer zu recht=fertigen sein. Ich habe die christliche Religion und die griechische Götterlehre vermischt angewendet, ja, selbst an den maurischen Aberglauben 10 erinnert. Aber der Schauplatz der Handlung ist Messina, wo diese drei Religionen teils lebendig, teils in Denkmälern fortwirkten und zu den Sinnen sprachen. Und dann halte ich es für ein Recht der Poesie, die verschiedenen Religionen als ein kollektives Ganze für die Einbildungskraft zu behandeln, in welchem alles, was einen eigenen Charakter trägt, eine 15 eigene Empfindungsweise ausdrückt, seine Stelle findet. Unter der Hülle aller Religionen liegt die Religion selbst, die Idee eines Göttlichen, und es muß dem Dichter erlaubt sein, dieses auszusprechen, in welcher Form er es jedesmal am bequemsten und am treffendsten findet.

Sizilien.

Nirgends, lehrt eine traurige Erfahrung, sieht man die Leidenschaften 20 und Laster der Menschen ausgelassener toben, nirgends mehr Elend wohnen als in den glücklichen Gegenden, welche die Natur zu Paradiesen bestimmte. Schon in frühen Zeiten stellten Raubsucht und Eroberungsbegierde dieser gesegneten Insel nach; und so wie die schöpferische Wärme dieses Himmels die unglückliche Wirkung hatte, die abscheulichsten Geburten der Tyrannei 25 an das Licht zu brüten, hatte selbst auch das wohltätige Meer, welches diese Insel zum Mittelpunkt des Handels bestimmte, nur dazu dienen müssen, die feindseligen Flotten der Mamertiner, der Karthager, der Araber an ihre Küste zu tragen.... Ein barbarisches Gemisch von Sprachen und Sitten, von Trachten und Gebräuchen, von Gesetzen und 30 Religionen zeigte noch jetzt von ihrer verderblichen Gegenwart.

(From *Universalhistorische Übersicht.* Säkular Ausgabe, XIII. 149--150.)

APPENDIX II

Extracts from Schiller's Correspondence on 'Die Braut von Messina.'

II, a.

Ich teile mit Ihnen die unbedingte Verehrung der Sophokleischen Tragödie, aber sie war eine Erscheinung ihrer Zeit, die nicht wieder kommen kann, und das lebendige Produkt einer individuellen bestimmten Gegenwart einer ganz heterogenen Zeit zum Maßstab und Muster aufdringen, hieße die Kunst, die immer dynamisch und lebendig entstehen und wirken muß, eher töten als beleben. Unsere Tragödie, wenn wir eine solche hätten, hat mit der Ohnmacht, der Schlaffheit, der Charakterlosigkeit des Zeitgeistes und mit einer gemeinen Denkart zu ringen; sie muß also Kraft und Charakter zeigen, sie muß das Gemüt zu erschüttern, zu erheben, aber nicht aufzulösen suchen. Die Schönheit ist für ein glückliches Geschlecht; aber ein unglückliches muß man erhaben zu rühren suchen.

(To Professor Süvern, July 26, 1800. Jonas, *Schillers Briefe*, VI. 175—176.)

II, b.

Ich habe große Lust, mich nunmehr in der einfachen Tragödie nach der strengsten griechischen Form zu versuchen, und unter den Stoffen, die ich vorrätig habe, sind einige, die sich gut dazu bequemen. Den einen davon kennst du, die Malthefer; aber noch fehlt mir das Punctum saliens zu diesem Stück, alles andere ist gefunden.... Ein anderes Sujet, welches ganz eigne Erfindung ist, möchte früher an die Reihe kommen; es ist ganz im Reinen und ich könnte gleich an die Ausführung gehen. Es besteht, den Chor mitgerechnet, nur aus 20 Szenen und aus fünf Personen. Göthe billigt den Plan ganz, aber es erregt mir noch nicht den Grad von

Neigung, den ich brauche, um mich einer poetischen Arbeit hinzugeben. Die Hauptursache mag sein, weil das Interesse nicht sowohl in den handelnden Personen, als in der Handlung liegt, sowie im Ödipus des Sophokles; welches vielleicht ein Vorzug sein mag, aber doch eine gewisse Kälte erzeugt. Noch habe ich zwei andere Stoffe, die zu ihrer Zeit gewiß auch an die Reihe kommen, aber sich bisjetzt der Form noch nicht haben unterwerfen wollen. Der eine davon ist Warbeck....

(To Körner, May 13, 1801. Jonas, VI. 277.)

II, *c.*

Ich arbeite jetzt mit ziemlichen Ernst an einer Tragödie, deren Sujet du aus meiner Erzählung kennst. Es sind die feindlichen Brüder oder, wie ich es taufen werde, die Braut von Messina. Über dem langen Hin- und Herschwanken von einem Stoffe zum andern habe ich zuerst nach diesem gegriffen und zwar aus dreierlei Gründen: (1) War ich damit, in Absicht auf den Plan, der sehr einfach ist, am weitsten. (2) Bedurfte ich eines gewissen Stachels von Neuheit in der Form und einer solchen Form, die ein Schritt näher zur antiken Tragödie wäre, was hier wirklich der Fall ist, denn das Stück läßt sich wirklich zu einer äschyleischen Tragödie an. (3) Mußte ich etwas wählen, was nicht de longue haleine ist, weil ich nach der langen Pause notwendig bedarf, wieder etwas fertig vor mir zu sehen. Ich muß auf jeden Fall am Ende des Jahres damit zu Stande sein, weil es Ende Januars zum Geburtstag unsrer Herzogin aufgeführt zu werden bestimmt ist. Alsdann geht es hurtig an den Warbeck, wozu der Plan jetzt auch viel weiter gerückt ist, und unmittelbar nach diesem an den Wilhelm Tell, denn dies ist das Stück, von dem ich Dir einmal schrieb, daß es mich lebhaft anziehe.

(To Körner, September 9, 1802. Jonas, VI. 414.)

II, *d.*

Gegen die reiche Abwechselung Ihrer Beschäftigungen sticht meine auf einen einzigen Punkt gerichtete Tätigkeit sehr dürftig ab, auch kann ich Ihnen das Resultat meiner Einsamkeit nur durch die Tat beurkunden. Ich habe ein mißliches und nicht erfreuliches Geschäft, nämlich die

Ausfüllung der vielen zurückgelassenen Lücken in den 4 ersten Akten nun beendigt, und sehe auf diese Weise wenigstens 5 Sechsteile des Ganzen fertig und säuberlich hinter mir, und das letzte Sechsteil, welches sonst immer das wahre Festmahl der Tragödien=Dichter ist, gewinnt auch einen guten Fortgang. Es kommt dieser letzten Handlung sehr zu statten, daß ich das Begräbnis des Bruders von dem Selbstmord des andern jetzt ganz getrennt habe, daß dieser jenen Actus vorher rein beendigt als ein Geschäft, dem er vollkommen abwartet, und erst nach Erledigung desselben, über dem Grabe des Bruders, geschieht die letzte Handlung, nämlich die Versuche des Chors, der Mutter und der Schwester, den D. Cesar zu erhalten, und ihr vereitelter Erfolg. So wird alle Verwirrung und vorzüglich alle bedenkliche Vermischung der theatralischen Ceremonie mit dem Ernst der Handlung vermieden. Übrigens haben sich im Lauf meines bisherigen Geschäfts noch verschiedene bedeutende Motive hervorgetan, die dem Ganzen sehr dienen.

(To Goethe, January (26?), 1803.   Jonas, VII. 6.)

II, *e.*

Mein erster Versuch einer Tragödie in strenger Form wird Ihnen Vergnügen machen; Sie werden daraus urteilen, ob ich, als Zeitgenosse des Sophokles, auch einmal einen Preis davon getragen haben möchte. Ich hab' es nicht vergessen, daß Sie mich den modernsten aller neueren Dichter genannt und mich also im größten Gegensatz zu allem, was antik heißt, gedacht haben. Es sollte mich also doppelt freuen, wenn ich Ihnen das Geständnis abzwingen könnte, daß ich auch diesen fremden Geist mir zu eigen machen können. Ich will indes nicht leugnen, daß mir ohne eine größere Bekanntschaft, die ich indes mit dem Äschylus gemacht, diese Versetzung in die alte Zeit schwerer würde angekommen sein. Vielleicht ist Ihnen nicht bekannt, daß eine Übersetzung des Prometheus, der Sieben von Theben, der Perser, und der Eumeniden von Stolberg, noch in seiner bessern Zeit gemacht, jetzt herausgekommen. Ich kann nicht leugnen, sie hat mir einen hohen Eindruck von Äschylus gemacht, wieviel auch von seinem Geist mag verloren gegangen sein.

(To Humboldt, February 17, 1803.   Jonas, VII. 13—14.)

II, *f.*

Hier bringe ich Ihnen endlich wieder etwas Neues und wünsche, daß es Ihnen Vergnügen machen möge. Es ist nach der Strenge der alten Tragödie gemacht, eine einfache Handlung, wenig Personen, wenig Ortver= änderung, eine einfache Zeit von einem Tag und einer Nacht, vornehmlich aber der Gebrauch des Chors, so wie er in der alten Tragödie vorkommt; auf ihn ist die Hauptwirkung der Tragödie berechnet. Die Darstellung wird nicht schwer sein, da die Reden des Chors nicht mit Musik begleitet werden, ein etwas feierlicherer und pathetischerer Vortrag der lyrischen Stellen, eine belebte Aktion auch bei denen, welche nicht selbst reden, und eine möglichst symmetrische Disposition der Figuren möchte das Wesent= lichste sein.

(To Iffland, February 24, 1803. Jonas, VII. 17.)

II, *g.*

Sie haben durch Ihr Außenbleiben die Hoffnungen vieler Freunde getäuscht, die Sie lieben und verehren, und manches Plänchen, das auf Ihr Hiersein berechnet war, scheitern gemacht. Unter diesen war auch eins von mir, das auch Goethen sehr am Herzen lag—es ist eine Tragödie von mir, mit dem Chor der alten Tragödie, vorhanden, worin dieses wirksame Organ der alten Bühne nicht ohne Erfolg versucht worden ist. Ich sende das Stück mit heutiger Post nach Berlin an Iffland, von dem Sie es zu lesen bekommen können. Wir hielten es nicht für unmöglich, die lyrischen Intermezzos des Chors, deren fünf oder sechs sind, nach Gesanges Weise rezitieren zu lassen und mit einem Instrument zu begleiten. Übrigens verließen wir uns auf Ihr sachverständiges Gutachten und auf die Eingebungen Ihres Genies. Ihr Wegbleiben zernichtet nun zwar diese Hoffnung und wir werden das Stück mit sammt den Chören bloß deklamieren lassen. Vielleicht aber interessieren Sie sich doch für diese Arbeit und Sie überraschen uns einmal mit einer musifalischen Ausführung derselben.

(To Zelter, February 28, 1803. Jonas, VII. 18.)

II, *h.*

Nur ein paar Zeilen heute über den ersten Eindruck Deines neuen Werkes. Gestern abends kam es, und noch hab' ich es kaum zweimal gelesen.

Es hat einen hohen Rang, däucht mich, unter Deinen Produkten. Mir ist kein modernes Werk bekannt, worin man den Geist der Antike in einem solchen Grade fände. Der Stoff geht ganz unter in der Hoheit und Pracht der poetischen Form. Aber ein solches Gedicht wird nur mit unbefangener Seele und im gesundesten, kraftvollsten Zustande des Geistes genossen. Rechne hier nicht auf lärmenden Beifall der jetzt lebenden Menge, aber auf dauernden Ruhm bei echten Kunstfreunden der künftigen Geschlechter. Nächstens mehr, wenn ich mehr über Dein Werk gedacht habe.

(From Körner, February 18, 1803. *SK.* II. 433.)

II, *i.*

Durch Dein neues Werk ist mir zuerst recht anschaulich geworden, wieviel die dramatische Darstellung durch den Chor gewinnt. Es gehört zur Würde der Handlung, daß der Einzelne von einer Gruppe teilnehmender Menschen umgeben wird. Malerei und Musik kennen die Vorteile solcher Gruppen sehr gut, aber die moderne dramatische Poesie stellt ihre Hauptpersonen in den wichtigsten Momenten einem unbedeutenden Vertrauten gegenüber. Du hast Dich nicht begnügt, Deinem Chor eine untergeordnete Rolle zu geben. Er wird in einigen Momenten selbst handelnd. Auch gewinnt Dein Gemälde an Reichtum durch die Verschiedenheit des Charakters in beiden Chören.

In der Behandlung des Chors hast Du mehr Ähnlichkeit mit Äschylus als mit Sophokles und Euripides. Bei jenem ist mehr Leidenschaft, bei letzteren beiden ist mehr Ruhe in dem Chor. War es vielleicht ein Kunstgriff der späteren dramatischen Kunst, das Lebendige der Handlung durch den Kontrast der ruhigen Betrachtung zu heben? Auch war es vielleicht Bedürfnis, bei der wilden Leidenschaft der handelnden Personen, die man besonders in einigen Stücken des Euripides findet, in den Chor ein

Gegengewicht zu legen. Bei Äschylus aber, so wie bei Dir, unterscheiden sich die Hauptpersonen durch Hoheit und Würde, nicht durch die Heftigkeit des Affekts. Dein Cesar selbst ist nur in einem einzigen entscheidenden Momente von Leidenschaft überwältigt. Auch beim Sophokles findet man bei den handelnden Personen nirgends so wilde Mordlust, wie in mehreren Stücken des Euripides. Sollte vielleicht das spätere Athen einen heftigern Reiz bedurft haben? War es etwa nicht mehr empfänglich für einfache Größe?

Beim ersten Lesen Deines Stückes habe ich gar nicht an eine Aufführung gedacht. Aber wenn man sich länger damit beschäftigt, entsteht die Frage, wie unter den günstigsten Umständen und bei einem Zusammentreffen der größten Talente der Chor auf dem Theater gegeben werden könnte. Manches könnte gesungen werden, wenn es allein stände. Aber da das ganze Stück gesprochen werden muß, so würde ich auch den Chor sprechen lassen, aber immer eine Person nur auf einmal, außer bei einzelnen Worten und kurzen Sätzen, wodurch der Gedanke der Menge auf einmal laut wird. Drei bis vier Personen, die die vordersten des Chors sind, teilen sich in die Rede. Einer fällt oft dem andern ins Wort und endigt die Phrase. Hauptstellen wie solche:

> Wir gehorchen, aber wir bleiben stehn

und dergleichen werden vom ganzen Chor wiederholt. In dem Ideenkostüm Deines Chors ist etwas Gewagtes. Griechische Mythologie findet sich neben katholischen Religionsbegriffen. Wolltest Du vielleicht ein allgemeines poetisches Kostüm gebrauchen, so wie es ein Malergewand gibt? Die Darstellung gewinnt dadurch an Reichtum in einzelnen Stellen, aber ich weiß nicht, ob die Gestalten des Chors im Ganzen nicht dadurch etwas an Bestimmtheit verlieren.

Der Gedanke scheint mir sehr glücklich, daß Du im Moment der Begeisterung bei dem Chor griechische Rhythmen eintreten läßt, und den Reim gebrauchst, wo sich die Rede des Chors mehr dem Gespräch nähert. Auch hat mich die Mannigfaltigkeit und Wahl Deines Rhythmus gefreut.

Unter den einzelnen Figuren fesselt die Mutter—eine echte Niobe— besonders die Aufmerksamkeit. Ihre Hoheit, die im schrecklichsten Moment in eine Art von Trotz übergeht, wird gleichwohl nie unweiblich. Manuel und Cesar kontrastieren auf eine feine Art. Manuel ist nur durch die Liebe milder geworden, indem sie ihn glücklich machte. Bei Cesar blieb die stürmische Begierde ohne alle Befriedigung. Beatrice ist eine holde

Erscheinung, deren Wirkung zwischen den schauderhaften Szenen sehr wohl tut.

Die Fabel ist einfach, aber doch reichhaltig; das ganze Geschlecht ist zu einem tragischen Gemälde ausgesucht, und der harte kraftvolle Vater im Hintergrunde gehörte auch mit zum Ganzen. Schauderhaft ist besonders die Entstehung des größten Unglücks aus löblichen Handlungen. Unter den Fällen, wo ein einfaches Mittel eine große Wirkung hervorbringt, ist mir besonders die Stelle in der Erwähnung des Boten lieb, wie der Einsiedler seine Hütte anzündet.

(From Körner, February 28, 1803.   *SK.* II. 434—435.)

II, *k.*

Was Du über mein Werk schreibst, mußte mich sehr freuen, weil ich gerade das hinein legen wollte, was Du Dir aus dem Werke herausnahmst. Wegen des Chors bemerke ich noch, daß ich in ihm einen doppelten Charakter darzustellen hatte, einen allgemein menschlichen nämlich, wenn er sich im Zustand der ruhigen Reflexion befindet, und einen specifischen, wenn er in Leidenschaft gerät und zur handelnden Person wird. In der ersten Qualität ist er gleichsam außer dem Stück und bezieht sich also mehr auf den Zuschauer. Er hat, als solcher, eine Überlegenheit über die handelnden Personen, aber bloß diejenige, welche der ruhige über den passionierten hat: er steht am sichern Ufer, wenn das Schiff mit den Wellen kämpft. In der zweiten Qualität, als selbsthandelnde Person, soll er die ganze Blindheit, Beschränktheit, dumpfe Leidenschaftlichkeit der Masse darstellen, und so hilft er die Hauptfiguren herausheben.

Das Ideenkostüm, das ich mir erlaubte, hat dadurch seine Rechtfertigung, daß die Handlung nach Messina versetzt ist, wo sich Christentum, Griechische Mythologie und Mahomedanismus wirklich begegnet und vermischt haben. Das Christentum war zwar die Basis und die herrschende Religion, aber das griechische Fabelwesen wirkte noch in der Sprache, in den alten Denkmälern, in dem Anblick der Städte selbst, welche von Griechen gegründet waren, lebendig fort, und der Märchenglaube, sowie das Zauberwesen schloß sich an die maurische Religion an. Die Vermischung dieser drei Mythologien, die sonst den Charakter aufheben würde, wird also hier selbst zum Charakter. Auch ist sie vorzüglich in den Chor gelegt, welcher einheimisch und ein lebendiges Gefäß der Tradition ist. Was du in Vorschlag bringst, um den Chor auf dem Theater darzustellen, wird hier wirklich in Ausübung gebracht werden.

(To Körner, March 10, 1803. Jonas, VII. 24.)

II, *l.*

Vor acht Tagen ist die Braut von Messina hier zum ersten Male gegeben und vorgestern wiederholt worden. Der Eindruck war bedeutend und ungewöhnlich stark, auch imponierte es dem jüngeren Teil des Publikums so sehr, daß man mir nach dem Stück im Schauspielhause ein Vivat brachte, welches man sich sonst hier noch niemals herausnahm. Über den Chor und das vorwaltend Lyrische in dem Stücke sind die Stimmen natürlich sehr geteilt, da noch ein großer Teil des ganzen deutschen Publikums seine prosaischen Begriffe von dem Natürlichen in einem Dichterwerk nicht ablegen kann. Es ist der alte und der ewige Streit, den wir beizulegen nicht hoffen dürfen. Was mich selbst betrifft, so kann ich wohl sagen, daß ich in der Vorstellung der Braut von Messina zum erstenmal den Eindruck einer wahren Tragödie bekam. Der Chor hielt das Ganze trefflich zusammen und ein hoher furchtbarer Ernst waltete durch die ganze Handlung. Goethen ist es auch so ergangen, er meint, der theatralische Boden wäre durch diese Erscheinung zu etwas Höherem eingeweiht worden.

(To Körner, March 28, 1803. Jonas, VII. 29—30.)

II, *m.*

Bei der Braut von Messina habe ich, ich will es Ihnen aufrichtig gestehen, einen kleinen Wettstreit mit den alten Tragikern versucht, wobei ich mehr an mich selbst als an ein Publikum außer mir dachte, wie wohl ich innerlich überzeugt bin, daß bloß ein Dutzend lyrischer Stücke nötig sein würden, um auch diese Gattung, die uns jetzt fremd ist, bei den Deutschen in Aufnahme zu bringen, und ich würde alles dieses für einen großen Schritt zum Vollkommenen halten. Übrigens aber werde ich es vor der Hand dabei bewenden lassen, da einer allein nun einmal nicht hinreicht, den Krieg mit der ganzen Welt aufzunehmen. Meine zwei nächsten Stücke werden Ihren Wünschen vermutlich um vieles mehr entsprechen. Das erste, welches ich diesen Sommer ausarbeiten will, ist die Geschichte des Warbeck, der sich unter Heinrich VII von England für einen Herzog von York ausgab...das zweite Stück ist Wilhelm Tell.

(To Iffland, April 22, 1803. Jonas, VII. 34—35.)

II, *n.*

Der Himmel segne Sie, teurer Freund, für den Gedanken, uns Ihr Trauerspiel im Manuscript zu schicken! Ich sehne mich unglaublich danach. Ich bin im Voraus sicher, daß Ihr Ringen mit den Alten nicht vergebens gewesen sein wird. Aber warum wollten Sie nur leisten, was jene leisteten? Es ist einmal unverkennbar: wir haben mehr als sie, und es ist möglich, dies Mehrere poetisch darzustellen. Sie waren bloß, was sie waren. Wir wissen auch, was wir sind, und blicken darüber hinaus. Wir haben durch die Reflexion einen doppelten Menschen aus uns gemacht. Ich denke Sie mir mit der ganzen Stärke und dem ganzen Reichtum, den dieser Vorteil gewährt, in den Realismus der Alten zurückgekehrt, und so entsteht freilich der höchste Genuß, ein unendlicher Inhalt in einer nach reinen Kunstforderungen beschränkten Form. Und so wird Ihr neues Stück sein. Immer werden Sie, wenn man Sie wahrhaft würdigt, der Schöpfer einer neuen Poesie heißen; einer Poesie, welche die Schranken der bisherigen durchbricht, sich eine neue, aber durch sich selbst geregelte Bahn bricht. Was Sie in jeder Gattung gemacht haben, hat ein Siegel geistiger Größe und Tiefe, das man sonst nicht findet. Was ich erst von Ihnen sagte, gilt auch von Ihren Arbeiten. Sie leben und weben mit aller Frische und Realität der Wirklichkeit doch in einem reineren und ätherischeren Element als andere. Sie sind erzeugt und erhalten sich durch Ideenkraft und bringen sie wieder hervor. Ihre Poesie verliert nicht an Anschaulichkeit und Innigkeit; aber sie gewinnt an Erhabenheit. Ja der Gewinn in diesem wird größer, je mehr Sie nur an jenes denken; und darum ahnde ich, was Ihre Braut von Messina sein muß.

(From W. von Humboldt, April 30, 1803. F. C. Ebrard, *Neue Briefe W. v. H.'s an Schiller.* 1911. 319—320. His fine appreciation of Schiller's drama is contained in his letter to Schiller dated Oct. 28, 1803.) See A. Leitzmann, *Briefwechsel zwischen Schiller und Humboldt.* Stuttgart. 1900. 307—314.

It is the best critical discussion of the play by one of the great contemporaries of Schiller and a master of literary criticism. Unfortunately it is too long to be reproduced in this place.

II, *o.*

Am 14. und 16. ward die Braut von Messina mit Würde, Pracht und Bestimmtheit gegeben. Gegenfüßler? Etliche! Totaleffekt? Der höchste, tiefste, ehrwürdigste! Die Chöre wurden meisterhaft gesprochen und senkten wie ein Wetter sich über das Land. Gott segne und erhalte Sie und Ihre ewig blühende Jugendfülle!

(From Iffland, June 18, 1803. Urlichs, *Briefe an Schiller*, 526.)

II, *p.*

Dies durfte wohl der Dichter einmal schildern,
Wir danken ihm, daß er's vollbracht;
Doch geben wir so trostlos herben Bildern
Von minder klugem Pinsel gute Nacht.
Was Er uns brachte, bleibt uns wohl empfohlen,   5
Er fesselt uns mit zart und strengem Sinn,
Was unerfreulich macht Er zum Gewinn,
Was Er getan, soll keiner wiederholen.

* * * * * * *

These lines were subsequently replaced by two stanzas, the concluding portion of which runs:

Vergebens willst du dir's vernünftig deuten;
Was soll man sagen, wo es bitter heißt: 10
Ganz gleich ergeht's dem Guten wie dem Bösen!
Ein schwierig Rätsel, rätselhaft zu lösen.
Uns zum Erstaunen wollte Schiller drängen,
Der Sinnende, der alles durchgeprobt.
Gleich unsern Geist gebietet's anzustrengen,   15
Das Werk, das herrlich seinen Meister lobt. —
Wenn Felsenriffe Bahn und Fahrt verengen,
Um den Geängsteten die Welle tobt,
Alsdann vernimmt ein so bedrängtes Flehen
Religion allein von ew'gen Höhen.   20

Goethe, *Maskenzug vom 18ten Dezember*, 1818 (Weimar Edition, Vol. XVI. 480 and 289.)

APPENDIX III

Parallel Passages from Aeschylus (Humboldt), Schiller and Goethe.

III, *a.*

Auf nun, und schlinget den Reigen!
Lasset ertönen
Den grausen Gesang!
Singt, wie den Sterblichen
Unsre Schar des Schicksals Lose verteilt: 5
Wie sie, strenges Recht zu üben, sich freut!
Denn, wer in schuldloser Reinheit
Seine Hände bewahret,
Den besucht nie unser Zorn;
Fern von Unglück durchwallt er das Leben.   10
Aber, wer, wie dieser, frevelnd
Hände des Mordes birgt,
Dem gesellen wir uns rächend bei,
Zeugen wahrhaft den Erschlagenen gegen ihn,
Fordern von ihm das vergossene Blut.   15

Strophe 1.

Mutter, die du uns gebarest,
Nacht den Schauenden und Blinden,
Mutter, hier die Erinnyen!
Unsre Ehre schmälert Letos Sohn,
Reißt aus unsrer Hand den Flüchtling,   20
Den des Muttermordes Frevel
Unserm Rächerarm geeignet.
Über dem geweihten Opfer
Sei dies unser Lied! Sinnberaubend,

Herzzerrüttend, wahnsinnhauchend,   25
Schallt der Hymnus der Erinnyen,
Seelenfesselnd, sonder Leier,
Und des Hörers Mark verzehrend.

Antistrophe 1.

Denn des Schicksals Richterausspruch
Gab zum sichern Eigentume   30
Dieses Los uns. Wessen Frevlerarm
Mordend unschuldvolles Blut verspritzt,
Dem zu folgen, bis er zu den
Schatten walle. Aber sterbend
Wird er nicht der Banden ledig.   35
Über dem geweihten Opfer
Sei dies unser Lied! Sinnberaubend,
Herzzerrüttend, wahnsinnhauchend,
Schallt der Hymnus der Erinnyen,
Seelenfesselnd, sonder Leier,   40
Und des Hörers Mark verzehrend.

Epodos.

Plötzlich aus der Höhe stürzend,
Hemmen wir des flücht'gen
Bösewichts unsichern Schritt.
Unter seiner Untat Bürde   45
Wankt in irrem Lauf sein Fuß,
Und er sinkt; und sieht es
In des Wahnsinns Irrtum nicht.
So umhüllt mit Blindheit ihn der Frevel,
Da des Unglücks tiefes Dunkel seinem   50
Hause das Gerücht entgegenstöhnt.

AESCHYLUS, *The Eumenides.*

The translation of this Chorus was made by
Wilhelm von Humboldt (1793).

17—2

III, b.

. . . .

. . . .

So schreiten keine ird'schen Weiber,
Die zeugete kein sterblich Haus!
Es steigt das Riesenmaß der Leiber
Hoch über Menschliches hinaus.

Ein schwarzer Mantel schlägt die Lenden,   105
Sie schwingen in entfleischten Händen
Der Fackel düsterrote Glut;
In ihren Wangen fließt kein Blut.
Und wo die Haare lieblich flattern,
Um Menschenstirnen freundlich wehn,   110
Da sieht man Schlangen hier und Nattern
Die giftgeschwollnen Bäuche blähn.

Und schauerlich gedreht im Kreise,
Beginnen sie des Hymnus Weise,
Der durch das Herz zerreißend dringt,   115
Die Bande um den Sünder schlingt.
Besinnungraubend, herzbetörend
Schallt der Erinnyen Gesang,
Er schallt, des Hörers Mark verzehrend,
Und duldet nicht der Leier Klang: 120

„Wohl dem, der frei von Schuld und Fehle
Bewahrt die kindlich reine Seele!
Ihm dürfen wir nicht rächend nahn,
Er wandelt frei des Lebens Bahn.
Doch wehe, wehe, wer verstohlen   125
Des Mordes schwere Tat vollbracht;
Wir heften uns an seine Sohlen,
Das furchtbare Geschlecht der Nacht!

Und glaubt er fliehend zu entspringen,
Geflügelt sind wir da, die Schlingen   130
Ihm werfend um den flücht'gen Fuß,
Daß er zu Boden fallen muß.

So jagen wir ihn ohn' Ermatten,
Versöhnen kann uns keine Reu',
Ihn fort und fort bis zu den Schatten,   135
Und geben ihn auch dort nicht frei."

So singend tanzen sie den Reigen,
Und Stille, wie des Todes Schweigen,
Liegt überm ganzen Haufe schwer,
Als ob die Gottheit nahe wär'.   140
Und feierlich nach alter Sitte
Umwandelnd des Theaters Rund
Mit langsam abgemeßnem Schritte,
Verschwinden sie im Hintergrund.

SCHILLER, Die Kraniche des Ibykus, ll. 101—144.

III, c.

Iphigenie.   Sage mir
Vom Unglückſel'gen! Sprich mir von Oreſt!—   1050

Oreſt. O könnte man von seinem Tode sprechen!
Wie gärend stieg aus der Erschlagnen Blut
Der Mutter Geist
Und ruft der Nacht uralten Töchtern zu:
„Laßt nicht den Muttermörder entfliehn!   1055
Verfolgt den Verbrecher! Euch ist er geweiht!"
Sie horchen auf, es schaut ihr hohler Blick
Mit der Begier des Adlers um sich her.
Sie rühren sich in ihren schwarzen Höhlen,
Und aus den Winkeln schleichen ihre Gefährten,   1060
Der Zweifel und die Reue, leis herbei.
Vor ihnen steigt ein Dampf vom Acheron;
In seinen Wolkenkreisen wälzet sich
Die ewige Betrachtung des Geschehnen
Verwirrend um des Schuld'gen Haupt umher.   1065
Und sie, berechtigt zum Verderben, treten
Der gottbeſäten Erde schönen Boden,
Von dem ein alter Fluch sie längst verbannte.
Den Flüchtigen verfolgt ihr schneller Fuß;
Sie geben nur, um neu zu schrecken, Rast.   1070

GOETHE, Iphigenie auf Tauris, III. 1, ll. 1049—1070.

APPENDIX IV

Priamus Laomedontis filius cum complures liberos haberet ex concubitu Hecubae Cissei sive Dymantis filiae, uxor eius praegnans in quiete vidit se facem ardentem parere, ex qua serpentes plurimos exisse. id visum omnibus coniectoribus cum narratum esset, imperant quicquid pareret necaret, ne id patriae exitio foret. postquam Hecuba peperit Alexandrum, datur interficiendus. quem satellites misericordia exposuerunt, [eum] pastores pro suo filio repertum expositum educarunt eumque Parim nominaverunt. is cum ad puberum aetatem pervenisset habuit taurum in deliciis. quo cum satellites missi a Priamo ut taurum aliquis adduceret venissent, qui in athlo funebri quod ei fiebat poneretur, coeperunt Paridis taurum abducere. qui persecutus est eos et inquisivit quo eum ducerent. illi indicant se eum ad Priamum adducere * qui vicisset ludis funebribus Alexandri. ille amore incensus tauri sui descendit in certamen et omnia vicit, fratres quoque suos superavit. indignans Deiphobus gladium ad eum strinxit; at ille in aram Iovis Hercei insiluit. quod cum Cassandra vaticinaretur eum fratrem esse, Priamus eum agnovit regiaque recepit.

Hygini Fabulae, XCI : Alexander Paris.

APPENDIX V

BIBLIOGRAPHY.

THE books marked with an asterisk have been seen or consulted by the present editor. The following list does not lay any claim to absolute completeness, but it is hoped that no book or article of real importance for students has been overlooked. The titles of most of the English and German School editions have been considerably shortened in order to save space. Only translations into the English language have been enumerated. Hardly any books or articles published before 1870 have been mentioned in the following lists, except the translations enumerated under B. For earlier criticisms and articles on Schiller's drama full information is easily obtainable in Karl Goedeke's Grundrisz zur Geschichte der deutschen Dichtung (new edition of the Schiller portion by Max Koch), Vol. v (1893), § 255, pp. 227 sqq.

A. EDITIONS.

a. THE PRINCIPAL GERMAN EDITIONS.

Die Braut von Messina oder die feindlichen Brüder, ein Trauerspiel mit Chören von Schiller. Tübingen. Cotta. 1803. (The first edition was followed by many others. See A. Hettler's and P. Trömel's works, and also M. Koch in the second ed. of Goedeke's Grundrisz, v (1893), 227.)

*Die Braut von Messina, ed. H. Oesterley, in K. Goedeke's Historisch-Kritische Ausgabe. Vol. XIV. 1—128 and Introd. v—vi. Stuttgart. Cotta. 1872.

*Die Braut von Messina, ed. K. Goedeke, in Cotta's Bibliothek der Weltlitteratur. Schillers Werke. Vol. VI. pp. 145—248 and Introd. 6—8. Stuttgart. No year. [Also in Cotta's Handbibliothek. Vol. 110.]

*Die Braut von Messina, ed. O. Walzel, in Cotta's Säkular-Ausgabe. Vol. VII. pp. 1—120 and Introd. vii—xxi. Stuttgart. No year [1905].

*Die Braut von Messina, ed. W. v. Maltzahn, in Hempel's 'Deutsche Klassiker.' Schillers Werke. Vol. v. (New ed. Berlin. 1889.) pp. 257—344 and Introd. 248—254.

*Die Braut von Messina, ed. L. Bellermann, in his ed. of 'Schillers Werke.' Kritisch durchgesehene und erläuterte Ausgabe. Vol. v. pp. 169— and Introd. 161—168. Leipzig. Bibliographisches Institut. No year.

*Die Braut von Messina, edd. R. Boxberger and A. Birlinger, in J. Kürschner's 'Deutsche National-Litteratur. Historisch-Kritische Ausgabe.' Vol. 123, 1 (Schillers Werke, VI, 1). pp. 13—134 and Introd. 3—12. Stuttgart. No year.

*Die Braut von Messina, ed. Arthur Kutscher, on the basis of the old Hempel edition in the 'Goldene Klassiker-Bibliothek.' Vol. v, 243—330 and Vol. x, 61—63 (notes). Deutsches Verlagshaus. Bong and Co. No year. Berlin, Leipzig, Wien, Stuttgart.

*Die Braut von Messina, ed. Albert Leitzmann, in Hesse's 'Historisch-Kritische Ausgabe' of Schiller's collected works in 20 volumes. Vol. VII, 273—375 and Vol. XX, 251—261 (notes). Leipzig. No year.

b. German School Editions.

*1. Seb. Englert (in Brunner's Sammlung). Bamberg. Buchner. 1899.

*2. R. Franz. Bielefeld and Leipzig. Velhagen and Klasing. 1906.

*3. H. Heskamp (7th ed. by Schmitz-Mancy). Paderborn. Schöningh. ⁷1906.

*4. F. Hülskamp. Münster. 1882; ⁵1905.

*5. A. Kleffner (in Aschendorff's Collection). Münster i. W. Aschendorff. 1902.

*6. H. Leitzmann. Leipzig. Hesse. No year. See under *a*.

*7. J. Pölzl (in 'Hölder's Classiker-Ausgaben'). Wien. Hölder. ²1888.

*8. J. W. Schäfer. Stuttgart. Cotta. 1874. New ed. 1886.

*9. J. Trötscher (in 'Graesers Schulausgaben'). Wien. 1885. Now Leipzig. Teubner. No year.

*10. K. Tumlirz. Leipzig. Freytag. 1895.

*11. Veit Valentin (in 'Schillers und Valentins Deutsche Schul-Ausgaben,' No. 20). Dresden. Ehlermann. 1896.

12. G. Wendt. Berlin. Grote. 1870.

c. AMERICAN SCHOOL EDITIONS.
(with an introduction and notes in the English language).

*1. William Herbert Carruth. New York, Boston and Chicago. No year [1901 ?]. (In ' The Silver Series of Modern Language Text-Books.')

*2. A. H. Palmer and J. G. Eldridge. New York. Holt and Co. No year [1901 ?].

d. FRENCH SCHOOL EDITIONS.

*1. E. Scherdlin. Paris. Hachette. 1879; ⁶1899.

2. M. Schnaufer. (Expliquée, littéralement traduite par A. Regnier.) Paris. Hachette. 1907.

B. ENGLISH TRANSLATIONS.

*1. William Taylor (of Norwich). Act IV, Sc. 4 in his 'Historic Survey of German Poetry.' London. 1830. Vol. III, 229—230 (lines 2268—2309). Reprinted in H. E. Goldschmidt, German Poetry with the English versions of the best translators. London and Edinburgh. 1869. pp. 162—165.

*2. Ch. Hodges. Translated and Original Poems. In 2 volumes. Coblentz. 1834. Vol. I, 95—116 (here lines 294—770 only are given). Vol. II contains only original poems. In 1836 Hodges published (at Munich) another volume of 'Original Poems.' In this he included the following translations from 'Die Braut von Messina,' ll. 1—293, 777—1562, 2590—2840 (end). Thus from the two volumes taken together it appears that about two-thirds of Schiller's drama have been rendered, lines 1563—2589 being omitted. The translation is in the Library of the British Museum.

*3. George Irvine. The Bride of Messina. A tragedy from the German of F. v. Schiller. London. 1837.

*4. Anonymous. The Bride of Messina or the hostile Brothers. A tragedy with Choruses by F. Schiller. German and English. München. P. Jacob Bayer. 1838. Changed into: München. Georg Franz. 1839.

*5. A. Lodge. The Bride of Messina. A tragedy with Choruses. London. 1841. 3rd ed. 1863 (in Bohn's Standard Library).

6. J. Towler. Carlsruhe, Bielefeld. 1850.
7. E. Allfrey. London. 1876.
*8. A new verse translation of the Choruses, which is hitherto un-published, was kindly placed at my disposal by the translator, Mr Frank C. Nicholson, of Edinburgh.

See also : *Thomas Rea. Schiller's Dramas and Poems in England. London. 1906. pp. 91—96, 144, 149.

C. LANGUAGE AND METRE.

*L. Rudolph und K. Goldbeck. Schiller-Lexikon. Berlin. 1869. Vol. II, 354 sqq. (Schiller's language is treated by Goldbeck.)
*Oskar Weise. Aesthetik der deutschen Sprache. Berlin. 1909. Chapter 19 : Schillers Sprache, pp. 177 sqq.
*Albert Fries. Beobachtungen zu Schillers Stil und Metrik in der Zeit seiner dichterischen Reife, in 'Studien zur vergleichenden Literaturgeschichte.' Vol. v (1905). Ergänzungsheft. pp. 303—330.
*Otto Behaghel. Zum Gebrauch des Beiworts bei Schiller, in 'Wissenschaftliche Beihefte zur Zeitschrift des Allgemeinen Deutschen Sprachvereins.' Heft 26 (1905), 180—198. Followed by
*Hermann Wunderlich. Zur Sprache im 'Tell' und in der 'Braut von Messina,' *ibid.* pp. 199—207.
*Friedrich Zarncke. Über den fünffüssigen Iambus, mit besonderer Rücksicht auf seine Behandlung durch Lessing, Schiller und Goethe. I. Leipzig. 1865. (Now more easily accessible in Zarncke's 'Goetheschriften.' Leipzig. 1897. pp. 406—409.)
*Eduard Belling. Die Metrik Schillers. Breslau. 1883. In various places. (See also Wackernell in the 'Zeitschrift für deutsche Philologie.' XVII, 46 sqq.)
*H. Draheim. Schillers Metrik. Berlin. 1909. pp. 84—90.
*H. Henkel. Der Blankvers Shakespeares im Drama Lessings, Goethes und Schillers, in the 'Zeitschrift für vergleichende Litteraturgeschichte,' I, 321—327.
*Otto Harnack. Über den Gebrauch des Trimeters bei Goethe, in his 'Essays und Studien zur Literaturgeschichte.' Braunschweig. 1899. pp. 126 sqq., especially p. 128.
*Fr. Vogt. Von der Hebung des schwachen *e*, in 'Forschungen zur deutschen Philologie,' Festgabe für Rudolf Hildebrand. Leipzig. 1894. p. 173.
*J. Minor. Neuhochdeutsche Metrik. Strassburg. 1893 ; ²1902.

D. COMMENTARIES.

*II. Düntzer. Erläuterungen zu den deutschen Klassikern. Vol. 52. 5th edition, revised by A. Heil. Leipzig. No year.

*A. Zipper. Erläuterungen zu den Meisterwerken der deutschen Litteratur. Vol. 5. Leipzig. Reclam's Universal-Bibliothek. No. 3812.

*C. Weitbrecht. Schiller in seinen Dramen. Stuttgart. 1897. Chapter IX. pp. 269—299.

*L. Bellermann. Schillers Dramen. Beiträge zu ihrem Verständnis. Berlin. [1]1891. Vol. II, 307—420. [3]1905. Vol. III, 1—116. (Here the most important older writings are quoted.)

*II. Gaudig. Wegweiser durch die klassischen Schuldramen. Part II (Schiller), 224—311. (Part V of the most useful work: Aus deutschen Lesebüchern.) Gera and Leipzig. 1893.

*M. Krafft. Schillers 'Braut von Messina' für Schule und Haus erklärt. Cassel. 1881.

Aug. Hagemann. Schillers 'Braut von Messina' (Vorträge für die gebildete Welt. I). Riga and Leipzig. 1883; [3]1888 (Spandau-Berlin).

*H. Bulthaupt. Dramaturgie des Schauspiels. Oldenburg and Leipzig. [8]1902. pp. 407—432.

R. Peters. Schillers 'Braut von Messina' (Vol. 22 of 'Die deutschen Klassiker, herausgegeben von E. Kuenen und M. Evers). Leipzig. 1902.

E. REMARKS ON THE PLAY IN SOME OF THE BEST LIVES OF SCHILLER AND HISTORIES OF LITERATURE.

(Brahm's, Minor's, and Weltrich's Lives of Schiller which are in course of publication do not yet treat of the *Bride of Messina*.)

*K. Hoffmeister. Schiller's Leben, Geistesentwickelung und Werke. Stuttgart. 1840. (In various places. See the Index.)

*F. Wychgram. Schiller dem deutschen Volke dargestellt. With many illustrations. Bielefeld and Leipzig. 1895. pp. 455—469.

*E. Müller. Regesten zu Friedrich Schillers Leben und Werken. Leipzig. 1900. pp. 151—163.

*L. Bellermann. Schiller. Leipzig, Berlin, Wien. 1901. With many illustrations. pp. 221—226.

*Otto Harnack. Schiller. With ten portraits. Berlin. ³1905.
pp. 366—382.
*Eugen Kühnemann. Schiller. München. ³1908. pp. 546—562.
*Karl Berger. Schiller. Sein Leben und seine Werke. München.
Vol. II (1909), 598—642 and 780—781.
*Thomas Carlyle. The life of Fr. Schiller. London. Chapman
and Hall. pp. 151—152. (See H. Conrad, 'Carlyle and Schiller,'
in 'Vierteljahrschrift für Litteraturgeschichte.' Vol. II (1889),
195—228, especially p. 208.)
*Calvin Thomas. The Life and Works of Friedrich Schiller. New
York. 1902. pp. 387—404.
*John G. Robertson. Schiller after a century. London. 1905.
pp. 115—118.

*Carl Leo Cholevius. Geschichte der deutschen Poesie nach ihren
antiken Elementen. Leipzig. 1856. Vol. II, 182—188.
*H. Hettner. Geschichte der deutschen Litteratur im achtzehnten
Jahrhundert. Braunschweig. ⁴1894. Vol. III, 3, pp. 300—306.
*G. Gervinus. Geschichte der deutschen Dichtung. 5th ed. 1874.
Vol. v, 625—627.
*A. Koberstein. Geschichte der deutschen Nationallitteratur.
5th ed. Leipzig. 1872. Vols. III—V. (See the Index at the
end of Vol. v.)
*K. Goedeke. Grundrisz zur Geschichte der deutschen Dichtung.
Aus den Quellen. 2nd ed. Dresden. 1892—3. Vol. v, § 255.
(A most valuable survey of the literature on the play by Max
Koch.)
*Wilh. Scherer. Geschichte der deutschen Litteratur. 9th ed.
Berlin. 1902. pp. 604—608 and 780. (There is an English
translation of this work by Mrs F. C. Conybeare. New ed. Oxford.
1906. Vol. II, 220—224.)
*F. Vogt and M. Koch. Geschichte der deutschen Literatur von
den ältesten Zeiten bis zur Gegenwart. ²1904. Vol. II (by Max
Koch), pp. 329 and 559.
*Kuno Francke. A history of German Literature as determined by
social forces. London. 1901. pp. 393—394.
*John G. Robertson. A history of German Literature. Edinburgh
and London. 1902. pp. 393—395. Outlines of the History of
German Literature. Edinburgh and London. 1911. pp. 174—175.

*Jakob Minor. Zur Geschichte der deutschen Schicksalstragödie und zu Grillparzers 'Ahnfrau,' in the 'Jahrbuch der Grillparzer-Gesellschaft,' IX (1899), 1—85.

*Jul. Braun. Schiller im Urteil seiner Zeitgenossen. Berlin. Vol. III, 285—360, and in a few scattered later places.
*Albert Ludwig. Schiller und die deutsche Nachwelt. Berlin. 1909. (In various places. See Index.)

F. DIVERSA.

*C. G. Wenzel. Aus Weimars goldenen Tagen. Dresden. 1859. pp. 242—246. (Here some of the older literature and also older illustrations and musical compositions are mentioned.)
*C. Wurzbach von Tannenberg. Das Schiller-Buch. Wien. 1859. (Gives a full account of the older literature.) Nos. 783—845.
*Paul Trömel. Schiller-Bibliothek. Leipzig. 1865. pp. 87 sqq.
*August Hettler. Schillers Dramen. Berlin. 1885. Nos. 26—79.
*Jahresberichte für Neuere Deutsche Litteraturgeschichte. (Stuttgart, now) Berlin. Yearly. Since 1892.

*Gustav Freytag. Die Technik des Dramas. Leipzig. ⁴1881.
*Hermann Unbescheid. Beitrag zur Behandlung der dramatischen Lektüre. Berlin. ²1891. (In various places.)
*Rudolf Franz. Der Aufbau der Handlung in den klassischen Dramen. Hilfsbuch zur dramatischen Lektüre. Bielefeld and Leipzig. 1892. pp. 87—89 and 418—424.
*Paul Goldscheider. Lesestücke und Schriftwerke im deutschen Unterricht. München. 1906. (In many places. See Index.)
*Paul Goldscheider. Die Erklärung deutscher Schriftwerke in den oberen Klassen höherer Lehranstalten. Berlin. 1889. (In various places.)

*Julius Petersen. Schiller und die Bühne. Ein Beitrag zur Litteratur- und Theatergeschichte der klassischen Zeit. Berlin. 1904. (Palaestra XXXII.) In various places.
*Eduard Genast. Aus Weimars klassischer und nachklassischer Zeit. Erinnerungen eines alten Schauspielers. Neu herausgegeben von Robert Kohlrausch. 3rd ed. Stuttgart. No year. I, 83—87.

*Robert Prölss. Geschichte der dramatischen Litteratur und Kunst in Deutschland von der Reformation bis auf die Gegenwart. Leipzig. 1883. Vol. II, 111—112.

---

*Ch. Andler. Les deux sources médiévales de la 'Fiancée de Messine.' Contained in a volume written by miscellaneous contributors under the title 'Études sur Schiller.' Paris. 1905. pp. 25—40. (But see Euphorion, XV (1908), 786—787; Litteraturblatt für germanische und romanische Philologie, XXX (1909), 358—359.)

Arnoldt. Über Schillers Auffassung und Verwertung des antiken Chors. Programme. Königsberg. 1893.

*Ernst Bergmann. Das dramatische und tragische Problem in Schillers 'Braut von Messina,' in 'Neue Jahrbücher f. d. Klass. Altertum, Geschichte und deutsche Litteratur,' IX (1902), 129—146.

*Ernst Bergmann. Zur Geschichte der 'Braut von Messina,' in 'Die Grenzboten.' 1903. pp. 213—221, 273—281.

*Ernst Bergmann. Die Verknüpfung der Handlung in Schillers 'Braut von Messina.' Programme. Braunschweig. 1903.

*Ernst Bergmann. Ist die 'Braut von Messina' eine Schicksalstragödie? Programme. Braunschweig. 1906. (Contains a very careful grouping and discussion of previous essays dealing with the same question.)

*Walter Bormann. Schiller als Dichter der 'Braut von Messina,' in Otto Sievers' 'Akademische Blätter.' Braunschweig. 1884. pp. 672—715.

O. Brosin. Schillers 'Braut von Messina' vor dem Richterstuhl der Kritik. Programme. Liegnitz. 1872.

*Konrad Burdach. Schillers Chordrama und die Geburt des tragischen Stils aus der Musik, in 'Deutsche Rundschau.' Vol. 142 (1910), 232 sqq., 400 sqq. and Vol. 143 (1910), 91—112.

*Julius Burggraf. Schillers Frauengestalten. Stuttgart. ²1900. pp. 385—411.

*Julius Burggraf. Schillerpredigten. Giessen. ²1909. No. 12. pp. 200 sqq.

A. Buttmann. Die Schicksalsidee in der 'Braut von Messina' und ihr innerer Zusammenhang mit der Geschichte der Menschheit. Berlin. 1882.

*W. H. Carruth. Fate and Guilt in Schiller's 'Die Braut von Messina,' in 'Publications of the Modern Language Association of America.' Vol. XVII (New Series, Vol. X), 105—124. Baltimore. 1902.

*Paulus Cassell. Schiller's 'Braut von Messina,' edited (after Cassell's death) by H. Krüger, in 'Studien zur vergleichenden Litteraturgeschichte.' Ergänzungsheft zu Vol. v (1905), 246 sqq.

*Starr Willard Cutting. Concerning Schiller's treatment of fate and dramatic guilt in his 'Braut von Messina,' in 'Modern Philology.' Vol. v (Jan. 1908), 347—360.

*Franz Diebitsch. Zur Führung der Handlung in Schillers 'Braut von Messina.' Programme. Neustadt (Ober-Schlesien). 1901.

*Th. Distel. Zur ersten Aufführung der 'Braut von Messina' in Lauchstädt, in 'Studien zur vergl. Litt. Gesch.' Ergänzungsheft zu Vol. v (1905), 350—354.

*Paul Dörwald. Schillers 'Braut von Messina,' in 'Aus der Praxis des deutschen Unterrichts in Prima.' Berlin. 1908. pp. 133—167.

*H. Draheim. Das physiologische Rätsel in Schillers 'Braut von Messina,' in 'Zeitschrift f. d. deutschen Unterricht.' Vol. xix (1905), 594—596.

*Richard Fester. Schillers historische Schriften als Vorstudien des Dramatikers, in 'Deutsche Rundschau.' Vol. 138 (1909), 148—158.

Isaac Flagg. An analysis of Schiller's tragedy 'Die Braut von Messina' after Aristotle's 'Poetic.' Dissertation. Göttingen. 1871.

*J. Baptist Gerlinger. Die griechischen Elemente in Schillers 'Braut von Messina.' Ein Beitrag zur deutschen Litteraturgeschichte. Neuburg. 1852; ⁴1892.

G. Gevers. Über Schillers 'Braut von Messina' und den 'König Oedipus' des Sophokles. Programme. Verden. 1873—4.

*H. Gloël. Schicksal und Charakter in Schillers 'Braut von Messina,' in 'Zeitschrift für das Gymnasialwesen.' Vol. 59 (1905), 66—74.

*F. Hahne. Die Charaktere Manuels und Cesars in der 'Braut von Messina,' in 'Neue Jahrb. f. d. Klass. Alt., Geschichte und Deutsche Literatur.' Vol. xiii (1904), 443—453.

*Erich Harnack. Über das Problem der Vererbung in Schillers 'Braut von Messina,' in 'Internationale Wochenschrift.' Vol. iv (1910), 1120—32.

*J. Imelmann. Symbolae Joachimicae. Anmerkungen zu deutschen Dichtern. Berlin. pp. 16—19.

*Gustav Kettner. Schillerstudien. pp. 51—53 (previously in 'Zeitschrift für deutsche Philologie.' Vol. xx (1888), 49—54).

*Eugen Kilian. Schillers Massenszenen auf der Bühne, in the 'Marbacher Schillerbuch,' ii (1907), 108 sqq.

*Victor Kiy. Themata und Dispositionen zu deutschen Aufsätzen und Vorträgen im Anschluss an die deutsche Schullektüre. Berlin. 1895. Vol. ii, 139—184.

*Robert Kohlrausch. Schillers 'Braut von Messina' und ihr Schau-platz, in 'Deutsche Rundschau.' Vol. 122 (1905), 118—127.

*Josef Kohm. Schillers 'Braut von Messina' und ihr Verhältnis zu Sophokles' 'Oidipus Tyrannos.' Gotha. 1901.

M. Landau. Die feindlichen Brüder auf der Bühne, in 'Bühne und Welt.' Vol. IX (1906?), 189—192 and 236—241.

*F. Liebrecht. Zur Volkskunde. Heilbronn. 1879. pp. 474—480.

*Ernst Maass. Die 'Braut von Messina' und ihr griechisches Vorbild, in 'Deutsche Rundschau.' Vol. 134 (1908), 64—76.

*O. Nietzsche. In wie weit lässt sich Schillers 'Braut von Messina' für das Verständnis der griechischen Tragödie verwenden? Programme. Görlitz. 1897.

*K. Olbrich. Die Chöre in Schillers 'Braut von Messina,' in 'Neue Jahrbücher für das klassische Altertum, Geschichte und deutsche Literatur.' Vol. 15 (1905), 463—464.

*R. Petsch. Chor und Volk im antiken und modernen Drama, in 'Neue Jahrbücher' etc. Vol. 13 (1904), 57—79, especially pp. 77—78.

*R. Petsch. Freiheit und Notwendigkeit in Schillers Dramen. München. 1905. pp. 249—269.

August Rosikat. Über das Wesen der Schicksalstragödie. Programmes. Königsberg. 1891; 1892.

*G. Sachse. Zur aesthetischen Beurteilung von Schillers 'Braut von Messina,' in 'Zeitschrift f. d. d. Unterricht.' Vol. 17 (1903), 512—518.

August Schneegans. Schillers sizilianische Dichtungen [in the 'Augsburger Allgemeine Zeitung.' Nos. 306—313]. 1881.

*Ferd. Schultz. Meditationen. Vol. 1 (3rd edit.). Dresden. 1905. (Contains : (1) Welche Motive des Sophokleischen König Ödipus benutzte Schiller in seiner 'Braut von Messina'? (Med. No. 29), and (2) Das Schicksal in der 'Braut von Messina' (No. 42).)

*Heinrich von Stein. Goethe und Schiller. Beiträge zur Aesthetik der deutschen Klassiker. Leipzig. Reclam. No. 3090. pp. 96—98.

Warncke. Zur Behandlung der 'Braut von Messina.' Programme. Myslowitz. 1908.

*R. Wegener. Aufsätze zur Litteratur. Berlin. ²1884. pp. 1—84.

*E. Wilisch. Schillers Verhältnis zu den beiden klassischen Sprachen, in 'Neue Jahrbücher' etc. Vol. XIV (1904), 39—51.

*W. Wittich. Über Sophokles' 'König Oedipus' und Schillers 'Braut von Messina.' Programme. Cassel. 1887.

*Theobald Ziegler. Freiheit und Notwendigkeit in Schillers Dramen,

in the 'Marbacher Schillerbuch.' Vol. I. Stuttgart und Berlin.
1905. pp. 32—41.

---

*K. Goldbeck and L. Rudolph. Schiller-Lexikon. Erläuterndes
Wörterbuch zu Schiller's Dichterwerken. 2 Vols. Berlin. 1869.
*Gottfr. Fritzsche, Max Moltke, and Moritz Zille. Schiller-
Halle. Alphabetisch geordneter Gedanken-Schatz aus Schiller's
Werken und Briefen. Leipzig. 1870.
*Heinrich Stickelberger. Parallelstellen bei Schiller. Burgdorf.
1893.

---

*Albert Schaefer. Historisches und systematisches Verzeichnis
sämtlicher Tonwerke zu den Dramen Schillers, Goethes, Shakespeares, Kleists und Körners. Leipzig. 1886.
*Hans Knudsen. Schiller und die Musik. Dissertation. Greifs-
wald. 1908.

---

*Schillers Briefwechsel mit Körner. Von 1784 bis zum Tode
Schillers. 2nd edition ed. Karl Goedeke. 2 Vols. Leipzig.
1874. Vol. II. Also the edition of the correspondence in Cotta's
'Bibliothek der Weltlitteratur.'
*Briefwechsel zwischen Schiller und W. v. Humboldt. 3rd
enlarged edition by Albert Leitzmann. Stuttgart. 1900. And
*Neue Briefe Wilhelm von Humboldts an Schiller
(1796—1803) bearbeitet und herausgegeben von Friedrich Clemens
Ebrard. Berlin. 1911. See the Indexes to both editions.
*Briefwechsel zwischen Schiller und Cotta, ed. Wilh. Vollmer.
Stuttgart. 1876.
*Briefwechsel zwischen Schiller und Goethe, ed. Wilh. Vollmer.
4th ed. 2 parts. Stuttgart. 1881. (A good popular edition in
4 small volumes, with introd. and full Indexes by Franz Muncker,
forms part of Cotta's 'Bibliothek der Weltlitteratur.')
*Schillers Briefe, herausgegeben und mit Anmerkungen versehen
von Fritz Jonas. Kritische Gesammtausgabe. Deutsche Verlagsanstalt. Stuttgart. Leipzig. Berlin. Wien. No year (since
1892). Vols. VI and VII. (See Index at the end of Vol. VII.)
*Briefe an Schiller, ed. L. Urlichs. Stuttgart. 1877. pp. 509—
536. (This edition is far from being complete.)
*Julius Petersen. Schillers Gespräche. Berichte seiner Zeitge-
nossen über ihn. Leipzig. 1911. (See the Index.)

INDEX TO THE NOTES

For EU product safety concerns, contact us at Calle de José Abascal, 56–1°, 28003 Madrid, Spain or eugpsr@cambridge.org.

www.ingramcontent.com/pod-product-compliance
Ingram Content Group UK Ltd.
Pitfield, Milton Keynes, MK11 3LW, UK
UKHW020451240426
470322UK00016B/294